Technology and the Future of Work

Technology and the Future of Work

Paul S. Adler

Editor

New York   Oxford
OXFORD UNIVERSITY PRESS
1992

Oxford University Press

Oxford   New York   Toronto
Delhi   Bombay   Calcutta   Madras   Karachi
Petaling Jaya   Singapore   Hong Kong   Tokyo
Nairobi   Dar es Salaam   Cape Town
Melbourne   Auckland

and associated companies in
Berlin   Ibadan

Copyright © 1992 by Oxford University Press, Inc.

Published by Oxford University Press, Inc.,
200 Madison Avenue, New York, New York 10016

Oxford is a registered trademark of Oxford University Press

Library of Congress Cataloging-in-Publication Data
Technology and the future of work / Paul S. Adler, editor.
p. cm.   Includes bibliographical references and index.
ISBN 0-19-507171-9
1. Employees—Effect of technological innovations on.
I. Adler, Paul S.
HD6331.T419   1992
331.25—dc20   91-17526

9 8 7 6 5 4 3 2 1

Printed in the United States of America
on acid-free paper

Preface

Competitive firms share a common trait—they create a good match between their technology, people and organization, and they sustain it with well-meshed business, technology and human resource strategies. Too many firms, however, lack that match, and therefore realize only a fraction of the potential of the new process technologies. They don't invest enough or effectively enough in workforce training; they antagonize employees and unions by excluding them from the planning and implementation process; and they fail to prepare for new technologies with long-term strategic plans. The acceleration of technological change makes these handicaps increasingly debilitating in an era of intensified global competition.

This book addresses the influence of new technologies on work and the resulting challenges for business organizations. It seeks to answer four major questions:

- What new types of job content and work organization will be needed for the effective use of the new process technologies?
- What new skill formation approaches will prepare people for their new roles in more automated work settings?
- What types of employee relations will ensure the effective design of technology and its effective use in the workplace?
- how will leaders weave together long-term business, technology and human resource strategies that can respond to these challenges?

The individual chapters began as briefing papers for a seminar at Stanford University in March 1990 with the same title as the present book. The seminar brought together 200 senior managers and union leaders from U.S. industry, and 50 leading researchers from the U.S., Europe, and Asia. In preparation for the seminar, and as seminar organizer, I commissioned some of the researchers to prepare the briefing papers which, in revised and edited form, are presented here to a wider audience.

The seminar also addressed another, complementary question: what guidelines will help system developers ensure the optimal usability of the new technology implementations? A companion volume addressing this question, edited by Terry Winograd and me, *Designing Technology for Usability* will be published by Oxford University Press.

The seminar was conducted under the auspices of the Stanford Integrated Manufacturing Association. Funding was provided by several Association sponsors: Apple Computer, Inc., Digital Equipment Corp., Ford Motor Co., General Motors Corp., Hewlett-Packard Co., and IBM Corp. Representatives from these companies helped shape the agenda, and to several of them I owe my special gratitude for their contribution to the planning effort: Reesa Abrams, Chris Duncan, Al Jones, Frank West, and Stuart Winby. Stanford faculty colleagues Elliott Levinthal, Warren Hausman and Dick Scott provided valuable guidance and support. Susan Sweeney's help with the logistics and Cecilia Wanjiku's secretarial support were indispensable; their endurance was remarkable. To Greg Tong I owe special thanks for his editorial help in refining successive drafts. Thanks too to Herb Addison at Oxford, for his encouragement and patience throughout. Above all, this book is the fruit of the contributing authors. Their responsiveness to the concerns and suggestions voiced in the editing process made the editor's job a pleasure.

Tarzana, Calif.   P.S.A.
October 1991

Contents

Contributors, xi

1. Introduction, 3
   Paul S. Adler
   Stumbling Backwards into the Future, 4
   The Emergent View, 6
   Overview, 9
   Two Key Themes, 13

2. Automation and Competency Requirements in Manufacturing:
   A Case Study, 15
   Larry Hirschhorn and Joan Mokray
   The Context: The Westfield Plant, 16
   Model of Competence, 18
   Skills: A Function of Tools and Problems, 20
   Hierarchy of Skill Layers, 24
   The Roles of Direct and Indirect Personnel, 27
   The Role System and the Principle of Complementarity, 34
   Mapping Competencies, 42
   Summary, 43

3. Skill and Occupational Changes in U.S. Manufacturing, 46
   Paul Attewell
   Theories of Skill and Occupational Change, 46
   Empirical Studies of Long-Term Occupational and Skill Change, 57
   Recent Occupational and Skill Change in Manufacturing, 60
   The Future, 80
   Conclusion, 82

4. Automation and Work in Britain, 89
   Peter J. Senker
   British Debates on Automation and Skills, 90
   Policy Analysis: 1950s to 1970s, 91
   Labor Process Analysis, 95
   The British Contextualist Critique, 96
   Automation and Skills in the 1980s, 99

Managers' Influence on Technology and Work Organization, 103
Conclusion, 106

5. New Concepts of Production and the Emergence of the
   Systems Controller, 111
   Horst Kern and Michael Schumann

   The Automobile Industry: A New Personnel Policy, 113
   Machine Manufacturing Industry: Centers of Craft
     in Reconstruction, 120
   The Chemical Industry: The Skilled Production Worker is
     Accepted, 125
   Electrical and Electronic Products: About to Take the Great
     Leap?, 129
   Systems Controllers as a Key Group within the Workforce, 133
   Long-Term Trends in Germany's Work Structure, 140
   Conclusion, 141
   Appendix: Work and Skills in the History of
     German Industrial Sociology, 142

6. Institutions and Incentives for Developing Work-Related
   Knowledge and Skill, 149
   David Stern

   Competitiveness, Automation, and Learning on the Job, 149
   The Spectrum of Institutions for Developing
     Work-Related Knowledge and Skill, 152
   Schools, 154
   Corporate Training, 164
   Learning-Intensive Production, 169
   Some Policy Implications, 177

7. Issues in Skill Formation in Japanese Approaches
   to Automation, 187
   Robert E. Cole

   Contextual Factors Influencing Approaches to Automation and
     Worker Training, 188
   Approaches to Skill Formation in Japanese Manufacturing, 194
   Reasons for Worker Support and Management Adoption of
     Microelectronic Applications, 197
   Training Strategies for Automation, 201
   Japan's Approach, 208

8. Technology, Industrial Relations, and the Problem of
   Organizational Transformation, 210
   Robert J. Thomas and Thomas A. Kochan

   History of Debates on New Technology and Industrial Relations, 212
   Integrating Human and Technical Attributes in Production, 218
   Changes in Industrial Relations Theory and Practice, 225
   Conclusion, 228

9. Union Initiatives to Restructure Industry in Australia, 232
Max Ogden

A New Union Strategy, 232
Macro Elements of Union Strategy, 238
Enterprise-Level Elements of Union Strategy, 248
Strategic Unionism, 256
Conclusion, 260
Appendix A, 261
Appendix B, 266

10. Transforming the Routines and Contexts of Management, Work, and Technology, 269
Claudio U. Ciborra and Leslie S. Schneider

Formative Context, 270
The Firm as a "Thinking Organization", 271
Levels of Learning, 272
Strategies for Innovation and Change, 282
Conclusion, 288

11. Innovation and Institutions: Notes on the Japanese Paradigm, 292
Thomas B. Lifson

Forms, Forces, and Institutions, 294
The Evolution of Organizational Forms in Japan, 298
Innovation in Interfirm Systems, 303
Innovation in Administrative Networks, 307
Adapting the Japanese Paradigm to the American Context, 313

Name Index, 321
Subject Index, 327

Contributors

Paul S. Adler is currently Associate Professor at University of Southern California School of Business Administration. He began his education in Australia and moved to France in 1974, where he received his doctorate in Economics and Management while working as a research economist for the French government. Before coming to USC in 1991, he was a Visiting Scholar at the Brookings Institution, a Visiting Assistant Professor at Columbia University, a Postdoctoral Research Fellow at the Harvard Business School, and Assistant Professor at Stanford University. His principal research interests are in the management of new technologies in production and engineering operations.

Paul Attewell is Professor of Sociology at the Graduate Center of the City University of New York. His major interest is in the sociology of organizations and of work, and his most recent research has focused on the ways that work roles and organizational practices are changing in the wake of computerization in a sample of nearly 200 New York area firms.

Claudio U. Ciborra is Professor of Management Information Systems and Director of the MIS Department of Theseus Institute, in Sophia Antipolis, France, and at the University of Trento, Italy. He received his degree in Electrical Engineering from the Milan Polytechnic and has been a Fulbright Scholar at the University of California, Los Angeles, and Harvard University. He has published widely and consults in organizational analysis of information technology, economics of organizations, and organizational change.

Robert E. Cole is Professor of Sociology and Business Administration at the University of California, Berkeley. He received his Ph.D. in sociology from the University of Illinois in 1968. Professor Cole is a longterm student of Japanese work organization, having written widely on the subject. His most recent monograph appeared in 1989 and was entitled *Strategies for Learning: Small Group Activities in American, Japanese and Swedish Industry*. His current research activities focus on the relation between quality improvement and organizational practices.

Larry Hirschhorn is a principal at the Wharton Center for Applied Research in Philadelphia. He consults to business and industry on such issues as technology implementation, organization design, and the management process. He is the author of *Beyond Mechanization,* a study of automation and socio-technical system; *The Workplace Within,* a study of the psychology of work in post-industrial settings; and *Managing in the New Team Environment,* a practical guide for managers in team-based settings. Hirschhorn's current consulting and research focuses on the design of knowledge work and the challenges of new product development. He is a member of the Society for Manufacturing Engineers, the OD Network, and the International Society for the Psychoanalytic Study or Organizations.

Horst Kern is Professor of Sociology at the University of Göttingen, Germany, and Presient of the Soziologisches Forschungsinstitut Göttingen (SOFI). His research in industrial sociology focuses on the restructing of industries, including international comparisons. He has also published on methodological problems and the history of sociological thought.

Thomas A. Kochan is the George Maverick Bunker Professor of Management and a Leaders for Manufacturing Professor at M.I.T.'s Sloan School of Management. He came to MIT in 1980 as a Professor of Industrial Relations. In 1988 he was appointed Area Head for the Behavioral and Policy Sciences Area in the Sloan School. From 1973 to 1980 he was on the faculty of the School of Industrial and Labor Relations at Cornell University. He also served one year as a consultant to the Secretary of Labor in the Department of Labor's Office of Policy Evaluation and Research. He received his Ph.D. in Industrial Relations from the University of Wisconsin in 1983. Since then he has served as a third-party mediator, factfinder, and arbitrator and as a consultant to a variety of labor management committees and groups. He has done research on a variety of topics related to industrial relations and human resources management in the public and private sector. His recent books include: *Challenges and Choices for American Labor,* 1984; *Human Resource Management and Industrial Relations,* 1985; and *The Transformation of American Industrial Relations,* 1986; *Collective Bargaining and Industrial Relations, 1988.* In 1988 the *Transformation* book received the annual award from the Academy of Management for the best scholarly book on management.

Thomas B. Lifson received his Ph.D. in Sociology at Harvard University in 1978. He also holds an A.M. in East Asian Studies from Harvard and an M.B.A. from Harvard Business School, where he was a Baker Scholar. He has taught at Harvard and the Columbia University Graduate School of International Affairs. He works as a management consultant for U.S. and Japanese multinational firms. He is currently Visiting Professor at the Japanese National Museum of Ethnology.

Joan Mokray's undergraduate degree is in Political Science form the University of California, Berkeley, and her graduate degree is from Harvard Business School. She is currently Technical Resource Development Manager for Low-End Systems Manufacturing at Digital Equipment Corporation. Before joining Digital, Joan worked for Potlatch, International Paper, General Electric, and Syntex.

Max Ogden is Australian Council of Trade Unions Officer for Skill Formation and Work Organization. In this capacity he advises and works with affiliate unions on restructing and implementing their new agreements at the enterprise level, including the introduction of new technology. He has been active in the union movement since starting work as an apprentice. From 1972 to 1984 he was the first full-time education officer in the Victorian branch of the Amalgamated Metal Workers Union. From 1984 to 1989, when he took up his present position, he was national industrial democracy officer for the Metal Workers. He has been interested in, and studied the issues of, work organization, skill, technology, and industrial democracy since the late 1960s. He has spoken widely and contributed to the debate on these issues in Australia and abroad. He is a lifelong socialist and for 25 years was a member of the Communist Party, most of that time in the national leadership, until resigning in 1984. He is now a member of the Australian Labor Party.

Leslie Schneider is Director of TECnet, Research Assistant Professor at the Tufts University College of Engineering, and Associate Director of the College's Manufacturing Engineering Program. She holds a Ph.D. from Stanford University. She has served as a consultant to both private- and public-sector organizations on the design and implementation of manufacturing technology, and she has designed and implemented a variety of computer-based conferencing systems.

Michael Schumann is Professor of Sociology at the University of Göttingen, Germany, and Director of the Soziologisches Forschungsinstitut Göttingen (SOFI). His main area of research is in industrial sociology. He has published widely on trends in rationalization, changes in workers' behavior, and industrial policy.

Peter J. Senker graduated in economics from Cambridge University in 1957. Until 1971, he worked in economics, industrial market research, and consultancy, mainly in the Philips electronics group. He was awarded an IBM Fellowship at the Manchester Business School in 1971. Since 1972, he has worked as a Senior Fellow at the Science Policy Research Unit, the University of Sussex, leading a research program on the implications of technological change for skills and training.

David Stern is an economist whose research deals with education and human resources. His writings include two books: *Managing Human Resources, The Art of Full Employment* (Auburn House, 1982) and

Adolescence and Work (Erlbaum, 1989; co-edited with D. Eichorn), in addition to numerous articles. He is associated with the National Center for Research in Vocational Education at the University of California, Berkeley. Currently he is engaged in two research projects about how work and learning take place at the same time. One project is a study of companies involved in learning-intensive production (with Clair Brown and Michael Reich). The other is a longitudinal study of how students' paid employment affects their subsequent success in school and work (with Charles Hopkins, James Stone, and Martin McMillion). His chapter is based in part on these projects, supported by the National Center for Research in Vocational Education.

Robert J. Thomas (Ph.D. 1981, Northwestern University) is Leaders for Manufacturing Associate Professor of Organization Studies at the Sloan School of Management of the Massachusetts Institute of Technology. His recent publications include: *Citizenship, Gender and Work* (California, 1985), "Participation and Control: A Shopfloor Perspective on Employee Participation" (*Research in the Sociology Organizations*, 1990), "Microchips and Macroharvests: New Technology and Labor Relations in Agriculture" (*Workers, Managers and Technological Change*, 1987), "Blue Collar Careers" (*The Handbook of Career Theory*, 1989), and "Technological Choice: Union–Management Cooperation in New Technology Design" (*Industrial Relations*, forthcoming). He is currently completing a book entitled *The Politics of Technology*.

Technology and the Future of Work

1

Introduction

Paul S. Adler

To the extent that businesses plan for the workforce implications of new process technologies that they introduce, it is often in a largely unconscious manner. The fantasy that often governs this unconscious process might be called the "de-skilling myth": received wisdom and wishful thinking encourage many managers to believe that new technologies will permit them to get along not only with proportionately *fewer* workers—a perfectly reasonable assumption in many cases—but also with workers who are on average *less skilled and doing narrower jobs.*

There are, of course, some cases where de-skilling occurs. But an emerging body of research suggests first, that the use of new technologies will in general be more profitable when entrusted to more highly skilled employees, and second, that as a result, firms generally, although not always, "muddle through" to an implementation approach premised on upgraded skills and broader jobs.

The difficulties experienced by many United States firms in international competition suggests that this muddling through process is often, at least in the case of the United States, far too protracted and erratic. This book aims to clarify the changes in job content and work organization needed for the effective implementation of new technology, and to identify the implications of this upgrading for skill formation, employee relations, and strategic leadership.

This book brings together a set of papers on these themes, commissioned as background briefing for a seminar conducted at Stanford University on March 28–30, 1990. The seminar was attended by 200 leaders from industry and 50 researchers, including the papers' authors. The enthusiastic response to the seminar encourages us to believe that the set of issues was well-defined and that the papers deserve wider circulation.

The authors were selected because they present a new, emerging generation of research on technology and work. The purpose of the book is to give this new generation greater visibility, and thus allow it to be better scrutinized for its strengths, weaknesses and policy implications.

This introduction will expand on the nature of the technology and work problem as experienced in industry, and then discuss some limitations of the currently dominant research approaches. It is against this industrial and intellectual backdrop that we can better appreciate the novelty and promise of the new generation of research.

STUMBLING BACKWARDS INTO THE FUTURE

In many firms today the dominant technology–people–organization model combines indifference and blind faith: indifference to the crucial role played by the three-way interaction among technology, people, and organization in the effective implementation of automation, and blind faith that technology can by itself sustain or restore competitiveness.

These models—if model is the right word—leave many organizations without a strategy for the joint development of their technical, human, and organizational resources. Line managers, human resource staffs, engineers, and workers are left to muddle through without strategic guidance. These models thus severely impede industry's ability to tap the potential benefits of new process technologies. In some cases, such models lead businesses to staff automated systems with overly qualified personnel out of an exaggerated fear of potential technical difficulties. More often, they lead to staffing systems with undertrained personnel out of misplaced hopes that technology can somehow eliminate the need for skilled users. Too many firms thus stumble backwards into the future.

This lack of clear direction is reinforced by, and in turn reinforces, confusion in the broader public discussion on what to expect from new technologies. This confusion is due in large measure to the way that the fear of some mirrors the fantasy of others that new technologies will finally allow machines to supplant human expertise. Such fears and fantasies mislead us on both the quantitative issue of technology's impact on the number of jobs and on the qualitative issue of technology's impact on the nature of work.

On the quantitative side, the factory of the future will be much more productive and will thus employ fewer people in proportion to the volume of the plant's output. Some observers therefore fear that the acceleration of technological change will increase aggregate national unemployment rates. In most cases, however, such productivity increases will allow price reductions that open new markets and thereby create more jobs. The primary threat to jobs is not too fast a pace of technological change, but a pace that is too slow in comparison with the competition. In contrast to the automation debate that raged in the United States during the 1960s, this proposition is now fairly commonly accepted. The appropriate policy response to unemployment is still a topic of public debate, but the role of technology has been de-emphasized.

Qualitative issues occupy the center stage of the public debate about technology today and they are therefore the primary focus of this volume. The papers collected here study the type of jobs and organizations that the effective use of new technologies will require. The contributors believe there is now ample evidence to refute decisively the fear/fantasy that the factory of the future will be staffed by a majority of low-skilled button pushers and a handful of high-level engineers. Such images contrast strikingly with the real experience of highly automated facilities. Naturally, the precise workforce skill requirements vary according to product, process, market, and strategy. And sometimes a small proportion of jobs are "de-skilled," creating both opportunities and problems. But more automated operations almost invariably rely on higher levels of expertise in the majority of jobs.

The lack of skills, not a surplus of skills, has proved to be the most common stumbling block in automation projects. This challenge to the skill base of the organization poses, in turn, important challenges for the firm's skill-formation efforts, for its employee relations policies, and for its strategic leadership.

Although academic research has played a useful role in clarifying the quantitative employment issues, several factors have impeded its ability to contribute to our understanding of the qualitative issues.

First, as compared to the 1950s and 1960s, United States research in the 1980s has devoted less attention to the theme of technology and work. In part, this de-emphasis is due to a shift over the last two decades U.S. industry's focus away from production towards finance and marketing. In Europe, technology and work issues have been much more politically controversial and have therefore attracted greater academic attention.

Second, when researchers' attention has turned to these issues, it has often focused on a single narrow facet of the problem, reflecting the growing specialization in academic research. Industry, however, needs guidelines for managing the whole set of interrelated issues that arise in implementing new technologies.

Third, insight into the technology–people–organization issues has also been impeded by the tendency of contemporary theory to focus on causal factors other than technology itself. Any hint of "technological determinism" has become suspect. Yet industry often confronts its technology–people–organization problems in precisely this technologically deterministic form: Knowing that they will need to implement new generations of equipment, industry leaders seek guidance on the organizational changes needed to yield the maximum benefits from these investments.

Finally, over the past few years researchers have focused increasingly on the differences rather than the similarities between organizations and countries. Recent academic social theory has tended to shy away from the task of formulating broad generalizations and has tended to focus on the incommensurability of different historical trajectories. When viewed from the vantage point of the international competitiveness problem, however, research needs to help us draw lessons from other countries' experience.

In sum, as the rate of technological change accelerates, the need grows more pressing for conceptual frameworks capable of making sense of the challenges we face. In this context, the weakness of conventional academic research—above all, its inability to cast light on the broader, longer-term trends associated with technological change—has become increasingly burdensome.

Technology is, of course, not the only factor that adds urgency to the task of developing new technology–people–organization models. Pressures for better integration of product and process design, new competitive conditions and market demands, demographic trends, and cultural shifts also contribute. But the premise of this collection is that technology is one of the key forces undermining the old models, and as such, deserves sustained attention.

THE EMERGENT VIEW

The contributors to the present volume are diverse in their orientations, but they share an awareness of the importance of technology's influence on the range of effective options available to organizations. They also share an interpretation of the evidence available on the general nature of technology's influence, namely that a broad process of workforce skill upgrading and organizational redesign will be needed to ensure the effective deployment of new process technologies.

To the casual observer, unaware of the tenor of research on automation and skill over the past two decades, such an upgrading proposition may seem self-evident, but the emergence of a research stream that takes this proposition as its premise represents a remarkable turn for the international research community.

Research on automation and work has gone through three major generations since the Second World War. A brief sketch of each of them will highlight the novelty of the emergent fourth generation.

The first generation, in the 1950s and 1960s, was dominated by authors such as Blauner (1964), Woodward (1958), Touraine (1954), and Mallet (1963), who—despite considerable differences in nuance among them—all saw automation leading to a broadening of job and upgrading of skills relative to the limited jobs requirements of the assembly line. The chemical refinery control room seemed to exemplify the future of work in the eyes of these researchers.

Partly because of the prominence of less-skilled workers in the resurgence of industrial conflict in the late 1960s, and partly because of the internal limits of the older research—the optimism of which seemed based almost exclusively on the narrow base of continuous process industries—the second generation of research, conducted in the 1970s, was dominated by a very different approach. A series of theoretical and empirical studies originating in different countries expressed a striking convergence on the proposition that automation's potentially favorable effect on skill requirements was often not realized. Frequently inspired by Marx's analysis of the labor process, authors such as Braverman (1974) in the United States, Freyssenet (1974) in France, Beynon and Nichols (1977) in the United Kingdom, and Kern and Schumann (1972) in Germany all argued various forms of a single thesis: capitalist societies tend to de-skill work in their constant search for lower production costs and greater control over a potentially recalcitrant labor force.

"Technological determinism" was the dogma that this second generation assailed. The implementation of the same technology would have, they argued, very different effects in different types of societies. A long-run decline in average skill levels both for individual jobs and for the labor force as a whole—in some authors' frameworks, a decline conjugated with the creation of a smaller number of highly skilled positions—was the diagnosis of the past and the prognosis for the future of advanced capitalist societies. The assembly line seemed to be the key image of the future of work for these researchers.

The polemical intent in this proposition was fairly evident. In the absence of systematic statistics, case studies were used to great effect to show: (1) a frequent gap between workers' capabilities and job requirements (skill underutilization), (2) instances in which profitability did seem to call for de-skilling, and (3) other instances in which managerial ideologies and political concerns led to de-skilling at the expense of efficiency. The microdynamics of power relations within the firm became the focus of attention and the premise for broad claims about trends in skill requirements.

Even its partisans, however, had some difficulties with this de-skilling thesis. In particular, doubts began to crystallize around the multitude of skill upgrading counter-examples and around the implicit assumption of managerial omniscience and omnipotence. Moreover, none of the larger-scale statistical studies offered any support for the de-skilling diagnosis (Spenner, 1983).

A third generation of research therefore emerged, which progressively veered away from the "big generalizations" and from the question of broader trends. In tune with a growth of skepticism among influential thinkers concerning anything resembling historical "laws of development," the focus turned even more resolutely to the microdynamics of changes in technology and work. For this "contextualist" generation, which attained dominance in the late 1970s and early 1980s, and which today remains the dominant school of thought, there was no valid generalization possible concerning long-run trends in skills, nor a fortiori concerning the technology–work relationship.

This skepticism generated very worthwhile research into the "social construction" of skill definitions—the idea that the distinction between skilled and unskilled is often more political and ideological than economic and technical—and into the host of local factors (balance of political power, union organization, market conditions) that could override any direct effect technology might have on skills. The group around the French journal *Sociologie du Travail* can, in this respect, be compared to the research of Edwards (1979) in the United States and Gallie (1978) in Great Britain (see also the collection edited by Knights et al., 1985) in their focus on the impact of relative bargaining power and specific market conditions on automation, staffing, and labeling. The dominant image of the future of work in this research is that of a kaleidoscope of complex patterns, constantly shifting and forming no overall tendency.

Over the past five years or so, a change of tone has become audible. In the wake of nearly two decades of economic turbulence, the dynamism of work reorganization efforts and the extensiveness of industrial restructuring seem to call for new efforts to reach viable, if modest, generalizations. Data on aggregate skill levels and case studies are increasingly being read not only as counter-evidence against the de-skilling thesis, but as evidence for a distinct net upgrading trend. Moreover, the new research highlights an important, if mediated, influence of technology on skill requirements.

Some of this research is still struggling to confess the radicalness of its departure from the preceding generation's rejection of generalizations regarding skill trends and a causal role for technology. Nevertheless, the new generation focuses increasingly on the weight of competitive pressures to adopt more productive work systems and the resultant long-run trends towards upgrading in skill requirements.

In a sense, this new focus represents a return to some of the themes of the first generation, but it also retains important lessons from the intervening work. From the labor process research, the new generation has retained an appreciation of the fact that in the context of a market economy these upgrading tendencies will typically manifest themselves in a somewhat chaotic manner, often leaving pockets of de-skilling and layoffs that may indeed call for policy remedies. From the contextualist research, the fourth generation has retained a sensitivity to the importance of variations across national and organizational contexts and the influence of many intervening variables.

In the new research, however, class conflicts and local variability, important as they are, do not preclude an overall shift towards higher skills stimulated by the competitive pressure to implement new technology more effectively. In the new paradigm, competition forces firms to seek out more productive combinations of machine and human capacities. In this process the outcome is, more often than not, an upgrading of skill requirements. Firms, regions, and countries that ignore this relationship suffer a critical competitive handicap.

If "technological determinism" means that all machines have specific work content and work organization written into them, then the doctrine is clearly too simplistic to be of much use. A "softer" form of technological determinism, however, would argue that upgrading and de-skilling modes of implementation are not equally productive and that the competitive pressure to adopt more efficient job designs with new technologies generates some determinate and important trends in skill and work organization. The new generation articulates such a "soft" technological determinism—one that neither underestimates the causal roles of other variables nor telescopes the time frame required for technological constraints to manifest themselves.

The new research, freed from the de-skilling presumption and from the exclusive concern with the microdynamics of power relationships and the sources of local variation in skill outcomes, seems to have found a new vigor and relevance. It appears able to address both the positive tendencies associated with the introduction of new technology and to provide more insightful critiques of the associated problems.

OVERVIEW

These premises explain the structure of this volume. The sequence of chapters is designed to highlight a primary causal chain leading from growing automation opportunities to competitive pressure to use automation effectively, to the need to adapt work content and work organization, to new training practices, to new industrial relations policies, and finally to new approaches for the strategic management of technology.

Causal chains running in the opposite direction are certainly not absent. Nevertheless, the working assumption of the papers in this volume is that we can better apprehend the dynamics of modern society, at least in its longer-term contours, by distinguishing the central currents—as summarized in this causal chain—from the secondary eddies.

The structure of the book also reflects the editor's home in the United States. The U.S. case is at the center of most of the papers. Even when the subject of their papers is the experience of another country, the U.S. authors were asked also to explore the implications for U.S. industry.

The first four chapters address the job content and work organization most effectively associated with new process technologies. They look at engineers, technicians, workers, and managers in manufacturing and design and ask how we can characterize the impact of technology on the content of their work, what types of old skills have become obsolete and what new ones have been created, what new job categories are needed, and what forms of organization are most effective in the use of new process technologies.

The case study by Larry Hirschhorn and Joan Mokray of "Auto-

mation and Competency Requirements in Manufacturing" lays the
foundation for the volume by presenting the results of a survey of
workers and managers at a Digital Equipment Corporation plant that
has experienced several waves of automation. The chapter highlights
the duality of skills (job content) and roles (work organization) as
components of "competence." The authors conclude that, for workers
to be competent (effective) in their use of new forms of automation,
they need both new upgraded skills and new broadened roles in the
organization's division of labor.

Paul Attewell's chapter on "Skill and Occupational Changes in U.S.
Manufacturing" shifts the focus from the plant level to U.S. manufacturing as a whole. Attewell critically reviews recent U.S. research
on technology and skill, and presents new data on the shifts in the
occupational structure of U.S. manufacturing that confirm an upgrading
trend. He also discusses in more detail recent qualitative research on
a number of occupations experiencing technological change.

Horst Kern and Michael Schumann analyze the German experience
of "New Concepts of Production and the Emergence of the Systems
Controller." In a surprising and sweeping revision of their landmark
1972 study of German industry—which concluded that automation
seemed to be associated with de-skilling and skill polarization—Kern
and Schumann have more recently argued that the current trend in
German industry is towards workforce upgrading. This is most clearly
visible in the emergence of a new job category—"systems controller"—
in many automated settings. They present here some new survey data
on the diffusion of this new type of work in the auto, machine
manufacturing, chemical, and electrical and electronic producuts industries.

Peter Senker's study of "Automation and Work in Britain" argues
a dual thesis. On the one hand, Senker's own research and that of
a growing number of his British colleagues highlight the need for higher
skills and broader roles for the effective use of new manufacturing
and engineering automation. On the other hand, British management,
he argues, has been reticent to adopt these new policies, and as a result,
the payoff to new technology investments has often been disappointing.

The next two chapters focus on how firms can meet the need for
new competencies. They ask what education, recruitment, selection,
training, and development approaches are needed to build the skills
and prepare people for the roles associated with technological change,
and how these approached interact with the external general and
vocational education system.

David Stern's chapter on "Institutions and Incentives for Developing
Work-Related Knowledge and Skill" reviews the range of institutions
and practices that contribute to the development of the skills of the
U.S. workforce. He summarizes several bodies of research—in economics, education policy, and cognitive psychology—on the relative roles

of general education, vocational education, corporate training, and the production process itself. His discussion of "learning–intensive production" and new approaches to off–the–job training—approaches that teach by involving students in solving real problems encountered in their jobs, and that thus constitute what Stern calls "doing by learning"—poses a fundamental challenge to the economists' assumption that training always represents a short–term cost to the employer.

Robert Cole's study of "Issues in Skill Formation in Japanese Approaches to Automation" examines the general patterns of skill formation that underlie the very broad diffusion of reliable advanced technologies in Japan. These skill–formation practices reflect a strategic focus on skills that contrasts with the dominant United States approaches. The Japanese strategy results from the conjunction of a historical tradition of long-term employment relationships and the current pressure of labor shortages. Japanese human capital investment fosters both basic knowledge and application–oriented skills; it puts great emphasis on multiskilling. Cole's analysis reveals the systematic way in which Japanese firms weave together policies of automation, skill building, and employee relations through learning strategies designed to diffuse best practices. As a result, Japanese workers show relatively little resistance to new technology and Japanese firms can more effectively exploit their new equipment.

The next two chapters focus on the influence of technology on employee relations. They ask what kinds of employee relations are needed for the effective implementation of automated systems, and what involvement employees and unions should have in the design of jobs, of skill formation policies, and of the automated systems they will use.

Robert Thomas and Thomas Kochan, in "Technology, Industrial Relations and the Problem of Organizational Transformation," argue that deriving competitive advantage from new technologies on a sustained basis will require a fundamental change in the U.S. industrial-relations system. The traditional industrial-relations model is based on a clear separation of the rights and duties of labor and management and assumes a basically antagonistic relationship between the parties. A new model will need to encourage mutual commitments to building skills and to pursuing production improvement opportunities. This will require strengthening the voice and role of employees as stakeholders in the corporation. Thomas and Kochan outline some of the major obstacles to the emergence of this new model.

Max Ogden is an official at the Australian Council of Trade Unions, and his chapter on "Union Involvement to Restructure Industry in Australia" presents an extraordinary story, little known outside Australia. With the election of a Labor Party government in 1983, the unions saw the need and the opportunity to shift their traditional focus on the distribution of wealth to a joint focus on both the production and the distribution of wealth. Rather than adopting a defensive posture focused on technology's potential negative effects on specific segments of the workforce, the unions have increasingly seen new technology, work upgrading, and skill formation as essential to international competitiveness and prosperity. Positioning themselves as representatives not of sectional interests but of society's general interest, the unions have become key players in defining national, industry-level, and company-level restructuring strategies.

The last two chapters focus on the implications of the constellation of issues addressed in the preceding chapters for the strategic management of the firm. They ask what types of strategies will enable companies to orchestrate the joint development of human and technical resources, and how industry leaders will weave together long-term business, technology, and human resource strategies.

Claudio Ciborra and Leslie Schneider, in "Transforming the Routines and Contexts of Management, Work and Technology," address the question of how organizations can make the major, as opposed to incremental, changes that often seem necessary for firms to capitalize on the competitive potential of new technologies. Whereas much of the strategy literature focuses on the need to ensure an appropriate fit among strategy, technology, and organization, it is largely silent on the enormous difficulties many firms experience in regaining this fit after a major change in technology. Ciborra and Schneider argue that these difficulties are inherent in the process of "second-order learning." Much of an organization's existing strategy–technology–structure "package" is invisible to the organizational actors, since it has become a set of background assumptions and institutional arrangements that are taken for granted. These assumptions thus become a "formative context" that shapes the members' understanding of the range of alternatives, and often precludes precisely the radical changes required by the new circumstances. Ciborra and Schneider show the power of the formative context using two cases of automation, and discuss a range of policies that can facilitate second-order learning.

Thomas Lifson's contribution on "Innovation and Institutions: Notes on the Japanese Paradigm" argues that Japanese competitiveness, especially the ability to upgrade products and processes continuously, is facilitated by the extensive use of collaborative networks of firms and individuals. Tracing the historical evolution of Japanese organizational forms, he contends that Japanese industry exploits a broader range of the institutional spectrum than U.S. industry. In the United States, strategic options are typically framed in terms of a choice between two basic organizational forms—markets or hierarchies, buy or make—whereas in Japan, a more extensive reliance on norms of reciprocity facilitates the development of collaborative networks between and within firms. The competitiveness and effectiveness of this arrangement will, Lifson argues, encourage its adoption to a growing number of American firms.

TWO KEY THEMES

Taken together, these essays demonstrate the potential relevance and rigor of the emergent fourth generation of research. The perspective of this fourth generation allows us to move to a new level of understanding of the dynamic processes currently reshaping industry. In particular, the new perspective highlights two themes among the determinants of competitive performance: competence and learning.

The effective use of new technologies will require a workforce with both higher skills and broader roles, and hence the theme of competence. Much prior research and pragmatically-oriented literature has focused on one facet to the exclusion of the other. However, the conclusion that emerges from these papers is that it is the combination of new skills and roles that will give employees the kind of competence required to use new technologies most effectively.

The effective use of new technologies also requires that the business firm be substantially reconfigured to support a process of continuous learning. Many of the new technologies are programmable and therefore more malleable than preceding generations, making the ability to extend their capabilities on a continual basis an increasingly important competitive factor. An accelerating rate of change in both technology and the business environment further emphasizes the importance of learning in a second sense—the ability of the organization to adapt rapidly to successive generations of new tools and new tasks—as a competitive factor.

It is becoming increasingly obvious that, to compete effectively, firms need to develop comprehensive long-term strategies for building their "knowledge assets," that is, for jointly managing the interdependent development of the knowledge embodied in technical systems and the knowledge accumulated by employees. Clearly, the success of firms in developing this new approach depends to a great extent on changes in the broader social, political, and institutional context. To preserve its focus, this book unfortunately leaves this issues in the background. But equally clearly, industry itself has a key role to play in shaping the future. This volume helps us assess the prospects.

REFERENCES

Beynon, H. and J. Nichols. *Living with Capitalism*. London: Routledge–Kegan Paul, 1977.
Blauner, R. *Alienation and Freedom*. Chicago: University of Chicago Press, 1964.
Braverman, H. *Labor and Monopoly Capital*. New York: Monthly Review Press, 1974.
Edward, R. *Contested Terrain*. New York: Basic, 1979.
Freyssenet, M. *Le processus de dequalification–surqualificatioin de la force de travail*. Paris: Centre de sociologie urbaine, 1974.
Gallie, D. *In Search of the New Working Class*. Cambridge: Cambridge University Press, 1978.

Kern, H. and Schumann, M. *Industriearbeit und arbeiterbewusstsein*. Frankfurt A. M.: Europaische Verlagsanstalt, 1972.

Knights, D., H. Willmott, and D. Collinson (eds.) *Job Redesign: Critical Perspectives on the Labour Process*. Hampshire, UK: Gover, 1985.

Mallet, S. *La Nouvelle Classe Ouvriere*. Paris: 1963.

Spenner, K. "Deciphering Prometheus." *American Sociological Review*. December, 1983.

Touraine, A. *L'Evolution du travail aux usines Renault*. Paris: 1954.

Woodward, J. *Management and Technology*. London: 1958.

2

Automation and Competency Requirements in Manufacturing: A Case Study

Larry Hirschhorn

Joan Mokray

Skills, know-how, education base, work ethic, knowledge, abilities, competence, empowerment, responsibility: the proliferation of articles with keywords such as these is symptomatic of a growing concern. As companies invest in automated equipment and increase the rate at which they introduce new products, they need workers who can solve production problems; analyze trends, quality and output; learn to control new machinery quickly; and communicate effectively with engineers and marketing people. What forces shape these new requirements? What helps workers meet them? What can managers do to stimulate the corresponding abilities?

Skills, education base, work ethic, and so forth: the proliferation of the terms themselves is also symptomatic of a theoretical and conceptual problem that compounds the practical one. Although there is a substantial overlap among these terms, the differences suggest real uncertainty as to where the most urgent needs are located and how they can best be met.

Addressing these practical and conceptual questions in parallel, this chapter reports a pilot case study of the Digital Equipment Corporation's (DEC) Westfield computer manufacturing plant. Through in-depth interviews, we tried to assess when and why workers feel competent and what factors help them act and work in a competent manner. Our effort to make sense of what people were telling us in these interviews led to the development of a new theoretical framework. The methodology for this study thus derived from the tradition of "grounded theory," in which facts do not test a prior theory but rather inform the development of theory, and the emergent theory helps clarify the meaning of the facts.

These interviews revealed that "to be competent in the job" was a central concern of both workers and their managers. This concern encompassed both an objective level of performance capability and a subjective experience of effectiveness. When we tried to make sense of the cluster of factors that emerged in these interviews as critical to competence, we found that many of the previously mentioned keywords can be grouped into two facets of competence: skills and roles. Competence resulted from the joint presence of the relevant skills—knowledge, know-how, abilities, and so on—and the appropriate roles—work ethic, empowerment, responsibility and so forth.

This chapter is divided into six sections. In the first, we provide a brief description of the Westfield plant. In the second, we present our model of competence, showing how competence is shaped through the interaction of a worker's skills with the role he or she performs. In the third, we examine in detail how the tools used by Westfield workers and the problems they solve have evolved to create a new profile of skills. In the fourth, we synthesize these findings into a hierarchical model of skills. In the fifth, we show how the role system at Westfield shapes a new pattern of interaction between "direct" and "indirect" labor, a pattern we call "dynamic complementarity." We elaborate on this idea in the sixth section, showing how it relates to existing organizational design theories. In the seventh, we show how the new roles and the new skills interact to define a particular set of competencies. A seventh section summarizes our argument.

THE CONTEXT: THE WESTFIELD PLANT

Employing 1250 people, with some 400 shopfloor workers, DEC's Westfield plant makes circuit boards and the metal frames and covers for computers. It has gone through two process technology revolutions in the past decade— surface-mount technology for printed circuit boards and computer numerical control for punch presses—while also supporting DEC's frequent introduction of new products to the marketplace. Thus, Westfield workers have had to master new machines as well as learn to produce a succession of new products.

Surface-mount technology has significantly changed the way in which printed circuit boards (PCBs) are produced. In the past, using "through-hole" techniques, workers inserted components onto a board, placed component leads in the correct positions, and then placed the boards in a solder bath to connect the different parts electrically. It was assembly work, and "direct" personnel (shopfloor workers) used their eyes and hands deftly and intensively to ensure that components were placed in the proper holes with the correct front-to-back orientation.

As board density grew, engineers first developed a system to allow workers to continue hand mounting components using magnifying glasses and dental tweezers. But leads were easily bent when the boards were transported, and almost every mounted component had to be "tweaked" to create a functioning board. As densities reached over 200 components per board, hand assembly became infeasible.

Surface mount automates the process of producing circuit boards. Workers lay solder paste onto a board using a silk-screening process. Components are then automatically placed, an infrared oven melts the solder paste over the leads, and then the workers inspect the boards. Workers no longer assemble boards. Instead, they monitor the critical variables of an automated process. While automatic, the machinery is far from perfect, and workers must check the height of the solder paste, the speed with which it is applied, the size of the silk-screen holes, and the temperature profile of the oven. Since little is visible to the naked eye, workers set up the machines using software commands and check the process by analyzing data. Monitoring, analyzing, and checking becomes particularly important because repairing boards has become almost impossible: manually removing or reorienting a poorly placed component would destroy the component and the board. The workers produce quality boards by monitoring their production, not by repairing defective products.

As for sheet metal operations, in the 1960s, workers themselves shaped the sheets using a die as a guide or template. In the early 1970s, Westfield progressed to computerized control. A computer tape loaded by a worker controlled the press so that workers did not have to change the die or manually move a sheet. Holes were punched continuously and the worker's role involved checking the tools in the turret and setting up the job.

At the time of our interviews, a new generation of equipment was being installed. Workers were no longer loading tapes into the punch press; instead, data for directing the press were directly downloaded from a central computer. In setting up the job, workers now had to check the program to ensure that it was accurate. Thus, workers who once manually worked a press now controlled its operation by checking the data that directed the machine's action and by monitoring the press to make sure its actions conformed to the engineer's specifications for the resulting sheet. The work had become information intensive.

Our Interviews

To understand how workers, supervisors, managers, and engineers had adjusted to this new technological environment and how different employees understood what kinds of knowledge, skills, and abilities they needed to work effectively within it, we conducted in-depth semistructured interviews with 23 employees, 15 direct personnel (shopfloor workers), and 8 indirect personnel (managers, engineers, and support staff). We chose people who had worked for a significant number of years in the plant and had experienced many of its changes.

We asked such questions as, "When do you feel competent and why?," "If you could construct a curriculum to become more competent, what courses would you take?," and "What other roles would you like to try here at the plant?" We also requested that they "Describe a curriculum of study your boss should take." During the interviews, we took handwritten, close-to-verbatim notes, and then analyzed their contents for general themes, as well as specific hypotheses, as we began to understand the patterns of responses. Finally, a draft of our findings was reviewed by the interviewees themselves.

MODEL OF COMPETENCE

The key result of our analysis of these interviews is that competence is shaped by skills and roles. In turn, skills are shaped by the plant's technical infrastructure, and roles by the plant's social system (see Fig. 2.1).

As Figure 2.1 suggests, the skills workers need are shaped by the tools they use and the problems they face. Workers facing difficult problems using simple tools need significant skills. Similarly, those working with powerful tools may still need significant skills especially when they must solve continually changing problems. Changes in skill requirements therefore result from changes in both tools and problems.

While workers may be very skilled, their ability to act skillfully is shaped by the roles they occupy. If, for example, a worker were highly skilled but had little authority to exercise this skill or did not get the resources and information needed to deploy it, the person would feel

Figure 2.1. Competence Is a Function of Skills and Roles

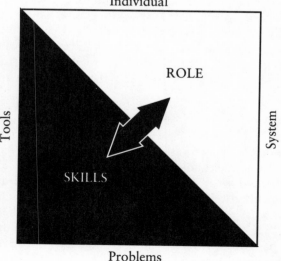

incompetent and be unable to act in a competent manner. The role occupied by the worker makes the worker incompetent despite the skills he or she possesses. The role the individual occupies is, we posit, shaped by both the system of role relationships that sets the bounds for any given role and the particular choices the individual makes in taking a role. People occupying the same official roles may exercise the role differently; one may take more initiative within its bounds, another may "work to the book." Thus, two people with the same skills occupying the same official role may not appear to be equally competent.

Why use the term *competence*? What value does it offer? As this model suggests, the concept of skill alone is insufficient to understand a person's efficacy at work. Skills, our research led us to believe, must always be potentiated by the context in which they are exercised. They are not specific to a job, or to a person, but result from the interaction among system, person, and job. Competence is the outcome of a combination of action, choice, process, and design. Questions about how competency requirements are changing in the context of the automated factory should therefore evoke a complex reflection on experience. By focusing on competence rather than skills, we can explore not only the technical requirements of a job but how and whether people are authorized to meet those requirements.

Indeed, when we asked people to describe when and how they felt competent, they frequently responded with considerable emotion. The word *competence* itself evokes experience of one's personal efficacy as well as one's objective skills and abilities. One shopfloor worker, recounting an incident when she felt competent, noted:

> *The metals department brought in a broken piece of equipment. My mentor wasn't there. I took the equipment, no promises. I took it apart, found out what was wrong, and I fixed it. I was so proud. It wasn't so complicated, but I did it on my own and I was proud.*

Another said:

> *If equipment has been down all night, and if I can get it up in a half hour, I feel really good. Competence is how good you are at your job. I am judging myself. My feelings have a lot to do with whether I feel good. Good confidence makes you feel competent.*

A third described when he felt competent:

> *When I can put production out. It's frustrating when machines break down. You feel very incompetent and can't do it. I'm not so incompetent, but I should have been able to keep it running.*

These responses, which so directly link feelings to performance, suggest that the experience of competence involves the whole person, that is, the person interacting with tools, problems, and others in his or her environment.

SKILLS: A FUNCTION OF TOOLS AND PROBLEMS

Changes in skill requirements reflect changes in tools and problems. We will characterize the changes in tools in a little more detail before addressing the problems aspect.

Tools

Consider the development of the punch press at Westfield—from manually controlled presses where workers changed dies by hand and pushed and pulled on metal, the plant progressed to the new computer-controlled presses where information was downloaded electronically and tools and dies automatically appeared in the right sequence.

Four changes were evident in the transformation. First, the tool system itself became integrated, with fewer distinct parts. Second, there was less disjunction between the raw materials and the tools for transforming them. In contrast to an oldtime metalworker who experienced the ongoing tension between hammer and metal—indeed his skills consisted of his ability to apply hammer to metal—the new worker does not experience the stress between the two because the tool interacts continuously with the metal in a computer-controlled system. Instead, the new worker observes the consequences of this interaction.

Third, as tools and materials are integrated, workers cannot get direct sensory data from their interplay but instead must get data from an interface such as a computer screen or a paper report. Fourth, as tools became integrated and linked more continuously to the materials, workers shifted their focus and broadened their perspective. Rather than focusing on the instantaneous interaction between tools and materials, the workers observed a broader pattern of events.

These same distinctions apply to changes from through-hole to surface-mount technologies. The separate stages of pasting, placing, and soldering are integrated. The insertion equipment interacts continuously with the board. Workers get data from the various interfaces—the oven readings and the testing at the end of the process—and workers monitor the whole process rather than any single part.

Table 2.1 summarizes these shifts in the nature of tools.

Problems

As workers used increasingly automated tool systems, we might anticipate that the problems they must solve became simpler. However, in responding

Table 2.1. The Changing Nature of Tools

From	To
A single tool	A system of tools
A discontinuity between material and tool	A seamless interaction of material and tool
Sensory feedback at the juncture of tool and material	Cognitive feedback at an interface between the system and the person
Tools that narrow the worker's focus	Tools that broaden the worker's focus

to our requests to describe the nature of the problems they encountered in everyday operations, the workers at Westfield did not highlight any growing simplicity but rather the increasingly abstract nature of the problems. They noted that they were more often using their heads than their hands. Moreover, despite access to more information through the automated systems, many emphasized their need to rely more on memory to control production.

We asked workers whether their work depended more on their heads than in the past. Almost all said that it did. However, what was more striking were the ways in which people described how and why they relied more on their heads. People typically noted how they had to cope with greater variety and complexity and consequently had to remember more. Consider the following statements.

- "It's memory work today. You have to remember what to do, when to do it, and how to do it. Every problem is a little different. Before it wasn't as complicated. It was simpler work. You had fewer kinds of parts, fewer processes."

- "Work is now a mental strain. There's more to remember. There's lots of new tooling, lots more paper work. "

- "You have to think—there are so many components. You need to think through the right orientation. It's stressful, because you really have to concentrate. In the old days you only had to memorize the right polarity. Now there's lots to remember."

- "Maintenance is more head. Before we did more mechanical tweaking. Now you're in computers. The programs are in your head. Even the manuals. One program is linked to another, and you have to remember how. It has never been so complicated."

- "Now it's heads more. There's lot of different equipment and to

run it you have got to use your head. You have to think before
you randomly push buttons. We had to think before, but it's different
now. Before it was soldering. Today you concentrate on a quality
product. Before your hands made the quality product. Now the
machine makes it and you watch through an interface."

- "I think there's more thought now. No, it's a different type of
  thinking. There's less handling. And we can do more operations
  at one time than ten years ago. In the past it would have been
  a single operation for each person."

- "If you build a product with the Omni [the surface mount machine]
  and you notice all the chips are off target, you can either build
  and then manually move all of them or use your head and go into
  the terminal. More thinking is required."

As these remarks suggest, people are both describing a new problem
domain as well as new mental abilities required to perform effectively—
to be competent. The problem domain presents more variety and
complexity. The circuit boards are more compact and densely packed; the
range of tools as well as their interconnectedness has grown; workers'
span of operations had also grown; and workers now focused on the
quality of the product, in addition to getting the product out. As the
last quotation suggests, workers used their heads by "going into the
terminal," that is, by identifying and solving a problem in the abstract
rather than manually correcting it.

Given the much greater data availability in the automated environment, the emphasis on memory seems almost paradoxical, as does the
belief of some of the direct personnel that work was more mentally
straining and demanding. Consider, however, the nature of a manual
skill. When working with their hands, operators depend less on memory
and more on the direct "feedback" from physical materials. A carpenter
sawing a piece of wood does not execute a predetermined sequence
of actions but rather modifies her actions as she observes the succession
of cuts. Her skill is defined by the automaticity of her response to the
changing feel of the wood and saw. By contrast, when machines control
component placement, the problems confronted by direct personnel
work are less routine and resolution is less automatic. Workers set up
the work, inspect the work, and troubleshoot the flow of work. Instead
of tactile stimuli guiding routine actions, workers must depend on
explicit knowledge and forethought concerning the conditions and
parameters that shape the production run. To plan ahead, monitor,
and inspect, they must bring to mind—that is, consciously remember
and picture in the abstract—the whole nature of the run.

One shopfloor worker expressed this shift in thinking and working
in a particularly interesting way. Describing how he had become more
skilled over his ten years at the plant, he noted that, "Ten years ago

I was in the learning mode, so I was using my head to grasp what I was seeing. Now I use my head to reach my goals. I'm constantly thinking ahead." He described this shift as the consequence of his own maturation, but we suspect it also reflects his adaptation to the changing technological profile of the plant. Direct personnel now focused less on the immediate transformation of materials—gluing, placing, and twisting—than on the flow, its control, and on the results of the total process. Mental work becomes more important because automation leads workers to step to the side of the core production process in order to control a broader range of operations.

Table 2.2 highlights how technology has changed the problem domain at Westfield.

Skills

By linking tools to problems, we can understand how skill requirements have changed at Westfield. Tools create increasingly abstract representations of increasingly integrated operations, and the problems that workers must solve in the performance of their tasks reflect the increasingly systemic character of operations. Skills therefore become more "head based" and linked to the activities of controlling, planning, and consciously remembering. Table 2.3 highlights these shifts.

In sum, direct personnel must master a greater range of problem situations, and this quantitative shift also restructures the problem domain. Working with a system of tools ultimately linked together by the computer, the direct personnel must focus increasingly on flow and pattern rather than on the single piece and the particular puzzle it may present. In turn, this shift in the problem domain requires a new set of skills. In controlling the production process instead of simply working within it, direct personnel must focus on the goals of a particular

Table 2.2. The Changing Nature of
Problems to Be Solved by Workers

From	To
A few parameters	Many parameters
Correcting variances	Preventing variances
Sustaining levels of output	Sustaining quality
Puzzles: a single piece	Patterns: the flow, the linkages
Within a single operation	Across several operations

Table 2.3. Technology's Impact on the Nature of Skills Required

From	To
Doing	Controlling
Responding	Planning
Tacit knowledge	Explicit knowledge— knowing what you know
Enacting one's knowledge	Remembering one's knowledge
Awareness	Awareness of one's awareness

run and rely more on their explicit knowledge rather than the tacit knowledge embedded in manual skills. Consequently, direct personnel became more aware of the focus and limits of their awareness and experienced this as an increasing emphasis on their capacity to remember.

HIERARCHY OF SKILL LAYERS

A further insight into the nature of technology's impact on skills emerged from our interviews. In discussing how the nature of skill requirements had evolved at Westfield, interviewees indicated that, with the shift from a focus on discrete steps to a focus on the overall flow, they found the greatest challenge to be in higher cognitive functions—in the domain of thinking, remembering, and planning, rather than just doing. We identified five "layers" of cognitive functions ranging from lower- to successively higher-order skills.

The layer closest to the work itself is "doing," the actual performance of a work task. But the performance of any task needs always to be informed by a second, higher-order layer of skill—"controlling." Some examples of controlling skills are techniques like JIT (just–in–time) or SPC (statistical process control). The third layer of skill is "learning"—the experience of stepping back from the task to reflect on it and to improve performance over time. Controlling a task is a resource for learning; it provides the data that allows the worker to recognize patterns. The true value of JIT and SPC, as implemented by more advanced users, is in driving this continuous learning. The fourth layer of skill is "design"—the process of innovation, or designing new systems. And finally, the fifth layer is "valuing"—understanding how to evaluate alternative designs.

Technological Change and the Skill Layer Hierarchy

As new technologies are introduced, established ways of doing, controlling, and learning are rendered partially obsolete. Responding to the challenge of re-creating the needed skills requires discovering new patterns in the new contexts. With the acceleration of technological change at Westfield, the skill-building challenge intensified at all five levels and for all categories of employees, but the challenge was growing relatively faster for the higher-order skill layers.

This shift from doing to planning led us to posit a developmental ladder as a model of how different types of skills emerge in the factory setting. Mapping the logic of a developmental processes onto this ladder of successively higher skills—doing, controlling, learning, designing and valuing—suggests four hypotheses about skills development:

1. A higher-order skill is needed for the effective deployment of the skill that lies below it on the ladder. Thus, for example, to do an activity like assembling a PCB, a worker must implicitly control her doing, that is, guide her hand or get feedback from the pressure of her hand against a component.

2. Workers become more skilled as they master the relevant higher-order skills, that is, as they move up the ladder.

3. Workers master these higher-order skills by making them explicit, by taking them out of the tacit background of their activity and making them the focus of their attention.

4. As technological change accelerates, workers must develop the skills higher on the ladder.

To see these relationships at work, consider the following sequence. A manual worker on an assembly line performs a simple task, such as placing a knob next to a dial, and controls the task implicitly, simply by directing his hand movements. Now imagine that this assembly process is automated and the worker monitors an automated assembly workstation. In this situation the worker explicitly controls the task by examining a printout, watching a gauge, and correcting a setting. Whereas before, "controlling" was the tacit background requirement for "doing," it now becomes visible, explicit and the focus of attention.

Let us move further up the ladder of skills. A worker, expert at monitoring a particular machine, has learned to monitor it through an implicit process of adaptation. By making small mistakes, for example overcorrecting or undercorrecting in steps of the process, the worker has learned to fine tune the process so that the resulting product meets the appropriate specifications. As technological change accelerates, however, machine controls are modified or replaced more frequently, and workers can no longer rely on an implicit process of adaptation. They must explicitly think of themselves as learners using particular methods, tools, and skills to learn how the machine process and its controls interact. Thus, for example, using statistical process control, workers can track how their control actions affect a process. SPC amplifies and accelerates their learning by providing an explicit record of their control actions. Thus, they become aware of the learning process itself.

Moving further up the ladder, as managers and engineers face the prospects of continually improving machines and modifying the system of controls, workers must become increasingly conscious of their creative or inventive talents. When workers adapt a new control system to a machine, they are implicitly designing an optimal configuration. Tracking variances in the resulting product, they may discover that a particular control strategy is insufficient. For example, when using a particular feedstock or metal, they might find it better to have controls at the front end in order to reduce variances at the back end. As the technological change process and the continuous improvement process accelerate, managers need workers to collaborate with engineers to design and modify machines as well as learn to control them. In this situation, the worker's implicit capacity to design is made explicit. Explicit design replaces implicit modification. Like operators and technicians in a pilot plant, workers then increasingly focus on designing the production process itself.

Finally, as workers become increasingly involved in design, they must become increasingly aware of the tradeoffs in creating an industrial process. The process of designing a process or product is always based on some concept of what is valued and why. Should a more costly process be adopted that reduces defects to close to zero, or are some types of defects acceptable because customers are more interested in costs and can easily obtain replacement parts? Should the process be designed so that it can produce products with a wide variety of characteristics, or should it be designed to produce products that meet a very narrow set of specifications? Workers must know how to value different configurations and link these valuation schemes to different company strategies.

Skill Planning

As technological change accelerates, the challenge to workers' skills is not only at the doing and controlling levels but also and increasingly at the higher levels of learning, designing, and valuing. Our study of Westfield suggests that workers have been successful at transforming their doing and controlling skills, and, with the introduction of more explicit control tools such as SPC, workers are building their learning, designing, and valuing capabilities. As Westfield confronts the new technologies, workers' abilities at the creating and valuing levels are becoming increasingly important.

Our framework can be used to help human resource staffs plan for future training programs. Human resource planners currently use task, job, and competency analysis methodologies to assess what skills workers need to do their jobs. These tools do not *plan for the future* so much as they *assess the present*. But increasingly we need to be able to predict what skills workers will need in the future.

Working with the company's technology planners and engineers, the human resource professional can assess the current state of worker skills, the pace of technical and marketplace changes that might lead workers to take up higher-level challenges, and the rate at which workers are currently developing new skills. Using the skill-ladder concept, the human resource professional can in effect ask: What is the current status of worker activity, in what directions is it changing, at what rate is it changing, and how might technological changes accelerate this rate or modify the direction of change? With these questions answered, the human resource professional can then plan a sequence of training activities that help workers develop skills at the appropriate levels on the ladder.

We would also advance a related hypothesis of significance to skills planning: Specific lower-order skills are associated with specific higher-order skills. For people to learn how to perform a given set of tasks effectively, they must tackle a whole "slice" through all five layers of skills. Two complementary arguments for this hypothesis seem compelling, or at least plausible enough to warrant further research:

1. Lower-order skills are "brittle" without their higher-order counterparts. Doing skills, for example, cannot be applied in contexts that differ even slightly from the context in which the skills were learned unless they are complemented by their higher-order counterparts, since it is these higher-order skills that allow the user to adapt to the new context.

2. Conversely, the higher-order skills cannot be effectively learned "in the abstract," divorced from the types of contexts in which they will be applied. The exercise of the lower-order skills constitutes these contexts.

This approach might allow curriculum design and skill formation planning to move beyond the currently dominant "Chinese menu" approach, where skills at different levels are tackled without regard to their interconnection.

THE ROLES OF DIRECT AND INDIRECT PERSONNEL

Our model suggests that to deploy their skills competently workers must take up roles and be part of a role system that supports their ability to perform skillfully. What kind of role system supports workers' ability to control, learn, and create? To answer this question, we asked workers and managers when and why they felt competent, and then assessed the kind of roles they were implicitly portraying when describing their moments of competent performance.

We found striking differences in the way in which indirect and direct personnel answered these questions. Our data suggest that workers feel most competent when they are participating in a role system that supports what we call a *dynamic complementarity* between direct personnel and indirect staff. Workers could successfully undertake their tasks when the indirect staff buffered them from some of the broader uncertainties and disruptions that product and process innovation introduced. Workers want the indirect staff to be competent in their management of the introduction of products and processes so that workers can be competent in the complementary tasks of controlling the resulting machine process. In this section, we argue that:

1. Westfield is a dynamic system, constantly breaking in new products and developing new processes.

2. The factory as a whole faces two primary tasks: first, bringing innovations to Westfield and linking them to the work of the factory, and second, securing a steady-state flow of product in the face of the disruptions that innovations create.

3. Innovating and controlling tasks complement each other. The success of each shapes the success of the other. Indeed, the interaction of the two determines the factory's rate of learning and how far that learning can progress.

4. The two complementary tasks affect how direct and indirect labor take up different but complementary roles.

5. Workers can deploy their skills competently only when the role system as a whole supports this dynamic complementarity.

Let us explore these propositions in greater detail.

When Workers Feel Competent

To explore workers' experience of competence, we asked them to assess when and why they felt competent, when and why they felt less than competent, and what barriers stood in their way to becoming more competent. The difference in responses from direct and indirect personnel was striking.

In general, we found that direct personnel felt competent when the wider system of work and organization supported rather than disrupted their activities. They believed that the wider system of management and organization should, like a user-friendly tool, be transparent to them. This transparency would allow them to control their work while

feeling autonomous in executing it. By contrast, the indirect staff—
support technicians, engineers, supervisors, and managers—felt competent when they could act upon this infrastructure, when they could
communicate information and ideas to help shape a context that facilitated
the direct personnel's work. The context, the set of relationships, *was*
their work.

Consider the comment of a production manager describing when he
felt particularly competent:

> *I feel particularly competent when I begin to see my vision brought
> to fruition, when I can bring a variety of functions together and
> have them focus on a goal. When I first began in this job, I felt
> incompetent because I didn't know how to do it. When people
> felt my vision, I began hearing people talk about common goals
> and it started to work. The people's talk made me feel the effectiveness
> of my vision.*

This statement highlights three features that shaped the manager's
experience of feeling competence: (1) the manager's ability to influence
others, (2) evidence in the use of his language and ideas by others,
and (3) a view of his task as creating goals and shaping a context.

Now consider the following statement (part of which we quoted
earlier) from a shopfloor worker, a calibration technician:

> *I feel particularly competent in the parts I know the best, where
> I'm educated the most. Our field is so wide, it's hard to say you
> know everything, but there are areas you know more about. I
> have little victories if I can accomplish something on my own
> without technical assistance. That adds to my competence and
> confidence. The metals department brought me a broken piece
> of equipment. My mentor wasn't there. I took the equipment, no
> promises. I took it apart, found out what was wrong, and fixed
> it. I was so proud. It wasn't so complicated, but I did it on my
> own and I was proud. I hated to give it up. I wanted to sign
> it.*

This statement highlights a very different experience of competence. Not
surprisingly, this experience is focused on machines and objects. The
proof of competence lies in the ability to repair an object, to make
it work or fit, to put things back into the flow of production. The
experience of competence is linked to a sense of being autonomous,
to working without supervision.

We found that the difference in remarks was, in general, reproduced
across the set of all the people we interviewed. Thus, when we asked
when they felt competent, some supervisors among the indirect staff
said: "You can walk away from the job and the group is still successful",
"During the team meetings, I feel good because I am not dominating.
. . and I am seeing the team take more ownership", "I have competence

in understanding, listening and helping people. I know this by people being willing to come to me."

By contrast, direct personnel responded: "When I am fixing a job to my standards", "When I am able to do things without asking questions, and I have to rely on myself and my knowledge", "When I was doing major repairs, I got work out at my own pace and I felt satisfied with the day", and "The days I have no problems, everything goes super, machines run well, and the tapes are correct."

Of course, each group wanted the work to run smoothly, but direct personnel focused on the smooth flow of materials whereas indirect personnel focused on the regular flow of information and communication and on the development and reproduction of relationships that shape work.

To examine this difference in greater detail, we analyzed the responses to the question "When do you feel competent?" and the complementary question, "When do you feel incompetent?" and placed answers in one of two categories: "Competence is experienced as the ability to work autonomously, without disruption," and "Competence is the ability to work with others or through others." Table 2.4 shows that the majority of responses from direct personnel fell into the first category and that responses from indirect personnel favored the second.

Supporting Role Systems

Autonomy clearly is much more important for direct than for indirect personnel. How might we interpret this finding, and how can we use it to describe a role system that supports workers' competence? At first glance, we might think that direct personnel are simply asking for less supervision, that they want to be left alone. But answers to the question of how their managers could improve belied this interpretation, and brought out another distinctive difference between the two groups. The answers tended to fall along a continuum, from wanting bosses to be more active and offer more

Table 2.4. The Nature of Competence and Incompetence

	Direct personnel	Indirect personnel
Competence		
Autonomously	11	6
Through others	1	6
Incompetence*		
Autonomously	11	4
Through others	3	9

* Numbers add to greater than 23 due to multiple coding of certain answers.

direction, to asking their bosses to step back and let go. Thus, on the passive side, we had such comments as "Be in tune, develop communication skills, be a coach," "Supporting us in what we feel and need, knowing us as individuals," and "Ability to listen, sit still long enough to listen." On the active side, people said such things as "How to be a boss and not a buddy," "Show up more often," and "To ensure things happen, without too much bureaucracy—just do it!"

Using the "active–passive" contrast, we coded people's responses, again distinguishing between indirect and direct personnel, in Table 2.5.

Direct personnel wanted a management that managed more, that made decisions, was aware of what was going on, understood people's jobs, and communicated more frequently. By contrast, indirect personnel were relatively more interested in a management that was less intrusive and that "let go."

The apparent contradiction between these two findings—the direct personnel's wish for more autonomy *and* more management—was clarified by the answers to a third question. In their assessments of the barriers to becoming more competent, we found that direct personnel focused on the problems of resources and stability, whereas indirect personnel focused on problems of turf, relationships, and communication. Thus, for example, direct personnel mentioned such factors as "too many changes," "machines going down," "inadequate resources," and "too little training." Indirect personnel mentioned such things as, "lots of fence building and tree hugging," "not getting enough information," "underdeveloped teams," and "the organization is too functional." As Table 2.6 shows, the answers of the two groups differed significantly. Direct personnel focused on the system's ability to deliver resources and stability, and indirect personnel focused on the texture or shape of the relationship system itself.

This analysis helps us understand our prior findings. To direct personnel, autonomy meant the ability to work without undue disruption and with adequate support. They felt autonomous when the context that shaped their work was supportive rather than intrusive. They wanted management to be responsible for creating such a context. They therefore wanted an active management, not in the sense of one that intruded

Table 2.5. "How could managers improve?"

	Active*	Passive†
Direct personnel	9	5
Indirect personnel	4	4

* "Decide," "do," "know us," "be there," "communicate."
† "Facilitate," "listen," "let go."

Table 2.6. Barriers to Being Competent*

	Resource	Instability	System	Self	Other
Direct personnel	5	4	0	1	2
Indirect personnel	0	0	5	1	0

* Numbers do not add up to 23 because of incomplete answers by some respondents.

into their work, but one that understood the everyday life of the factory and could provide the resources and information direct personnel needed to be productive.

In asking for a stable context, we might at first suppose that direct personnel were simply conservative, that is, they longed for stability in the face of an increasingly unstable environment. But in their answers to the question, "What training curriculum would you design for yourself?," direct personnel recognized that their wider environment was changing rapidly:

- "Our field is so wide it is hard to say you know everything."

- "I need organizational skills. You never know where this job will take you."

- "I want an AA degree in computer technology because computers are always changing."

- "I like to do diagnosing. It makes me unhappy not to troubleshoot. The new technologies are coming. What are they? I would like to be trained for them."

Workers were aware that their jobs were changing significantly, that they were using their heads more than their hands, and that they must manage an increasingly varied and complicated production system.

The Complementary Tasks of Integration and Control

Instead of conservatism, we therefore suggest a different interpretation of the workers' request for stability, namely that they wanted a stable context, a user-friendly relationship system, that would allow them to control the production process better and maintain it in a steady state. Such a task became all the more challenging and important as the indirect personnel's task became one of innovating, bringing new products and processes to the shop floor, and reworking relationships so that innovations were accepted and integrated into the old system. In sum, the more indirect personnel innovated, the more direct personnel were challenged in their task of control and the more they pressed for an environment that supported their ability to respond to the challenge.

Indeed, Westfield, the oldest and largest manufacturing plant in the DEC system, has had to manage an accelerating and often disruptive set of changes and discontinuities. As the primary manufacturing unit of the DEC system, Westfield has borne the brunt of the product revolutions in the computer field, from the early production of simple circuit boards to DEC's more complex Vax system and its (unsuccessful) efforts to penetrate the personal computer market. These successive shocks have continually disrupted the plant's social and technical systems.

Indirect personnel, we suggest, have internalized this history. When indirect personnel were asked about the curriculum they would design for themselves, they highlighted their need to develop nontechnical competencies, that is, competencies that would give them a broader understanding of the plant's business environment and help them function more effectively in the plant's dynamic and unstable social system. For example, one of the indirect staff wanted more understanding of organizational development; a second wanted skills in interfacing with and convincing others; a third sought an understanding of the wider corporate picture; and a fourth, an understanding of how decisions were made. These were the competencies the indirect personnel believed they needed to help stimulate and integrate innovations in Westfield's sociotechnical environment.

As Table 2.7 shows, both direct and indirect groups acknowledged that they were working in a dynamic context, that everyone had to learn more because the context around them was changing. But direct personnel wanted a curriculum that gave them more technical knowledge and depth, whereas indirect personnel wanted both contextual knowledge—knowledge about the organizational context and the business objectives of the plant—and knowledge about working with and influencing others.

In sum, the direct personnel's wish for a stable context and more active management is no indication that they were conservative. On the contrary, they knew they were working in a dynamic context where tools and problems change. Their wish reflected an appreciation of their primary task to control production in the face of innovation, and their

Table 2.7. Focus of Desired Curriculum for Self

	Technical knowledge	Social relations	Business objectives
Direct personnel	11	4	1
Indirect personnel	3	3	6

Table 2.8. Dimensions of Competence

Direct personnel feel competent when:	Indirect personnel feel competent when:
They become more technically knowledgeable	They develop more social knowledge about the systems
They can overcome barriers and disruptions to the steady state	They can overcome social divisions and organizational turfs
They actively solve problems	They can influence others to master a problem
They act autonomously	They act through others

belief that management must help them by creating a stable and orderly context for their work of control. Table 2.8 summarizes this succession of findings.

THE ROLE SYSTEM AND THE PRINCIPLE OF COMPLEMENTARITY

Our argument thus far points to the following hypothesis. In describing their roles during moments of competence, workers were describing a system that supported what we have come to call a *dynamic complementarity* between direct and indirect roles. The key role of indirect personnel is to stimulate change and integrate innovation into the plant system, while the key role of direct personnel is to control the resulting innovation so that the plant can produce a steady flow of products. In other words, underlying the differences we have noted in the roles of direct and indirect personnel, there lies a fundamental complementarity between the responsibilities of those—primarily indirect personnel—whose primary task is to integrate new technologies into the plant, and the responsibilities of those—primarily direct personnel—whose main task is to control the production system. Control tasks are geared to maintaining a steady state, and progress is measured by the ability to meet short-term schedules. Innovation is geared to creating a context, a set of linkages, that can support a new product or process. To be successful, the innovators must work to a series of deadlines shaped by a planning horizon that extends farther into the future than the direct personnel's daily, weekly, and monthly production goals. While innovators must manage networks to develop new social linkages, controllers must work within a relatively stable boundary because they do not want organizational instabilities to compound disruptions in the machine system (see Table 2.9.).

Table 2.9. Dynamic Complementarity

	Integrating innovations	Controlling systems
Time horizon	Long-term planning horizon	Daily, weekly, monthly schedules
Outcome	New supportive linkages	Production within cost
Relational context	Networks cross-functional areas	Boundaries
Competence	Communicative	Technical

These contrasts were visible when we asked interviewees to draw a picture of themselves in relationship to the people and functions they work with every day. While most drew a direct representation of their physical work environment, a few saw their task as a projective one and drew more abstract images of their roles in a relationship system. Four indirect and three direct staff drew such projective pictures. As shown in Figure 2.2, all three direct personnel drew themselves at the center of a surrounding system. However, as the set of pictures in Figure 2.3 shows, a production manager and a supervisor put himself at the periphery of a circle, and a supervisor put themselves in a cluster of relationships lacking clear visual definition and boundaries. The direct personnel drew a role system that contained them, whereas the indirect personnel drew a role system that lacked clear structure or one that they helped to contain.

Figure 2.2. Images drawn by direct personnel in response to the question: "Draw a picture of yourself in relationship to your work unit, the people and the functions you work with every day."

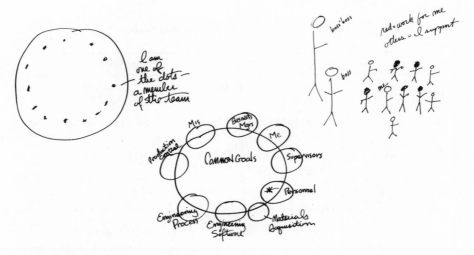

Figure 2.3. Images drawn by indirect personnel in response to the question: "Draw a picture of yourself in relationship to your work unit, the people and the functions you work with every day."

Reciprocity and the Role System

Our argument suggests that the competence of each group depends on the competence of the other. Tasks, and therefore roles, are reciprocally interdependent. To understand this, consider the following "vicious circle" scenario. Indirect personnel introduce a new machine but do so with insufficient planning. As a result, direct personnel lack the manuals and training to control the machine effectively. The machine breaks down more frequently than expected, creating further disruption as raw materials pile up and final product deliveries are late. Troubled by the resulting imbalance of inputs and outputs, indirect personnel become preoccupied by tasks associated with changing production plans and delivery schedules, further reducing their ability to help the direct personnel acquire the training and skills they need.

In this vicious circle, direct personnel cannot control production because indirect personnel fail to integrate the innovation—the new machine—into the sociotechnical system of the plant. Indeed, direct personnel's answers to our question, "When do you feel *in*competent?," point to the salience of such a scenario. Their answers emphasized the themes of disruption and what they experienced as mismanagement: "when machines keep going down," "when management is loaning people out, moving them around and putting people in jobs way beneath them," and "when they introduce new processes and expect us to know the process without adequate training." In the extreme case, the new machine is abandoned.

A second scenario suggests how the two groups may create a stable situation in which the innovation is only partly integrated into the factory. Consider the following hypothetical case. Indirect personnel introduce a new machine and provide direct personnel with training. However, direct personnel are unable to work together to solve downtime problems and thus fail to meet production schedules. Supervisors and support staff are drawn into the task of keeping the machine functioning and, as a result, cannot focus on developing the delivery, purchasing, and quality control programs they need to support production. As a result, the machine is only partly integrated into the plant system. Using supervisors on the shopfloor, the plant community can "put the product out," but it is unable to develop the infrastructure needed to realize fully the machine's contribution. Indirect personnel do not feel competent because they are not facilitating but doing, and direct personnel do not feel competent because they have not developed operational autonomy.

In this scenario, the direct personnel's difficulties lead to successively smaller and smaller increments in the level of integration and control, so that at some point neither group can stimulate the other group to improve. This is the point where organizational learning stops. Direct personnel are making just enough mistakes, so that indirect personnel, to correct them, cannot continue the work of improving the infrastructure for regulating and maintaining the innovation. The organization is walking up a down escalator just fast enough to keep them in the same place.

Finally, the two groups may interact to create a "virtuous circle" of development. Consider the following scenario: Indirect personnel introduce the innovation and provide a high level of training. Consequently, direct labor succeeds in establishing a basic level of control over the machine system. They can address bottlenecks or problems in the support system surrounding the machine, such as an unresponsive maintenance staff, problems with delivery, or subtle gaps in training. This leads the indirect personnel to link the machine system to the plant's sociotechnical arrangements even more effectively by, for example, working with the maintenance groups, developing additional training materials, or ensuring a more steady flow of high-quality raw materials. Experiencing even fewer barriers to effectiveness, direct personnel can then further fine-tune their capacity to control the machine system. The process becomes self-amplifying.

What are the conditions that make this third scenario possible? Our interviews suggest that the answer is a process of sustained reciprocity, whereby information and communication flow freely between the two groups so that each shapes its own actions on the basis of what both it and the other group has learned. This is the distinctive feature of the third scenario: The plant community learns through a double process in which each group learns both from its *own* experience (for example,

direct personnel assess why they have difficulty controlling production)
and from the *other's* experience (for example, the indirect staff learns
about the limits of its training initiative from direct personnel's difficulties in controlling production).

These three scenarios thus highlight the complementarity between
the two groups. Direct personnel can control production effectively only
when indirect personnel provide a supportive and stabilizing context,
which includes the training, information, and resources required to
control a new process or to introduce a new product. Similarly, indirect
personnel can be effective in introducing new technologies only when
the direct personnel can perform their controlling tasks autonomously
or without much supervision. Each needs the other to support and
stimulate its own specific competence.

Four Models of Organization

In the context of our original model, we can now ask what kind of role
system supports workers' capacity to be competent. How should the role
system be designed to enable workers to perform competently in a system
of dynamic complementarity?

To answer these questions, it is useful to differentiate between four
models of organization: the classical hierarchical, bureaucratic Weberian
model; the matrix model; the sociotechnical model; and the model of
complementarity. Table 2.10 situates these in a simple two-dimensional
matrix contrasting the number of hierarchical levels and degree of
functional specialization.

Sociotechnical systems theory (STS) has provided an increasingly
popular alternative to classical bureaucracy in the design of jobs to
help workers control modern technology. At its core, STS proposes
a model based on a strategy of reducing differences between managers
and workers and among workers themselves. The former is expressed
in the principle of self-management, the latter in the principle of
multiskilling.

Our analysis suggests that these two principles may no longer be
adequate under the current conditions of rapid ongoing technological
change. Practitioners and researchers who first developed the principles
of sociotechnical design were addressing relatively stable settings in
which workers, once freed from the burdens of supervision, could
control the predictable variances in the production process and teach
each other needed skills. However, as factories take up product and
process innovations with greater frequency, workers must develop skills
that no team member has yet mastered. Moreover, to integrate innovation into the factory, indirect and direct personnel must become more
specialized in their orientation and more dissimilar, but they must also
become more tightly linked.

Table 2.10. Four Forms of Organization

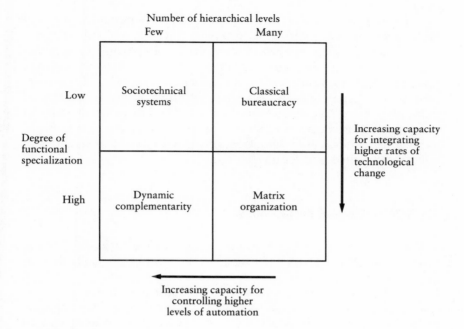

Number of hierarchical levels

	Few	Many
Low	Sociotechnical systems	Classical bureaucracy
High	Dynamic complementarity	Matrix organization

Degree of functional specialization

Increasing capacity for integrating higher rates of technological change

Increasing capacity for controlling higher levels of automation

The matrix form of organization, through its multiplicity of reporting links, enhances the organization's ability to integrate specialized forms of expertise. But because it preserves the bureaucratic model's multiple layers of authority, it does little to ensure that the distinctively unpredictable variances characteristic of highly automated operations are controlled close to their source.

The dynamic complementarity model that we have discerned at Westfield solves the problem of integrating specialized functions and controlling complex operations in the following way. Personnel work in specialized functions, the differences among which grow as technical change progresses. However, because the number of levels in the organization is low and people have high authority in their roles, the levels in the organization where conflicts can be resolved are sufficiently close to the level of work that information and decisions can flow easily among the divided parts. The new organization can therefore reduce hierarchical differences while increasing the distinctiveness of its functional parts. The authority that people are given in lower-level roles stimulates the processes of reciprocity—communication, information flow, meeting processes—that foster the excellence of the divided parts while linking them in and through a process of improvement and learning.

The Role System

Let us now summarize our argument. Workers are skilled when they can
perform the tasks of controlling, planning, thinking, and remembering,
but they can do so only when they inhabit a role system that supports
relationships of dynamic complementarity between direct and indirect
personnel. Such a system depends on a particular distribution of authority,
on a set of reciprocal linkages among functions, and on an ongoing process
of learning. Table 2.11 summarizes the changes in the role system required
to support worker competence. We need to design role systems that highlight
learning, reciprocity, and dynamic differences between groups, where authority
is both distributed and locally focused.

The Role System and the Individual

This description of the new role system helps us define the kinds of modal
roles individual workers should take up to support the role system as well
as their own competency.

As Table 2.12 suggests, workers in the automated factory face the
challenge of taking up their roles in a distinctive way that supports
not only their own competence but the competence of the plant community
as a whole. If they were to fail in assuming this role, because they

Table 2.11. Technology's Impact on the Role System

	From	To
Differences between roles	Established to create stability	Established to facilitate change
Authority	Concentrated and globally focused	Distributed and locally focused
Flow of materials and information	Linear	Reciprocal
Principle of control	Establish dependencies between groups	Manage interdependent decisions between groups
Central Task	Learn in order to perform	Perform in order to learn

find it difficult or because management does not provide adequate support, they would create problems for other groups. As the table suggests, the principle of dynamic complementarity requires that people take up their roles while consciously considering others whose work is complementary. This means for example, that one must learn from those who are different, that to promote system performance one must highlight different perspectives and points of view, and that one cannot simply consider one's role as the end point of one's focus but rather as the starting point.

When people find it difficult to take up their roles in this way, the plant system as a whole faces a series of chronic difficulties. For example, people who cannot challenge one another in the process of collaborating will engage in turf wars; people who cannot learn from differences will experience information overload; and people who see their role simply as a job will allow work and information to fall through the cracks.

Table 2.12. Changing Roles in the Automated Plant

From	To	Frequent transition problems
Doing a job	Taking a role	"Things" slipping through cracks
Mind one's own business	Mind other people's business	Turf wars
One's domain	One's vantage point or perspective	Culture clash
Cooperative	Collaborate	Problem avoidance
Minimize conflict	Highlight differences, challenge others	Chronic conflict
Learn from those who hold jobs like yours	Learn from those who hold jobs different than yours	Information overload, loss of meaning
Roles are established by a system of relationships	Roles establish the system of of relationships	Felt loss of authority throughout, isolation

MAPPING COMPETENCIES

Let us once again turn to our original model of competence. New technologies mean new skills in planning, thinking and controlling, and new roles of dynamic complementarity for focusing and realizing the full potential of those skills. Together, the new roles and the new skills define the worker competencies needed in the new manufacturing environment.

Working with this model, we can begin to predict what specific competencies—specific combination of skills and role behaviors—workers need to perform effectively. In Table 2.13, we have placed skills in the rows and role behaviors in the columns. We can then ask what kind of competent performance links the two.

Consider, for example, the intersection of "Control production" with "Mind other people's business." We can interpret this competence in the following way: To control production in one's domain, one must know what others who influence one's work are doing, and must in

Table 2.13. Competence Is a Function of Skills and Roles

SKILL \ ROLE	Mind other people's business	Consider one's role as a vantage point	Highlight differences; challenge others	Learn from those different to you	Help shape a system of roles
Control production					
Plan					
Develop explicit knowledge					
Remember; bring to mind the variety of situations that need controlling					
Be aware of how one attends to situations					

turn be able to influence them; one cannot successfully control production without attending to the set of stakeholders who shape one's work.

Similarly, consider the intersection of "Plan" and "Learn from those who are different from you." We can interpret this competency in the following way: Plan with other people and functions in mind; in planning production, learn how people in other functions and groups are affected by one's planning activities; take their point of view.

Finally, consider the intersection of "Highlight differences, challenge others" with "Develop explicit knowledge." We can interpret this competency in the following way: Understand what one knows and test this with others; make one's own knowledge explicit by testing it against the knowledges and practices of others; highlight the differences to discover one's distinctive contribution to the community's general stock of knowledge.

As these different examples suggest, we can develop a competencies profile by mapping skill requirements onto the role behaviors that support skilled performance. This mapping process calls attention to how a particular skill needs to be applied through a particular set of relationships. It thus highlights how competent performance is embedded in the relationship between people and tools, between the social and the technical.

SUMMARY

People perform competently when the skills they have are supported by the roles they take. Our pilot study of Westfield suggests that tools and problems changed at Westfield in such a way that workers increasingly performed controlling and planning tasks. However, to perform these tasks competently, they needed a role system that created a process of dynamic complementarity between direct and indirect personnel. Such a system helped the plant community balance the tasks of innovation and control as new products and processes constantly disrupted the shopfloor's ability to maintain a steady flow of output. Dynamic complementarity could work only when the role system distributed authority, encouraged specialization, linked divided functions through a process of reciprocal interaction, and valued learning as an outcome of performance.

By examining such a role system, we then described the kind of role–appropriate behaviors workers needed to assume to support dynamic complementarity. At a fundamental level, workers needed to take up their roles as starting points or vantage points rather than as complete descriptions of their jobs. Then, by performing their work, they became attuned to the influence they had on others and the influence others had on them. Moreover, by mapping these behaviors back onto skill requirements, we created a particular competency profile. Such a profile highlighted how people's competence—ability to accomplish their work skillfully—depends on the social system that supports their efforts. The competency profile thus shows how social and technical forces together shape performance.

The model we have developed here was based on a pilot research project. Our findings and the concepts we developed to explain them thus point to a program for research. Such a program might be based on the following questions.

1. As workers face increasingly automated environments, how can we understand the new sources of mental stress they face? For example, the workers in our interviews suggested that memory and remembering became more important. How general is this finding, and what other cognitive processes (such as focusing or broadening one's attention, and troubleshooting or predicting future events) become important as well? Can we develop models of the structure of such mental activity and the relationship between this structure and technology? We might expect that tasks in a highly computerized plant might emphasize anticipating, and the worker's attention might need to be broadly rather than narrowly focused. By contrast, we might expect that in a less automated plant workers would devote more time to troubleshooting problems rather than anticipating errors, and focus their attention more narrowly.

2. Can the skill-hierarchy concept be tested and refined? What determines when workers need to develop higher-level skills? Does the skill hierarchy describe the developmental history of skill formation in a particular plant? For example, is it the case that workers' ability to design machines (using their creating and valuing skills) depends on their previously established skills in learning, controlling and doing? Or can a factory "jump" a level on the hierarchy, going, for example, from expertise in controlling directly to valuing and use the latter stage to force learning at the "jumped" or "skipped" level? Can human resource professionals use the skill hierarchy to predict future needs rather than simply to prepare workers for current jobs?

3. In other plants facing accelerating product and process innovation, would we find the kind of complementarity among factory and office, shopfloor and management that we described here? More generally, can our model of complementarity be used to assess the impacts of technical change beyond the shopfloor? Can we use the concept of complementarity to describe the relationships between managers and engineers, or between engineers and marketing people?

4. Do the concepts of the role and role system developed here fit with the way in which people take their roles in "best practice plants"? If people take up roles as vantage points or starting points for understanding and interacting with the system of roles around them, what training or education has prepared them for this stance?

These are, of course, only some of the questions our pilot project has suggested. Much remains to be done to understand the dynamics of technology and work.

3

Skill and Occupational Changes in U.S. Manufacturing

Paul Attewell

Many important changes have occurred in U.S. industry with the introduction of new technologies in manufacturing—computer-integrated
manufacturing, computer-aided design (CAD) computer-controlled materials handling, and manufacturing resource planning (MRP). This chapter
characterizes the resulting changes in the skill requirements and occupational mix of U.S. industry, with special emphasis on recent developments
in the United States. It locates recent technological advances and their
human resource implications within broader processes that have been
unfolding over several decades, and suggests some prognoses for the decades
ahead.

The chapter begins with the larger context, first reviewing the competing
theories about skill change and technology that currently inform scholarly
research. This is followed by an empirical overview of skill and occupational trends since the turn of the century. Recent developments
in manufacturing, including an assessment of the human resources
implications of new technologies, are the subject of the third section
of the chapter. The fourth section discusses projections for the next
two decades.

THEORIES OF SKILL AND OCCUPATIONAL CHANGE

Capitalism, according to the economist Schumpeter, is a system characterized by "creative destruction." It is creative because profit seekers are
pushed to develop novel products, to implement new process technologies
to cut production costs, and to set up new firms to fill emerging market
niches. It involves destruction because this process implies the abandonment
of outmoded technologies and obsolete products, the devaluation of costly
investments and hard-won skills, and the decline or bankruptcy of firms
that have fallen behind.

Given this vision, one might expect scholars to view the technical
skills and knowledge of the workforce as subject to a continual process

of obsolescence and replacement, where old skills are rendered unnecessary by technological change, and where new challenges for learning
result in new skills. This viewpoint, which might be called one of "skill
replacement," has been advocated especially by labor historians and
historically informed sociologists (Penn and Scattergood, 1985; More,
1980; Samuel, 1977).

The Historical Perspective

These researchers view skill changes as incessant, protracted, and man-
ageable, rather than revolutionary or cataclysmic. They note that even the
most important innovations, those that ultimately remake whole industries,
take decades to diffuse through an industry. For example, mechanized
weaving, which launched the Industrial Revolution in Britain, and which
showed clear advantages over hand weaving, took four decades to displace
fully the prior technology. The implication of such decades-long transitions—and such lengthy transactions are also the rule for more recent
innovations—is that skill transitions will be gradual, and can, in principle,
be absorbed within normal processes by which new generations of workers
are educated and trained and older generations retire or move between
firms.

Where technological transitions have generated a huge cost in human
suffering, the reasons have rarely been that workers skilled in the old
technology were unable to retrain for the new, or that a new technology
came on line too fast to be absorbed. Instead, one finds three types
of problems. The first, for which the introduction of mechanized weaving
is the classic example, arose where whole communities remained committed to the old technology, did not move to the new factories, and
were slowly squeezed into penury by the technologically more advanced
competition. A second situation, typified by the mechanization of U.S. steel
production in the late nineteenth century, occurs where a new technology is bitterly fought by craft unions who view it (sometimes accurately)
as intended to de-skill them, and where, after protracted strikes, skilled
workers lose their struggle and return to lower-level or narrower skill
jobs at reduced pay. The third situation, distressingly frequent in recent
years in the United States, occurs when plants with old technology
are not technologically modernized, but are instead slowly run down
or milked for available return, after which the plants are closed and
replaced by more technologically advanced plants in other regions or
countries (Perrucci and Targ, 1988). None of these three situations is
a problem of skill or knowledge acquisition *per se*.

Another relevant observation by scholars is that innovative technologies are rarely, if ever, bought as a piece and then installed. Instead,
the typical situation involves a lengthy period after the initial introduction of the technology, during which substantial modification of

the original machinery occurs, and changes in materials, product design, work flow, and staffing patterns often prove necessary. This modification is often so extensive that some scholars argue that every firm in essence reinvents its own new technology (Clark, 1987). While perhaps an overstatement, this point speaks to an to an important skill issue. A firm embracing major new technologies is committing itself to a lengthy period of experimentation, skill development, and organizational learning. This process often requires a more highly skilled and more committed workforce than is the case for an already established, mature technology because of the flexibility, initiative, and willingness to learn and relearn that are demanded of the work force. Later, when the technology is thoroughly mature, skill levels may decline, unless a string of further innovations follows.

The Compensatory Perspective on Skill

Furthermore, historically oriented scholars have tended to emphasize the multidimensionality of skill. Researchers have often noted that skill involves a mix of manual and sensory capacities, workplace knowledge, and cognitive skills. In this sense, skill is multi-dimensional, or alternatively one might say people have multiple skills or multiple elements of skill. During a major change in work, such as one caused by new machinery, certain elements of skill may become irrelevant and disappear. But this will not automatically de-skill the job as a whole because other important elements remain intact, and because new kinds of skill are often needed to operate the new technology (More, 1980; Samuel, 1977). Instead of skill degradation, these scholars offer an image of reformulation and replacement of elements of skill.

An example of skill replacement and reformulation, and of the importance of the multiple dimensions of skill, may be found in the history of the skilled metal machining trades. In the nineteenth century, before the introduction of standard parts, fitters and related trades saw their elite status as grounded in their ability to create "one-off" parts. They used hand tools (and some simple machinery) to obtain an exact fit. The introduction of increasingly powerful general purpose machine tools (lathes, milling machines), seemed to threaten the manual skills, and memoirs record worker fears in the early years of this century that machine tools would "de-skill" them (Watson, 1935).

In reality, the reduction in dexterity requirements was balanced by the acquisition of new skill elements that allowed fitters, tool and die makers, and other skilled machinists to retain their status as the most highly skilled of the blue-collar occupations (Watson, 1935, pp. 212–15; USGPO, 1938). The new machine tools involved more complex forms that were cut to finer tolerances, requiring enhanced conceptual skills in setup, measurement and calibration, and working from blueprints (More, 1980, pp. 184–92). The cutting speeds of the new machines increased substantially such that cutting could easily go wrong because of minor variations in hardness within the metal being machined. A machinist's sense of touch and feel therefore became very important as the craftsman could sense a change in the material through vibration, and alter the feed and speeds to avoid a broken tool or miscut piece. This new tactile element or dimension of skill became central to the definition of a superior machinist.

Decades later, the introduction of computer numerically controlled machine tools threatened this tactile vibration-sensing element of skill. Machinists whom I interviewed after the introduction of Mori–Fanuc machining stations were very concerned that their work would be rendered unskilled by these machines, which could cut astonishingly complex forms to fine tolerances at high speed. The new machines were enclosed in safety hoods, and the machinists no longer physically held onto anything during machining.

In the shop I studied, however, new skills emerged that allayed these fears. Machinists programmed their own machines, and also ran several machines simultaneously. Machines rarely provided good cuts the first time, and so the machinists spent time modifying and improving programs, which required considerable conceptual work. And in place of their tactile sense, machinists developed the ability to discern, within a noisy environment, muffled sounds that indicated something was about to go wrong (see also Zicklin, 1987, p. 459). I observed machinists leaping to hit red emergency stop buttons, based on this intuitive auditory sensibility, just in time to prevent expensive tools and work from being chewed up.

A "compensatory theory of skill" (Penn and Scattergood, 1985) emphasizes the obsolescence and replacement of elements of skill, as in the preceding example. It does not state that changes in skill levels, whether upgrading or de-skilling, are impossible. It simply notes that, given the multidimensionality of many skills, partial change rather than total transformation is likely, and that, given the pace of technology diffusion, skill changes tend to be evolutionary rather than revolutionary.

The Social Determination of Skill

A final and important insight provided by recent scholarship on the labor process is that skill in the workplace is socially determined (Turner, 1962; Jones, 1982; Penn, 1982, 1983; Penn and Scattergood, 1985). This is an easily misunderstood idea. It is helpful, at the outset, to separate and distinguish the idea of a *skill* from the idea of a *skilled job*. In the first case, one focuses on aptitudes and the complexity of particular tasks, and the skill needed to perform each task. The second case concerns an occupation that is socially labeled and remunerated as a "skilled job."

Scholars who propose a social determination of skill argue that the social labeling of a job as skilled is not simply a matter of whether it contains tasks that are complex and therefore require skills. Rather, the constitution of a job as skilled depends on the ability of those in the occupation to control various processes at the workplace. A skilled job is defined by rules about who can and who cannot do certain tasks (demarcation); rules about length of training or apprenticeship, staffing levels and promotion ladders, closeness of supervision and prerogatives over decision making, and the ability to sustain a high rate of pay.

The success of an occupation in protecting its social definition as skilled depends on more than the level of complexity of its tasks. It also has to do with the formal and informal organization at work, including the solidarity of those in the occupation and whether they are unionized, whether they are strategically well placed within the work flow of the factory and can cause great disruption if they strike, whether their speciality is in short supply or can be easily replaced, and their relationship to other workers or work processes.

Viewed in this fashion, skill is not only an objective measure of the complexity of certain tasks, but is also a attribute of jobs, an attribute governed by complex political struggles in the workplace. This perspective makes sense of the fact that skilled occupations are very concerned about demarcation (who is allowed to do certain tasks) and fight against dilution (refusing to allow noncraft workers to do even the most unskilled part of craft work) for they are concerned with control over a certain area of work, not just with the complexity of certain tasks.

The distinctiveness of a social-deterministic view of skill can be seen when it is compared to a more traditional task-analytic approach. Task analysis assumes that skill is an objective aspect of a job and can be measured scientifically. Typically this is done by rating the complexity of the job's tasks on dimensions such as complexity in dealing with people, data and things. Then one determines the overall skill entailed in the job by calculating the average complexity of these various dimensions, or a weighted sum of the scores for each dimension (Kohn and Schooler, 1983). A technology is then considered to have de-skilled or upgraded according to whether a job's score goes down or up.

In contrast, for a social determinist, the (socially acknowledged) skill of a job may depend on control over its one or two strategically most important (or socially most prestigious) tasks, and may have nothing to do with other more routine aspects of the work, or with its average complexity. Technological change, even if it reduces mean complexity, may not be viewed as de-skilling by those who do the work if the prerogatives and control of the occupation were not infringed upon. Conversely, skilled workers may feel very threatened by the loss of a particular task element that is important to their claims to skill even if the technologically reorganized job were to offer what is on average more complex work.

The key debate between task analysts and social determinists is over the question of whether having strategic power in the workplace can allow an occupation to attain a skilled status, even if there is no underlying "real" skill (complexity) in its work. H. A. Turner (1962) comes closest to arguing that a skilled job with no real skills is possible. More (1980, pp. 163–65) and others argue against this, viewing control over at least some complex tasks are necessary if a craft is to retain its status.

Unidirectional Changes in Work

Those scholars who offer a social-deterministic, multidimensional view of skill and a compensatory or skill-replacement perspective on technological change tend to treat skill change as incessant and evolutionary, with no necessary overall direction, because they view change as the result of many forces acting at cross purposes (Littler, 1982). Within any given occupation, skill levels will fluctuate over the years, as some technological changes make the work more demanding while others simplify work tasks. This perspective sees the skill level of the whole economy as a relatively placid body of water, with minor eddies but no major currents.

However, other scholars of industrial skills and know-how reject this view. They emphasize, instead, unidirectional changes in the skill level of work over time (for example, a steady process of skill upgrading) that affect numerous occupations across the whole economy. These skill changes may alter the fit between work demands and worker skills, creating disjunctures in which past practices and skills do not smoothly transmute to satisfy future needs. Mismatches may develop in which the available workforce lacks the requisite knowledge and abilities or, on the contrary, has underutilized skills and abilities.

The vision of substantial unidirectional changes in skill is shared by two otherwise quite opposed schools of thought. On the one side, the "de-skilling school" identifies a long-term tendency toward the simplification of work and the destruction of skill. This process, these researchers believe, leads to a mass of overqualified and underchallenged employees whose native intelligence and acquired knowledge are not utilized in the workplace and who therefore become alienated from their work (Braverman, 1974; Burris, 1982).

On the other side, one finds a number of researchers who believe that new technologies are more demanding in terms of the skills and knowledge required of employees. They view work as being "upgraded" by technology. Among the latter, some are concerned that large proportions of our workforce lack the basic skills needed for efficient work in a technologically complex workplace, and are also deficient in more

specialized skills (such as statistical reasoning for quality control) that
cannot be easily learned without the basic educational grounding. These
scholars therefore anticipate shortages of qualified employees, or, alternatively, envision industry having to provide substantial training to
bring a poorly educated workforce "up to speed."

These two extremes, one that sees work as too simple for workers
and the other that posits the reverse, have been with us for decades,
perhaps centuries. There has been a tendency for popular and scholarly
opinion to swing, pendulumlike, from one to another, especially during
periods of rapid technological change.

Thus, the de-skilling thesis appeared in the earliest decades of British
industrialization, when the destruction of craft skill by mechanization
became part of the "machinery question" (Marx, 1867; Berg, 1982). It
was revived in the United States during debates at the close of the
nineteenth century over the displacement of hand by machine labor,
and reappeared in the 1970s and 1980s with fears that computer
technologies represented the *coup de grace* for skilled blue-collar (and
also for much white-collar) work (Braverman,1974; Zimbalist, 1979).

Conversely, the advent of mechanization in the 1950s and 1960s
led to fears of technological unemployment, and to concerns that new
automated jobs required higher and more cognitively oriented skills
that might be in short supply. Walker (1957, p. 195) wrote of industry's
need for "skills *different in kind*: skills of the head rather than of the
hand; of the logician rather than the craftsman; of nerve rather than
of muscle; of the pilot rather than the manual worker; of the maintenance man rather than the operator." In the late 1980s, this idea
was revived in modified form with the concept of a "skills mismatch,"
particularly in cities where large numbers of high school dropouts
coexisted with job openings requiring high school or college-level skills
(Kasarda, 1986, 1988; Blackburn et al., 1989).

Despite their apparently contradictory beliefs, both the "de-skilling
thesis" and the "upgrading" school provide valuable insights into the
dynamics of technological change and skill formation. The weaknesses
of both occur when something that is true for one particular kind of
work setting, or fraction of the population, is (inappropriately) generalized to the skill mix of the economy as a whole.

The De-skilling Thesis

The de-skilling school views management and labor as opponents in an
irreconcilable conflict. Management, these researchers argue, uses mechanization and automation as occasions for increasing its leverage over the
work force. Mechanization simplifies work processes, and results in the
division of once-complex craft tasks into separate routinized steps, filled
by cheaper, less skilled labor. This produces cost savings, of course, but

de-skilling theorists stress the implications for control rather than cost. Low-skill employees are more tractable and more easily replaced than their skilled predecessors, whose special knowledge and skills provide strategic resources in struggles with management. Mechanization is therefore an occasion for removing such knowledge, skill, and conceptual responsibilities from production employees, and transferring it to technical professionals, or to others less troublesome from managers' point of view.

From the de-skilling perspective, technological progress results in a steady degradation of work, an unending simplification of tasks, and an erosion of employees' conceptual and decision-making respon-sibilities. For the bulk of employees, work becomes limited to executing routines and procedures laid down by others. The need for a conceptual understanding of one's work disappears; thus employees become ig-norant of how their own work fits into the larger picture, are unwilling or unable to show initiative, and are alienated from their work.

When theorists of the de-skilling school look for evidence of a historical simplification of work, and for proof of a managerial policy of de-skilling, they are apt to point to the advent of Taylorism or Scientific Management in the early part of this century and its subsequent legacy, expressed in managerial attitudes and in the design of machines and work processes. Taylorism, with its emphasis on the "one best way" of organizing tasks and its belief in the superiority of work processes designed by engineers, held production workers' conceptual skills and trove of knowledge in low esteem. Far from seeking initiative from employees, it sought speed and regularity in the performance of narrow tasks. Motivation was to be purchased via piece-rate incentives or close supervision.

The legacy of Taylorism is widespread in the United States. In its most benign form, it consists of a preference for detailed job descriptions and procedures manuals; a tendency to design new work processes to be as simple and straightforward as possible—idiot-proof—in the belief that gains in speed will outweigh losses in motivation and quality; and a pervasive assumption that production workers really do not need to know very much about their machines, the materials with which they work, sources of quality problems, and so on. Taylorists are more comfortable delegating all such conceptual tasks to specialists, whether they be maintenance technicians, supervisors, or quality-control staff.

The vision of work offered by the de-skilling school is a very bleak one. It implies a long-term erosion of craft work, with a steady increase in the proportion of employees who are unskilled or semiskilled. Scholars within this tradition do not limit the analysis to blue-collar work but find analogous processes occurring within clerical work, which they view as increasingly fragmented and routinized (Crompton and Jones, 1984; Glenn and Feldberg, 1977). Nor do they see much hope in the creation of new skilled professional or technical occupations that take on the conceptual tasks that were formerly integrated with execution work on the shop or office floor. They believe the same processes of rationalization and simplification that have degraded craft and manual labor may be turned upon professional workers. Computer automation may reduce the discretion and decision making skills of loan officers, insurance examiners, and others. Computer-aided design (CAD) would affect engineers' skills, and physicians would be affected by artificial-intelligence diagnostic software (Perrolle, 1985, pp. 163–72).

The de-skilling thesis, although it has many adherents among U.S. and foreign scholars, has been subjected to intense criticism on both theoretical and empirical grounds (summarized in Attewell, 1987a; Wood, 1982). Its view that managers have a central interest in utilizing technology to undermine craft labor is an overgeneralization. Historically one can indeed find cases where technological change was a conscious policy for undermining the power of strong craft unions by de-skilling the work. The reorganization of steel production in the late nineteenth century is one example (Stone, 1974). The automation of newspaper composition and printing in recent decades is another example of de-skilling (Wallace and Kalleberg, 1982), although this has been disputed (Martin, 1981; Cockburn, 1983). But there is little evidence that a policy of de-skilling is the norm.

Indeed, firms often embark on programs of major innovation with very little understanding, or even thought, of what the consequences will be for skill levels, or for the occupational composition in the firms (Butera, 1984; National Academy of Sciences, 1986; Majchrzak, 1988). The central managerial goal behind innovation is more likely to be cost reduction or keeping up with the competition, and this sometimes proves to require a more skilled and more expensive work force, especially where the new technology is complex, error prone, or requires more setup, testing, or maintenance time (Attewell, 1987).

Commentators have also pointed out that craft labor does not take technologically induced de-skilling lying down. Industrial strife, or the threat of it, often molds the implementation of new technologies. Compromises are struck that may prevent or at least lessen de-skilling. And in industries where craft labor has historically been powerful, one frequently finds a situation where management prefers a policy of "responsible autonomy" on the shopfloor to one of de-skilling and strife (Friedman, 1977).

The belief that technological change is or has been aimed primarily at craft labor, or at the most complex of tasks, has also been criticized. As a practical matter, it is frequently easier to automate out of existence work that is already narrow and repetitious rather than complex and varied. This implies that the brunt of technological change is felt by low-skilled labor, and that new production technologies can reduce the proportion of low-skill jobs in some situations.

The implication of these and other criticisms of the de-skilling thesis is that new production technologies do not have a single, across-the-board effect on skills or on the occupational mix of an industry's work force. Different production technologies will have very different impacts on skills (Clark et al., 1988). And, most important, identical technologies can be and are implemented in a variety of ways, some of which enhance skill, whereas others de-skill. Tasks may be grouped to make simpler or more complex jobs; workers may be given discretion over speed of machines, or they may be denied such discretion. In one firm, setup, routine machine maintenance, or programming may be given to specialists, while in another, these tasks remain integrated with the operator's duties (Wilkinson, 1983). Job rotation and job ladders (or their absence) also affect skill acquisition (Lee, 1981).

The thrust of such observations is that the skill outcomes of technology are more a matter of managerial and designer philosophy and choice than the de-skilling thesis implies. Controlling the workforce via de-skilling is only one possible managerial goal, and one that is sometimes absent and sometimes subordinated to other goals. Skill outcomes also depend to a considerable extent on the contingencies of shopfloor politics, and there is a large additional unplanned component in which serendipitous events during the technology implementation process affect staffing and skills. The critics therefore confront the determinism of the de-skilling thesis with a much more fluid and nondeterministic view of skill dynamics.

The Upgrading Thesis

The "upgrading" approach to technology impact provides, in many ways, a mirror image of the pessimistic de-skilling approach. Where de-skilling theorists pay attention to the impact of technology upon more highly skilled workers, upgrading theorists view technology as automating the lowest, most routine activities out of existence (Giuliano, 1982; Hirschhorn, 1984). The elimination of such tasks within any given job would result in an upgrading, as the employee concentrates on the more challenging and complex aspects of the old job. When looking at combinations of occupations within a given industry, the upgrading thesis suggests that employment in the lower-level occupations will shrink, either in proportion or absolutely, as process technologies eliminate routine work.

Where de-skilling theorists were sensitive to the loss of certain dimensions or aspects of manual skill, upgrading theorists have pointed to the emergence of new, different types of skill as production technologies change. In the 1950s and 1960s, researchers of this school examined the impact of (precomputer) automation upon blue-collar job skills, in the wake of concerns that "hard automation" (specialized machine tools) would remove skill from machinists and others. They concluded to the contrary that there had been a net upgrading of skill levels (OECD, 1965, p. 30; Crossman, 1966, p. 21; Baldwin and Schultz, 1954, p. 121; Clague and Greenberg, 1962; Mann, 1962).

The upgrading came from several sources: an increase in the importance of maintenance skills for automated equipment; a shift from manually guiding machines to monitoring by sight and sound; overseeing several machines that were working simultaneously; an increase in the complexity of forms cut and of tighter tolerances made possible by the new machines; and an increase in responsibility, for operator negligence or sloppiness could easily turn expensive items into scrap. Shifts in the kinds of skills employed at work were especially clear where processes moved from batch production to continuous flow or process technologies as a result of technological progress. Manual workers in process plants no longer had to move at a pace dictated by machinery. Instead, they became monitors and troubleshooters for automated processes. These roles often required a more intellectual orientation toward the work (Blauner, 1964; Faunce, 1965).

This perception of increased cognitive demands and complexity has also been echoed by more recent studies of computerized work settings (Hirschhorn, 1984; Penn and Scattergood, 1985; Attewell, 1987; Clark et al., 1988). In addition, researchers have stressed the increased responsibility often required in computerized jobs (Adler, 1986a; Hirschhorn, 1984). As isolated machines are integrated into continuous processes, and data are shared among interlinked databases, the importance of accuracy and vigilance increases. Mistakes become more costly because what once would have produced isolated problems, today becomes magnified into system disasters.

The theories of the de-skilling and upgrading schools point to several mechanisms by which new production technologies may, in principle, change the skill composition of individual occupations and the economy-wide level of skills. One cannot, however, deduce from purely theoretical premises the overall outcome of these various mechanisms for de-skilling, re-skilling, and upgrading because the theories cannot estimate the magnitudes of the various effects. In addition, one has to carry out a rather complex process of aggregation that combines (1) skill changes within individual jobs over time, (2) skill shifts due to changing relative sizes of occupations within an industry (such as changes in the relative proportions of craft and semiskilled employees), and (3) skill changes due to different growth rates of various industries that employ different kinds of workers (for example, the growth of fast foods versus manufacturing). Such analyses are empirical tasks. The next section reviews empirical studies of economy-wide shifts in skills.

EMPIRICAL STUDIES OF LONG-TERM
OCCUPATIONAL AND SKILL CHANGE

Direct measurement of skill levels across large numbers of occupations requires a complex method for assessing skill and task complexity. In the United States, the most common approach has been to use the U.S. Department of Commerce's Dictionary of Occupational Titles (DOT). Since 1949, inspectors from the United States Employment Service have visited workplaces, observed workers, and coded their tasks on several dimensions of complexity.

Spenner (1983, 1985) has reviewed 11 such studies. While de-skilling was documented in some studies within individual occupations, none of them have found de-skilling across the occupational spectrum as a whole. Upgrading was reported by some studies, but not to a substantial degree. The impression given by the DOT studies is of great stability in the skill mix of the economy over recent decades. These findings cannot be viewed as definitive, however, because some experts are quite critical of the measurement and sampling weaknesses of the DOT (Cain and Treiman, 1981). The most conservative course is to view them in the light of the remainder of the research to be reviewed here.

An alternative method of assessing skill changes involves national sample surveys of employees or managers who have experienced technological changes in the workplace, asking respondents to assess the impact of these changes on various dimensions of work life. Although subject to various biases due to inaccurate recall and perceptions distorted by a general sense that technology is progressive, such surveys have the merit of asking those most immediately affected rather than depending on analysts who spend short periods of time observing any given job. Almost all general surveys of this type report upgrading and considerable satisfaction with the results of technological change on the part of the large majority of affected employees (Mueller, 1969; Response Analysis Corporation, 1983; Verbatim Corporation, 1982; Bednarzik, 1985).

Skill can also be measured by educational requirements. Rumberger (1981) examined educational requirements of jobs across the whole economy from 1960 to 1976, as determined by DOT inspectors. He found that the shifting employment distribution over this period "favored more skilled jobs. . . . Overall the average skill requirements of jobs increased in this period, but at a slower rate than in other periods." (Rumberger, 1981, p. 578). In more recent work, Levin and Rumberger (1986) combined present-day educational requirements for each job with Bureau of Labor Statistics occupational projections for the period 1982–1995. Their analysis suggested that the educational requirements for the workforce as a whole in 1995 will differ very little from those in 1982. Thus, the educational data suggest an upgrading since 1960, but no sudden or dramatic increase in demands for educated labor created by more recent advances in the information revolution.

Long-Term Economy-Wide Occupational Change

Looking backward, popular commentators often discern an industrial shift from manufacturing to service in twentieth-century society, but this paints a potentially misleading picture of occupational change. First and foremost, one should be struck by the stability of manufacturing employment in a century when other sectors were undergoing much greater changes in their share of employment. At the turn of the century, about one-quarter of the U.S. workforce was employed in manufacturing, compared with slightly under one-fifth today. This drop is nowhere as dramatic as the shift out of agriculture (from nearly one-third of employment at the turn of the century to about 5 percent today), or the rapid growth in social services (principally government, health, and education) and in business services (finance, insurance, and real estate).

The most striking occupational changes since the turn of the century are those reflecting the extraordinary expansion of white-collar work: from about 20 percent of the workforce at the beginning of the century to 60 percent today (*Monthly Labor Review*, February, 1988, p. 20). This white-collar expansion included the creation of millions of clerical jobs held by women, but it also encompassed a large expansion of professional and technical jobs (from 4.2 to 15 percent of our work force), and an increase of managers, who constitute nearly 10 percent of today's employees.

One must avoid the trap of assuming that the historical shift to white-collar employment is simply a result of a shift away from manufacturing toward more information-intensive industries, for the white-collar revo-

Figure 3.1. Non-Production Employment in U.S. Manufacturing

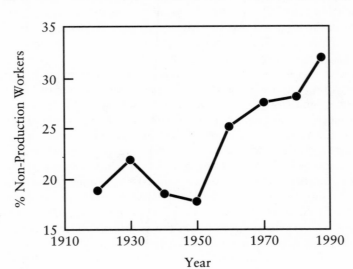

lution has also occurred within manufacturing. The proportion of nonproduction labor in manufacturing has climbed from around 18 percent in 1920 to 32 percent today (Figure 3.1). In manufacturing, as elsewhere, the share of managerial, professional, and clerical labor in the workforce approaches that of production labor.

The economy-wide movement toward an educated and credentialled white-collar labor force is read by many scholars as implying a substantial upgrading of the skills and aptitudes of American workers today compared with their grandparents, and is one reason that the de-skilling thesis has been greeted with skepticism. A second reason is that the occupational composition of blue-collar labor also fails to support a de-skilling conclusion. If mechanization were to result in the replacement of craftworkers by machine tenders, one would expect to see a substantial shrinkage over the long term in the proportion of craftworkers. Instead, one finds that craftworkers constituted about 29 percent of nonfarm manual workers in 1900; today they are over 40 percent (Attewell, 1987, p. 333; Penn, 1986). Scholars debate who exactly should be counted as a craftworker, and those who advance the de-skilling position insist that foremen and occupations like auto mechanic should be dropped from the craft category (Braverman, 1974). But even with such statistical manipulations, the resulting numbers fail to document a substantial decline in craft labor over this century.

Wright and Singelmann (1982) advanced an analysis that attempted to reconcile the upgrading observed in economy-wide occupational statistics with the de-skilling thesis advanced by Braverman. Their logic was that the observed upgrading (from 1960 to 1970) was due to the rapid growth of relatively high-skill industries or sectors (such as education and medicine), creating many higher-skill jobs. But within individual industries, they suggested, a process of occupational degradation or de-skilling was nevertheless occurring. The de-skilling, their data showed, was masked by the intersectoral shifts in employment toward higher-skill sectors. However, if the rapid growth of education, government, and other high-skill areas were to slow down (as they believed might be the case), then aggregate skill levels would fall as the underlying de-skilling tendency reasserted itself.

In a reanalysis using data spanning 1960–1980, Singelmann and Tienda (1985) found this not to be the case. The growth of high-skill sectors such as education and government did indeed slow down after 1975, and the effects of sectoral growth therefore became less central in determining the skill mix of the whole economy, but shifts within industries in the 1970s were nevertheless toward higher-level occupations and not de-skilling. This shift bolstered job creation among professional technical and managerial workers (although at a slower rate than earlier decades). The overall trend since 1960 has therefore been toward higher-skill employment.

RECENT OCCUPATIONAL AND SKILL CHANGE IN MANUFACTURING

The past 15 years have been tumultuous ones for much of U.S. manufacturing. It has weathered intensified international competition, two severe
recessions, sudden gyrations in energy and raw materials costs, movement
of some assembly jobs overseas, an acceleration in the rate of plant closings,
and a period of rapid technological change in many domestic plants.

Because these multiple events overlapped in time, it is quite difficult
to attribute observed changes in the occupational makeup of manufacturing to one of these causes rather than to another. The approach
I will take is first to present my analyses of occupational data for
manufacturing as a whole. These will provide a sense of the major
shifts in occupational composition for manufacturing from 1976 to
1989. I will then discuss studies of technology impact. These studies
are usually based on site visits and surveys of samples of firms, often
selected because of their use of state-of-the-art technologies. I will draw
upon others' research as well as my own study of a sample of firms
in the New York area.

Occupational Data

Data obtained from the Bureau of Labor Statistics' establishment surveys
show a slowdown in the growth of total manufacturing employment since
1970 and an absolute decrease in the past decade (Figure 3.2). Present
total manufacturing employment in the United States is around 19 million.

Figure 3.2. U.S. Manufacturing Employment 1910-1989

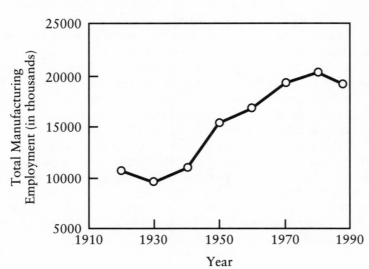

Even as total employment has been slowing down, nonproduction worker employment has grown, both proportionally (because production jobs are being lost) and in absolute numbers (with new nonproduction personnel being hired). This growth has become more marked since 1980. Today nonproduction employment amounts to over 33 percent of manufacturing jobs.

Given the traditional focus on blue-collar labor in manufacturing, it is easy to underestimate the importance of the shift to non production labor. Given the size and expense of the white-collar component of today's manufacturing, it should be stressed that attempts to increase productivity and reduce costs require increased attention to white-collar productivity and overhead costs more generally.

Managers whom I have interviewed, when shown the figures on the growth of nonproduction labor, have offered three explanations: (1) that they reflect an explosion in paperwork and bureaucracy stemming in part from governmental regulation and in part from the heavy paperwork burden in today's multidivisional firm; (2) that intensified competition requires a greater sales effort and therefore increased employment in sales and customer support; and (3) that computerization and related technological developments in production expand the number of professional and technical personnel.

At first glance, these explanations seem very reasonable. However, when one decomposes the growth in nonproduction labor into occupational groups, one finds that this "common sense" view of what is going on is inaccurate.[1]

Figure 3.3. Clerical and Adminstrative Employment in Manufacturing

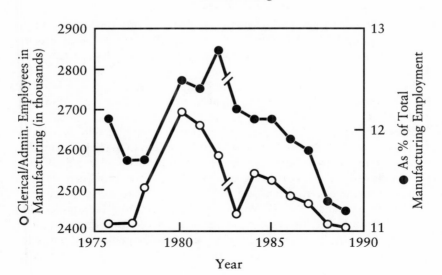

Figure 3.4. Sales Occupations in Manufacturing

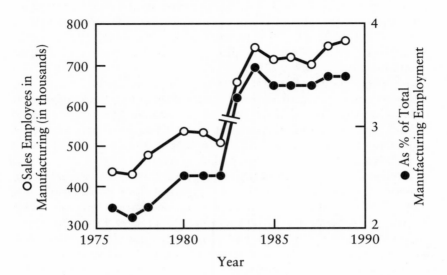

Year

Regarding the first explanation—that the expansion of nonproduction employment reflects a worsening paperwork burden—survey data suggest that manufacturing has been very successful in reining in its clerical and administrative component. In absolute numbers, clerical/administrative employment today is at about the same level as in 1976. Moreover, as a proportion of total employment, it has shrunk (Figure 3.3). Thus clerical/administrative labor is not the cause of the expansion of nonproductive labor in recent years.

The idea that increases in sales staff have contributed to the expansion of non production employment is partially true, as demonstrated by Figure 3.4. Sales-force employment has grown from about 350,000 to 750,000 since 1976. But sales is a quite small part of manufacturing employment (less than 4 percent today), and so is not the central factor in burgeoning overhead costs.

Neither is the expansion of professional and technical employment the key. Such jobs have grown, from around 2 million to 2.5 million since 1976 (Figure 3.5).

These changes, however, are dwarfed by the increase in the size of management. The number of managerial workers in manufacturing has nearly doubled, from approximately 1.2 million to over 2.5 million, over a period of 15 years (Figure 3.6). Very little has been written, either in the research literature or in the popular press, about this expansion of management beyond complaints of "middle-management bulge." If anything, attention has focused on the idea that American corporations are successfully slimming down management by removing layers of the corporate hierarchy. The occupational survey data suggest

Figure 3.5. Professional and Technical Occupations
in Manufacturing

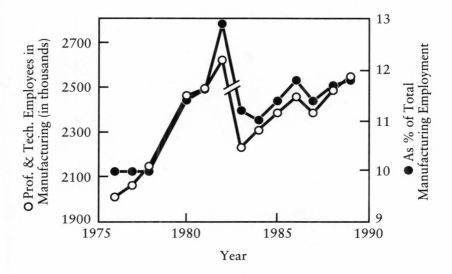

Figure 3.6. Managers in Manufacturing

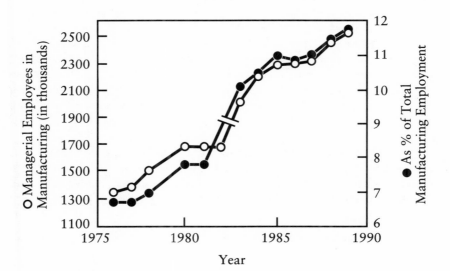

this diet has not had a noticeable effect in manufacturing as the numbers of managers continue to climb.

The occupational data on production worker employment in manufacturing are unfortunately not detailed. One can only compare two broad categories: craftworkers and machine operators. However, the comparison is instructive. Figure 3.7 shows a substantial increase in

Figure 3.7 . Ratio of Craft to Machine Operators
in Manufacturing

the ratio of craft to production workers since 1976, indicating an upgrading of the production work force. This increase reached a plateau around 1985, and the ratio of craftworkers to machine operatives remains well above that in earlier years.

In part, the shift toward craftworkers results from the loss of low-level assembly and machine operator jobs to plants abroad. One attempt to assess the magnitude of occupational and employment consequences of recent changes in international trade is in a U.S. Department of Labor publication (1978). But the shift also reflects a change in the nature of production work in the most highly automated plants in the United States.

In sum, the occupational employment data for manufacturing since 1976 show a process of upgrading through occupational redistribution. Higher-skill occupations are growing relative to lower-skill ones in both production and non production employment.

Studies of Production Worker Skills

A shopfloor production worker in a modern manufacturing plant is potentially affected by the computer revolution in numerous direct and indirect ways. An employee's day's work may appear initially in the form of a printout, stating what is to be done in what order. Manufacturing Resource Planning (MRP) software may generate a detailed Bill of Materials list for the employee. Raw materials or subassemblies are likely to be delivered by someone responding to a computerized inventory system, and such materials, as well as finished work, will be tracked by bar-code readers. Supervisors may come by to discuss variances in actual production or cost-accounting data generated by a computerized management information system (MIS). And, of course, the production worker may be tending or monitoring an automated machine with digital readout.

This kind of idealized description of a highly automated plant, while accurate in one sense, misses something important about the experience of automation in many, if not most, of today's workplaces. The shift from mechanized to automated equipment is only partial in most factories. Hence the shopfloor is covered with a mix of automated and conventional equipment. Computer numerically controlled machine tools sit next to conventional lathes and milling machines, manual insertion of electronic components and manual soldering next to automated insertion machines and wave soldering units, and so on. The machinery often comes from diverse manufacturers and represents different generations of technology. Early numerical control (NC) tools sit next to brand new machining centers; machines from several different companies sit side by side. The social or organizational technologies of the workplace are similarly diverse: reporting and inventory control systems are an overlapping mix of computerized, written, and face-to-face communications.

This diversity and incompleteness of automation has certain important implications for skill and human resource needs in today's factory, implications that sometimes are missed by researchers who study a state-of-the-art plant or observe the skills of a person working at one highly automated machine. Many of the snags and problems of today's workplace occur because it is difficult to integrate highly computerized systems with mechanized ones. An automated machine may go down, and force workers to transfer the job to different or less automated machines. Computerized schedules for work flow may fall out of synch with conditions on the shopfloor and require a quick resetup. Bottlenecks can appear because of the very different speeds and capacities of different equipment. An accurate computerized inventory system that fails to initiate a needed delivery of materials can force the employee to figure out some workaround.

Where different technologies coexist, production personnel may have to be proficient on a range of machines, each with its own idiosyncrasies and demands (Zicklin, 1987). They cannot give up old skills for new, but must have both. This undoubtedly places the greatest demands on maintenance personnel, who today are faced with a mixture of mechanical, electronic, and pneumatic devices. This is frequently also the case with skilled machinists, whose daily work takes them from machining centers to conventional tools, and it even affects operators, who become much more useful when they are able to transfer from one type of machine to another as the need arises.

Besides polyvalent skills, in the sense of being proficient on multiple machines, workplaces in the throes of modernization require a higher degree of flexibility and commitment on the part of production personnel than might be the case for more mature, stable, and homogeneous technologies. Shopfloor workers have to work around the snags in work flow that abound in highly integrated factories. When they encounter problems with new machines, they find that maintenance staff are not yet omniscient experts (or are busy elsewhere). This places a premium on troubleshooting and learning on the part of even the lowest-level employees.

Hirschhorn (1984) and Adler (1986a, 1986b) have characterized the increased responsibility demanded of workers in new technology settings. They suggest that responsibility, care, attention, and initiative have increased in importance for production jobs in highly automated plants. Automated machines and modern integrated work processes are not necessarily more *error prone* than earlier technologies, in the sense that errors occur more often than in less automated or less integrated machine systems, but highly integrated systems tend to be more *error sensitive*, in the sense that errors can have ramifications through the parts of an interdependent system and therefore cause greater problems. Workers need to act responsibly to minimize the resulting risks. For example, failing to enter materials taken from the stockroom into the inventory computer will throw off the accuracy of inventory and ordering software and can cause costly delays when material supposed to be in stock cannot be found. The traditional practice of keeping a "kitty" of completed work under one's bench to be reported on the next day, instead of as soon as it is finished, distorts MIS production data and wreaks havoc with MRP. Keeping a personal stock of raw material under one's bench throws off inventory software and MRP.

All these "vices" have been common for decades in nonautomated plants. What has changed is that, in more highly integrated plants, their negative impacts are worse because the organizational "buffers" or slack that allows errors to be absorbed have been eroded in the attempt to increase efficiency. Thus, there is less extra inventory under computerized MRP, so any "ghost stock" is a greater problem. In a factory aiming for rapid delivery, unexpected machine breakdowns wreak greater havoc than in a traditional factory with a bulging warehouse or long delivery times. Managers using scheduling software to optimize the flow of work from machine to machine, and to minimize down time, find unexpected breakdowns more problematic than a conventional firm that operates with lots of extra machine capacity. Firms seeking to gain a reputation for high-quality products find that "it is no longer cost-effective to inspect quality after the fact" and instead require workers to take responsibility for the quality of their own operations (Adler and Borys, 1988, p. 14).

In sum, the increased interdependency of the modern plant, and the greater cost of the equipment, place a higher emphasis on reducing uncertainty and avoiding errors. This requires greater responsibility and initiative on the part of shopfloor workers.

The Machine-Tool Case

This diagnosis has, however, been debated, and it is instructive to review these debates in order better to understand the complexity of any prognosis for the future. Research on the case of numerically controlled machine tools offers an exceptionally rich spectrum of views.

There is convincing evidence that one of the goals of those who designed numerical control was to de-skill machine jobs. This aspect was certainly a major selling point in marketing the technology (Noble, 1984; Shaiken, 1984). Certainly, companies who adopted it expected to be able to use less skilled employees on the machines (Ayres and Miller, 1982; Lund et al., 1978; Lundgren 1969). This expectation was based upon the fact that NC lowered the manual motor and perceptual skill requirements since the operator no longer needed to guide the machine through its cutting path.

However, NC machines required programming, which required substantial new cognitive skills, and the processes of proofing programs and editing them to correct for errors or to improve quality became very important. Furthermore, the maintenance of NC technology proved considerably more complex than that for conventional equipment, requiring a richer mix of mechanical, electronic, and sometimes pneumatic skills (Swords-Isherwood and Senker, 1980; Senker, 1981).

Judgments as to whether overall skill requirements were increased, decreased, or stayed constant therefore depend in part on the ways that analysts measured and then compared the new cognitive and maintenance skills with the loss of motor skills. According to the weight assigned by the researcher, very different conclusions can be reached (see the discussion of Crossman et al., 1966, and Hazelhurst et al., 1969, in Adler and Borys, 1988).

In many plants, especially in the early years of numerical control, the conceptually demanding tasks of programming and even setup and proofing were turned into separate jobs filled by technicians or by highly skilled former machinists specially trained in programming. Maintenance of NC machines became yet another specialty. This new division of labor created substantial problems for researchers who want to say whether numerical control upgrades or degrades skill. Those scholars whose focus was solely on the machinist tended to view early NC as de-skilling the machinist because of the apparent loss of motor or manual skills. Researchers concerned with the skill demands of the overall workforce (machinists plus programmers plus maintenance) were equally emphatic that there was no aggregate loss in skill, but rather a redistribution of skilled work among jobs (Jones, 1982). Others have called the new pattern a polarization of skill between a group of highly skilled programming and maintenance staff and a mass of semiskilled operators (Burns, 1984).

The extent to which conceptual and manual tasks were separated into different jobs varied widely, in part, because of varying managerial policies. Kelley (1986) identified three contrasting styles of NC implementation—scientific management, technocentric participative, and worker-centered participative—that dramatically affected how the cognitive work in NC was allocated. In part, the division also stemmed from firm and product characteristics. Small plants and small-batch production were associated with giving the programming, proofing, and editing tasks to operators (Hartman et al., 1983; but see Kelley, 1986, p. 228).

Where programming and operation of NC machine tools are combined in one job, most scholars would agree that the result is occupational upgrading, in that the new skills exceed even those of skilled machinists on conventional equipment. Some researchers have therefore focused on assessing the frequency with which programming is combined with operating and on estimating the efficiency effects of such a combination.

For the mid-1970s, Kelley's (1984) analysis of 221 manufacturing plants indicated that no operators were programming their machines and that relatively few were setting up their machines. This would suggest that operators were effectively de-skilled, but there are important caveats. First, the punch tape controls and programming languages of the early period of NC were not conducive to easy operator programming, whereas today's machines with Manual Data Input make it much easier for operators to program. And second, there is good ethnographic evidence that even in shops where the formal division of labor proscribed operators from set up, proofing, and programming, operators were informally performing these tasks so as to get their work done (Wilkinson, 1983; Shaiken et al., 1984; Noble, 1984, pp. 240–45, 262, 269–76). This evidence shows that operators used override buttons on NC machines to gain control of cutting and feeding speeds, learned to read punch tape, and surreptitiously edited programs to improve performance. Programs written in the back office rarely performed adequately the first time; they had to be edited, and operators seemed best positioned to do this.

Evidently, the separation of conceptual work from operator work envisioned by designers and early adopters of numerical control was a mirage. The knowledge and initiative of skilled machinists proved important for firms to get the best out of the technology.

This lesson took a long time to sink in. Noble (1984) detailed the ways in which large firms like General Electric (GE) and General Motors (GM) initially attempted to implement NC as a de-skilling technology. They offered lower pay rates for NC operators, and kept setup and programming as separate jobs. These policies caused great friction with unionized labor, as well as managerial dissatisfaction over the low productivity of NC. GE and other firms then experimented with a very different division of labor, designing jobs that combined set up, programming, and other conceptual skills with the manual aspects of machining. Noble (1984) characterizes these as technical and economic successes. They proved highly problematic for some managers, however, because they bolstered the skills and leverage of union labor. At GE, the best known of these enrichment programs was quashed (Noble, 1984, pp. 280–307).

There are several indications that the de-skilling approach to numerical control has become less common over time, and that the practice of encouraging operators to set up, proof out, and edit is spreading. First, early attempts to employ a lower grade of labor at lower pay rates (see Williams and Williams, 1964) seem to have collapsed by the 1980s. According to national survey data, today's NC operators are paid on average at the same level as the top category of machinists on conventional machines (Adler and Borys, 1988).

Second, the technology itself has shifted to enable operator programming, proofing and editing. Modern machining centers are programmable at the machine. According to Kelley and Lan (1990), by the mid-1980s, this change in technology had increased considerably the amount of programming performed by machine operators. In about 56 percent of the sites with programmable automation, operators routinely wrote programs for new parts, and in 75 percent of sites operators programmed new parts at least occasionally. The number of machine operators informally proofing and editing programs at their machines was probably even greater.

Third, "pay for knowledge" schemes are spreading. In these schemes, operators earn higher rates because they take on quality control, maintenance and other tasks requiring broader skills (*Wall Street Journal*, 1985).

Fourth, the trend in this area of manufacturing is towards "flexible manufacturing"—the ability to produce different products on the same set of machines. This results in shorter production runs, and more programming and setup work, which in turn demands more worker skill (Sabel, 1982; Piore and Sabel, 1984; Hirschhorn,1984; Kaplinsky, 1984).

Finally, contemporary machinists working on the most modern type of machining centers characterize their own work as equal in skill, and in some ways more skilled than their prior work on conventional machine tools (Zicklin, 1987).

The High-Skill Strategy

Two other kinds of research suggest that the strategy of employing a high-skill workforce will spread and perhaps dominate U.S. manufacturing establishments in the future.

First, studies of successful advanced manufacturing technology (AMT) plants in the United States, indicate that these plants stressed a highly skilled production work force. Cutting-edge AMT plants combine programmable automation with MRP and various forms of process planning software with CAD, and with the use of automated materials handling technologies. Such plants are by no means typical of U.S. manufacturing, but they provide a guide to future trends.

Firms obtain the high-skill mix of the AMT production workforce by being very selective about the educational and skill background of their workers at entry. Moreover, these plants are investing considerably more resources in training efforts than has been the U.S. norm. In a national survey of manufacturing establishments, Majchrzak (1986) found that "training needs dramatically increase as equipment is integrated." Last, the firms assign these employees to jobs that are broader in scope than those in traditional manufacturing (National Academy of Sciences, 1986).

In a study of 16 North American plants operated by U.S. companies, a National Academy of Sciences panel contrasted AMT technologies with the earlier technologies they replaced in terms of human resource demands. The panel found:

- Machine operators' responsibilities broadened in scope to include routine maintenance and service; troubleshooting and debugging; simple programming of NC machines; increased responsibility for quality, including statistical quality control and an emphasis on prevention; increased operator decision-making on scheduling and machine use. Machine operators also ran multiple machines simultaneously.

- A greater degree of teamwork, leading to fewer job titles and more cross-training. Greater interdependence between employees and work groups, leading to increased importance of interpersonal and co-ordination skills.

- A managerial structure that was less hierarchical than in traditional manufacturing, with more delegation of operating decisions. Considerable efforts were made to build a committed workforce and a partnership between management and labor (National Academy of Sciences, 1986).

This picture of successful Advanced Manufacturing Technology plants based on a high-skill, high-commitment strategy is corroborated by other studies of successful state-of-the-art factories (Majchrzak,

1988; Susman et al., 1988), but it must be stressed that the strategy of skill development described does not occur "automatically" with the technology. It was either a conscious choice when the plant was designed or (more commonly) it evolved through experimentation and experience with AMT.

There is little in the short run to prevent managers who are committed to a de-skilling or Taylorist philosophy from attempting to organize AMT using low-skill production labor with narrow job classifications and no job rotation. Clearly, some firms have done so, for there are research reports of AMT plants in which operator discretion was very low (Gerwin, 1982), tasks were unchallenging and narrow (Gent and Weinstein, 1985), and manual and conceptual tasks were rigorously separated (Jones, 1984, 1985, 1989). These firms have had to pay the costs of such a strategy: more operator stress and lower motivation.

A second indication that the high-skill strategy is proving to be more successful is found in cross-national studies of AMT. West German manufacturing has for historical reasons favored a higher-skilled workforce with a high proportion of craftworkers. This tradition has been carried over into AMT plants (Dostal and Kostner, 1982). Comparisons of German plants with their French and British counterparts indicate that productivity is considerably higher in the German plants and that this difference can be attributed to their higher skills (Hartmann et al., 1983; Sorge et al., 1983; Daly et al., 1985).

One issue that has received relatively little attention in discussions about production worker skills is the demand placed upon workers by statistical quality control methods. Increasingly, operators are becoming responsible for monitoring quality, diagnosing error, and developing improvements (Pullen, 1976). Cole (1979, pp. 135–55) has given a detailed description of the statistical quality control procedures carried out by production workers in Japanese manufacturing. His description is impressive, not only for its demonstration of the degree of initiative and responsibility of the employees, but also for its delineation of the mathematical knowledge demanded of those workers. The quality control methods assumed that operators understood elementary probability theory, that they were familiar with the idea of statistical variance, standard deviations and other statistical measures, and that they could grasp quasiexperimental approaches to diagnosing possible sources of error (Cole, 1979; p. 139 fn). For Japanese approaches to quality control by teams of operators (as distinct from a specialized staff function) to become current in the U.S., firms would have to upgrade the conceptual skills of most of their employees significantly.

Clerical and Support Staff Skills

Although increasing productivity on the shopfloor and managing the skills of the blue collar workforce are central concerns of manufacturing management, the continued growth of nonproduction labor suggests that we should be equally attentive to what is happening in the factory office. The most significant changes in clerical jobs have occurred as firms have shifted from computerized batch processing of data to interactive, real-time, on-line processing. In characterizing the changes that have occurred in these jobs, I will summarize earlier research that I carried out as part of a study of a representative sample of nearly 200 New York–area firms (Rule and Attewell, 1989). For a more complete description of how the picture I draw below is related to the larger literature on office automation, the reader is referred to Attewell (1987a, 1987b, 1989).

In interactive processing, each transaction is entered individually into the computer, which immediately makes calculations and adjusts data records to reflect the newly entered transaction. By contrast, during batch processing, large numbers of transactions are accumulated over time, coded in a standard format for computer input, and run in one block, say, once a month.

The shift from batch to interactive computing has changed clerical jobs in several ways. First, under interactive computing, work is distributed more evenly throughout the day or month. Employees are no longer rushing to meet month-end or other deadlines for calculating receivables and preparing drafts or checks, as was the case under most batch systems. Second, jobs that were very narrow and repetitious under batch processing have become somewhat broader.

Interactive computing, in addition to allowing a worker to move easily from one task to another via software, also allows information entered into one database to be moved, without human intervention into another database. Thus, for example, an entry made into accounts payable can be automatically used to update the general ledger, or a customer order entry may interface with inventory, and generate a production order, possibly resulting in a purchase order for more raw materials, and so on.

Before the introduction of interactive computing and integrated databases, processes like those just described involved work separated into stages. Paper was typically carried from one person to another. Inventory had first to be checked before a decision was made to produce more product. Then raw-materials inventory had to be studied, and then perhaps a purchase order authorized for more materials. These practices tended to result in an organization of paper flow and decision processes into long sequences, each stage of which was the responsibility of a different person. Thus, the properties of manual paperwork tended toward or were enhanced by Tayloristic designs that involved sequencing, simplifying, and fragmenting white-collar work. This fragmentation was carried over into batch computer processing.

By contrast, the capacity of interactive computing to link, update, and transfer calculations from multiple databases in a fraction of a second have made it feasible and efficient to integrate diverse tasks into one job in a way that would not be feasible with manual or batch processing. It enables a clerk, for example, to do order entry, check inventory, and monitor customer credit from one terminal, whereas batch processing would probably have involved different clerks consulting different printouts in different physical locations. In short, interactive computing facilitates the integration of tasks into broader jobs.

As the number of linked databases increases, the complexity of jobs often increases because of the greater number of choices. At the same time, the demand for rapid access to information also has risen because systems give an up-to-date picture of many of a firm's most important activities. But not all the people seeking information are skilled enough to access the information themselves. Thus, it becomes feasible and sensible to develop specialized jobs for employees who mediate between the computer system and other people, such as customers or salespeople, who do not know the intricacies of the system.

The technology makes it possible to have jobs that combine retrieving information from the system for other people, with clerical-like data entry into the system. Such jobs have rapidly proliferated in recent years, and offer a new and different type of clerical work.

To summarize: I have identified four properties of modern interactive computing that have consequences for clerical work:

1. Distributing work more evenly through the day and month;

2. Facilitating easy movement from one data-processing task to another;

3. Facilitating the aggregation of previously sequenced tasks into broader jobs; and

4. Encouraging job designs that combine data retrieval and data input.

In my New York research, I found many clerical jobs that had assumed these characteristics. For example, some accounts-receivables clerks, who had previously spent almost the entire work day typing bills or invoices, were alternating among three tasks: entering billing data, posting checks as they were received, and telephoning customers to increase the collections of past-due bills. Clerks whose previous duties had consisted primarily of typing order information received from salespeople were now able to enter orders into the computer, check inventory, give an estimated delivery date, and sometimes also check the customer's credit or payment history. Some also acted as customer-service representatives, answering customer queries on the status of their orders. In these and other examples, interactive computing has modified many low-level clerical functions primarily by enabling previously separated tasks to be joined.

Clerical personnel filling these jobs also required a broader and more detailed knowledge than their clerical predecessors. Managerial informants pointed out that when clerks were working on systems that linked with financial records, production orders, and inventory data, and when they handled inquiries from managers and customers about availability or production status, the clerks needed to have a good understanding of the various records they were accessing and of the firm's activities that those records represented. This stood in contrast to the narrow parochialism of many clerical jobs of an earlier era.

Finally, these jobs in interactive, highly integrated information systems required more responsibility and care from clerks. Erroneous or sloppily entered data will rapidly pollute integrated databases, throwing off accounts receivable, inventory and other information. Errors were therefore more serious in their consequences and often more difficult to undo.

Taken together, these consequences of interactive information systems have been altering many clerical jobs, requiring more knowledge and demanding a greater degree of care and responsibility. This is upgrading, and it has led to a proportionate growth in higher-paid, higher-skilled clericals and a relative shrinkage of the lowest most routine level of clerical jobs in many firms and industries (Attewell, 1987a).

Designers and Drafters

Another area of work that has been affected by information technology is the process of design. CAD systems are software packages, run on mainframe computers or on powerful workstations, that use interactive computer graphics. They enable drafters and designers to "draw" at the computer, modify designs, and to use the numerical power of the computer to calculate different perspectives or views of the object designed. Many CAD systems in use at present provide two-dimensional images. More sophisticated versions allow three-dimensional representation. Some can compute engineering characteristics of the design as the design is being created, and some can decide on tooling to be used in manufacturing the designed part (CAD/CAM).

CAD was widely expected to revolutionize the design and drafting process, and hence affect the job content of designers' and drafters' work. As part of their sales pitch, vendors of these systems claimed that CAD made design and drafting much faster, and that it would yield considerable labor savings. This view was corroborated by engineering researchers such as Kidd and Burnett (1981, p. 1), who claimed, "It has been proven conclusively many times that CAD can improve the productivity of the designer/draftsman by factors of between 2:1 and 5:1 depending upon the applications."

Based on such estimates, Leontief and Duchin (1986, pp. 38–40) predicted that the number of drafters would drop to 63 percent of their 1978 level by 1990, and (under one of their scenarios) "no human drafters are required by the year 2000." Other scholars believed that the loss would mainly fall on designers, much of whose work might be shifted to less skilled drafters using CAD. Alternatively, CAD might reduce the room for creativity by designers, by limiting them to minor modifications of vast computer libraries of predesigned parts (Shaiken, 1984, pp. 218–27).

CAD has been used in many U.S. manufacturers with large design staffs for nearly a decade, although in most design/drafting departments the transition to CAD has been gradual, and manual and computer-aided design still coexist. There has by now been sufficient time to see whether the anticipated occupational, skill, and employment effects have come to pass.

It seems clear that many of the early expectations have proved false. Far from declining, the total number of drafters employed in the United States has risen from 296,000 in 1978 to 348,000 in 1986. Bureau of Labor Statistics projections (that are also influenced by predictions that CAD results in large productivity gains) suggest that the number of drafters will probably continue to rise to about 354,000 by the year 2000 (Silvestri and Lukasiewicz, 1987, p. 52).

Salzman (1989) has examined the use of CAD and the employment of engineers and drafters in the two U.S. industries that are the heaviest users of the technology: aerospace and automobiles. Although investment in CAD increased sixfold between 1977 and 1986 in those industries, Salzman showed that the employment of drafters almost doubled in aircraft manufacturing and almost tripled for automobile manufacturing in the same period—a period that saw overall employment in those industries stagnating or declining.

The prophecies that CAD could allow unskilled employees to replace designers ignored important limitations in the technology and masked the critical importance of designers' skills in the successful use of CAD. Salzman's (1989) case studies of CAD in printed circuit board design illustrate this point. Several firms had believed the claims of vendors and attempted to use CAD for design with a less skilled workforce. In every case the result was a disaster, and boards took many months to design. One limitation of the de-skilling strategy was that the CAD software itself was full of complex bugs that well-experienced users knew how to work around. Less skilled CAD users were slowed to a crawl by the same problems.

Another limitation was that designs based solely on computer algorithms proved inferior because the algorithms were not as subtle or knowledgeable as human experts. Skilled designers overrode the machine, using their expertise to enhance designs and to avoid mistakes. Less skilled operators could not do this, and generated very poor quality work. Simultaneously, greater demands were being made for more complex designs and tighter tolerances, which again placed a premium on human skills.

The experience with CAD mirrors that with numerical control and other new technologies. Early attempts to sell CAD technology in terms of labor displacement and de-skilling were believed by employers at first. Subsequent attempts to use the technology with fewer and less skilled workers often backfired, leading to an increasing realization that the technology works best when it complements human skills instead of replacing them. The fact that a high-skill workforce seems to operate the equipment most successfully is slowly but steadily emerging across industries (Majchrzak and Salzman, 1989; Forslin and Thulestedt, 1989; Badham, 1989; Adler, 1989; Manske and Wolf, 1989).

Managerial Skills

Even before the computer revolution, scholars found it difficult to describe the skills and cognitive demands of managers (Sayles, 1979). There are so many kinds of manager—from chief executive to first-line manager, from head of a specialist staff department to manager of an operations department—that generalization is difficult. The problem is compounded when one tries to characterize management in today's computerized environment, for firms vary greatly in the diffusion and impact of computerization.

Given this problem, I offer here a thumbnail sketch, based largely on my own field research on a sample of New York–area firms, in which I highlight those trends I believe to be most common and most relevant to our interest in the future skills of middle- and lower-level managers in manufacturing industries.

One of the most dramatic recent changes in the managerial work process is the proliferation of computerized management information systems that capture a mass of transactional and production data from the office and factory floor. The fineness of detail of these data is far greater than that available in previous systems. The data are also far more up to date, reflecting yesterday's production (and in some cases information that is a few minutes old), where a prior generation of managers made do with information on last week's or last month's activity. Today's MIS data are more accessible and more malleable than before. A manager can call up information on aggregate sales orders, production volume, or inventory, and then zoom in to see information on individual transactions or orders. A manager can often demand custom-designed tabulations of the data (or can download to a spread-sheet) for particular analytical purposes.

Since this kind of MIS offers a detailed representation of a firm's activities and of a manager's own area of jurisdiction, managers can, for the first time, monitor and administer on the basis of numerical data rather than direct observation or verbal reports. No one gives up these other forms of information, but the balance shifts toward quantitative information, and, for some managers in some cases, MIS data become their "primary reality." The contrast is most clearly seen when one compares today's MIS with earlier batch and manual record systems. The older systems reflected historical data that were useful for upper managers who wanted to know how the firm did last month, but were of limited use to lower level managers involved in today's production. As a result, an operational manager obtained current information either by walking around the shopfloor and seeing for him/herself, or from meetings with foremen and others who would alert the manager to problems.

With on-line MIS, operational managers report that they are more knowledgeable and feel more informed about what is going on inside their jurisdiction. They say that they monitor production more continually and in more detail via MIS than they did under earlier systems. Previously, errors or problems were often caught long after they had occurred, for example, when costing data became available for a prior month's production, or when accounts were closed at the end of a month. Given such time lags, problems often could not be undone; one could only change policies or staff to make sure the problem did not recur. By contrast, with on-line MIS, even minor deviations from the norm jump to a manager's attention, and since the data are only hours or a day old, it is feasible to intervene and reverse the problem virtually as it is happening. Since errors are no longer faits accomplis, managers can and do intervene at an earlier stage, before problems become irreversible.

This change in availability of information is drawing many managers into a more activist style of management. As they spend more time scrutinizing short-term fluctuations in productivity or sales MIS data, operational managers are increasingly likely to notice emerging problems themselves, and are therefore less dependent on subordinates to inform them of shopfloor problems. This method of using data also tends to draw some managers into greater experimentation with work routines, such as shifting people and processes around to increase productivity. With on-line MIS data, the effects of even minor tuning of work processes may be seen by comparing production before and after a change in staffing or procedure. Thus, where managers might once have left established work routines to supervisors and skilled workers, some are now tempted to try new ones, and are thereby drawn further into thinking about the details of daily work life.

Of course, some managers have always been interventionists, while others, even after the introduction of computing, do not track MIS data so closely or involve themselves with manipulating production processes. My point is that modern MIS systems appear to encourage or tempt managers to be more interventionist, as they provide the tools to evaluate interventions. I contend that they are shifting the norm toward a more interventionist style for operations management.

According to managers themselves, the availability of good information, along with spreadsheets and forecasting tools, has facilitated
advance planning and strategic thinking. They report being better able
to analyze the costs and benefits of buying a new machine or increasing
staff. They also say that they are better able to prioritize interventions
and investments. The availability of cost-accounting data, for example,
has allowed them to see that changing one fabrication step will have
a bigger payoff, summed across numerous product lines, than mod-
ernizing another step.

So far, I have described what amounts to the development and
intensification of a quantitative information culture within many U.S. firms
as a result of modern information systems and computer tools. This
change clearly places new skill demands on managers to access and
manipulate MIS data through spreadsheet and other analytical
software. Equally importantly, managers cannot function effectively in
such a context without understanding some of the theoretical principles
behind MRP, production scheduling, forecasting methods, and statistical quality control. Managers have therefore had to extend both their
practical and conceptual skills.

Most of the nearly 200 managers interviewed experienced this transition
positively because they they had mastered the needed skills. Managers
reported that MIS and related developments had given them a sense
of heightened awareness and cognitive control over activities within
their jurisdiction.

However, there was also a dark side to this information culture. Some
managers reported having to spend more time than necessary preparing
data analyses because spreadsheet models (and sometimes fancy pre-
sentational graphics) have become *de rigeur* for almost any budget
request or other initiative. Some complained that decisions that would
once have been made by a lower-level manager on the basis of "gut"
knowledge, and approved by a superior who trusted the subordinate's
judgment, now require elaborate quantitative rationales. This consumed
hours of an already pressured day, and led some managers to fudge
assumptions to fit their goals.

Other managers complain that higher-level executives, scanning MIS
data, tried to micromanage. However, my survey data indicate that
this centralization of decision-making, long predicted as a result of
computerization, is not widespread. Only a small proportion of managerial
respondents experienced it; most reported more delegation and greater
autonomy than before.

Finally, some managers complained that executive decisions as to
investment and resource allocation overemphasized quantitative measures of departmental performance even when these poorly reflected
the efforts and particular position of one department versus another
(Attewell, 1986).

We see in these negative aspects a potential "tyranny of numbers"
in managerial work as a result of computerization. It is one negative

outcome of technological change, but it varies widely from firm to firm. It does not, for most managers, outweigh the positive aspects of computerization.

A more widespread managerial complaint about highly computerized, highly integrated plants concerned a loss of control, or more accurately a greater degree of lateral dependence in the organization. With MRP and related computerized forms of inventory management and production planning, the activities of different parts of the firm were drawn more tightly together. When these technologies prove successful, delivery times were shorter, inventory levels were lower, and excess machine capacity was lower. This improved efficiency resulted in an erosion of autonomy for individual departments because they were subjected to a master schedule. They had less slack or buffers (extra time, people, machine capacity); so they had less ability to absorb unexpected changes. Delays or problems from other operational areas therefore spread right through the system, causing carefully constructed schedules to be thrown out the window.

The end result of this was that managers (and others) in successfully automated highly integrated plants reported spending more of their time dealing laterally with other departments. They had to scan for problems elsewhere that might affect their own department, coordinate with others over unexpected changes in tight schedules, become concerned over quality issues that rebound on their own jurisdiction, and so on. This was quite demanding. It required superior interpersonal skills on the part of managers, whose success depended on being able to gain cooperation from departments over which they had no direct authority. It also required that managers have a broad knowledge of other departments' activities in order to make intelligent demands or make helpful suggestions. And it placed a premium on quick improvisation.

Within their own departments' operations, managers reported having to keep abreast of new machinery and software, and having to manage a more sophisticated workforce whose initiative and good will are essential. In essence they are having to manage processes of technological change and organizational and individual learning alongside their usual responsibilities for daily operations.

In sum, new technologies are challenging the talents of lower and middle managers. Many of the skills required are not new in an absolute sense—handling lateral ties has always been a significant element in managerial work (Sayles, 1979). But there is evidence that these skills have increased in importance. In an alternative formulation, one can say that uncertainty has increased for many managers, making the skills described more central to the average manager's work. Perhaps the added burdens in these areas explain the rapid expansion in the number of managers since the early 1970s that was documented earlier in this paper.

THE FUTURE

Forecasting occupational trends is a risky pursuit because forecasts are highly dependent upon assessments of future gross-national-product (GNP) growth, the future penetration of imports, and export levels, as well as technological factors. Past experience suggests that Bureau of Labor Statistics (BLS) projections have been accurate, if one were to confine oneself to a decade ahead and the larger occupational groups. Prediction error is substantially greater for detailed occupations. Thus, in this section, I will summarize BLS forecasts up to the year 2000, insofar as they bear on issues of skill and occupational composition.

Under moderate growth assumptions, employment in the U.S. economy is expected to grow by over 21 million jobs between 1986 and 2000. This is only about half the employment growth rate for 1976–86. The slowdown reflects BLS expectations of an average growth rate of 2.4 percent per annum in GNP, a shrinkage in young entrants to the labor force as the baby boom turns into the baby bust, and some fairly optimistic assumptions regarding future productivity growth.

Manufacturing employment will continue to shrink as a proportion of total employment, from around 19 percent today to about 15 percent in the year 2000. This represents an absolute decline in manufacturing employment from 19 million in 1986 to 18.2 million in 2000. (The peak was around 21 million in 1979). This shrinkage should prove considerably less traumatic than the period we have just experienced for the annual rate of loss (1986–2000) will be about one-fifth the rate for the period 1979–86 (Personick, 1987).

Despite the loss of employment, the BLS projects strong output growth for manufacturing as a whole (2.3 percent per annum), and an even brisker expansion for durable manufactures. (This optimism may be misplaced, because it is based in part upon an extrapolation of figures that show a strong growth in productivity for manufacturing over the past decade. Several scholars have argued that those figures seriously overstated productivity gains in manufacturing. (Mishel, 1988; Dennison, 1989).

In terms of occupational groups, the BLS anticipates further growth in managerial, professional, and technical employment, a shrinkage in clerical and administrative support occupations, a small growth in precision production and craft employment, and declines in "other production jobs"—a category that includes machine operators, assemblers, material movers, and laborers. Overall, these estimates represent a modest shift toward higher-skill categories within both white- and blue-collar employment in manufacturing. This mirrors the trend in the larger economy, where higher-skill jobs, and jobs requiring the most education and training, are expected to grow more rapidly than the workforce as a whole through the end of the century (Personick, 1987; p. 33).

Even though manufacturing employment as a whole will shrink, the redistribution of employment to higher-level occupations will result in growth in certain manufacturing occupations. Engineering will add 165,000 employees by the year 2000, managers, 85,000, and technicians, 70,000. The greatest shrinkages, according to the BLS, will occur for machine setters, operators, and hand assemblers (Silvestri and Lukasiewicz, 1987, p. 50).

Given these projections, what are the implications for skill formation and the availability of skilled labor? First, there is little reason to expect systematic shortages in the decade ahead for manufacturing occupations, given the stagnant-to-declining employment pattern for the sector as a whole. One possible exception is for computer specialists. The BLS anticipates a great deal of investment in computer-aided manufacturing alongside continued rapid growth in the computer-services part of business and professional services. There is therefore potential for competition between industrial sectors for systems designers and analysts, programmers, and software developers.

Another possible area of shortages concerns skilled machinists. Given projected trends requiring more of these workers, one might anticipate worse shortages of the most skilled craftspeople in the decades ahead. However, this is a complex and contentious issue. Complaints of shortages of skilled machinists appear to have been chronic for 30 years (Noble, 1984, p. 39). Unemployment rates for these specialists have been quite low, consistent with an image of shortages. Nevertheless, Rosenthal (1982) has shown that the wages of skilled machinists have not been bid up, as one would expect if chronic shortages were to have persisted, and the number of completed apprenticeships has been declining. These conflicting findings leave even experts stumped.

In earlier sections, I stressed the diffusion of computer technologies within manufacturing and the skill demands this places upon blue- and white-collar employees. While these computer skills are quite real, there is little evidence to suggest that manufacturers will face shortages of computer-literate employees. The National Commission for Employment Policy (1986) and Goldstein and Fraser (1985) combined assessments of computer skills for detailed occupations with occupational projections to 1995. They concluded that Group 1 jobs, requiring lengthy training in computers, will constitute only 1 percent of employment. Group 2 jobs, requiring brief training and occasional programming, will constitute 7 percent of the labor force, and group 3 jobs, requiring operation of computer-based equipment with standard software, will make up 23 percent of the U.S. labor force. They argue that Groups 2 and 3 are successfully learning these skills primarily on the job, and that there are few indications that bottlenecks or skill shortages are occurring for these occupations, nor would one expect shortages to manifest themselves in the near future.

The situation may be different for more specialized skills needed in advanced manufacturing technology plants, but here we see a pattern of in-house training and/or collaborations between industry and educational establishments for training employees (Majchrzak, 1986; National Academy of Sciences, 1986; Deutsch, 1987). Although the burden for training falls upon employers, there is no indication of serious shortfalls in the making.

One final area of concern in manufacturing involves general education—the literacy and numerical skills of nonprofessional and nontechnical employees. This is a complex issue. On the one hand, several studies have pointed out that the United States compares very favorably with its international competitors on some measures of human resource quality, such as the proportion of high-school graduates, proportion of the workforce with a college education, and so on (Report of the President's Commission on Industrial Competitiveness, 1985, Vol. 2, pp. 45–47). These findings suggest that manufacturers will not face problems locating educated labor.

On the other hand, some educational researchers have pointed to distressingly low functional levels of literacy and numeracy, even among those with high-school education (Appleby et al., 1989). If, as these researchers suggest, a large majority of high-school juniors were unable to calculate a simple percentage problem, there will be difficulties ahead when these students confront statistical quality control and similarly demanding tasks in the workplace.

The skills problem is most severe for the least educated portion of the American population. Especially in the northern cities, there appears to be a skills mismatch, in the sense that a decreasing number of jobs are available for high school dropouts and others with a weak basic education while the number of dropouts is increasing (Kasarda, 1988). In the past, manufacturing provided many of the jobs for this least educated urban stratum, but such opportunities are shrinking. Many unskilled jobs have been lost overseas and to Southern nonurban areas. Moreover, as detailed above, the most technologically advanced manufacturing remaining in the U.S. is increasingly selective about its workforce and requires higher levels of skills (National Academy of Sciences, 1986; Hirschhorn, 1984).

In the future, either these least educated of our citizens will face a future with few employment prospects, or employers will have to make extraordinary efforts to train them in the basic literacy and numeracy skills needed on the job.

CONCLUSION

As we have seen, there is great contention among scholars as to the direction that occupational change and skill will take as a result of technological change. Sophisticated theorists have offered models that provide convincing mechanisms for upgrading, de-skilling, and skill replacement and reformulation. My own belief is that all these mechanisms and processes exist simultaneously, and that one cannot select a true theory on deductive or logical grounds alone.

The issue is not which theory is right, but which processes dominate in a given era, and why. Empirical evidence suggests that the particular conjuncture of changes in industry mix, international competition, and shifts in products and production processes have favored upgrading for the past decade or two in the economy as a whole. Upgrading has been mirrored in manufacturing, where employment shrinkages in work processes utilizing the more routinized kinds of labor have coincided with the introduction of complex integrated manufacturing systems that demand a more skilled work force.

While the main currents of technological and occupational change seem to propel manufacturing towards a higher-skill work force, this does not mean that countereddies are absent, or that individual firms may not fight the current and pursue de-skilling strategies. On the contrary, evidence suggests that a range of managerial strategies coexist, even with regard to the staffing of the most advanced manufacturing establishments.

It will take some time for a "best practice" to emerge, and even then perhaps a minority of manufacturers will survive holding onto a form of staffing and skill distribution at odds with the rest. But at present, the trend seems clearly to be toward a higher-skill, high-commitment work force, and indications are that this will persist for the next decade or two.

NOTES

1. A technical note: The data presented in figures 3 through 7 in this chapter are derived from the Bureau of Labor Statistics household survey of Americans. One difficulty is that the occupational classification used in this series changed between 1982 and 1983 to reflect new census occupational classifications. This created a discontinuity in the data, represented by a gap on the graphs. The most conservative way to read these graphs is to examine first the trend for the years 1976–82, and then look at the trend for 1983–89, that is, ignore sudden jumps between 1982 and 1983, and concentrate on the trends on both sides of the discontinuity. In those cases where the same trend is apparent in both periods (1976–82, 1983–89) one may be confident that the effect is not an artifact of the classificatory change. So, for example, the increase in managers (Figure 3.6), and the increase in ratio of craft to operators (Figure 3.7) occurred both before and after the change in classification, and are consequently trustworthy.

REFERENCES

Adler, Paul. 1986a. "New Technologies, New Skills." *California Management Review* 29:9–28.

Adler, Paul. 1986b. "Rethinking the Skill Requirements of New Technologies." In Dale Whittington (ed.). *High Hopes for High Tech*. Chapel Hill, N.C.: University of North Carolina Press.

Adler, Paul. 1989. "CAD/CAM: Managerial Challenges and Research Issues." *IEEE Transactions on Engineering Management* **36** (3):202–15.

Adler, Paul, and Bryan Borys. 1988. "Bringing Technology Back In: Theoretical and Empirical Issues in the Relationship between Technology and Work in the Machining Case." Unpublished, Stanford University, Department of Industrial Engineering and Engineering Management.

Appleby, Arthur, Judith Langer, and Ina Mullis. 1989. *Crossroads in American Education: A Summary of Findings.* Princeton N.J.: National Assessment of Educational Progress and Educational Testing Service.

Attewell, Paul. 1986. "Imperialism in Complex Organizations: The Role of MIS data in resource allocation decisions." *Sociological Theory* **4** (Fall):115–25.

Attewell, Paul. 1987a. "The De–Skilling Controversy." *Work and Occupations* **14** (3):323–46.

Attewell, Paul. 1987b. "The Impact of Office Automation on Work: Insights from a Multisite Study." Paper prepared for the meetings of the International Sociological Association. New Delhi.

Attewell, Paul. 1989. "The Clerk De–Skilled: A study in False Nostalgia." *Journal of Historical Sociology* **4** (2) (December):357–88.

Ayres, R., and S. M. Miller. 1982. *Robotics: Application and Social Implications.* New York: Harper and Row.

Badham, R. 1989. "Computer-Aided Design, Work Organization and the Integrated Factory." *IEEE Transactions on Engineering Management.* **36**, 3:216–26.

Baldry, C. 1986. *Computers, Jobs, and Skills: The Industrial Relations of Technological Change.* New York: Plenum.

Baldwin, George, and George P. Schultz. 1954. "Automation: A New Dimension to Old Problems" Industrial Relations Research Association. Proceedings of the 7th Annual Meeting. December.

Bednarzik, Robert W. 1985. "The Impact of Microelectronics on Employment: Japan's Experience." *Monthly Labor Review* **108** (9) (September):45–48.

Berg, Maxine. 1982. *The Machinery Question and the Making of Political Economy.* Cambridge: Cambridge University Press.

Blackburn, M. ,L., David Bloom, and Richard Freeman. 1989. "The Declining Economic Position of Less–Skilled American Males". Working paper No. 3186. Washington D.C.: National Bureau of Economic Research.

Blauner, Robert. 1964. *Alienation and Freedom.* Chicago: Chicago University Press.

Braverman, Harry. 1974. *Labor and Monopoly Capital.* New York: Monthly Review Press.

Burns, B. 1984. "Factors Affecting the Introduction and Use of Computerized Numerical Control Machine Tools." Paper presented to the International Conference on Human Factors in Manufacturing. London, April 3–5.

Burris, Beverly. 1982. *No Room at the Top: Underemployment and Alienation in the Corporation.* New York: Praeger.

Butera, F. 1984. "Designing Work in Automated Systems: A Review of Case Studies." In F. Butera and J.E. Thurman (eds.). *Automation and Work Design.* New York: Elsevier Science.

Cain, P. and D. Treiman. 1981. "The DOT as a Source of Occupational Data" *American Sociological Review* **46**:235–78.

Clague, Ewan, and Leon Greenberg. 1962. "Employment," In *American Assembly Automation and Technological Change.* Englewood Cliffs, N.J.: Prentice Hall. pp. 114–31

Clark, Peter. 1987. *Anglo–American Innovation.* London: Methuen.

Clarke, Jon, Ian McLoughlin, Howard Rose, and Robin King. 1988. *The Process of Technological Change.* Cambridge: Cambridge University Press.

Cockburn, C. 1983. *Brothers: Male Dominance and Technological Change.* London: Pluto Press.

Cole, Robert E. 1979. *Work, Mobility, and Participation: A Comparative Study of American and Japanese Industry.* Berkeley, Calif.: University of California Press.

Crompton, R., and G. Jones. 1984. *White Collar Proletariat.* London: Macmillan.
Crossman, E.R.F.W. 1966. *Automation, Skill, and Manpower Predictions.* U.S. Department of Labor, Seminars on Manpower Policy and Programs. Washington, D.C.: USGPO.
Daly, A., M. Hitchens, and K. Wagner. 1985. "Productivity, Machinery and Skills in a Sample of British and German Manufacturing Plants." *National Institute Economic Review* 111.
Dennison, Edward. 1989. *Estimates of Productivity Change by Industry.* Washington, D.C.: Brookings Institution.
Deutsch, Steven. 1987. "Successful Worker Training Programs Help Ease Impact of Technology." *Monthly Labor Review* 110 (11) (November):14–20.
Dostal, Werner and Klaus Kostner. 1982. "Beschäftigungsveränderung beim Einsatz numerisch gesteuter Werkzeugmaschinen" (Employment changes with the use of numerically controlled machine tools). *Mitteilungen aus der Arbeitsmarkt- und Berufsforschung* 15:443–49.
Faunce, William. 1965. "Automation and the Division of Labor" *Social Problems* 13 (Fall):149–60.
Forslin, J. and B. M. Thulestest. 1989. "Computer-Aided Design: A Case Strategy in Implementing a New Technology." *IEEE Transactions on Engineering Management* 36 (3):191–201.
Friedman, A. L. 1977. *Industry and Labour: Class Struggle at Work and Monopoly Capitalism.* London: Macmillan.
Gent, M., and A. Weinstein. 1985. "Effects of Auto Plant Technology Change on Worker Outcomes: A Path Analysis." Paper presented at the meetings of the American Institute of Decision Sciences, Las Vegas, Nevada, November.
Gerwin, D. 1982. "Do's and Don'ts of Computerized Manufacturing." *Harvard Business Review* (March–April):107–16.
Giuliano, V. 1982. "The Mechanization of Office Work" *Scientific American* 247 (3):148–65.
Glenn, Evelyn, and Roslyn Feldberg. 1977. "Degraded and Deskilled: The Proletarianization of Clerical Work." *Social Problems* 25:52–64.
Goldstein, Harold, and Bryna Shore Fraser. 1985. *Training for Work in the Computer Age.* Washington, D.C.: National Commission for Employment Policy.
Hartmann, G., I. Nicholas, A. Sorge, and M. Warner. 1983. "Computerized Machine Tools, Manpower Consequences and Skill Utilization: A Study of British and West German Manufacturing Firms." *British Journal of Industrial Relations* 21 (2):221–31.
Hirschhorn, Larry. 1984. *Beyond Mechanization: Work and Technology in a Postindustrial Age.* Cambridge, Mass.: MIT Press.
Jones, Bryn. 1982. "Destruction or Redistribution of Engineering Skills. The case of Numerical Control." In Stephen Wood (ed.). *The Degradation of Work?* London: Hutchison. pp. 179–200
Jones, Bryn. 1984. "Computer Integrated Manufacturing: Two Faces of Control." Paper presented at La Table Ronde sur L'Informatisation de la Production dans les Industries, Aix-en-Provence, December 14–15.
Jones, Bryn. 1985. "Flexible Technologies and Inflexible Tools: Impossible Dreams and Missed Opportunities." Paper presented to the 1985 SME World Conference on the Human Aspects of Automation. Cambridge, Mass., September 8–11.
Jones, Bryn. 1989. "When Certainty Fails: Inside the Factory of the Future." In Stephen Wood (ed.), *The Transformation of Work?* London: Heineman. pp. 44–58
Kaplinsky, R. 1984. *Automation: The Technology and Society.* London: Longman Harlow.
Kasarda, John D. 1986. "Jobs, Migration, and the Emerging Urban Mismatches." In Michael McGeary and Laurence Lynn Jr. (eds.), *Urban Change and Poverty.* Washington, D.C.: National Academy Press. pp. 148–98
Kasarda, John D. 1988. "Population and Employment Change in the United States: Past Present and Future." In *A look Ahead: Year 2020.* A report of the Transportation Research Board. Washington, D.C.: National Research Council. pp. 83–148

Kelley, Maryellen R. 1984. "Tasks and Tools: An Inquiry into the Relationship Between Tasks, Skills, and Technology with Application to the Machining Labor Process." Ph.D. thesis. Sloan School of Management, MIT.

Kelley, Maryellen R. 1986. "Programmable Automation and the Skill Question: A Reinterpretation of the Cross–National Evidence." *Human Systems Management* 6:223–41.

Kelley, Maryellen, and Xue Lan. 1990. "Does Decentralization of Programming Responsibilities Increase Efficiency: An Empirical Test." Working Paper 90–13, School of Urban Affairs, Carnegie Mellon University.

Kidd, John, and David Burnett. 1981. "CAD/CAM Interfaces." Technical Paper MS81.386. Dearborn, Michigan: Society of Manufacturing Engineers.

Kohn, Melvin L., and Carmi Schooler. 1983. *Work and Personality*. Norwood, New Jersey: Ablex.

Lee, David. 1981. "Skill, Craft, and Class: A Theoretical Critique and a Critical Case." *Sociology* 15 (February):56–78.

Lee, G. L. 1989. "Managing Change with CAD and CAD/CAM" *IEEE Transactions on Engineering Management* 36 (3):227–33.

Leontief, Wassily and Faye Duchin. 1986. *The Future Impact of Automation on Workers*. Oxford: Oxford University Press.

Levin, H. and R. Rumberger. 1986. *Educational Requirements for New Technologies: Visions, Possibilities and Current Realities*. Working Paper 86. Stanford, Ca.: Stanford Education Policy Institute.

Littler, Craig. 1982. *The Development of the Labour Process in Capitalist Societies*. London: Heinemann.

Lund, R. T., C. J. Barnett, and R. M. Kutta. 1978. *Numerically Controlled Machine Tools and Group Technology*. Report number 78-2, Center for Policy Alternatives, MIT.

Lundgren, E. R. 1969. "Effects of NC on Organizational Structure" *Automation* 76 (January):44–47.

Majchrzak, Ann. 1986. "The Effect of CAM Technologies on Training Activities" *Journal of Manufacturing Systems* 5 (3):203–11.

Majchrzak, Ann. 1988. *The Human Side of Factory Automation*. San Francisco: Jossey-Bass.

Majchrzak, A. and H. Salzman. 1989. "Social and Organizational Dimensions of Computer-Aided Design." *IEEE Transactions on Engineering Management* 36 (3):174–79.

Mann, Floyd. 1962. "Psychological and Organizational Impacts" In *American Assembly Automation and Technological Change*. Englewood Cliffs, N.J.: Prentice–Hall. pp. 43–65

Manske, F., and H. Wolf. 1989. "Design Work in Change: Social Conditions and Results of CAD Use in Mechanical Engineering." *IEEE Transactions on Engineering Management* 36 (4):282–92.

Martin, R. 1981. *New Technology and Industrial Relations in Fleet Street*. Oxford: Clarendon Press.

Marx, Karl. 1867. *Das Kapital* I. English edition, New York: International Publishers, 1975.

Mishel, Lawrence. 1988. *Manufacturing Numbers: How Inaccurate Statistics Conceal U.S. Industrial Decline*. Washington, D.C.: Economic Policy Institute.

More, Charles. 1980. *Skill and the English Working Class, 1970–1914*. London: Croom Helm.

Mueller, E. 1969. *Technological Advance in an Expanding Economy: Its Impact on a Cross–Section of the Labor Force*. Ann Arbor, Mich.: Institute for Social Research.

National Academy of Sciences. 1986. Committee on the Effective Implementation of Advanced Manufacturing Technology. *Human Resource Practices for Implementing Advanced Manufacturing Technology*. Washington, D.C.: National Academy Press.

National Commission for Employment Policy. 1986. *Computers in the Workplace: Selected Issues*. Washington, D.C.: NCEP.

Noble, David F. 1984. *Forces of Production*. New York: Alfred Knopf.

Organization for Economic Cooperation and Development. 1965. *The Requirements of Automated Jobs*. Paris: OECD.

Penn, Roger. 1982. "Skilled Manual Workers in the Labour Process." In Stephen Wood (ed.), *The Degradation of Work?* London: Heinemann.

Penn, Roger. 1983. "Theories of Skill and Class Structure." *Sociological Review* 31 (1):22–38.

Penn, Roger. 1986. "Where have all the Craftsmen Gone?: Trends in Skilled Labor in the United States of America Since 1940." *British Journal of Sociology* 37 (4):569–80.

Penn, Roger, and Hilda Scattergood. 1985. "De–skilling or Enskilling?: An Empirical Investigation of Recent Theories of the Labor Process." *British Journal of Sociology* 36 (4):611–30.

Perrolle, Judith. 1985. *Computers and Social Change*. Belmont, Calif.: Wadsworth.

Perrucci, Carolyn, and Dena Targ. 1988. *Plant Closings: International Context and Social Costs*. New York: Aldine de Gruyter.

Personick, Valerie. 1987. "Industry Output and Employment Through the End of the Century" *Monthly Labor Review* 110 (9)(September):30–45.

Piore, M., and C. Sabel. 1984. *The Second Industrial Divide*. New York: Basic Books.

President's Commission on International Competitiveness. 1985. *Global Competition: The New Reality*. Washington, D.C.: USGPO.

Pullen, R. 1976. "A survey of manufacturing cells." *Production Engineer*, September.

Response Analysis Corporation. 1983. *Office Automation and the Workplace*. Minneapolis, Minn.: Honeywell, Inc.

Rosenthal, Neal. 1982. "Shortages of Machinists: An Evaluation of the Information." *Monthly Labor Review*. (July):31–36.

Roy, Robin, and David Wield. 1986. *Product Design and Technological Innovation*. Milton Keynes, England: Open University Press.

Rule, James, and Paul Attewell. 1989. "What Do Computers Do?" *Social Problems* 36 (3):225–41.

Rumberger, R. W. 1981. "The Changing Skill Requirements of Jobs in the U.S. Economy" *Industrial and Labor Relations Review* 34:578–90.

Sabel, C. 1982. *Work and Politics*. Cambridge: Cambridge University Press.

Salzman, H. 1989. "Computer Aided Design: Limitations in Automating Design and Drafting." *IEEE Transactions on Engineering Management* 36 (4):252–61.

Samuel, Raphael. 1977. "The Workshop of the World: Steam Power and Hand Technology in Mid-Victorian Britain." *History Workshop* 3 (Spring):6–72.

Sayles, Leonard. 1979. *Leadership: What Effective Managers Really Do and How They Do It*. New York: McGraw Hill.

Senker, Peter. 1981. *Maintenance Skills in the Engineering Industry: The Influence of Technological Change. A report prepared for the engineering industry training board*. EITB occasional paper. British Government Documents.

Shaiken, Harley. 1984. *Work Transformed: Automation and Labor in the Computer Age*. New York: Holt Reinhardt Winston.

Shaiken, H., S. Kuhn, and S. Herzenberg. 1984. "Case studies on the Introduction of Programmable Automation in Manufacturing." In *Computerized Manufacturing Automation: Employment, Education, and the Workplace* 2(A). Office of Technology Assessment. Washington, D.C.: USGPO.

Silvestri, George, and John Lukasiewicz. 1987. "A Look at occupational Employment Trends to the Year 2000." *Monthly Labor Review* 110 (9)(September):46–63.

Singelmann, Joachim, and Marta Tienda. 1985. "The Process of Occupational Change in a Service Society: The Case of the United States, 1960–80." In Bryan Roberts, Ruth Finnegan, and Duncan Gallie (eds.), *New Approaches to Economic Life*. Manchester: Manchester University Press. pp.48–67

Sorge, A., G. Hartmann, M. Warner, and I. Nicholas. 1983. *Microelectronics and Manpower*. Berlin: Gower.

Spenner, Kenneth. 1983. "Deciphering Prometheus: Temporal Change in the Skill Level of Work." *American Sociological Review* 48:824–37.

Spenner, Kenneth. 1985. "The Upgrading and Downgrading of Occupations: Issue, Evidence, and Implications for Education." *Review of Education Research* 55:125–54.

Stone, Katherine. 1974. "The Origins of Job Structures in the Steel Industry." *Review of Radical Political Economics* 6 (Summer):61–97.

Susman, Gerald, James W. Dean, Jr., and Se Joon Yoon. 1988. *Advanced Manufacturing Technology and Organizations: A Study of 185 Pennsylvania Firms in Six Metal-Working Industries.* Center for the Management of Technological and Organizational Change, College of Business Administration, Pennsylvania State University.

Swords-Isherwood, N. and P. Senker. 1980. *Microelectronics and the Engineering Industry: The Need for Skills.* London: Frances Pinter.

Turner, H. A. 1962. *Trade Union Growth, Structure, and Policy.* London: George Allen and Unwin.

United States Department of Labor. 1978. *The Impact of International Trade and Investment on Employment:* A Conference on the Department of Labor Research Results. Washington, D.C.: Bureau of International Labor Affairs.

United States Government Printing Office. 1938. *Job Descriptions for Machine Jobs.* Prepared by the Job Analysis and Information Section, Division of Standards and Research, U.S. Department of Labor.

Verbatim Corp. 1982. *The Verbatim Survey: Office Worker Views and Perceptions of New Technology in the Workplace.* Sunnyvale, Calif.: Verbatim Corp.

Walker, Charles. 1957. *Towards the Automatic Factory.* New Haven: Yale University Press.

Wall Street Journal. 1985. "Work-Rule Programs Spread to Union Plants" p. 6, Tuesday, April 16.

Wallace, M., and A. Kalleberg. 1982. "Industrial Transformation and the Decline of Craft: the Decomposition of Skill in the Printing Industry." *American Sociological Review* 47 (3).

Watson, W. F. 1935. *Machines and Men: An Autobiography of an Itinerant Mechanic.* London: George Allen and Unwin.

Wilkinson, B. 1983. *The Shopfloor Politics of the New Technology.* London: Heinemann.

Williams, Lawrence, and C. Brian Williams. 1964. "The Impact of Numerically Controlled Equipment on Factory Organization." *California Management Review*, 25–34.

Wood, Stephen (ed.). 1982. *The Degradation of Work?* London: Heinemann.

Wood, Stephen (ed.). 1989. *The Transformation of Work?* London: Unwin Hyman.

Wright, E. O., and J. Singelmann. 1982. "Proletarianization in the American Class Structure," pp. 176–209. In M. Burawoy and T. Skocpol (eds.). *Marxist Enquiries: Studies of Labor, Class, and States* (a special supplement to *American Journal of Sociology* 88).

Zicklin, Gilbert. 1987. "Numerical Control Machining and the Issue of De-skilling." *Work and Occupations* 14:(3):452–66.

Zimbalist, Andrew. 1979. *Case Studies in the Labor Process.* New York: Monthly Review Press.

4

Automation and Work in Britain

Peter J. Senker

This chapter discusses the implications of automation for work organization and skills in Britain's engineering industries. These industries are engaged in the manufacture of metal goods and mechanical engineering products such as machine tools; electronics, including components; consumer goods; defence products and systems; industrial capital equipment and office equipment; instrument engineering; motor vehicles; and aerospace equipment. As in all advanced industrial countries, these industries play important economic roles as producers and employers. Their performance is heavily dependent on their success in implementing automation, and on the availability of an adequate supply of appropriate skills among the labor force.

It is within engineering industries that some particularly important and interesting automation technologies such as numerical control (NC), computer numerical control (CNC), computer-aided design (CAD), and robotics have diffused most extensively. The skills implications have excited considerable interest among research sponsors in Britain, including the Engineering Industry Training Board (a statutory body charged with the responsibility of encouraging appropriate training in these industries), which supported such research for more than 20 years.

A substantial body of research therefore exists on these engineering industries. This research shows that the proportion of scientists and technologists has been rising relative to technicians, craftsmen, and operators. Moreover, the less skilled occupations have witnessed the fastest rates of employment decline (Fidgett, 1983; Khamis, et al., 1986).

This chapter reviews British research on automation and its implications for work organization and skills in the manufacturing industry over the past 30 years, with a focus on the engineering industries. A plausible conclusion to be drawn from this research is that the efficient use of automation requires an upgrading of employees' skills. In Britain, however, forces pushing in this direction, such as competitive pressure, have often been counteracted by powerful conservative forces—in particular by the negative attitudes of many British managers towards the training needed to unlock automation's potential.

BRITISH DEBATES ON AUTOMATION AND SKILLS

The participants in British debates on automation and work have entered the fray with many differing objectives and perspectives. It is helpful to understand these points of view in order to put their findings into context. For the purposes of this chapter, British research is placed into three categories related to those utilized by Adler and Borys (1989) in discussing the history of research on the skills implications of numerical control: (1) task-level analysis focused on the objective requirements of effective use of automation; (2) labor process analysis in the Marxist tradition; and (3) analysis of the social conventions surrounding skill and the variability of automation–skill relationships across organizations.

Task-level analysis of the technological requirements of automation is included here in a broader category of policy research. The general aims of policy research are to help industry and government education and training planners devise programs to cope with changing skill requirements. The policy label is used to group together research based on various theoretical perspectives that has been undertaken with a heavy emphasis on influencing policy in addition to making academic contributions. Such research has continued in Britain from the beginning of the period under consideration—the mid-1950s—until the present, as it has in the United States. The work of James Bright and Paul Adler in the United States, the work of Prais and colleagues at The National Institute for Economic and Social Research and of Martin Bell and his successors at the Science Policy Research Unit at the University of Sussex in the United Kingdom, discussed later in this chapter, can all be placed in this category.

The principal purpose of Marxist literature is not so much policy prescription as critique. Braverman's work on automation and skill helped revive British Marxists' interest in the concept of the alienation of workers from capitalism. Adler (1987) argues that the polemical intent in the work of Braverman and his followers led them to a narrow focus on situations in which technology was deliberately used by capitalists to de-skill jobs. Nevertheless, this research stream has highlighted some important factors that counteract the rationality often assumed by many of the policy-oriented task-analysis school. Empirical research in the United Kingdom based on this perspective includes the research of Kaplinsky (1982) and Baldry and Connolly (1986) on computer-aided design.

The third and most recent approach views skill requirements as the consequences of complex interactions that are often context and organization specific. This stream of research sees these interactions as variable enough to make generalizations about the automation–skill relationship impossible. The work of Bryn Jones (1982), Buchanan and Boddy (1983), and Hartmann et al. (1984) can in this sense be classified as "contextualist." These analysts insist that the implications of technology for work are variable depending on the social, political, and industrial relations and the cultural contexts in which they are implemented.

POLICY ANALYSIS: 1950S TO 1970S

In 1956, the British Government published a report on the effects of automation that identified many issues still important more than 30 years later (Department of Scientific and Industrial Research, 1956). In many respects, its analysis foreshadows the conclusions of more recent policy-oriented analyses.

The importance of skills was recognized in the report, which claimed that it was "reasonably certain" that the ratio of managers, supervisors, and technicians to operatives would be greater in automated plants. The report contrasted this conclusion with hypotheses then current that automation would demote skilled workers by eliminating the need for their skills, or alternatively that the jobs created by automation would be too highly skilled for the displaced operatives to take on even with training. Effective maintenance in an automated plant, the report recognized, required a shift to preventive maintenance from fault repair in order to minimize downtime and keep production going. Implementing such policies was likely to require increases in the ratio of skilled maintenance staff to operatives.

Lilley's research (1965, pp. 274–75) led to similar conclusions:

Automated production needs large numbers of skilled craftsmen— maintenance engineers, electricians and electronic engineers, tool-makers and the like—whose role is to keep the automatic machinery in good working order. But maintenance electricians and good production engineers do not grow on trees. A very extensive and very powerful education system is needed to produce them. . . [T]echnology is now changing so fast that we can no longer be content with educating young people once and for all. . . but must rather think in terms of the continued reeducation of most people every few years to cope with the new technological tasks as they arise.

A few years later, Fyrth and Goldsmith (1969, pp. 39, 62–63) suggested that:

Automation is coming more quickly and on a much larger scale than steam engines did. . . . One result of automation which demands change in education is that by the end of the century unskilled and repetition workers will scarcely be needed. . . Machines and

*methods of production, social institutions, social problems, the
arts and human knowledge change so quickly that the only person
adequate for work or living is becoming the one whose training
and education go on through life . . . [C]ertainly an apprenticeship
in which a boy learns a craft from the older generation and then
practices it for forty years is out . . . [W]hole crafts . . . will radically
change or disappear. Workers will have to train and retrain and
have an education which prepares them to change their jobs several
times in a working life.*

In the period 1968 to 1972, Bell (1972, p. 91) and his colleagues
conducted a general survey of the implications of technological change
for manpower requirements in a wide range of engineering industry
production processes. They concluded that many new technologies that
could have been useful were often being ignored because firms lacked
the knowledge necessary to use them. Technical development was producing an ever-widening range of new methods, techniques, and
processes. Their use would require frequent additional training for
technicians and technologists. This need arose more from the diversity
of technical development than its pace.

Bell's main concern was to study the implications of technological
change for the occupational structure of employment rather than for
skill requirements or training needs. His aim was to provide a basis
for forecasting the effects of changing technology on the numbers
required in the various occupational categories. One of his primary
objectives was to establish a more rigorous basis for such research. Bell
was dissatisfied with the analyses of previous writers such as Fyrth
and Goldsmith and Lilley on the grounds that: "they were not based
on any agreed set of concepts, and included nothing meriting the term
theory or *hypothesis*. The mass of empirical case-study material . . . lacks
structure and consistency of results."

Bell suggested that forecasts of the diffusion rates of the most important
types of new technology, combined with analysis of the skill requirements of each technology, could form the basis of forecasts of the future
occupational structure of the workforce. This approach assumes that
the physical characteristics of the technology largely determined firms'
skill requirements, an assumption considered further below.

Bell classified technological changes in manufacturing into changes
in materials, products, manufacturing processes, and management and
organization. He suggested that process change was most significant
in terms of its impact on occupational structure and that automation
would represent the most important aspect of process change in terms
of its manpower effects in the years following his study.

Automation in Machine Shops: Numerical Control

Bell's research was based directly on the earlier work of James Bright (1958) and Crossman (1966). Bright (1958, pp. 39–40) distinguished between level or degree of mechanization and the span of mechanization. The level of mechanization is high when machinery conducts a wide range of tasks automatically, for example, when machinery moves materials, selects items, manipulates them, and performs some actions to time limits and others to quantity limits. The span of mechanization is high when the whole sequence of activity is mechanized. And the penetration of mechanization is high when secondary or tertiary activities such as maintenance, setup, and scrap removal are also mechanized.

Bell did not take into account Bright's distinction between the analysis of entire manufacturing systems and individual workstations. In relation to the narrower context of individual workstations, Bell criticized Bright's classification of levels of automation for being unidimensional. He analyzed automation levels in three dimensions: the control function, the materials handling function of transferring workpieces from one workstation to another, and the application of nonhuman power sources to the transformation process itself. This taxonomy was subsequently applied by Bell and Tapp (1972) to the detailed study of the workforce implications of the automation of metal cutting. Their research was based on the assumption that technology was a major determinant of employment within occupational categories, and that social and economic processes would adjust the labor supply to the opportunities created and destroyed by new technology (Brady, 1986).

Bell and Tapp acknowledged that employment patterns were not rigidly determined by the nature of the production technology, and that "a host of other factors" such as batch size would affect the level of employment associated with a particular technology (Bell and Tapp, 1972, pp. 20–21). They acknowledged that "once a pattern, which is relatively intensive in the use of more skilled labor, is established, there are a number of forces at work to maintain that pattern." They also discussed a number of factors that were likely to result in de-skilling, including "reputed" shortages of engineering craftsmen and apprentice trainees. The demand for craft-trained employees to carry out functions away from the shop floor might leave fewer such employees available for machine operation. Once managers became more confident in using NC, they might be anxious to press for a less skill-intensive pattern of NC operation. Managers' attempts to de-skill might not meet strong resistance since craft-trained workers may reduce their demand for NC work once the novelty wears off. NC machining jobs may not make sufficient demands on craft-trained workers' skills and capabilities to satisfy their job expectations and aspirations (Bell and Tapp, 1972, pp. 112–13).

Bell and Tapp found that their data supported the view that patterns of employment associated with NC were remarkably similar to those found in conjunction with manual machine tools. Nevertheless, while their analysis was perceptive in many respects, the discussion of their results and the reasons they adduced to support them appeared no more rigorous than the previous analyses that Bell had criticized for their lack of rigor.

Factors that could have been significant, such as trade union policies, were scarcely mentioned, nor were issues of work organization discussed in detail. It is generally possible, for example, to reorganize work and to reallocate tasks between workers in different occupations when technology changes. Not only may the work be reallocated between occupations, it may also be reallocated between departments. Thus, any attempt to relate changes in technology in a machine shop to changes in the occupational structure within that machine shop is fraught with difficulties. Further, the adoption of new technology within one department of a firm, such as the machine shop, may have implications outside that department. For example, the increased precision offered by numerical control can reduce the need for fitters—the highly skilled craftsmen required to make fine adjustments to parts to ensure that they fit together.

Bell's methodology was restricted in the range of problems to which it could be applied. As he conceded, some modification would have been needed to make it capable of analyzing the implications of technological change in environments other than machine shops. A more significant restriction on its usefulness, however, was that the rigor applied principally to the analysis of task requirements with little comparable rigor applied to the social and organizational factors that shape employment patterns.

At about the same time as Bell conducted his study, Bradbury and Chalmers (1972) undertook a study of the differences between the skills needed to operate conventional manually controlled and numerically controlled milling machines. They classified skills as motor skills, perceptual skills, conceptual skills, and discretionary (decision-making) skills. The jobs involved in milling included setting up, operating and checking. The researchers assigned to each of these three tasks one of five degrees in each of the four skills, and thereby constructed skill profiles for both manual and NC jobs. Their analysis of eight pairs of jobs (one NC and one manual in each pair) in four companies showed that the most significant skill difference was between those firms that subjected NC machine tools to work planning and loading systems derived from those used for conventional machines and those that treated NC machines as expensive assets that should be loaded as continuously as possible. Firms used NC in different ways for different purposes, and work was organized in different ways in the various companies. The lack of overall pattern in skill changes arose largely from this fact. For example, some firms were using NC machines up to or even slightly beyond the limits of their inherent precision, and this could have imposed extra perceptual and conceptual loads on operators.

Like Bell and Tapp, these researchers noted that other variables such as batch sizes could affect skill needs. And the decisions and discretion required of operators depended on companies' inspection systems. One company assigned responsibility to inspectors for rigorous checking, while the others left varying degrees of discretion to operators. In addition, the skills required by operators were affected by the programmers' abilities: Where programmers were relatively inexperienced, setter-operators needed considerable skill to check programs, to advise programmers and to request modifications when necessary (Bradbury and Chalmers, 1972, pp. 128–31).

The authors did make some broad generalizations, but warned that there was no single pattern of skills common to all jobs. They found that in most cases there were appreciable increases in demands for skills resulting from NC use. In particular, there was increased demand for perceptual skills associated with vigilance, machine monitoring, and controls, and increased demand for conceptual skills associated with the interpretation of symbolic information in the form of part drawings, planning instructions, and calculations. They also found that in general NC resulted in some reduction in demand for motor skills and the associated perceptual load related to precision and accuracy of movement.

LABOR PROCESS ANALYSIS

Braverman's (1974) influence marks the next stage in automation and work research in the United Kingdom, as it had a few years previously in the United States. Marxist theory postulates that workers sell their capacity to work to employers who seek means of converting that capacity into work performance. According to Braverman, the solution to this problem is provided by Taylorism, which separates mental and manual labor. The mental labor is undertaken by managers who utilize "scientific management" techniques to plan in advance and in detail the tasks to be performed by each worker. Labor is reduced from its craft status to a series of simple tasks. Technology has a distinctive role to play in facilitating this reduction.

Prior to the development of numerical control, employers lacked the means to subject batch production in machine shops to scientific management. Instead, production was controlled by craftsmen exercising skills that took several years to acquire. With the advent of NC, speeds and feeds, for example, could be predetermined in the office by part programmers. According to Braverman, numerically controlled machine tools permitted employers to transfer machinists' skills to the office, and thus to gain detailed control over the production process.

Such analysis was embraced in the United Kingdom in the papers produced for the Conference of Socialist Economists in July, 1976 (Capital and Class, 1977). The first by the Brighton Labor Process Group (1977, p. 16) identified the three basic structural features of the capitalist organization of the labor process as: (1) the division of intellectual and manual labor, (2) hierarchical control, and (3) fragmentation/de-skilling of labor. Within this organization, control over the pace of work as well as its nature is theoretically placed under the control of management. This arrangement reduces labor costs, since unskilled labor typically costs less than skilled. The authors reject the view that the age of Taylorism, de-skilling, and alienation was a "transitional one and that we were now entering a new (post-industrial) era in which work will be characterized by higher skill and autonomy of the worker, by the dominance of supervisory, diagnostic, and cognitive rather than manual skills". They summed up their thesis with the statement that "there has been no change in the immanent tendencies of the capitalist labor process, beyond those analyzed by Marx" (Brighton Labor Process Group, 1977, pp. 22–24).

THE BRITISH CONTEXTUALIST CRITIQUE

While the labor process school attempted to reach broad generalizations, a more recent school of thought emerged that focused on the variability of technology-work configurations. Perhaps one of the most notable early contributions to this contextualist critique was that of Bryn Jones. Jones suggested that there were grounds for rejecting a unilateral motivation and capacity to de-skill on the part of capitalist management. He conducted a study (1982, p. 179) of firms using NC and reached the conclusion that "Even in a very small sample, mainly from one sector of engineering, there was sufficient variation among enterprises to confirm the decisiveness of product and labor markets, organizational structures, and trade union positions as independent influences on the forms of skill deployment."

Similarly, considering a wider range of computing technologies, Buchanan and Boddy (1983, p. 246) showed that the skills implications of the introduction of new technology were both complicated and highly variable:

> The changes in job characteristics that accompany technological change reflect partly the capabilities of the technology and partly the objectives and expectations of management. Computing technologies make demands on human information processing and decision-making skills, reduce the need for some manual effort and skill, and introduce new forms of work discipline and pacing. The extent to which responsibility, discretion, challenge and control increase, however, depends on managerial decisions about the organization of work.

It was in this spirit that Wilkinson (1983, pp. 10–16) attacked both the Braverman position and Bell's work in the United Kingdom. He criticized Bell's work for treating technology outside its social and political context: "Instead of discussing . . . the nature and availability of skilled labor within a firm and the way this might affect the choice and use of technology, the skilled labor is treated simply as a possible constraint." He criticized this approach for "depoliticizing technical change." He added, "The illusion of a consensus is achieved: it is in everyone's interest that the firm (or country) competes and survives, thus we must adopt the technology and accept its consequences, or else!"

Wilkinson presented two basic criticisms of Braverman's analysis that had been adduced by later Marxists: (1) the treatment of labor as totally acquiescent to managerial initiatives, and (2) the presentation of Taylorism as the fundamental practice of twentieth-century management. Wilkinson carried out four case studies and found wide variations in the way work was organized after new technology had been introduced on the shop floor. At one extreme, the management of an electroplating plant believed that its workers were unintelligent and unreliable. When the process was automated, the management ensured that the workers could not "interfere" with it by locking the control panel. In contrast, in another case, a company wished to purchase a CNC machine tool with manual data input facilities to allow the skilled craftsman operator to write his own program and to control the machine through his computer.

Wilkinson's case studies demonstrated that there were conflicts of interest in the implementation of new technology not only between workers and management but between different groups of workers and between different groups of managers. His work is important from the perspective of this paper because it demonstrates the difficulties of establishing and measuring the relative technical and economic efficiencies of alternative strategies.

While Wilkinson admitted that not all technical designs and working practices were economically feasible, he argued that technical and economic considerations only constrain but do not determine the outcome: "For instance, in the case of the machine tool manufacturer, the choice between manual data input (MDI) and conventional CNC—two very different designs—was not one between technical superiority and inferiority, but between 'retaining skill on the shop floor' and 'transferring skill into the office.'" Wilkinson pointed out that in general workers are concerned about their employers' efficiency and competitiveness, but an important part of the evidence from his case studies indicated that, while management's use of efficiency arguments is not always sinister and underhanded, British managers did sometimes use efficiency arguments to justify their wish to take control over production from machine operators.

Computer Numerical Control (CNC)

Rapid increases in the power of semiconductors and reductions in their costs made it possible to produce small, very powerful, relatively cheap minicomputers that could be used to control machine tools. The resulting computer-controlled machine tools (CNC) with a computer built into the machine tool allow for programming and editing by operators. In contrast, the hard-wired NC machine tools they replaced required programmers to produce and edit programs in offices away from the shopfloor.

While Wilkinson had considered one case study on CNC (reported in the preceding text), an Anglo-German research team concentrated on studying the implications of this new technology for organization and manpower, and tried to assess whether it was leading to de-skilling (see Hartmann et al., 1984). Their hypothesis was that the work traditions in different societies would not be changed as a consequence of technological change, but would be expressed in new ways, particularly as far as skills were concerned (Hartmann et al., 1984, p. 311). This hypothesis was verified by their study which found that CNC technology was extremely "malleable" and that there was no single simple effect of the use of CNC as such.

Like Bell in relation to hard-wired NC, they found that CNC had different effects according to such technical and economic factors as batch size, cutting technology, and machine type. For example, the allocation of programming tasks is strongly influenced by the time needed to write a program. In general, the longer it takes to write a program, the less likely are programming functions to take place on the shopfloor, because the program can only be made when the machine is idle. But this is not invariably the case, as some machines permit the operator to program the next job, and sometimes operators draft programs after working hours. In turning especially, the authors noted an increasing tendency for operators to program and perform programming-related functions such as speed and feed modification of previously prepared programs.

For such reasons, they concluded that the decision as to whether to allocate programming functions to shopfloor personnel or to technicians working in a separate office cannot be determined easily in accordance with clearly defined technical and economic criteria. There is considerable scope for societal factors to intervene. Indeed, the study found that there was a consistently greater use of operator programming in Germany, while separation of programming and operation was more usual in Britain. These general patterns exhibited stability over time and considerable continuity between NC and CNC policies.

The researchers related the patterns to the differentiation between craft and technician trainees in Britain, in contrast to German practices in which technician status is acquired by a further stage of training of workers who had previously received craft-training. In Britain, those performing planning and programming functions are granted white-collar status. In Germany, those functions are frequently carried out by blue-collar workers. The absence of a status barrier between programming and machine operation makes it possible to rotate German workers between craft and technical functions without any fear of losing status. In Germany, formal qualifications are common in both small and large firms, while in Britain there are very few formally qualified workers in small plants.

The researchers noted several tendencies common to both countries, especially trends to greater component variety and smaller batch size. As a consequence, CNC operators were likely to have to deal with a wider range of jobs and more frequent changes. This brought with it the need for greater skills relating to tooling, materials, feeds, speeds, faults, and breakdowns, which, in turn, required greater craft shopfloor skills rather than less. According to the authors, companies, particularly in Germany, were increasingly seeing the merits of craft skills. While the data were only indicative, it appeared that the German pattern of use of more skilled labor was more efficient and that there was a trend in this direction in both countries (Hartmann et al., 1984, p. 313). As Phillimore (1989, p. 85) suggests in relation to British machine shops, "there are clear examples of where the new technology has been used to de-skill workers in machine shops rather than re-skill them, although the commercial wisdom of such a policy is being increasingly questioned."

AUTOMATION AND SKILLS IN THE 1980S

Debate continues in Britain today. Indeed, it has been rekindled by disagreement over the impact of new forms of automation on maintenance and design.

Automation and Maintenance Skills

As automated equipment such as CNC machine tools comes into more widespread use, there is an increasing need for proper maintenance to ensure that the equipment fulfills its potential for economic production of high-quality goods. Kaplinsky (1984, p. 137) suggested that the maintenance of high-technology automated equipment had been de-skilled through the use of printed circuit board replacement procedures. If an automatic diagnostic system can signal the location of the faulty board, the maintenance task can be reduced to simply replacing the faulty board with a new one and either discarding the faulty board or sending it to a specialized department for analysis and repair.

Research in both the United Kingdom (Senker et al., 1981; Cross, 1984) and the United States (Office of Technology Assessment, 1984)

casts doubt on this de-skilling scenario. Certain maintenance tasks—
in particular, the replacement of printed circuit boards—do, indeed,
require little skill. But the maintenance of high-technology manufacturing systems more typically requires the ability to diagnose faults
efficiently and rapidly that are not so simply identified. Specifically,
defects are often concealed within hydraulic or mechanical
subsystems. Repair and maintenance people working with automated
equipment require less intimate knowledge of a single process or task,
but they need a general knowledge of more tasks.

Computer-Aided Design

In Britain until the 1940s, the aspiring apprentice tried to get into the
drawing office because it offered the terms and conditions of white-collar
employment with good chances of promotion. Many "draftsmen" (male
drafters) without University degrees gained access to professional and
managerial careers by achieving technical qualifications through part-time
study. Traditionally, in Britain, drafters completing their apprenticeships
started work as detail drafters, progressed to more complex drawing work,
and finally to design work. (In the context of the discussion in this section,
it is important to note that, for this reason, in Britain, the distinction between
drafters' and designers' work still tends to be blurred, although, as noted
below, designers in Britain increasingly are drawn from the ranks of
University graduates.)

By the 1960s, however, drawing office employment had become less
attractive for two principal reasons. First, improved conditions of service
on the shopfloor and lower pay differentials offered craft workers
benefits comparable to those of drafters. Second and more important,
easier access to higher education increased competition for the professional and management jobs to which drafters had previously
aspired. University-educated engineers bypassed the drawing office and
entered the engineering hierarchy as junior professionals, while drafters
languished in the drawing office (Arnold and Senker, 1982, pp. 27–
28).

Michael Cooley (1972) has suggested that the drawing office has
been downgraded in importance as a result of the finer division of
labor in engineering that began in the 1930s. He described how the
creative design element had become increasingly separated from the
work of executing drawings. The fragmentation of shopfloor jobs was,
according to Cooley, paralleled by fragmentation of the job of the
designer/drafter. Until the 1930s, drafters in Britain were responsible
for designing a component, stress testing it, selecting materials for it,
writing the specifications, and liaising with the shopfloor and
customers. But starting in the 1930s, these functions were progressively
broken down into separate jobs and taken over by various specialists,
such as stress testers, metallurgists, tribologists, methods and planning

engineers, and customer liaison engineers, leaving drafters with only the job of drawing (Cooley, 1972, p. 78).

In effect, in the Britain of the 1930s, drafters filled a general-purpose professional engineering and design role. As the whole process of design became more complex, the role of the drafter was split into higher functions—the specialists Cooley mentions, together with University graduate engineer designers—and lower level jobs—principally, drafters and support technicians.

Cooley criticized the whole process of specialization and division of labor, which he termed *fragmentation*, on which the industrial development of the past two hundred years has been based. He writes nostalgically of the millwright who "was capable of repairing any machine in the plant in which he worked. He could predict the failure rate of bearings, select the material for new ones, and in most cases manufacture them himself." By contrast, he argued, "CAD tends to de-skill the designer, subordinate the designer to the machine and give rise to alienation. Indeed, most computerized design environments begin to display those elements which are regarded as constituting industrial alienation, in particular powerlessness, meaninglessness, and loss of self and normality" (1987, p. 40).

Evidence supporting such views was provided by Chris Baldry and Anne Connolly on the basis of a study of seven leading CAD users in Scotland in the early 1980s (Baldry and Connolly, 1986, pp. 59–66). They found that much CAD work was repetitive and routine, involving details and enlargements of existing designs. Groups of drafters often worked on the same drawing, and few operators had the satisfaction of producing a complete drawing themselves. Operators had lost some elements of control over their work. The CAD system produced all drawing, labeling, and dimensioning in a standard format. Indeed, standardization of design is often a direct consequence of CAD use because CAD works most effectively if a library of standard parts and components is constructed in the computer's memory. Similarly, Kaplinsky (1982, p. 110) found that operators and management agreed that CAD reduced the skill component in drafting because it removed the craft elements associated with individually tailored layouts and lettering.

McLoughlin (1989), however, challenged Baldry and Connolly's findings on the basis of his own more recent case studies. While Baldry, Connolly, and Kaplinsky had cited the loss of manual craft skills in drawing as evidence of de-skilling, McLoughlin found that the new mental skills needed to use CAD usually compensated for the loss of manual skills. In response to the standardization argument, he pointed out that design is, in essence, a three-stage iterative process of basic conceptualization, analysis of design options, and detailed design and drawing. Most of the CAD systems in use in Britain are drafting systems, essentially electronic drawing boards serving only the third phase. They enable users to manipulate two-dimensional drawings and annotate

them. CAD systems are "shape processors" analogous to word processors, which aid writers but do not reduce the need for writing skills.

In addition, McLoughlin notes the increasing use of modeling systems
that support more directly the earlier, more creative phases. Computer
models act as malleable databases from which drawings can be extracted
and displayed. They allow designers to consider several design options
in some detail before deciding on a final design. They can also provide
data for downstream activities such as production and thereby eliminate
a great deal of routine work in recopying drawings. According to
McLoughlin, "Drawing by conventional means utilizes a number of
craft mental skills in manipulating the pencil, and involves a direct
relationship between the thought of a user to 'draw a line' and the
act of drawing." When CAD is used, "The craft skills used in actual
drawing are eliminated as lines of perfect quality and weight are drawn
automatically by the system. The relationship between the user and
the drawing thus becomes more indirect and abstract, requiring the
exercise of mental skills in understanding the capabilities of the system
and in selecting appropriate routines from the menu."

Our own interviews with a small sample of CAD users tended—
with some exceptions—to support McLoughlin's findings (Simmonds
and Senker, 1989). One user commented that CAD made his work
more routine, and some complained that CAD took away the satisfaction that could be derived from producing a good drawing. The
more common view, however, was that CAD increased the skills required
of the designer or drafter. The most common types of positive comment
made about CAD were that it made the work more interesting and
less routine, and that job prospects were liable to be better in companies
using CAD. For example, one CAD user commented:

*Working on CAD removes a lot of the tedium of the board but
also offers more avenues for being creative. It feels like you are
involved with a project rather than a drawing. Creativity is improved
with the greater freedom offered through, for example, the ease
of iteration and change, but it is limited by the level of expertise
you can develop and the poor level of system development.*

Another changed his unfavorable first impressions of CAD:

*I thought it took away a drafter's skills. But, after learning to
use CAD, I realized that the CAD 'only draws pictures.' It does
not take the skills of an engineer away; it enhances them. It does
not take drafting skills away. You need drafting skills to produce
good work on CAD. Advantages of CAD are that it is quick and
you can do more complicated things. . . . CAD makes life easier. It
would be a real pain to go back to the old ways of doing things.*

CAD only began to affect British engineering firms in the late 1970s
and early 1980s, and did not become really significant in British design

and drawing offices until the mid-1980s. Undoubtedly, engineering and design work has become much more specialized. It is doubtful, however, that the net result has been or will be de-skilling: There appears to be little evidence for Cooley's contention that CAD has de-skilled drawing and design work and would reduce the status of the drawing office still further. Indeed, our research in the early 1980s suggested that the "glamor" of CAD was likely to restore the status of the design function and to attract University graduates into design work (Arnold and Senker, 1982, p. 28).

MANAGERS' INFLUENCE ON TECHNOLOGY AND WORK ORGANIZATION

One might expect British managers to seek out examples of international best practice for adaptation to their own organizations' needs. Such efforts might have led to a fairly rapid convergence of British use of automation with international best practice. In reality, however, the rate of any such convergence has been slow. In part, this is due to inevitable barriers to the international diffusion of techniques and practices developed in very different environments. But there is strong evidence that the conservative attitudes of British managers are also to blame.

Many British managements have adopted automation fairly rapidly, but their enthusiasm often appears to have been motivated by an interest in automation for automation's sake. British managers have often neglected to consider the implications of automation for work organization, and in particular they have frequently paid insufficient attention to the need for training programs necessary to secure the maximum economic advantage available from the use of new technology (Institute of Manpower Studies, 1984; Coopers and Lybrand Associates, 1985). This is the most plausible explanation for the apparent discrepancy between British manufacturing industry's lag in efficiency and its relatively rapid rate of adoption of new technology.

An international comparison project by Campbell and Warner (1989) studied the implications for skills of the production of new microelectronics products in Britain and West Germany. Since the nature of the product often interacts with the nature of the production process to shape the pattern of tasks and skill requirements, Campbell and Warner studied two types of companies: "A" companies, producing information-processing products, and "B" companies, where information processing was not a primary attribute of their products.

In Germany, both categories of firms were deeply involved in the development and assembly of microelectronic components. In Britain, by contrast, nearly all type B companies were dependent on outside suppliers for microelectronics development and assembly, and there was therefore a marked polarization. Even larger British type A companies were moving away from component-level development and assembly towards an exclusive focus on systems integration work. They found that German mechanical engineering firms (type B companies) tended to develop in-house electronics skills, whereas British mechanical engineering firms tended to adopt the "noble" approach of buying their electronics controls from electronics firms.

The British strategy leaves the mechanical engineering firms in danger of subordination to electronics firms as the total value of electronics incorporated in products increases. To give a simple example: Specifying an appropriate washing machine control system demands detailed knowledge of heating and motor circuits switching, flows, temperatures, and speeds, and of how these pieces can be effectively controlled electronically. The proper specification of the electronics demands that the washing machine manufacturer's engineers understand both the operations of the machine they are designing *and* how an electronic system can perform the necessary control functions (Senker et al., 1988, p. 9). Since the ability to do this is often lacking in British mechanical engineering firms, their arms-length reliance on an outside electronics company is unlikely to result in a well-designed machine.

Child (1987, pp. 101–129) has charged that Britain "during its long period of relatively uninterrupted industrial and political development, has built up through progressive sedimentation, a solid structure of statuses, rules, and practices which now present a formidable barrier against organizational change." In his study, Child cited British managers' belief that new technology should be incorporated into existing structures and systems. The producers of new technologies and systems, he noted, reinforced this thinking by marketing their products on the basis of the ease with which they can be adapted to existing organizational characteristics. Organizational design was also influenced by established social norms, including those that viewed the stock of skills available in the labor market as a serious constraint on organizational innovation.

Undoubtedly, managements in Britain have presented decisions and proposals as being in the best economic interests of their organizations, especially in negotiation with trade unions. There are, however, grounds for questioning the accuracy of some of these claims in relation to the use of automation.

Our recent longitudinal study of CAD use by firms in the British engineering industry tended to confirm Child's analysis. CAD had diffused relatively rapidly in Britain, but few firms perceived their investment as a route to integrating design with production and other activities. Investments in CAD systems had often been justified through conventional payback and discounted cash flow analysis, where the key benefit was anticipated savings on drafting costs (Senker, 1984). Senior managers generally lacked the knowledge needed to guide a program of cross-functional integration, appearing to have a poor grasp of the technology and its implications for their organizations. CAD training tended to fluctuate in line with companies' financial performance. Few companies had provided refresher or updating courses, and several managers suggested that the failure to develop designers' skills was adversely affecting product design (Simmonds and Senker, 1989). Another study found that no provision was made for feedback to design from the experiences gained from building prototypes in many British firms. While this policy led to the need for increased skills in the drawing office, it has also tended to de-skill shopfloor workers. British managers tended to relieve skills shortages at higher levels by draining lower levels of more talented workers (Campbell and Warner, 1989).

In a previous study of British manufacturing firms' attempts to cope with the skills implications of automation, we found that decisions about the organization of work were often made by default. Management often installed systems based on information technology without giving much thought to the implications for work organization and skills (Senker et al., 1988). Our conclusions about the engineering industry in Britain were rather similar to Adler's (1987, p. 763) in the United States: "To the extent that skill requirements are planned for at the corporate level, it is largely in an unconscious mode." We reached similar conclusions in three case studies of the introduction of expert systems into British firms in different environments: industrial process control, repair of electronic printed circuit boards, and insurance offices (Senker et al., 1989).

The implications of this sedimentation are particularly visible for what Tidd (1991) calls "configurational" technologies—technologies such as numerically controlled machine tools, flexible manufacturing systems (FMS), and robotics that can be deployed in a very wide range of patterns. Tidd argues that it can be misleading to look for the "impact" or "implications" of configurational technologies on skills and work organization, as the experience of users and suppliers of robotic technology in the United Kingdom and Japan indicates clearly that existing work organization and skills are taken into account in the design of systems. Firms in the United Kingdom tend to assume that operators will have few skills, that products will not be designed for ease of assembly, that component quality will be poor, and that complex robotic assembly systems are needed to cope in such an environment. Rather than rely on the ability of operators, most British users have devoted a great deal of attention to making their systems "idiot proof." Tidd found that most managers thought the ability to carry out routine maintenance, clear blockages, and amend programs was beyond most operators (Tidd, 1991). The main benefits expected and experienced by robotic assembly users in the United Kingdom were improved productivity and better product consistency. Flexibility was not sought. Systems embodying sophisticated sensor-based technology were not generally used in a flexible way. In the United Kingdom, robotic assembly was a sort of sophisticated form of special-purpose automation. In practice, the U.K. model was expensive, unreliable, and inflexible because the technology was used to overcome organizational problems rather than to enhance flexibility.

Japanese industry, in contrast and paradoxically, used less complex technology more flexibly. For both numerically controlled machine tools and assembly robots, the development of lower cost, simpler machines by the Japanese was a major factor in the economically successful application of these technologies. The diffusion of assembly robots, for example, was more rapid in Japan. Both the design of the robots and the way they were typically applied differed substantially from typical British practice. In Japan, a high proportion of the assembly robots installed were of the relatively simple selective compliance assembly robot arm (SCARA) family. Japanese firms aimed to simplify operations for workers and to prevent operator error, rather than to replace workers. Robotic assembly in Japan relied heavily on operator involvement. In addition to using less sophisticated robots, the Japanese also used them more flexibly. For example, Tidd found that they were more inclined than British firms to use robots to assemble a wide range of product variants.

It seems that the Japanese approach to both the design of assembly robots and their implementation is far more effective from an economic point of view and represents current best practice. But despite the ready availability and evidence of the superiority of Japanese technology and management policies, there is no evidence of any convergence so far. Firms in the United Kingdom continue to develop and use ever more sophisticated systems. In the early 1980s, users in Britain and the United States claimed that available robots were simply "too dumb" and looked to breakthroughs in sensor technology to provide answers. More recently, attention has turned to endowing robots with more "intelligence" via the use of artificial intelligence techniques. British and American firms are energetically looking for answers to the wrong question.

CONCLUSION

In a riposte to contextualist attacks on technological determinism, Freeman (1987) argued that changes of the techno-economic paradigm based on combinations of radical product, process, and organizational innovations are more or less inescapable. He considers the adoption of Fordist mass-production and assembly-line techniques as one paradigm change, and the move to more flexible manufacturing processes involving information technology as a further change. Freeman suggests that competitive pressures in the world economy are so strong that once such a paradigm has crystallized, it would be hard for firms and countries not to conform. Technological choices in this situation become increasingly constrained, even while an element of social and political choice remains.

Even socialist countries, which have attempted to opt out of a pattern of technology characteristic of the capitalist countries, have after a decade or so been obliged to fall into step with worldwide trends, with minor differences. This was the case with the USSR. After intense controversy in the 1920s, it adopted Fordist assembly-line technology and even Taylorism in an attempt to catch up with and overtake the capitalist countries.

The evidence in this paper demonstrates, however, that there are substantial managerial, organizational, and social barriers to the international diffusion of "best practice" use of automation. The differences and delays that appear minor to Freeman can be of major significance. The case of the automobile industry is illustrative of the implications of the long time scale involved in the international diffusion of best practice. During the period 1960 to 1975, Japanese automobile producers evolved a radically new production system that was far more efficient. Yet it took until the late 1970s for the automobile companies in Europe and the United States to begin to respond to the proven competitive advantages of the Japanese system. And in the interim the U.S. and European manufacturers lost so much market share that they may not be able to catch up.

In anything but the very long term, there is therefore considerable scope for managerial discretion in designing and implementing new technologies. British management has been relatively progressive in terms of its willingness to invest in automation hardware and software; it needs to become more aware of the role of reorganization and extensive training and retraining in the effective use of automation.

The evidence that skill levels have increased over the past few decades in Britain is tenuous, but the evidence that skills *need* to change from more narrowly craft-based manual skills toward broader and more intellectual skills is compelling. Michael Cross has argued persuasively that the "single trade base" of British craft workers is a limiting factor during a period of change because their core knowledge and understanding bear less and less relation to the requirements of new and emerging jobs (Cross, 1984).

The general nature of the changes needed in staffing future factories is summarized in Table 4.1. Because such radical changes in jobs are occurring, workers at all levels, including managers, need to be able to cope with retraining. This means that they need more flexible minds, and flexibility requires higher levels of education and more frequent periods of education and retraining. Even if particular workers were not to need retraining for some years, management should still encourage them to continue their education to ensure that they retain their capacity to learn. In an environment of rapid technological change, a workforce accustomed to learning is a critical asset.

The efficient use of automation seems to call for upgrading the workforce. It is reasonably certain that the productivity of the British

Table 4.1. Patterns of Work in Present and Future Factories

Present pattern	Factory of the future
Single skills	Multiple skills
Demarcation	Blurring of boundaries
Rigid working practices	Flexible working practices
Operation mainly by direct intervention	Mainly supervision of advanced operations
High division of labor	Moves towards team work
Low local autonomy	High local autonomy and devolution of responsibility
Training given low priority	Training and organizational development given high priority

Source: Bessant and Senker (1987, p. 162)

workforce could be increased more rapidly if managements were to devote more time and resources to training and retraining their workforces. But pressures in this direction have been counteracted by the persistent negative attitude of British management toward training.

Using new technology to de-skill workers—unfortunately a relatively common managerial aim in Britain—results in inefficiency. If British industry is going to be able to compete effectively, managers need to regard automation as offering a means of enhancing workers' ability to produce high-quality products economically. The massive trade deficits in manufactured products experienced by Britain in 1989 bear witness to the costs of failing to invest adequately or wisely in education, training, and retraining.

REFERENCES

Adler, P. S. 1987. "Automation and Skills: New Directions." *International Journal of Technology Management* 2, 5–6;761–62.
Adler, P. S., and B. Borys. 1989. "Automation and Skill: Three Generations of Research on the NC Case." *Politics and Society* 17, 3:378–83.
Arnold, E., and P. Senker. 1982. "Designing the Future—The Implications of CAD Interactive Graphics For Employment and Skills in the British Engineering Industry." Watford: Engineering Industry Training Board Occasional Paper Number 9.
Baldry, C., and A. Connolly. 1986. "Drawing the Line: Computer-Aided Design and the Organization of the Drawing Office." *New Technology, Work and Employment* 1, (1):59–66.
Bell, R. M. 1972. *Changing Technology and Manpower Requirements in the Engineering Industry*. Sussex University Press.

Bell, R. M., and J. Tapp. 1972. "Automation and the Structure of Employment in Machine Shops." Brighton: Science Policy Research Unit mimeo.

Bessant, J., and P. Senker. 1987. "Societal Implications of Advanced Manufacturing Technology." In T. D. Wall et al. (eds.). *The Human Side of Advanced Manufacturing Technology*. Chichester (and New York, Brisbane, Toronto, and Singapore): John Wiley.

Bradbury, J., and A. D. Chalmers. 1972. *Skill and Technological Change*. Final Report, Part 1, SSRC Project No. BH 133, Section 3. "Skill Changes Arising from the Introduction of Numerical Control of Milling." Univ. Birmingham, Department of Engineering Production, pp. 104–94.

Brady, T. M. 1986. "New Technology, Manpower and Skills: Some Methodological Considerations." *New Technology, Work and Employment* 1, (1):77–83.

Braverman, H. 1974. *Labor and Monopoly Capital*. New York and London: Monthly Review Press.

Bright, J. R. 1958. *Automation and Management*. Cambridge, Mass.: Harvard University Press.

Brighton Labor Process Group. 1977. "The Capitalist Labor Process." *Capital and Class* 1.

Buchanan, D. A., and D. Boddy. 1983. *Organizations in the Computer Age*. Aldershot: Gower.

Campbell, A., and M. Warner. 1989. "Training Strategies and Microelectronics in the Engineering Industries of the U.K. and West Germany." Paper presented at Training Agency seminar on vocational education and intermediate skills. Manchester. 21–22 September.

Child, J. 1987. "Organizational Design for Advanced Manufacturing Technology." In T. D. Wall, C. W. Clegg, and N. J. Kemp, (eds.). *The Human Side of Advanced Manufacturing Technology*. Chichester: John Wiley.

Conference of Socialist Economists. 1977. *Capital and Class* 1.

Cooley, M. 1972. *Computer-Aided Design—Its Nature and Implications*. Richmond, Surrey: AUEW/TASS.

Cooley, M. 1987. "Human Centered Systems: An Urgent Problem for Systems Designers." *AI & Society* 1, (1):37–46.

Coopers and Lybrand Associates. 1985. *A Challenge to Complacency: Changing Attitudes to Training*. Sheffield/London: Manpower Services Commission/National Economic Development Office.

Cross, M. 1984. *Towards the Flexible Craftsman*. London: Technical Change Centre.

Crossman, E. R. F. W. 1966. "Evaluation of Changes in Skill Profile and Job Content Due to Technological Change." Working Paper. Univ. California, Department of Industrial Engineering and Operations Research.

Department of Scientific and Industrial Research. 1956. "Automation, A Report on the Technical Trends and their Impact on Management and Labour." London: HMSO.

Fidgett, T. 1983. *The Engineering Industry: Its Manpower and Training*. Watford: Engineering Industry Training Board.

Freeman, C. 1987. "The Case for Technological Determinism." In R. Finnegan, G. Salaman and K. Thompson, (eds.). *Information Technology: Social Issues, A Reader*. Open University Press.

Fyrth, H. J., and M. Goldsmith. 1969. *Science, History and Technology*, Book 2, Part III. London: Cassell.

Hartmann, G., I. J. Nicholas, A. Sorge, and M. Warner. 1984. "Consequences of CNC Technology: A Study of British and West German Manufacturing Firms." In M. Warner, (ed.). *Microprocessors, Manpower and Society*. Aldershot: Gower.

Institute of Manpower Studies. 1984. *Competence and Competition*. London/Sheffield: National Economic Development Office/Manpower Services Commission.

Jones, B. 1982. "Destruction or Redistribution of Skills? The Case of Numerical Control." In S. Wood, (ed.). *The Degradation of Work? Skill, Deskilling and the Labour Process*. London: Hutchinson.

Kaplinsky, R. 1982. *Computed Aided Design: Electronics, Comparative Advantage and Development*. London: Frances Pinter.

Kaplinsky, R. 1984. *Automation: The Technology and Society*. Harlow: Longman.

Khamis, C., G. Lawson & S. McGuire. 1986. *Trends in Manpower and Training in the Engineering Industry Since 1978*. Watford: Engineering Industry Training Board.

Lilley, S. 1965. *Men, Machines and History*. London: Lawrence and Wishart.

McLoughlin, I. 1989. "The Taylorisation of Drawing Office Work?" *New Technology, Work and Employment* 4, (1):27–39.

Office of Technology Assessment. 1984. *Computerized Manufacturing Automation: Employment, Education and the Workforce*. Washington, D.C.: DTA-CIT-235.

Phillimore, J. 1989. "Flexible Specialization, Work Organization and Skills: Approaching the Second Industrial Divide." *New Technology Work and Employment* 4, (2):79–91.

Senker, P. 1984. "Implications of CAD/CAM for Management." *Omega* 12, (3):225–31.

Senker, P., N. Swords-Isherwood, T. Brady & C. Huggett. 1981. *Maintenance Skills in the Engineering Industry: The Influence of Technological Change*. Watford: Engineering Industry Training Board.

Senker, P., J. Townsend, and J. Buckingham. 1989. "Working with Expert Systems: Three Case Studies." *AI & Society* 3:103–6.

Senker, P., M. Vandevelde, M. Beesley, and T. Hutchin. 1988. "Electronics on the Shopfloor. A Report on Electronics Skills and Training in the Engineering Industry in England and Wales." Watford: Engineering Industry Training Board.

Simmonds, P., and P. Senker. 1989. *Making More of CAD*. Watford: Engineering Industry Training Board.

Tidd, J. 1991. *Flexible Manufacturing Technologies and International Competitiveness*. London: Pinter Publishers.

Wilkinson, B. 1983. *The Shopfloor Politics of New Technology*. London: Heineman.

5

New Concepts of Production and the Emergence of the Systems Controller

Horst Kern and Michael Schumann

Lies have short wings, at least in the social sciences. Predictions are often contradicted by the subsequent course of social development. In 1984, with our book *The End of the Division of Labor?*, we presented an attempt at a prediction based on industrial sociology. At that time, we interpreted the situation of West German industry as one of radical transformation in which new approaches toward automation were being invented and implemented in a growing number of factories. We viewed this process as a fundamental change in the structure of industrial work, as a redistribution of living conditions in society, and as a challenge for politics. We forecast that new "concepts of production" were just around the corner.

The principal novelty of the new concepts of production lay in this: increased efficiency, we argued, demanded a relaxation of the division of labor through a policy of utilizing the intellectual capacities of the workforce in a more complex and tightly integrated work organization. The old Tayloristic correlation between increased efficiency and de-skilling was obsolete. To push this point to its logical conclusion, we predicted that the project of liberated, fulfilling work, originally interpreted as an anticapitalist project, was likely to be staged by capitalist management itself (admittedly in miniature version) in the name of efficiency (Kern and Schumann, 1989).

Our use of the notion "new concepts of production" differed from the projects discussed in the mid-1970s in West Germany under the heading "humanization of working life." In those days, industrial policy aimed to counteract negative changes in industrial work that were judged to be the "natural" impact of a politically unregulated, capitalist production process. This understanding of industrial policy would no longer be justified if what we claimed were true, since the diffusion of new concepts of production was leading not to the simplification of industrial work but rather in the opposite direction. Political regulation would still be necessary, but it would need to be rethought from different premises and changed perspectives.

Six years have passed since we initially published these ideas in Germany, providing enough time to test our prognosis. In view of the intervening developments, we submit that our predictions have proved largely accurate. This chapter reports some recent research results that support this claim.

Traditionally, the principal research technique of German industrial sociologists is based on a series of case studies. Case studies can identify new developments in a timely manner and describe them precisely, but they cannot be used to gage the scope of the change, its speed, nor its overall impact. Quantitative data are needed to complement qualitative findings. With this in mind, a research group in our institute—the Soziologisches Forschungsinstitut (SOFI)—devised a follow-up study to our book, *The End of the Division of Labor?*, in order to characterize developments in work organization and skill by means of more quantitative data obtained in field work or derived from official statistics.

In the following four sections, we sketch the results of this survey along with the findings of several new case studies in the automobile, machine-manufacturing, chemical, and electrical and electronic products industries (see Table 5.1). In the fifth section, the new type of job that has emerged under conditions of increasing automation in industry—the systems controller's job—will be analyzed in more detail. The sixth section summarizes our interpretation of the long-term trends in Germany's automation–skill–work organization practices. The conclusion argues that this German story is applicable on an international scale. An Appendix describes the historical and institutional background of our research.

Table 5.1. Sales and Employees in Selected Industries

Industry	Sales[a]	Employees[b]
Automobiles	175,381	825,573
Machine manufacturing	150,865	990,950
Chemicals	140,460	545,877
Electrical and electronic equipment	159,347	1,024,179

[a]In millions DM.
[b]Monthly average for 1988.
Source: Zentralverband der Electroindustrie, Statistical Report (1988).

THE AUTOMOBILE INDUSTRY: A NEW PERSONNEL POLICY

In spite of their profitability and growth, German automobile manufacturers believe their industry faces serious problems. According to them, prospects are worsening due to Japanese competitors and the expansion of production capacity all over the world. This assessment is common to high-volume producers and producers of luxury cars.

As a group, they have responded to these pressures in several ways. In marketing, they have refined their proven market strategy emphasizing high quality, reliability, advanced technology, and product variety. In manufacturing, they have redefined their vertical integration policy to ensure in-house control of operations considered important for competition and high value-added, and they outsource the rest; they have improved the logistics of production; and they have increased machine utilization through flexible working time, work on Saturdays, and night shifts.

Rationalizing the manufacturing process by improving machinery and work organization also remains important. In the area of technology, auto companies continue to expand the use of flexible automation, but in reality this transformation has taken different forms in the different areas of auto manufacturing. In stamping and machine shops—the areas that had already become highly automated over the past few years—the focus today is on improving automated control and on automating peripheral functions. In casting and painting, a dualistic structure prevails, combining high- and low-technology: Some years ago, it became possible to automate the main operations, but peripheral functions continue to be performed manually. Finally, the assembly process is slowly being automated: Since no German auto company is projecting a radical change in the level of assembly automation (except for the introduction of flexible automatic carrier systems), assembly will remain a low-technology area for some time to come.

The reorganization of work has differed according to the technology of the different areas. In low-technology areas, the predominant form of work is still direct manual labor. The change we observe now consists of hesitant steps toward job enrichment. In particular, factories plan to improve assembly work by integrating elements of quality control and of finishing work, as well as by increasing job rotation. Through these steps, the companies expect to be well prepared for a more complex and flexible assembly. Thus far, the most advanced solution developed has been the uncoupling of assembly lines with the use of automated individual carriers to transport assemblies.

In high-technology areas, the idea of an integrated work organization has gained much broader acceptance over the past six years since we identified the first steps in this direction. Integration here also means regrouping skilled indirect functions. At stake in this effort is the issue of the future localization of not only maintenance but also quality control, machine programming, and regulation of the work flow.

The decisive factor for the broad diffusion of the idea of integrated work roles is the conviction that a new kind of worker can guarantee maximum utilization of costly machinery. We call this worker *poly-valent* or multiskilled in the sense that he or she is able to carry out activities such as quality control and maintenance in addition to direct functions. Discussions about the integration of work roles in the high-technology areas have progressed beyond explorations of the general idea to specifications of the concrete forms and final scope of integration. We have found three competing forms of integration: First, and most frequently encountered, production workers are given more responsibility for some indirect functions. Second, we sometimes find the integration of production work and maintenance work in teams of workers collectively responsible for a whole system of automated machinery. These teams consist of highly skilled production workers *(Fertigungsmechaniker)*, maintenance mechanics, maintenance electricians, electronic specialists, and quality controllers. Third, in a smaller number of cases, maintenance workers themselves become responsible for the production process.

Implications for Work

There are few data on the long-term changes in work brought about by the trends in rationalization. Nevertheless, measurements in our new SOFI survey offer fairly precise indications of the current structure of work in automobile production. We will discuss published statistics first, and then our SOFI survey.

Published statistics reveal that the percentage of white-collar workers in the German auto industry increased from 20.2 percent in 1980 to 24.0 percent in 1988. The percentage of blue-collar workers dropped correspondingly from 77.2 to 72.5 percent. This decrease resulted mainly from a decline in direct blue-collar workers from 55.8 to 45.2 percent,

Table 5.2. Workforce in Automobile Industry 1980/88 (Percent)

Status	1980	1988
Blue collar	77.2	72.5
Direct	55.8	45.2
Indirect	21.4	27.3
White collar	20.2	24.0
In training	2.6	3.5
Total	100	100

Source: IG Metal: Betriebliche Daten und Untersuchungen über Löhne und Gehälter in der Automobilindustrie.

whereas indirect blue-collar workers—workers in maintenance, quality control, tool-making, and logistics—increased from 21.4 to 27.3 percent (see Table 5.2).

The new SOFI survey took a more detailed look at automobile work. We observe that despite automation, automobile work has remained essentially manual. More than three-quarters of the production jobs can be classified as "manual work in direct contact with the product"; these types of jobs include manual casting, manual painting, and manual assembly (see Table 5.3b). One of six production workers is specialized in "manual work on machines," meaning machine-feeding or tool setting. The "machine control work," implemented in the era of high mechanization, has already disappeared as result of further techno-logical progress realized through computer control—only in machine shops does one occasionally still find it. Finally, "systems control work" (the name we created to characterize the type of work that appears first with automated production) amounts to 5 percent of the production workforce in the car industry. This is still a small percentage but it is much larger than at the beginning of the 1980s when this type of work was almost nonexistent.

Judging by skill requirements, most production work in the auto industry is still unskilled (54 percent) and semiskilled work (34 percent) (see Table 5.3c). Yet the industry also has a noticeable share of skilled and highly skilled production workers at 12 percent of its workforce. Subdividing the workforce by function as well as skill level reveals that more than half of the systems control work is skilled or highly skilled work, whereas manual work in all its variants is essentially unskilled work (see Table 5.3d).

A note on our definition of skill is necessary. A worker is considered "skilled" (a *Facharbeiter*) if he or she performs a job that requires institutionalized vocational training and at least several months of on-the-job training. "Highly skilled" workers (*gehobener Facharbeiter*) are those who need the same training as "skilled" workers plus further professional training, such as a skilled metal worker with additional education in electronics. Institutionalized vocational training for blue-collar jobs in Germany is between three and three-and-a-half years long. The educational process is called "dual education" (*duale Ausbildung*) because it involves both apprenticeship (learning in a training department of an employer and/or by practical experience under skilled workers) and school education (a fifth of the training time is spent in a state school for vocational education). The institu-tionalized vocational education ends with an examination. The worker who passes the exam acquires the "certificate of proficiency" (*Facharbeiterbrief*).

In many cases, the training that production workers in the automobile industry have received exceeds the level of skills demanded by their present jobs. More than a third of the crews have finished job-relevant

Table 5.3. Industrial Work in the Automobile Industry

| (a) Total employees by area (n = 54,282) | (%) | Production Workers (n = 44,911) | | | |
		(b) Functions	(%)	(c) Skill requirements	(%)
Production	62	Manual work in direct contact with the product	77.5	Unskilled	54
Maintenance	6			Semiskilled (some months training on the job)	34
Quality control	7	Manual work on machines	17		
				Skilled (formal vocational education)	10
Preparatory/ finishing work	25	Machine control work	0.5		
		Systems control work	5	Highly skilled (formal vocational education and additional professional training)	2
Total	100	Total	100	Total	100

(d) Production workers by function and skills (n = 44,911)

	Manual-product (%)	Manual-machine (%)	Machine control (%)	System control (%)
Unskilled	56	62	3	3
Semiskilled (some months training on the job)	35	24	44	43
Skilled (formal occupational education)	8.5	8	45	36
Highly skilled (additional professional training)	0.5	6	8	18

Source: see Note 1.

vocational education, and, in some plants, more than half. This "overqualification" gap between capabilities and job demands could, however, promote further innovations in work organization.

Looking Ahead

By combining the findings of our first statistical measurements with those of our new case studies, we believe we can make some forecasts. In the case studies, we investigated the work structures of "pilot projects," those departments whose work structures prefigured future developments ac-

Table 5.4. Production Work in the Automobile Industry Divided into Processes — Average versus Pilot Projects

	High-tech areas				Dualistic areas				Low-tech areas			
	Stamping		Machine shops		Body assembly		Painting		Sub-assembly		Final assembly	
	A	B	A	C	A	D	A	E	A	F	A	G
Functions (%):												
Manual-product	—	—	6	—	81	44	95	80	80	7	100	100
Manual-machines	86	—	68	10	14	—	2	—	12	13	—	—
Machine control	—	—	3	—	—	—	2	—	—	—	—	—
Systems control	14	100	23	90	5	56	1	20	8	80	—	—
Total	100	100	100	100	100	100	100	100	100	100	100	100
Skill Requirements (%):												
Unskilled	52	—	45	6	56	44	64	40	434	22	55	—
Semiskilled	36	—	28	4	33	—	30	40	44	3	35	100
Skilled	12	100	17	—	9	12	5	10	10	50	10	—
Highly Skilled	—	—	10	90	2	44	1	10	3	25	—	—
Total	100	100	100	100	100	100	100	100	100	100	100	100
n	2,480	8	8,597	83	8,879	18	6,000	20	4,604	93	14,259	213

A = average for process.
B–G = Pilot projects, i.e., work structures that indicate future development.
B = stamping systems (Stufenpressen).
C = CNC-transfer lines.
D = robot lines.
E = automated painting lines.
F = automated assembly lines.
G = flexible carrier assembly.

Source: see Note 1.

cording to management planning and theoretical knowledge. Comparisons between the pilot project structures and the present state of industry give some insight into development trends. Once again, we differentiate among the various areas of auto production because each area has its own specific dynamic (see Table 5.4).

In high-technology areas (stamping, machine shops), auto companies will continue to have a rather homogeneous workforce, with almost all workers being skilled or highly skilled systems controllers. We expect the automation of peripheral functions to eliminate manual work, and any residual manual operations to be integrated into the core jobs. On modern stamping systems (*Stufenpressen*), we can already observe crews in which all workers are skilled systems controllers. In machine shops, where the shift from the traditional transfer lines to the CNC lines has just begun, 90 percent of the workforce are highly skilled systems controllers.

Distributing the small number of remaining manual functions among the systems controllers instead of concentrating them in specialized jobs for unskilled workers is more efficient, since it reduces passive work; in other words, it reduces the time spent by systems controllers merely waiting to intervene. This distribution of tasks also responds to the demands of most factory councils (*Betriebsrat*). Resistance most likely will come from the systems controllers themselves, who prefer not to be responsible for unskilled routine operations. However, their preference in this regard has not been respected in the past.

Evidence is thus accumulating for the prediction that systems control work will gain more importance in the high-technology departments and that, within the next 10 to 15 years, new bastions of skilled production work will develop in these departments. For a traditional mass-production industry like the auto industry, an industry marked by decades of Fordism, this will be a spectacular development.

The situation is quite different in departments with dualistic high-tech/low-tech structures, namely body assembly and painting. Further rationalization in these areas will aim at higher, or more complete, automation, but this thrust will be limited by the nature of the work. More than half (56 percent) of the people working on lines equipped with robots are already systems controllers, and most of them are highly skilled workers. But the other half do unskilled work. On automated painting lines, only 20 percent of the workforce are systems controllers, whereas 80 percent continue to do manual work (partly unskilled, partly semiskilled).

In these areas, rationalization does not lead to fundamental structural change. Automating more than the core processes is not currently possible. A lot of grinding, polishing, painting, and repair remains manual work. Attempts to enrich these operations by combining them with more attractive ones are hampered by a lack of attractive additional functions, since maintenance operations are rare, quality control is quite simple, and the idea of integrating finishing work is inapplicable because these activities are themselves the finishing operations.

In these departments, future development is therefore likely to take the form of small high-technology islands with skilled systems control jobs amid a larger sea of simpler manual work. Insofar as the demarcations between these two segments of the workforce are accentuated, sharp social conflicts can be expected.

The situation in the low-technology departments—assembly—is again quite different. As automation advances, work structures will be turned upside down by the substitution of skilled for unskilled workers. In one subassembly pilot project, for example, 80 percent of the workers became skilled or highly skilled systems controllers. Yet there is every indication that this technological change, although technically no longer difficult to make, will be slow to happen in most plants. The need for large investments makes management reluctant. Factory councils, alarmed by the danger of large labor-saving effects, act as an additional brake. What remains are projects to decouple the assembly line, to make work cycles more flexible, and to enrich jobs. But despite these measures, the work will continue to be dominated by manual assembly, although on a slightly higher semiskilled level.

One can question whether these changes in assembly departments are far reaching enough. There is a trend towards more complex products, more numerous models, and higher quality in the automobile market—a trend that seems to call for further restructuring of assembly work. To date, German producers have made changes only where changes seemed to be absolutely indispensable. For example, they initiated job-enrichment programs in body assembly and painting, but these programs did not create skilled jobs. Companies preferred instead to try to recruit well-educated workers (*Facharbeiter*) for the slightly changed assembly jobs. Quit rates, however, are high in the assembly divisions, since better-educated assembly workers leave relatively undemanding jobs as soon as they find an alternative.

In contrast to prevailing practice in Germany, assembly jobs can, however, be enriched to the point of transforming them into skilled work. The Uddevalla project started by Volvo in 1989 is one example of integrating work roles on a skilled level. While no German companies are currently planning anything quite so radical, plant designers are following the experiment closely and are moving cautiously in the same direction. One German auto company has recently opened a new assembly plant that goes significantly further than the plants opened between 1983 and 1987. In the latter, work structures remained traditional, with only slightly enlarged work cycles encompassing a few more subassemblies. The new plant moves toward a higher degree of work integration by locating a larger proportion of operations outside the assembly line, but unlike the Uddevalla plant it does not totally abandon the conveyor belt.

We assume that discussions on the future shape of the assembly process will continue, and that the idea of giving the responsibility for assembling a whole engine or even a whole car to one integrated team will become progressively more attractive. Factory councils are pushing in this direction, and managers will not be able to resist because they are also being pulled by the demands of the markets.

MACHINE MANUFACTURING: CENTERS OF CRAFT IN RECONSTRUCTION

In spite of excellent business results in the past, the German machine manufacturing industry, like the automobile industry, does not feel secure when it looks toward the future. (The machines produced by this industry include machine-tools as well as other kinds of industrial equipment such as printing presses.) West German machine manufacturers have strongly committed themselves to machine systems based on new technologies, but this market segment demands increasing investment. Given their capital base, it is difficult for midsize firms, which dominate machine manufacturing in Germany, to meet this investment challenge. Even if the German machine manufacturers continue to use their comparative advantage in customized products as well as they have in recent years, they will forfeit economic success in the long run if they do not also achieve cost savings by rationalization.

As in the auto industry, machine manufacturing companies try to achieve greater efficiency by expanding the time over which machinery can be utilized, by outsourcing costly components to specialized suppliers, and by implementing computer-based systems for planning and controlling the workflow. Product development and design, work planning, machine programming, and manufacturing need to be integrated and as much as possible put under feedback control.

Management is continuously updating the capital stock of their machine shops with CNC technology in order to lower costs without losing flexibility. But even if CNC technology makes automation and flexibility more compatible, we expect to see conventional and CNC metal-forming machines side by side for a long time. Among the machine manufacturers included in the SOFI sample, we found that a third of the factories (mostly small companies with not more than 100 employees) used CNC machines in less than 10 percent of their work (Table 5.5). The majority used CNC machines for 11–40 percent of their work, while 16 percent of the firms relied even more on this technology. CNC machinery in all these cases consists mainly of stand-alone machines, since flexible manufacturing systems are found in only the largest factories.

More integrated work roles are a second element of the rationalization of the machine manufacturing industry. Work at CNC machines normally combines feeding, controlling, and maintenance; in most factories it

Table 5.5. CNC Machinesin the Machine Manufacturing Industry

CNC machines as % of total machines	Size of plants			
	Under 100 employees (%)	100-500 employees (%)	Over 500 employees (%)	All factories (%)
0-10%	100	16.7	—	31.6
11-40%	—	58.3	100	52.6
over 40%	—	25.0	—	15.8
Total	100	100	100	100
n	4	12	3	19

Source: See Note 1.

also includes programming. Two types of worker involvement in programming were observed. Either the CNC operators workers became totally responsible for programming or a special programming department was responsible and machine workers were involved in testing, correcting and optimizing the programs. Sometimes both variants coexisted side by side.

Management's new vision goes beyond tools and roles to encompass the reorganization of the entire assembly process. Starting points for rationalization are the long and costly assembly cycles and the need to coordinate the assembly of mechanical, hydraulic, electrical/electronic, and software components. Both are problems induced by the growing complexity and diversity of the products.

Factories have reacted by improving their logistics and by modularizing their designs. Also, they have often separated the assembly process from the process of putting the assembly machines into operation ("installation") and concentrated the latter in a new highly-skilled job.

Implications for Work

Statistical data on the workforce in the machine manufacturing industry confirm these developments. The proportion of employees working in product design increased from 10.4 percent in 1980 to 12.4 percent in 1989 (Table 5.6). The changed ratio of fabrication to assembly is also interesting. In 1980, the fabrication machine shops were the biggest

Table 5.6. Workforce in the Machine Manufacturing Industry
1980–1989

Department	1980[a] All employees (%)	1989[b] (n = 5,866) All employees (%)	Blue-collar (as % of all employees)	White-collar (as % of all employees)
Production total of which	58.3	57.3	48.2	9.1
direct				
assembly	17.3	24.8	24.3	0.5
fabrication	21.6	18.7	18.2	0.5
indirect[c]	19.4	13.8	5.7	8.1
Logistics	4.6	4.5	1.8	2.8
Design	10.4	12.4	0.2	12.1
Administration	8.6	.8.1	1.3	6.8
Sales	8.7	9.9	1.5	8.5
Training staff	0.5	0.8	0.5	0.4
In training	8.9	7.1	5.7	1.4
Total	100	100	59.1	40.9

[a]Data from Verein Deutscher Maschinenbau-Anstalten
[b]Data from SOFI: see Note 1.
[c]Foreman, quality control, maintenance, etc.

sector, with 21.6 percent of the total workforce, whereas assembly employed only 17.3 percent. In 1989, fabrication employed 18.7 percent, while assembly employed 24.8 percent.

Looking at the functions performed by the workers (Table 5.7), we found that assembly work is manual work; machines are irrelevant in this area. Moreover, assembly work in the machine manufacturing industry is characterized by extremely long work cycles that include complex mechanical and electrical/electronic operations. Almost all assembly workers (92 percent) are skilled, and the majority of them are highly skilled.

In the fabrication shops, the main job category continues to be the traditional machine control worker. The systems controllers, who entered the scene with CNC technology, are still a minority. Traditional fabrication workers are often skilled (88 percent, most of them highly

Table 5.7. Production Work in the Machine Manufacturing Industry Divided into Processes

	Assembly (%)	Fabrication (%)
Functions:		
Manual— product	100	7
Manual— machines	—	11
Machine control	—	59
Systems control	—	23
Total	100	100
Skill requirements:		
Unskilled	2	5
Semiskilled	6	13
Skilled	48	59
Highly skilled	44	23
Total	100	100
n	1,743	1,274

Source: See Note 1.

skilled); systems controllers nearly always have the "certificate of proficiency" and most (53 percent) have some additional professional training (Table 5.8).

Looking Ahead

Future developments are easy to describe for the machining fabrication shops. The continued shift away from conventional technology toward CNC equipment and the parallel change from traditional machine work to systems control work will clearly lead to a higher average skill level. The increase reflects both the requirements of the new technology and the organizational adaptations that combine operating and programming functions in the same job.

The situation in assembly is more complicated, making future de-

Table 5.8. Industrial Work in the Machine
Manufacturing Industry

(a) Total employees by area (n = 3,860)	(%)	Production workers (n = 3,017)			
		(b) Functions	(%)	(c) Skill requirements	(%)
Production	78	Manual—product	61	Unskilled	3.5
Maintenance	4	Manual—machines	5	Semiskilled	9
Quality control	3	Machine control	25	Skilled	52.5
Preparatory/ finishing work	15	Systems control	9	Highly skilled	35
Total	100	Total	100	Total	100

(d) Production workers by function and skills (n = 3,017)

	Manual-product (%)	Manual-machine (%)	Machine control (%)	System control (%)
Unskilled	5	15	—	—
Semiskilled	6	40	12	2
Skilled	46	30	76	45
Highly skilled	43	15	12	53
Total	100	100	100	100
n	1,839	143	747	288

Source: see Note 1.

velopments more difficult to predict. The tendency toward more complex and more differentiated products will result in a demand for higher skills. The boundaries between mechanics and electricians/electronics specialists will become blurred. However, it is still unclear whether firms will create a hybrid *Facharbeiter* job that includes both functions.

Finally, new job categories are needed for the installation employees. They might remain classified as production workers, as is the prevailing practice. However, they do not directly modify the product in a tangible way. They check functions and the integration of mechanical, hydraulic, and electronic subsystems. Investigating and eliminating defects accounts for the large part of their working time. But the success of their work no longer depends on manual skill; a feeling for the peculiarities of the materials is no longer as important as their social and communication skills, since when they install the machine, they cooperate intensively with the customer's systems controllers. Thus, a new position is emerging within the machine manufacturing industry. Its characteristics still remain vague, but it will play a key role in the customer-oriented marketing policy of German machine producers.

THE CHEMICAL INDUSTRY: THE SKILLED PRODUCTION WORKER IS ACCEPTED

All chemical industry production involves the transformation of materials, but because the processes vary widely, there is no single typical state of automation. There are numerous procedures for changing the composition, structure, and properties of the materials. Other variables, like the volume of the product or the complexity of procedures necessary to produce it, complicate the picture. Nonetheless, some general characteristics can be identified.

First of all, the industry prospers by means of product innovation. Research and development leadership is typically more important for economic success than utilizing every last possibility of plant rationalization. The German chemical industry has done rather well in this respect. It is continually expanding; its returns are excellent; and its future prospects seem promising. Some specific products cause worry, but the resources provided by the overall success of the industry will enable firms to surmount these challenges.

The exception is admittedly the oil companies. Their market share has been declining for many years. The German oil refineries, built mostly in the 1960s, were designed for a product line that is no longer appropriate given present demand conditions which call for a larger proportion of light distillates. Oil companies are trying to adapt by energetically rationalizing their production processes and by enlarging the range of their product line.

Across a broad range of companies and departments, four problems are stimulating new discussions on technological and organizational change. First, customers are demanding increasingly higher quality standards, including better documentation of product features and more precision in important characteristics. Second, there is pressure to reduce production costs through savings in energy and materials. Third, there is political pressure for stricter norms in safety and environmental impact. Finally, there is the necessity to support product and process flexibility by means of personnel policy.

On the technological side, the most important response to these challenges is the replacement of traditional pneumatic and electronic controls with computer controls. But even in the more technologically advanced companies, the proportion of processes equipped with modern computer control does not average more than 10 percent. Moreover, these automatic systems normally control only core functions. The programming of total cycles, such as a whole production cycle in batch production or the whole set of operations putting a continuous process into, or out of, operation, has seldom been achieved.

The oil companies realized quite early that without far-reaching computer control they would not be able to respond to more complicated production requirements. Optimizing their complex production processes became even more urgent in the face of price pressure from foreign competitors. Computer control seemed unavoidable under these conditions, and for this reason high levels of automation became characteristic of the oil companies beginning in the early 1970s.

No one fundamentally questions the advantages of computer control in other parts of the chemical industry either, but it is more difficult to cost justify the required investment. Automation levels differ by product and process but, interestingly enough, the subdivision of parts of the industry into continuous processes and batch processes is not really important any longer as a differentiating factor. For some parts of the industry, especially pharmaceuticals and chemicals, the shift to extensive computer control is not currently on the agenda.

Regarding work organization, the situation is somewhat confused. The operator job in the control centers—the variant of systems control work characteristic of chemical processes—is defined as skilled work. The skill level for that work will increase even further as companies are demanding greater flexibility from their workers.

However, it is a matter of dispute whether the job differentiation between indoor control room operators and outdoor production personnel should be maintained. Working outdoors is currently a career step towards the position of general operator who alternates between work outside and inside. Whether the production workers should be (partly) responsible for maintenance, quality control, and programming is not a topic that the chemical industry discusses with the same enthusiasm as the automobile industry. At any rate, a broad reduction of the demarcations among the traditional jobs has, as of now, not been realized.

The oil companies, again, are an exception; as a matter of fact, they have implemented a new work organization that integrates maintenance work into production work, especially in mechanical operations. It is interesting that within the German system of industrial relations, a new collective bargaining agreement on work time encouraged this development. The working week in the oil industry is shorter than in other parts of the chemical industry. A fifth shift, necessary for running the processes around the clock, was introduced without hiring new workers, by integrating work roles based on increased skill levels.

In the long run, a redistribution of programming responsibility is also possible in the oil companies. Specialized staff responsible for programming in the plants do a better job if they take into consideration the practical knowledge of their operators. The oil companies might therefore demand more cooperation between "theoreticians" and "practitioners"—a solution similar to that in the machine-building industry in the area of machine programming and machine control.

Regardless of variations in the details of work organization, there is agreement within the whole industry with respect to the recruiting and training of workers. Everything points to a broad deployment of skilled workers educated according to a newly implemented industry-wide curriculum for skilled chemical workers. The reason given for this preference for skilled workers is often a technological one: that well-trained workers are more capable of mastering the more "abstract" operator task. A more convincing argument for the growing role of *Facharbeiter* appeals to a broader range of factors: More highly skilled workers are necessary not only to deal with technological complexity

Table 5.9. Industrial Work in the Chemical Industry

(a) Total employees by area (n = 2,631)	(%)	Production workers (n = 1,526)			
		(b) Functions	(%)	(c) Skill requirements	(%)
Production	58	Manual—product	25	Unskilled	30
Maintenance	22	Manual—machines	31	Semiskilled	31
Quality control	6	Machine control	11	Skilled	22
Preparatory/finishing work	14	Systems control	33	Highly skilled	17
Total	100	Total	100	Total	100

(d) Production workers by function and skills (n = 1,526)

	Manual-product (%)	Manual-machine (%)	Machine control (%)	System control (%)
Unskilled	38	57	4	7
Semiskilled	23	30	58	29
Skilled	28	1	37.5	32
Highly skilled	11	12	0.5	32
Total	100	100	100	100
n	380	469	177	500

Source: see Note 1.

but also to meet the increasing demands for quality, security, ecological soundness, and flexibility.

Implications for Work

As there are no official statistics on the workforce in the chemical industry, we have to rely on SOFI data for a picture of work changes. The data confirm our expectations: The proportion of systems controllers is already fairly high, at least for an industry in which production work was traditionally manual work. A third of all production workers perform this

Table 5.10. Production Work in the Chemical Industry Divided into Sectors

	Discontinous processes			Continuous processes		
	Type 1[a] (%)	Type 2[b] (%)	Type 3[c] (%)	Type 4[d] (%)	Type 5[e] (%)	Type 6[f] (%)
Functions:						
Manual— product	89	16	—	—	—	—
Manual— machines	5	42	34	26	11	9
Machine control	6	42	—	—	—	9
Systems control	—	—	66	74	89	82
Total	100	100	100	100	100	100
Skill requirements:						
Unskilled	—	5	32	17	9	2
Semiskilled	36	45	54	51	25	8
Skilled	44	40	—	32	62	29
Highly skilled	20	10	14	—	4	61
Total	100	100	100	100	100	100
n	82	86	35	41	103	245

[a] Laboratories without control engineering.
[b] Batch production with decentralized control.
[c] Batch production with centralized computer control.
[d] Continous process with simple control engineering.
[e] Simple continous process with centralized control.
[f] Complex continous process with centralized control.

Source: see Note 1.

new type of work (Table 5.9), mainly on the skilled (32 percent) or highly skilled (32 percent) levels.

"Manual work in direct contact with the product" and "manual work on machines" have diminished but not yet disappeared. They currently make up 25 and 31 percent of all jobs, respectively. On average, a third of production workers perform skilled or highly skilled work (17 percent highly skilled); the rest perform semiskilled (31 percent) or unskilled (30 percent) work.

We also looked at the differences among work structures of the various sectors of the chemical industry (Table 5.10). As differentiating criteria, we used "continuity of the process" and "technological level of process control." The work structures at the ends of the resulting range are simple to understand. Type 1 represents the production of chemical specialties in laboratories without control engineering. There we find mostly manual work in direct contact with the product, mainly on a high or very high skill level. On the opposite end are complex continuous processes extensively controlled by computers. In these, Type 6 work structures, 90 percent of the workers are systems controllers on the skilled or very skilled level, most of whom are in the highly skilled category. The work structures between these two extreme cases are less consistent and will be explored in further in future research.

Looking Ahead

To the extent that computer control advances, systems control work in the chemical industry will likely increase. Whether this trend will lead to the dominance of skilled work or not remains, as of now, an open question. In our statistical data, the skill level ranges from 14 percent *Facharbeit* in batch production with computer control up to 90 percent *Facharbeit* in complex continuous processes with computer control.

Based on these data, any prediction beyond the conclusion that skilled systems control work will expand is little more than speculation. One might add, however, that, if the chemical industry were to gain the character of a genuine skilled workers' industry, it would likely do so by following in the footsteps of the oil industry, namely by combining maintenance and programming functions with production work.

ELECTRICAL AND ELECTRONIC PRODUCTS: ABOUT TO TAKE THE GREAT LEAP?

Social research in West Germany (including our own in SOFI) has been, for reasons that need not be discussed here, excessively preoccupied with the three industries we have just discussed. We have therefore enlarged the range of our research in the past few years. One step was an additional survey on the change of production concepts and industrial work structures in the electrical and electronic equipment industry. This industry is at least as big as each of the other three industries (recall Table 5.1). Our study is still in progress, and our quantitative data has not yet been processed, but this section gives an overview and some information on a series of case studies.

In the past, this industry was a stronghold of Taylorism. An important exception to this was the segment producing complex capital equipment, which represents about one-third of the total industry employment (Table 5.11). We believe the old centers of mass production will change, but the move away from Taylorism will be characteristic only of certain segments. More precisely, the transformation will take place in fabrication and subassembly but not in final assembly, at least for the foreseeable future. In fabrication and subassembly, a trend has emerged similar to that in the other industries described. Comprehensive au-

Table 5.11. Map of the Electrical and Electronic Products Industry: Traditional Methods of Rationalization and Present Dynamics

	Standardized products	Standardized components	Complex equipment
Approximate share of industry employment	1/2	1/5	3/10
Fabrication			
Sub-assembly			
Final assembly			

Traditionally Tayloristic
Traditionally non-Tayloristic
Present dynamic: more need for flexibility
Present dynamic: new technologies and fundamental change of operations

Source: see Note 1.

tomation, both the more complete automation of tooling and the installation of complex interlinked lines for automated assembly, have caused a fundamental change in operations. Simple manual functions have disappeared almost entirely. The Tayloristic approach to work organization has become obsolete under the new conditions: the traditional polarized division of labor between a mass of unskilled labor and a minority of highly skilled specialists is no longer effective.

At the same time, we have observed a second trend in these same two segments—a trend that is not necessarily connected with greater automation, but that also produces an anti-Tayloristic effect. This second trend is towards increased flexibility in the work organization. But what are the alternative solutions that will replace Taylorism? In this respect, the situation is not yet clear.

Trust in Technology or Integrated Work Organization?

In our case studies of the electrical and electronic equipment industry, we identified two competing forms of work organization we call the *technocratic* model and the *integrated work organization* model. Neither has yet predominated.

The technocratic model attempts to maintain the traditional distribution of functions and skills between direct and indirect labor. Its protagonists are betting on new technology. That is, they propose to reduce operational risks through expert systems and the centralized control of both workflow and personnel based on close-meshed networks of computer data systems. While this model does not aim to create a totally automated factory, the specialists necessary for planning, controlling, and maintaining the processes are, as in the traditional model, located outside the factory, the assumption being that their presence in the manufacturing process is needed only sporadically. Concentrating these expensive specialists outside manufacturing is seen as an effective strategy to minimize costs.

This technocratic model poses some problems. It overemphasizes the potential of technological solutions while underestimating the danger of breakdowns in complex manufacturing systems. In reality the specialists end up spending much of their time directly involved with the manufacturing process. This deviation produces unintended results. The indirect staff becomes overburdened by unplanned duties and as a result cannot accomplish their "normal" responsibilities, such as preventive maintenance. A vicious cycle ensues. An increasing number of external specialists becomes necessary, and the original cost targets are missed. Inasmuch as companies experience these consequences, we anticipate that the technocratic model will progressively lose its proponents.

The second model of adaptation currently under discussion in this industry falls under the heading of "integration." It is the reverse of

Table 5.12. Two Approaches to Integration

Defensive version: hidden traditionalism	Offensive version: optimistic view of change
Small range of integrated functions	Large range of integrated functions
Integration according to the principle: skilled specialists for process control and semiskilled workers for residual functions	Integration according to the principle: skilled specialists and semiskilled workers jointly control the process
Integration by addition	Integration by amalgamation
Preserving traditional division of labor	Reducing division of labor, new design of responsibilities
Polarization of skills within operating staffs	Operating teams

the traditional structure characterized by the externalization of skilled and indirect functions. In the second model, functions such as maintenance, quality control, and planning are integrated into production work, which has been totally reshaped as a result of automation.

This integrated work organization model plays an increasingly important role. Firms are experimenting with many versions of it that vary by scope and method of integration. One extreme can be described as a defensive path to integration, whereas the other represents an offensive path. These two paths are described in Table 5.12. Which of the two will finally prevail is not easy to determine. In the following, we evaluate the pros and cons of both versions.

First, the defensive version is a relatively costly way to integrate work. It also raises many difficulties in the area of social integration. The defensive version is inconsistent because it attempts to integrate functions that are traditionally separated from production by means of cosmetic corrections, without restructuring the production process. Because it does not integrate far enough, it often fails.

Second, the offensive version encourages highly skilled workers to engage in jobs located in production. Such workers can be attracted to jobs that offer broader responsibilities and higher skill level requirements. Integration "from the top down," that is, the transfer of indirect functions into production, is combined with integration "at the bottom," that is, the aggregation of distinct production tasks into single jobs. Costly specialists can be better utilized in this version of the integration model. It creates a flexible work organization that is open to further adaptations.

Third, the offensive version demands more worker training and retraining. The traditional demarcations between occupations are undermined. The separation of training curricula for metal workers and electricians has already been repealed, but in the offensive integration strategy further changes are needed. Companies must use new, more integrated, curricula in their training departments, and they have to shape training policies to their specific needs, for example, by integrating training related to equipment with training related to materials and processes, and laying more stress on the development of interpersonal communication skills. In addition, the continuing training of those employees involved in restructuring becomes more important. Firms, however, have been restricting their training activities to select groups of highly skilled specialists. Thus, the availability of sufficient numbers of appropriately skilled workers is a bottleneck on the road to offensive integration.

SYSTEMS CONTROLLERS AS A KEY GROUP WITHIN THE WORKFORCE

In the four industries we have discussed, a new type of job—systems controller—has appeared whose number will increase. This work is mediated by automated machinery: The making of the product is almost completely transferred to the technical system, and the worker's job is to ensure that the system functions as efficiently as possible.

Human work—which the traditional sociology vocabulary called the *labor process*—and the making of the product—traditionally called the *production process*—are decoupled in this new configuration. That is, they no longer coincide in time and activity. The systems controller in automated production embodies these changes.

The emergence of this type of job has reshaped the work structure in the oil industry, where it first evolved, and is currently reshaping the work structures of other industries where it appeared later and on a smaller scale. The spread of systems control work is surely one of the most important change in German manufacturing over the past decade. Synthesizing our industry studies, we can identify the key features of this kind of work from a sociological perspective.

Functions

Traditionally, machines were guided by workers. Workers defined the rules, initiated and coordinated the actions, and regulated performance. Modern automation means that all of these functions are performed by the technical system. Of course, in many situations, the technical system is still somewhat dependent on human action as well. However, these interventions by the worker no longer consist of directly shaping material through fabrication or assembly, but of helping the machinery itself perform these functions. The worker supports the autonomy of the technical system and intervenes when machinery does not function optimally and when breakdowns occur. The worker's actions are in this sense subordinate to those of the technical system.

In cases of deviation from the optimal performance or of machine failures, the worker may take direct control of the process, but always with the aim of giving control back to the machinery as quickly as possible. The range of direct control goes from simply turning off an alarm to changing a parameter or even a whole program. Another type of intervention is maintenance, ranging from clearing a fault to making complicated repairs. When the technical system works perfectly, the main responsibility of a systems controller is to check and to service the machinery. The worker does a perfect job when he or she succeeds in anticipating deviations and breakdowns in the technical system and prevents them from taking place.

Skills

Observers of automated work often stress the importance of theoretical knowledge. They are right inasmuch as insight into very complex machine systems requires knowledge of fundamental principles: a skilled process worker in the chemical industry whose primary competence is in processing needs additional knowledge in mechanics and electronics; a production mechanic in the automobile industry might integrate some maintenance and quality-control knowledge; and a metal-cutting specialist combines traditional skills with a knowledge of the principles of numerical control. This theoretical competence cannot be taught through on-the-job training. Formal professional training, if possible in the form of a modernized *Facharbeiter* education, is necessary.

What is often not noticed however, is that being in charge of complicated equipment also requires empirical knowledge that the systems controller can acquire only in direct contact with the process day after day. Being in touch with the machinery day in and day out is the only way to acquire a feeling for its special "behavior"—a feeling that can be decisive for effective machine control. The ideal worker is a kind of scout—someone who is sensitive to the risks of breakdown, and who has quick reactions and the ability to improvise and take preventive action. Apart from theoretical knowledge, the systems controller needs distinctive empirical knowledge and behavioral skills so as to be able to close the remaining gaps in the technical system.

The salient characteristic of the systems controller's skills is thus the distinctive synergy of theoretical knowledge and practical experience. This combination of skills distinguishes systems controllers from personnel such as engineers and maintenance specialists, who rely primarily on more theoretical forms of knowledge.

That this practical experience is embedded in an elaborate theoretical framework hinders a relapse into the old habits of craft which would not be appropriate for work in a highly automated plant. The traditional crafts represented an area originally defined by the material they handled, such as metal, wood, and textiles. Later, they were also defined by the method used to handle their materials (toolmaker, mechanic, electrician). The new systems controllers integrate different traditional areas of expertise as well as some new skills. They are less materials oriented; the greater part of their skill base consists of technical and organizational procedures.

Mediating between theory and reality—the core of the systems controller's role—includes the task of ensuring the exchange of information between the different categories of workers. It is the systems controllers who, thanks to their continuous presence at the machinery, first notice irregularities. And it is the systems controllers' responsibility to communicate with the technical specialists such as engineers and maintenance personnel when the systems controllers cannot resolve the problem themselves and need external help. Social competence has thus become an important part of the systems controllers' skills.

Compared with traditional craftworkers, another difference is obvious. The systems controller is by no means the master of the production process that the craftworker was. Other personnel define the layout of the technical system, which means that others also define the points at which human intervention remain necessary and the types of intervention wanted. Compared with the traditional craftworker, the new systems controller has much less individual autonomy. Their level of functional interdependence is much higher. On the other hand, compared with the kind of work we became used to in the era of mass production, this new form of work is inherently more interesting. For these reasons, the new work situation is not a revival of earlier forms, and in particular, it is not a revival of craft production.

Supervision of Work

Four factors create problems in supervising systems controllers. First, in automated manufacturing, the main productive force is machinery. Human work gains its importance indirectly through a functionality best achieved when the least activity is necessary. Human work has to support the technical system's activity, not animate it.

Second, the work of systems controllers is often characterized by *ad hoc* measures. Improvisation is one of their critical skills. Because irregularities and breakdowns are by definition unexpected events, it is difficult to calculate in advance how one should best react. Defining standards is impossible under such circumstances.

Third, achievement can be assessed only by results, not by conduct. Nobody criticizes a systems controller for not having obeyed the rules if the outcome is felicitous. The rule book is thin, and it is very often the systems controllers themselves who write it.

Fourth, however effective the preventive maintenance program may be, interruptions are unavoidable and must be accepted as a necessary evil in complex, highly integrated technical systems. Whether interruptions occur, is, all things being equal, not an acceptable criterion for measuring the quality of the systems controller's work.

As a result of these four features of their work, systems controllers are not easy for management to supervise. The diffusion of this form of work forces management to develop new supervisory control techniques. Such techniques range from computer-based data systems to more simple devices to record actions and irregularities. More precise documentation of workers' actions could serve as the basis for further regulation of work and thus help management assign more responsibility to individuals.

The implementation of these ideas, however, remains difficult. There is no obvious linear relation between the behavior of systems controllers and the manufacturing outcome. The chain of cause and effect is very complicated and includes the complex behavior of the machinery and its interaction with organizational conditions. In addition, as improvisation and experimental behavior play such an important role in breakdown situations, the documentation of work activities will not justify reproaching workers for neglecting rules. We expect the documentation to be useful primarily for learning purposes and to help in avoiding recurrent problems.

Workers' Attitudes

From our interviews of systems controllers, we identified some distinctive attitudes toward work and factory. These workers often express a self-image of quasiprofessionals; that is, they see themselves as "modern" employees working in a complicated technical system using knowledge and practices acquired in a long and formalized education. They are interested in performing tasks that demand responsibility, self-direction, and a high level of skills. Their willingness to continue training is great.

They associate their occupation with technological and production targets (such as high efficiency and high quality), and they want to be involved in planning decisions and the design of work—areas not normally influenced by the rank-and-file employee. Finally, it is quite clear to them that they have some leverage on the labor market, that is, that the employer is unable to get along without their capabilities and cooperation.

In *The End of the Division of Labor?*, we described workers who exhibit such characteristics as "winners in the rationalization process." Whereas we ascribed the consciousness of being a winner primarily to maintenance specialists (particularly to electricians/electronic specialists) in the 1980s, we now can identify this same self-image in the systems controllers group among production workers as well.

Systems controllers see rationalization as more of an opportunity than a risk. Few of these workers fail to notice that rationalization also produces losers, and that this is its dark side. Often the process of rationalization is compared with a moving train onto which only those who are both well educated and able to continue their training can jump.

This interest in professional education is not politically motivated as it was for the German labor movement of the past, when knowledge was seen as a source of collective power. The systems controllers see education as a source of individual leverage in the labor market, as a way to advance their individual careers. Nonetheless, our interviews found proportionately few of these workers who displayed the mentality of people who elbow their way through the crowd. Most of them realized that it is difficult to jump onto the moving train without help, and that former winners can suddenly find themselves new losers.

The optimistic view that systems controllers have in general toward rationalization loses some of its conviction when it comes to the question of whether trends in rationalization are good for all workers. The controllers are skeptical about rationalization's effects on job security. Automation is usually seen as likely to eliminate manual work, but few were confident that new jobs would be created in sufficient number to compensate for this elimination. Accordingly, most systems controllers are sympathetic to social policies that provide remedial training and interim support for people who need retraining. Many systems controllers see a need for a new industrial policy to guarantee the balance job creation and destruction.

Relationship to the Unions

The systems controllers are not natural members of the union movement. It is impossible to mobilize these workers with the traditional argument— that the interests of workers are harmed through their subordination to capital and that the union is the champion of the oppressed.

While systems controllers are not totally content, many of their demands have been addressed. Systems controllers possess valued skills and therefore need not be concerned with being lost in a sea of workers looking for jobs and struggling to fulfill their basic needs; their wages are relatively high. They are not ruled by foremen who impose apparently arbitrary work norms; the systems controllers' work standards appear as the demands of technical system itself, and are therefore more acceptable. Finally, in contrast to the Tayloristic model of work, which does not value skills, the modern work process encourages these workers to accumulate knowledge and skills.

If systems controllers do show an interest in the traditional areas of collective bargaining—job security, wages, effort, and skills—they do so in a vague and abstract manner. Work stress and knowledge obsolescence are their major concerns. However, they are typically optimistic that they can meet these challenges individually, by means of individual bargaining, further training, job change, and advancement. While offering to help them in these efforts may sound like a politically astute move for unions, the systems controllers' requests are so situation-specific that do not easily fit into a comprehensive union program. There is nevertheless one issue that could be an exception. When it comes to wages and other tangible rewards, many systems controllers are not much concerned with actual amounts but are very anxious that the system of financial rewards be transparent. They passionately demand openness. They want to know, and they are disturbed by any power structure in factories and offices that remains a mystery to them.

Beyond the specific issue of compensation structure, systems controllers, like many other modern employees, want to be involved. The main fault they find with factory organizations is the participation gap: unclear evaluation criteria and goals, no opportunity for participation in strategic decisions, and lack of openness to unconventional proposals. They see themselves as knowledgeable actors whose knowledge is not adequately used despite their comprehensive work roles. They have been trained to be independent and responsible, but management only allows them to use these skills on the shopfloor; the organizational superstructure and its decision processes remain hierarchical.

This gap has been recognized by some more open-minded managers. Their response has been to open lines of communication through organization development initiatives, quality circles, and simplified decision paths. Nevertheless, real participation often fails because the traditionally privileged ranks fear change and experiments; the power structure is often too rigid. As a result, the desire for participation has not been satisfied.

For the unions, the participation gap offers an opportunity to mobilize modern workers. Unions could try to create a distinctive political image for themselves by attacking the obsolete elements of the power system and by arguing for more effective and more democratic decision-making processes. However, to pursue such a campaign in a way attractive to modern workers, the unions would need a more comprehensive and detailed model for bottom-up participation. To systems controllers, individual participation is primary: They resist what they sometimes see as the "codetermination bureaucracy." Instead of acting as mediators for the employees, unions should restrict themselves to the role of political brokers. Unions must try to enlarge the avenues through which employees can independently pursue their interests and, at the same time, be there to aid those who find themselves at a disadvantage.

Unfortunately, many union organizations have an internal participation gap just as problematic as those of business organizations. Unions will need appropriate internal structures to be credible advocates of workers interested in participation: flexible approaches, openness for experiments, and member participation, instead of monolithic organizations based on the principles of democratic centralism.

The unions must also present themselves as reliable protagonists of open-minded solutions in society. The systems controllers are "knowledge workers," very aware of their dual role as employees and members of society. This not only enables them to identify the deficiencies of the capitalist form of modern life, but, using their professional knowledge and competence, they can also recognize these deficiencies as unnecessary and as conquerable. In the workplace, these workers make decisions through careful deliberation, intellectual discipline, and independent judgement.

Performing the work of technical experts might lead systems controllers to become obsessed with technical, instrumental rationality—a form of reason ill-suited to complex political problems; however, in our interviews, we found that many systems controllers were able to avoid such narrow mindedness. We found skilled chemical workers who used their professional competence to advance a more general environmentalist critique and who, based on their technical knowledge, proposed less hazardous production systems capable of safe and ecologically balanced production. We found machine manufacturing specialists who, on the one hand, assembled labor-saving equipment, but who, on the other hand, criticized the single mindedness of much industrial planning, the gap between current processes and technical possibilities, and the underutilization of the humanizing potential typical of modern technologies. Their reflections were not narrowly technical and instrumental, but broadly social and holistic.

Systems controllers often saw the deficiencies of modern industry. They visited forests, and found them destroyed by pollution. They saw friends and relatives unemployed. Their professional training led them to conclude that such waste was not only morally reprehensible but also technically unnecessary. They are sympathetic to the argument that there is a need for greater "substantive rationality" in society. They are willing to examine new solutions and perhaps to involve themselves in advancing those solutions, even when they themselves do not benefit directly from them.

These developments bring not only challenges but also recruitment and mobilization opportunities for German unions. We believe that this kind of critical thinking will develop even further over time, and union policies should include, develop, represent, and strengthen it. Unions could define policies that build on these opportunities, but so far German unions have been reluctant to follow this route.

LONG-TERM TRENDS IN GERMANY'S WORK STRUCTURE

However complex the present course of industrial change in Germany may be, the constitutive elements exhibit a common feature: Workforce utilization is no longer limited by traditional Tayloristic–Fordist dogma. Nowhere in our empirical research did we come across an intensifying division of labor. The contrary trend predominates. Efficiency-improvement efforts are no longer based on further fragmentation of tasks. Instead, current efficiency efforts rely on the integration of functions and the design of jobs with broader responsibilities.

In *The End of the Division of Labor?*, we reported controversy within management about the pros and cons of this new approach. This controversy has since ceased. Inertia tends to maintain the traditional structures, but no one is promoting an alternative to the strategy of establishing a more integrated work organization.

Present Work Structures: Simultaneous Change and Stagnation

Industrial work is fundamentally changed where firms have answered the economic challenges that confront them by means of combining two strategies: flexible automation and integrated work organization. In these areas, there has been a radical substitution of machine and systems control work for manual fabrication and assembly work and the elimination of demarcations among production, maintenance, and quality control. Both changes are necessary for the expansion of the new type of skilled production work that we call *systems control work*.

Where, because of slower development on the technological side, workers have remained directly involved in fabrication and assembly, firms have found it more difficult to elude the legacies of Taylor and Ford. Yet even under such conditions we have observed attempts to integrate traditionally separate functions. These organizational changes, however, result not in highly skilled, but semiskilled, work that may be only little more complex than in the past. Upgrading here stops on a level far below the skilled tradesperson level. Further advances in these firms will require a second push. Swedish experiments, in which assembly work has been upgraded from semiskilled to skilled work, demonstrate that the additional push could come from the sociocultural environment. Volvo was pushed to adopt a more radical solution for its new Uddevalla assembly plant by the gap between the higher expectations that modern employees have of work and the meager satisfactions inherent in semiskilled labor.

Is Reprofessionalization on the Agenda?

The growth of the systems controller category among the blue-collar workforce suggests that average skill levels will continue to rise within German industry. Nevertheless, execution work will diminish radically and systems control work gain the upper hand only with comprehensive automation, that is, after both key operations and peripheral manufacturing processes are automated. This situation has been reached only in parts of the chemical industry, in the fabrication shops of the maching-building industry, and in the stamping and machine shops of the automobile industry. The new concepts of production are nevertheless spreading into low-technology areas, where they generally stimulate attempts at job enrichment and upskilling—albeit in restricted forms as of now. Even in a typical mass-production industry such as the automobile industry, the momentum for a further increase in worker qualifications already seems to be present.

A Plea for Political Regulation

Some political regulation is needed to ease this transition in worker qualifications. For some time, groups of workers with different skill levels and work opportunities will coexist in a situation with the potential for destabilizing conflict. Systems controllers, for example, are in a fortunate position, but workers in low-technology areas lack the same strategic leverage within the work process since their jobs do not allow them to influence the work process or to supervise themselves.

The industrial transition toward higher skilled workers therefore risks segmenting the workforce into a growing group of winners—the systems controllers—and a residual group of losers—the unskilled and semi-skilled workers who will decrease in number but will continue to be needed for the foreseeable future. For a few years, there may also be a middle group characterized by their slowly improving working conditions. Political regulation will be needed to avoid the risk of conflicts among the different groups, since such conflict could jeopardize the overall process of workforce upgrading.

CONCLUSION

Over the past two decades, West German production systems have undergone important changes as firms fought for competitiveness in a context of increased international competition. New concepts of production creatively combined new organizational forms with the possibilities offered by technological progress.

In this ongoing transition, there has been a clear trend towards the "humanization" of working life. While this trend cannot be interpreted as the "natural" concomitant of capitalist development—there is no simple relationship between humanized work and automation—management has found it increasingly difficult to improve efficiency by intensifying the division of labor. Management has therefore progressively reoriented its policies towards a greater integration of work, abandoning traditional demarcations among jobs. As a result, firms will increasingly be forced to contend with the new forms of worker consciousness emerging among the systems control workers.

These conclusions are based on data from West Germany and are, in a strict sense, valid only for this country. Obviously, the development of national industries is influenced by their specific social environments, including educational institutions, system of industrial relations, market structure, spatial patterns, producer and supplier relations, cultural and political legacy. Changes sensible in one environment are not necessarily so sensible for an industry operating under different institutional, cultural, political, and historical conditions. International comparative studies demonstrate that companies and industries can be particularly successful by utilizing their comparative advantages instead of adopting foreign methods.

Our reading of research results in other countries suggests, however, that there are important similarities among comparable German, Italian, and American industries in the implementation of automation technologies and in the structuring of work in automated manufacturing. The growing interlinkages between the national economies—subsystems of the world economy—seem to restrict the range of viable economic strategies. The story we tell in this paper is thus in all likelihood more than a specifically German one. Nonetheless, important differences still exist. The constraints imposed by the different environmental settings seem to be stronger in the area of work restructuring. As a result, we still find greater international difference between comparable industries in the area of work than in the area of technology. The transformation of work structures requires changes in the institutional context, in the education system and in the system of industrial relations; it is therefore by nature a long-term project.

APPENDIX : WORK AND SKILLS IN THE HISTORY OF GERMAN INDUSTRIAL SOCIOLOGY

One can trace German industrial sociology back to the end of the nineteenth century and "bourgeois" political economists such as Gustav Schmoller and Lujo Brentano (Kern, 1982). Disturbed by the politically disruptive concomitants of the Industrial Revolution (which in Germany came relatively late but very quickly), they tried to design a social policy to reconcile the growing mass of wage earners and bourgeois society. To justify their proposition that alienated workers could be socially integrated—in other words, that the workers did not automatically have to sympathize with the Marxist-led labor movement—and to identify changes in policy that would resolve the class conflict without fundamentally changing society, these academics and their successors (including Max Weber) carried out a series of social investigations known as *Enquêten des Vereins für Sozialpolitik* (Surveys of Social–Political Society). Among the societal problems studied in the surveys was the situation of workers in large manufacturing plants. Of particular interest were the changes in work and living conditions that resulted from capitalist rationalization and the ways in which the workers reacted.

In the late 1920s, Marxist social philosophers began to reexamine the premises of Marxist thinking and to reformulate Marxist theory. They were confused by the absence of socialist revolution in the industrialized capitalist countries, especially by the fact that the Russian revolution turned out to be an isolated event, and they were stimulated by the organizational and conceptual disunity within Marxism. Most of their work was theoretical but some included empirical research. The survey *Autorität und Familie* (Authority and Family) by Erich Fromm and others (1936) included an examination of whether the capitalist production process led to the decomposition of the working class and thus eroded collective identity. In the project *Die Arbeitslosen in Marienthal* (The Unemployed in Marienthal), Marie Lazarsfeld Jahoda and Hans Zeisel (1933) explored whether the experience of unemployment stimulated revolutionary actions or resulted in apathy and personal disorganization.

After World War II, sociology and empirical social research became established as an academic discipline in West German universities. At this point, the democratic elements in society became preoccupied by the urgent question of how to counteract the political narrow mindedness of the traditional industrial leaders that had had such disastrous effects during the Nazi period. One of their key objectives was to create a more democratic governance of German factories. Social scientists took up the topic. The question of whether the workers were prepared to participate constructively in democratic decision processes in factories was explored in research projects on workers' attitudes toward work, factory, technology, management, and society. Most of the leading German sociologists who started their careers around 1950 (including Heinrich Popitz, Theo Pirker, Burkart Lutz, Ludwig von Friedeburg) first won laurels in industrial sociology with research on *Technik und Industriearbeit* (Technology and Industrial Work), *Das Gesellschaftsbild des Arbeiters* (Workers' Image of Society), *Arbeiter, Management, Mitbestimmung* (Workers, Management, Codetermination), and *Betriebsklima* (The Social Climate in Factories).

Strains of all three generations of thought are still present in German industrial sociology and influence our thinking to this day. The social–political society generation contributed the construction of surveys as a flexible research method. The Frankfurt school of sociology offered a theory of society that we still use as a guideline, and the postwar industrial sociologists encourage our combination of political ideals with empirical research methods.

Postwar research was also inevitably shaped by the specific experience of Germany in the late 1950s and 1960s. At that time, the German economy was prospering. The German workforce benefited from progressively more job security, more opportunities for promotion, higher incomes, and shorter work time. These developments led some influential sociologists, such as Theodor Geiger (1949) and Helmut Schelsky (1956/1961, 1957), to predict the end of the class society and its transformation into an affluent society without social disparities. A large part of the public agreed with this interpretation. Since the principles of freedom and equality had gained general acceptance, even the blue-collar workers, it was argued, would become fully integrated into capitalist society. Not only was a convergence of incomes and lifestyles on a fairly high level expected, but occupations were to become more similar as well. The reduction of unskilled work was regarded as a natural concomitant of higher levels of automation, a process that had just begun in the factories and was still in a simple and rigid form. The caution with which workers acted politically at that time was quickly interpreted as proof of the dissolution of classes, but no effort was made to test alternative interpretations.

In 1964, we organized an extensive survey on the impact of technological change on industrial work and on workers' attitudes. We used this survey to evaluate some of the basic propositions of the classless society theory, focusing on changes in the work situation. Our method was based on the theoretical assumption that work was the central experience of social life in our society, and that it largely determined other social variables such as lifestyles and opinions.

After examining several industries, we became increasingly suspicious of the classless society theory. A cornerstone of the theory, the assumption of a simple correlation between technological progress and humanization of industrial work, turned out to be very weak. We found that the interplay between economic development, technological change, and work restructuring was much more complicated than we, like most of our colleagues, had assumed. Associated with the new, automated machinery being implemented at the time, the variety of industrial jobs was growing, not diminishing, and no simple tendency towards greater humanization was apparent.

We documented the development of semiskilled machine-control occupations, which had sprung up between the unskilled manual occupations and the traditional skilled occupations. In addition, we found that skilled work was not replacing unskilled work. On the contrary, the number of unskilled jobs remained stable and sometimes even grew when technological innovations where introduced. These innovations led to a rather small increase of skilled workers, primarily in the indirect areas. Often the work restructuring that resulted caused a double polarization: a polarization between many unskilled workers and a few skilled ones within shopfloor departments, and a polarization between a majority of primarily unskilled direct workers and a minority of skilled indirect workers. A Tayloristic work organization policy was still in force.

Regarding workers' attitudes, we found that these more heterogeneous work experiences did not erode the commitment to collective identity. Although some common beliefs were indeed dissipated when work situations became more differentiated, we saw that many elements of workers' traditional collective identity persisted. Irrespective of their specific jobs and of possible improvements in their working conditions and wages, nearly all workers remained committed to traditional views of technological change, views that originated in the old class consciousness. As people who need a job to earn a living, they viewed technological change as a threat to employment and thus as a danger for workers. Because this negative interpretation was often held even by workers who had benefited from technological change, we considered this as evidence of an ambivalent disposition with the potential for either social integration or social militancy.

Despite the contrarian nature of these conclusions, when we published them in our 1970 book *Industriearbeit und Arbeiterbewusstsein* (Industrial Work and Workers' Consciousness), the reception was primarily positive. The West German economy had experienced its first recession in the period 1967–68 and subsequently became less stable. In light of this new experience, more people had come to view the whole social system more critically. The idea that the prevailing model of society had lost its legitimacy (*Legitimationskrise*) rapidly gained ground. Public opinion was increasingly concerned with the gap between the wealth of the nation and the limited means of many of its citizens. Germans saw a rich industrialized country with declining job security, sustained business profits but incomplete worker protection laws, a lot of shiftwork, and a growing proportion of unskilled jobs. Social protest, including strikes, threatened to increase. The modernization of German society seemed to be faltering.

In the political arena, these perceptions promoted the reactivation of reform ideas. The Social Democrats received a new impetus, the Liberals adapted, and together they formed a new and electorally successful coalition with a reform agenda. The unions supported this reform policy electorally and in collective bargaining.

Our academic work helped to clarify these changes and suggested some ways of transforming reform ideas into social policy. The political influence of intellectuals in Germany is by no means high, but the design of the "humanization of working life" program was nevertheless influenced to some significant extent by our research.

The new political situation turned out to be highly conducive to the further expansion of social research. The task of identifying problem areas and points of conflict in society, including those accompanying technological change in industry, became a basic element of the reform agenda. Researchers such as ourselves were increasingly seen (although not necessarily esteemed) as suppliers of data necessary for the design of practical reform policy. Funding became more plentiful, and the social sciences' level of institutional visibility increased.

These advantages also created problems for the social sciences. There was a danger of becoming too involved in practical politics. Tracking the implementation of specific technologies, evaluating the results of reform activities, organizing the flow of information from research to policy—these tasks can be exciting for a scholar, but an agenda based exclusively on politically predetermined topics could stifle innovative research.

The research reported in this chapter was intended as a contribution to the effort to counteract these risks. In 1982, we formulated a plan to assess whether the trends we described in *Industrial Work and Workers' Consciousness* had continued or not. We discovered that there had, in the intervening years, been a substantial change in direction. The resulting story has been told in this chapter.

The first reactions to *The End of the Division of Labor?* within German industrial sociology were, frankly, often skeptical or even negative. (Important reviews were collected in Thomas Malsch and Rüdiger Seltz, 1987.) Some critics were upset by the fact that we now argued against the polarization thesis that we ourselves had promoted and that over the years had become broadly accepted among sociologists. Other critics criticized our data base, arguing that we had overemphasized some exceptional cases.

In the ensuing years, however, observers have come to agree that radical change is a key feature of the current industrial landscape in West Germany. And it is now rarely disputed that a growing number of enterprises are adopting these new concepts of production. Many German industrial sociologists today agree that, despite the restrictions, asymmetries, and contradictions involved, the new concepts are playing an increasingly central role in industrial development. The debate today is over the interpretation of this fact: Will Fordism be replaced or merely supplemented by these new concepts of production? Will skilled labor become the dominant type of industrial work? Or is there a shift towards new Fordism? Or perhaps neither model will prevail and we will see an increase in variety. Our (provisional) interpretation has been outlined in this chapter.

Of the criticisms that have been addressed to our work, the most fundamental perhaps are those that question the very relevance of industrial sociology for the understanding of modern society. André Gorz, for example, has argued that work is losing its central status within the structure and dynamics of modern society. We do not deny that the relationship between work and nonwork has fundamentally changed and that, as a result, the concepts of industrial sociology provide a less comprehensive foundation than they used to for an understanding of modern society. But we should not throw the baby out with the bath water. The future structure of society is being profoundly shaped by the emergence of these new concepts of production; they influence such key issues as the size of the gap between the winners and losers in rationalization and the intensity of conflicts within the working class. It is in the context of these new concepts of production that the social identity of workers is being formed; they thus also influence several other key issues such as the degree of autonomy at work and the use of free time. Understanding the new concepts of production is critical to our ability to forecast the future nature of both work and nonwork spheres.

NOTES

This chapter is based on research done in the Sociological Research Institute (SOFI) at the University of Goettingen. The following colleagues were involved in various surveys cited: Volker Baethge, Uwe Neumann, Roland Springer, Ulrich Voskamp, Klaus Peter Wittemann, Volker Wittke. We have drawn extensively on project papers co-authored with these colleagues.

1. Tables 3, 4, 5, 7, 8, 9 10 and part of Table 6 in this chapter are taken from Michael Schumann, Volker Baethge, Uwe Neumann, Roland Springer: Breite Diffusion der Neuen Produktionskonzepte - zögerlicher Wandel der Arbeitsstrukturen, SOFI Working Paper, Goettingen 1989. The data is from a special SOFI survey which is still in progress. The figures are representative for blue-collar work in West German automobile industry (n = 54,282 workers), the machine building industry (n = 3,860), and the chemical industry (n = 2,631). (In the latter two industries, data is still being collected.) Table 11 was taken from Ulrich Voskamp, Klaus Peter Wittemann, Volker Wittke: Elektroindustrie im Umbruch, SOFI Working Paper, Goettingen 1989. Table 12 summarizes some conclusions of discussions in our electrical industry research group.

REFERENCES

Friedeburg, L. V., et al. 1955. Betriebsklima. (The Social Climate in Factories.) Frankfurt-M.: Europäische Verlagsanstalt.

Fromm, E., et al. 1936. Studien über Autorität und Familie. (Studies on Authority and Family). Paris: Alcan.

Geiger, T. 1949. Die Klassengesellschaft im Schmelztiegel. (The Class Society in the Melting Pot.) Cologne/Hagen: Kiepenheuer.

Gorz, A. 1983. Les chemins du paradis. (Paths to Paradise.) Paris: Editions Galilée.

Gorz, A. 1988. Metamorphoses du travail. (Metamorphoses of Work.) Paris: Editions Galilée.

Kern, H. 1982. Empirische Sozialforschung. Ursprünge, Ansätze, Entwicklungslinien. (Empirical Social Research. Origins, Concepts, Trends.) Munich: C.H. Beck.

Kern, H. 1989. "Zur Aktualität des Kampfes um die Arbeit." (On the Relevance of the Struggle for Work.) In Kraemer, H. L. and C. Leggewie, (eds.). Wege ins Reich der Freiheit. André Gorz zum 65. Geburtstag. Berlin: Rotbuch-Verlag, pp. 200–24.

Kern, H., and M. Schumann. 1970. *Industriearbeit und Arbeiterbewusstsein.* (Industrial Work and Workers' Consciousness.) Frankfurt-M.: Europäische Verlagsanstalt.

Kern, H. and M. Schumann. 1984. *Das Ende der Arbeitsteilung?* (The End of the Division of Labor?) Munich: C. H. Beck.

Kern, H., and M. Schumann, 1989. "New Concepts of Production in West German Plants." In P. Katzenstein (ed.). *Industry and Politics in West Germany. Toward the Third Republic.* Ithaca, New York: Cornell University Press, pp. 87–110.

Lazarsfeld-Jahoda, M., and H. Zeisel. 1933. *Die Arbeitslosen von Marienthal.* (The Unemployed in Marienthal.) Leipzig: Hirzel.

Malsch, Thomas, and Rüdiger Seltz (eds.). 1987. *Die neuen Produktionskonzepte auf dem Prüfstand, Beiträge zur Entwicklung der Industriearbeit.* (The New Concepts of Production Being Put to the Test.) Berlin: Edition Sigma.

Pirker, T., *et al.* 1955. *Arbeiter, Management, Mitbestimmung.* (Workers, Management, Coeducation.) Stuttgart/Düsseldorf: Ring-Verlag.

Popitz, H., *et al.* 1957a. *Technik und Industriearbeit.* (Technology and Industrial Work.) Tübingen: Mohr.

Popitz, H., *et al.* 1957b. *Das Gesellschaftsbild des Arbeiters.* (The Workers' Image of Society.) Tübingen: Mohr.

Schelsky, H. 1956/1961. "Gesellschaftlicher Wandel." (Social Change.) In H. Schelsky (1965), *Auf der Suche nach Wirklichkeit. Gesammelte Aufsätze*, Düsseldorf/ Cologne: Diederichs, pp. 337–51.

Schelsky, H. 1957. *Die sozialen Folgen der Automatisierung.* (The Social Impacts of Automation.) Cologne: Diederichs.

Schumann, Michael, Volker Baethge, Uwe Neumann, and Roland Springer. 1989. "Breite Diffusion der neuen Produktionskonzepte—zögerlicher Wandel der Arbeitsstrukturen." (The Broad Diffusion of a New Model of Production—A Hesitant Evolution of Work Structures). *Soziale Welt* 41 (1990): 47ff.

Voskamp, Ulrich, Klaus Peter Wittemann, and Volker Wittke. 1989. "Elektroindustrie im Umbruch." SOFI Working Paper, Goettingen.

6

Institutions and Incentives for Developing Work-Related Knowledge and Skill

A greater emphasis on continual learning by employees appears to characterize some firms that successfully adapt to changing market forces and new technologies. This chapter outlines the roles of three mechanisms of skill formation in the United States—schools, corporate training programs, and what I will call *learning-intensive production*.

COMPETITIVENESS, AUTOMATION, AND LEARNING ON THE JOB

The strategic importance of human capital and continual learning has been highlighted by analyses describing how successful firms in Japan, West Germany, and certain other countries use production strategies that rely on, and continually cultivate, employees' problem-solving abilities (Aoki, 1984, 1988; Mincer and Higuchi, 1988; Soskice, 1989; Streeck, 1989). This section introduces the general theme of the chapter by arguing that in general the effective use of new technologies requires both a higher level of skill and a more active cultivation of continual learning in the production process.

A defining characteristic of the "flexible systems" proposed by Reich (1983), and the "flexible specialization" described by Piore and Sabel (1984), is their critical dependence on employees' skills in teamwork and problem solving. As Piore and Sabel put it, "a plant community of multi-skilled workers seems a precondition for agile maneuvering in a hostile world" (p. 213). Only by cultivating these skills can American employers succeed in entering what Reich calls the new "era of human capital." Similarly, Cohen and Zysman (1987) have argued that a strategy of "organized smarts" is probably the best way to reconcile the goal of a high wage economy with the imperative of international competition. Bailey's (1989a, b, c, unpublished) studies of four industries also found market forces leading to increased dependence on production workers' problem-solving skills. These broader responsibilities have brought changes in the kinds of skills required, as reflected in company-sponsored training. "Training requirements remain skills-oriented, but the skills are defined more broadly to include the ability to think about the process, as well as interpersonal and team skills" (National Academy of Sciences, 1986, p. 54).

However, not all researchers have concluded that more advanced technology requires higher levels of skill for employees. There is a tradition of thought in which the opposite hypothesis is considered more likely to be true, namely that firms use new technology to simplify work in order to reduce wages and make workers more interchangeable. Some case studies have substantiated this view. Spenner (1985), Burke and Rumberger (1987), the National Academy of Sciences (1987), and Attewell (Chapter 3, this volume) review the arguments and evidence in this "de-skilling" controversy, and conclude that, in general, the level of skill and knowledge firms expect employees to possess in order to operate a particular technology depends not only on the technology itself, but also on the kind of relationship that exists between the firm and its employees. Levin (1987) and Zuboff (1988) have explained how the effect of technology on skill demands in any particular workplace depends on managers' recognizing that new technology is likely to be more productive if employees are given responsibility for using it intelligently.

Although the introduction of automated technology itself has not always increased the level of skill demanded of production workers, much of the evidence indicates that effective use of new technology to keep lowering costs, improving quality, and reducing cycle times entails continual learning in and through the production itself. There are numerous accounts of firms succeeding with new technologies by involving production workers, engineers, and managers in a deliberate process of continual discovery and experimentation. In highly auto-mated manufacturing plants in the United States, Hirschhorn (1984) described how work has been organized to promote continual learning and problem solving by workers. A report by the National Academy of Sciences (1986) similarly points to the importance of teamwork, problem solving, and the capacity for continued learning on the part of production workers using advanced manufacturing technology in the United States. In firms employing such technology, information and decision making are brought closer to the production process itself. Employees, often organized in semiautonomous teams, have broad responsibility for monitoring production, trouble shooting, mainte-nance, and quality control (see also Thompson and Scalpone, 1985). In Japanese machine-tool firms using flexible manufacturing systems, Jaikumar (1986) found production workers had time purposely set aside for process-improving experiments, observation of machine behavior, and analysis of performance data. In Germany, Schultz-Wild and Kohler (1985) studied automated manufacturing plants and concluded there was a net advantage to organizing work in a way that allowed time for cross-training operators (see also Helfgott, 1988).

Recent research by cognitive scientists, psychologists and anthropologists on "situated learning" (Resnick, 1987a, b; Brown et al., 1989; Raizen, 1989) can help us understand the fundamental significance of this learning-intensive organization of production. This research suggests that learning through the work process itself may, in general, be the best way to acquire work-related knowledge and skill. In contrast, what is learned in classrooms, while useful in classrooms, does not readily transfer to actual work situations. A considerable number of empirical studies have now demonstrated the absence of correlation between school-taught knowledge and problem solving in the context of actual production (for a summary, see Raizen, 1989; for a recent example, see Scribner and Stevens, 1989). Scribner puts the point well:

> Skilled practical thinking incorporates features of the task environment (people, things, information) into the problem solving system. It is as valid to describe the environment as part of the problem-solving system as it is to observe that problem-solving occurs 'in' the environment. . . . [This view] emphasizes the inextricability of task from environment, and the continual interplay between internal representations and operations and external reality throughout the course of the problem-solving activity. (p. 42).

Sticht (1979, 1987) reports evidence of success with a kind of situated instruction called *functional context education*. Military trainees were taught reading skills in the context of technical training. Tests of general reading ability showed some improvement as a result of this instruction, but there were bigger gains on reading tests that contained items related to the technical content of the courses. Sticht concludes that "specific literacy skills can be developed and assessed for generalizability in the domain area that corresponds to what was taught" (1987, p. 3.18).

Some researchers are now giving renewed attention to apprenticeship as a model of efficient learning (Lave, 1988; Gott, 1988; Brown et al., 1989). At the same time, public policies are being formulated to make greater use of workplaces as a site for students' learning (William T. Grant Foundation, 1988; U.S. Department of Labor, 1989). In the description of schools in the following, special attention will be given to cooperative education, which is a time-tested method of learning from the work situation itself.

Despite the arguments in favor of situated learning, U.S. employers have not yet displayed much eagerness to take over more of the training business themselves. On the contrary, corporate spokespersons concerned about skill development have decried the necessity for employers to conduct education in basic academic subjects and have focused attention on improving schools (Committee for Economic Development, 1985; Kearns and Doyle, 1988). Given the perceived shortcomings or outright failure of schools, coupled with the theoretical advantage of situated learning, why have employers not tried to move more of the skill development effort into workplaces themselves? Obviously, training costs money, and firms seek to minimize costs. But, if the cognitive psychologists are right, employers could be in a better position than schools to use at least some portion of the training dollars cost effectively. The objective of this chapter is to review recent research into the respective contributions of schooling, corporate training, and learning-intensive production to the overall skill formation process.

THE SPECTRUM OF INSTITUTIONS FOR DEVELOPING WORK-RELATED KNOWLEDGE AND SKILL

Individuals may seek to acquire work-related skills and knowledge in various settings. These can be arrayed along a spectrum based on their proximity to actual production. At one extreme are school courses in academic subjects. At the other extreme is the work setting itself, which becomes a more important site for learning in places where technology or market forces have accelerated change in the work process. Between these two ends of the proximity-to-work continuum are vocational courses in schools, government-sponsored or subsidized training outside schools, formal instruction provided by employers, and work–school hybrids such as apprenticeship and cooperative education.

For a more concrete sense of how schools and firms participate in skill formation, consider Table 6.1. Here are manufacturing employees' answers to questions in the 1983 Current Population Survey about participation in training either to qualify for the present job or to improve skills since taking the present job (U.S. Department of Labor, 1985). A relatively large proportion of engineers and technicians say they went to school to get the skills or training required to obtain their present jobs, but large fractions of these groups also say they needed formal or informal on-the-job training (OJT). Formal OJT was relatively important for tool and die makers, machinists, repairers, and welders, many of whom have participated in formal apprenticeships. Operators and assemblers relied on informal OJT, either in the current firm or a previous one, to learn skills needed in the current job.

After obtaining their present jobs, relatively large proportions of engineers and technicians continued formal schooling or OJT to improve skills. In contrast, little or no further training of any formal kind is reported by machinists, welders, operators, or assemblers. This is a common pattern (Lillard and Tan, 1986): Employees who have completed more years of formal schooling before starting their careers also spend more time in continued formal training throughout their careers.

Mangum (1989) provides another representation of the spectrum of skill formation mechanisms. He maps the array of training sites by

Table 6.1. Participation in Training to Obtain Job or Improve
Skills, Selected Manufacturing Occupations:
Percent of Total Employment in Occupation

Occupation	Total	School	Formal OJT	Informal OJT
Industrial engineers				
obtain job	85	54	15	41
improve skills	51	21	23	18
Electrical and electronic technicians				
obtain job	88	48	19	39
improve skills	50	20	26	12
Industrial machinery repairers				
obtain job	63	14	18	40
improve skills	37	6	15	18
Tool and die makers				
obtain job	85	25	35	44
improve skills	40	17	10	17
Machinists				
obtain job	74	22	23	43
improve skills	33	7	10	18
Metal working and plastic working machine operators				
obtain job	46	6	7	37
improve skills	22	3	4	15
Welders and cutters				
obtain job	68	20	16	33
improve skills	25	7	5	13
Assemblers				
obtain job	24	4	4	18
improve skills	20	1	4	15

Source: U.S. Department of Labor, 1985: Tables 23 and 45

participants' age and perceived "ability" (see Figure 6.1). Adults spend
more of their time in work settings, as the diagram indicates, although
teenagers' employment rates have been steadily climbing since the early
1960s. The ability axis in Figure 6.1 could also be read as a socio-
economic scale. The mainstream consists of individuals who take a
mixture of academic and vocational courses (Wirt et al., 1989), who
go on to become, for example, secretaries, technicians, supervisors,
and skilled craft workers or machine operators and who receive in
these jobs a mixture of formal and informal OJT with very occasional
classroom courses.

Figure 6.1. Institutions of Employability Development

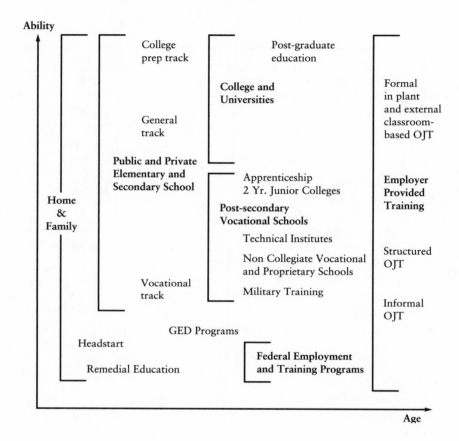

SCHOOLS

Americans look to schools as the main set of institutions for developing work-related knowledge and skill, and there is widespread agreement that preparing students for work is one of the schools' key missions. This section first reviews several kinds of evidence that schooling does contribute to economic productivity. At the same time, there seems to be something seriously amiss in American schools. American students perform poorly on achievement tests compared with students in other countries, even allowing for differences in the percentage of students in each country who take the tests (Bishop, 1989a). This section will therefore address several key weaknesses of the U.S. school system, and will describe some ideas for change. One of the most promising new forms of high school education attempts to integrate the academic and vocational sides of the curriculum, in addition to providing school-supervised jobs that let students apply and extend what they are learning in classrooms.

Schooling Boosts Economic Productivity

On average, individuals who have spent more years in school earn higher incomes. Around the world, the difference in earnings is generally high enough to pay at least a 10 percent real rate of return (often more) on the amount of time and money invested in schooling (Psacharopoulos, 1985). In the United States, recent trends show a growing monetary payoff to schooling at all levels. For instance, Levy (1988, p. 125) reports that for men in the 25–34 age bracket the annual earnings gap between men with 4 years of college and men with 4 years of high school grew from $3,925 in 1973 to $9,405 in 1986 (in constant 1987 dollars, including only men who were employed at least 1 hour during the year). Among women the gap grew from $4,962 to $7,742. The earnings difference has also widened between high school graduates and dropouts. Over the period from 1961 to 1981, among full-time working men aged 25 to 64, the difference grew from $2,387 to $4,489 (in constant 1981 dollars; Grant and Snyder, 1983, p. 191). Evidently, despite a temporary decline during the 1970s (Freeman, 1976), the economic payoff to staying in school remains large.

More direct evidence of education's contribution to productivity has come from studies of independent farmers, both in the United States and in other countries. Farmers with more schooling are more efficient (Jamison and Lau, 1982; Wozniak, 1987). While small farms seem far removed from automated factories, they are an excellent place to look for the direct effect of schooling on productivity because there would be no reason for a person who intended to become a self-employed farmer to stay in school unless it was economically useful. Furthermore, the kinds of improvised problem solving and practical innovation that help make small farmers successful bear some similarity to the trouble shooting and process improvement required of hourly employees in "factories of the future."

Outside the agricultural sector, evidence of education's contribution to productivity comes from studies showing that more highly educated labor is complementary with plant and equipment (Hamermesh and Grant, 1979), and in particular with new plant and equipment (Bartel and Lichtenberg, 1987). Mincer (1989) and Tan (1988) also have found higher average levels of education among employees in industries where productivity growth is high. These findings, and those for farmers, are consistent with the view (Schultz, 1975; Welch, 1970) that schooling enhances individuals' ability to improvise solutions for problems arising from use of new equipment or materials. Schooling pays off for those who are paid to think about how best to use new technology.

The conventional interpretation has been that this payoff to education reflects the value of skills that schooling develops (Denison, 1962; Jorgenson, 1984). Skeptical researchers have questioned whether earning differences really show any contribution of schooling to production (Berg, 1970; Arrow, 1973; Spence, 1973). Schools, they have argued, may simply be a mechanism for selecting more able individuals and certifying their ability to employers. More able individuals can get through school more easily, but the process may not make them any more productive. This argument implies that the additional earnings of people who have been to school longer exceed the actual contribution of schooling to total economic output.

However, more recent research has indicated that the additional earnings of more highly educated people are indeed an accurate measure of schooling's contribution to total output, without discounting for pre-existing ability. Schools contribute positively to economic productivity both by teaching people something and by screening abilities that are useful to certain jobs and not to others (Willis and Rosen, 1979; Garen, 1984).

Dissatisfaction with Schooling

With all this evidence of schools' contribution to the economy, one might expect that schools would be held in high esteem by employers and the public at large. However, this is not the case. A particularly heavy barrage of blame rained on American elementary and secondary schools in the 1980s, beginning with the celebrated Nation at Risk report (National Commission on Excellence in Education, 1983). Much of the criticism has focused on the schools' alleged failure to prepare young people for the workplace of today and tomorrow.

One might dismiss school bashing, like football, as a sport Americans particularly enjoy, observing that both drew large and enthusiastic audiences in the 1980s—except that there really are disturbing signs of poor performance by American students. Scholastic Aptitude Test (SAT) scores declined rather sharply and continuously from 1963 through 1979; the decline seems to have stopped in the 1980s, but the 16–year decline has not been reversed (Hanushek, 1986). According to Murnane (1988, p. 215), "a large part of the decline [in SAT scores] is due to an increase in the number of students with relatively low ability who are taking the test." However, scores on tests other than the SAT have also declined during the same period, and these downward trends are still "not well understood". Moreover, compared to students in other countries, American students in the 1980s have scored low on academic achievement tests (Lapointe et al., 1989), and the poor showing is not attributable to any disparity in the proportion of the relevant age groups who have been tested in the different countries (Bishop, 1989a).

To some extent poor performance comes from lack of trying, and this seems to be part of the problem with American students. Student apathy is chronic and widespread in U.S. schools, especially high schools. In a 1977 survey, high school principals in the United States cited "student apathy" as a serious problem more often than they cited lack of resources, bureaucratic regulation, or any other issue (Abramowitz and Tenenbaum, 1978, p. 86). Likewise, high school teachers report "lack of student interest" as the biggest problem for them (Goodlad, 1984, p. 72). The Goodlad study also asked high school students what was the "one best thing" about their school. The top choice was "my friends," by 34 percent of the students. Only 7 percent chose the "classes I'm taking," and 3 percent said "teachers"—while 8 percent chose "nothing"! (p. 77). A 1984 survey by the National Association of Secondary School Principals found the same thing: Friends and sports ranked much higher for students than did teachers, classes, or learning. The fact that high school students in the United States typically report spending as much time watching television during one weekday as they spend on homework in a whole week (Jones et al., 1983) likewise reflects little interest in school work.

Recently, Bishop (1989a) and Rosenbaum (1989) have suggested four structural reasons for the evident lack of motivation among American high school students. First, for students who go on to work after high school, the labor market rewards completion of high school but not higher grades or test scores. Bishop and Rosenbaum both review the empirical evidence showing that high school grades and test scores have little if any statistical correlation with employment or earnings after high school. Rosenbaum contrasts this lack of linkage here with the situation in Japan, where schools choose students with better grades to nominate for job openings assigned to the school by certain employers. Therefore, while American high school students who are not competing for admission to selective colleges do have a clear economic incentive to stay in high school until they are given a diploma, they have no practical reason to try to learn much while they are there.

Second, Bishop points out that rewarding grades or class rank creates zero-sum competition among peers, forcing many U.S. students into a choice between academic success and a happy social life in high school. Rosenbaum cites a report that one employer actually refused to consider hiring students with high grades, because of a concern that such students would be socially inept!

Third, Bishop notes the almost complete absence of special awards or recognition by schools for students who are not at the very top of their class. Many students in the unrecognized majority therefore reject official schools values. Rosenbaum reminds us that this dilemma was described by Stinchcombe 25 years ago. These features of American schools are not new.

Finally, for students who seek admission to selective colleges and universities, Bishop points out that aptitude tests are important but achievement tests are not. Compared with many other countries where college admission depends on a battery of achievement tests, in the

United States even college-bound high school students have less incentive to learn.

There are two approaches to increasing the incentives for learning. The first is extrinsic: Get students to work harder by making good grades and achievement tests a requirement for getting good jobs or going to college. The second is intrinsic: Get students to work harder by helping them want to learn.

Bishop and Rosenbaum make a number of practical suggestions that fall into the first category. One idea is to create documentation of what an individual high school student has done in a form that employers can quickly obtain. In fact, the Educational Testing Service (ETS) is currently developing a combined transcript/curriculum vitae that could be periodically updated and sent by schools to employers electronically or on paper (Rothman, 1989). The ETS project is actively supported by the National Alliance for Business and the American Business Conference.

The second approach is more subtle and probably more difficult than the first. How can a teacher who interacts with 150 students a day, and spends less than an hour with each one, find a way to make students hungry for knowledge of the subject? It can be done, as charismatic teachers occasionally demonstrate, but the structure and culture of the school militate against it.

Historically, the American high school took its present form during the period from roughly 1890 to 1935. High schools were transformed from elite academies to institutions of mass education. Compulsory schooling and child labor laws were enforced, and minimum wage laws enacted—all in response to the transition from a predominantly rural and agricultural to a predominantly rural and industrial economy. As the hierarchy of jobs in the industrial economy took shape, schools were seen as places to keep children safe from the dangers of low-level work in factories and sweatshops. Keeping children in school also kept them from competing for jobs against adult wage earners, and nourished hope that able children of immigrant or working-class parents could nevertheless rise into the ranks of managers and professionals.

In spite of John Dewey and others, the high school remained organized on the classical, subject-centered model that prevailed when it was still an elite institution. The curriculum is still organized that way, in large part because most colleges and universities are—and for reasons that have more to do with the perpetuation of academic specialties than with the world outside schools. So today, as Sizer (1984, p. 83) put it, "'Taking subjects' in a systematized, conveyor-belt way is what one does in high school. . . . The adolescents are supervised, safely and constructively most of the time, during the morning and afternoon hours, and they are off the labor market. That is what high school is all about."

Actually, increasing numbers of high school students have found their way back into the labor market for 20 or more hours a week during the school year. As discussed below, this provides an opportunity to "recontextualize" classroom learning for some students. But most students' coursework is unrelated to their current jobs. Classrooms, cut off from the world outside, remain boring places for many students much of the time.

This state of affairs never made much sense, but it was tolerated in previous decades when young people were a glut on the labor market. Now, however, the baby boom has entered middle age, and the small size of subsequent cohorts has created a new scarcity of young workers. In the U.S. labor market of the 1980s and 1990s, "warehousing" young people in schools is less tolerable than before. This may account for the current interest in altering incentive structures that have been allowed to undermine students' motivations for so long.

Vocational Education, Old and New

What can be done to cultivate students' interest in school? One early answer was vocational education, which became a common feature in American comprehensive high schools during the expansion of secondary schooling in the early decades of this century. Vocational education was seen, and continues to be seen, as a way to keep non-college-bound students interested in finishing high school (Bell, 1975; Weber, 1987; Kennedy, 1988). The practical content and relatively informal conduct of vocational shops and laboratories are seen as appealing to students who chafe in conventional academic classes (Goodlad, 1984). The fact that so many students elect to take vocational courses in high school is prima facie evidence that some students would have less reason to come to school if those courses were not available. There is also some statistical evidence that taking vocational classes has a significant, though small, effect on reducing the probability that a student will drop out of school (Mertens et al., 1982; Catterall and Stern, 1986).

While vocational education may help motivate some otherwise unmotivated students, it also has contributed to invidious tracking (Oakes, 1985). Federal laws have defined vocational education as preparation for occupations not ordinarily requiring a bachelor's degree. Although federal money pays only about 10 percent of the cost of vocational education, federal laws and regulations have had a major influence on shaping vocational programs. Most high school vocational classes are therefore oriented toward nonprofessional, nonmanagerial jobs. Since these jobs, on average, offer lower income and, in the eyes of some people, lower prestige than professional or managerial careers, vocational education can become stigmatized.

In response to this problem and to the academic "excellence" movement of the 1980s, instructional objectives for vocational courses have been expanded to include more proficiency in academic subjects. For example, the California State Department of Education has developed model curriculum standards and program frameworks for secondary vocational programs. Under the heading of General Employability Skills are standards and proficiencies in listening and speaking, reading, writing, grammar, capitalization and punctuation, spelling and vocabulary, whole number math, decimals and fractions, measurements and tables, and computer awareness, among others. In addition, standards and proficiencies that are specific to particular industries contain a certain amount of general, theoretical knowledge. For example, California high school students preparing for careers in financial services are expected to be able to "demonstrate an understanding of the nature of credit and its influence on the economy, business, and the individual."

Representatives of large employers have asserted that tomorrow's workers will need not only a solid foundation of basic academic skills and knowledge, but also general cognitive skills in problem solving and "learning to learn" (National Academy of Sciences, 1984; Committee for Economic Development, 1985). These objectives have also been incorporated into new vocational curricula. For instance, the Occupational Education curriculum developed in New York State includes an Introduction to Technology for grades seven and eight. This course features segments on using technology and technological systems to solve problems. Students are invited to learn about problem solving by taking on real projects such as improving air quality in the classroom, using a computer to transmit a text from one school to another, or designing a community service activity that addresses a local technological problem (University of the State of New York, 1987).

Vocational "academies," which organize the core academic curriculum of the high school around a vocational theme, are an important example of programs that combine academic subjects and general cognitive development with vocational education. For instance, some academies focus on computer-related occupations, others on electronics or health care. Each academy is organized as a school within a school, where students take most of their classes together, a team of teachers collaborate on curriculum, and local employers are directly involved in several important ways (Dayton et al., 1987).

The vocational academies in Philadelphia and California have selected students who had poor attendance, low grades, and few course credits at the end of freshman year, and who therefore seemed unlikely to finish high school. Evaluations of these academy students show that they have progressed more successfully through high school than other students in the same schools who had similarly poor records at the end of freshman year (Stern et al., 1988, 1989). Academies solve the motivation problem for some students by integrating a group of students and teachers, a school curriculum, and workplace applications into a more coherent whole. Academies also solve the tracking problem by including sufficiently rigorous academic content to enable students to go right to college if they wish.

Working Students and Cooperative Education

Since the advent of mass secondary education, discussions of school and work have assumed that the former precedes the latter. That was true for most students during the middle decades of the current century. However, it is not true now. Working for pay while in high school or college has increasingly become the norm in recent years. Greenberger and Steinberg (1986) have pieced together various government figures from 1947 to 1980 for 16 and 17 year olds who were attending school. Among boys, the labor force participation rate rose from 27 to 44 percent, and for girls it rose from 17 to 41 percent (p. 15). Labor force participation rates measure the fractions of a population who are employed or looking for work at a given point in time. Rates measuring cumulative work experience are higher. For instance, data from the 1980 High School and Beyond survey revealed that 80 to 90 percent of high school students had some kind of paid work experience by the time they graduated (Lewin-Epstein, 1981).

The employment rate of college students has also been rising. From 1959 to 1986, it rose from 35 to 56 percent among females, and from 50 to 57 percent among males (Stern and Nakata, 1991). For males and females combined, the percentage employed rose from 45 to 56. These numbers include part-time and full-time students between the ages of 16 and 34, at both two-year and four-year colleges. Most of the increase occurred during the 1970s, despite the relative surplus of young workers in that period due to the 1945–60 baby boom. The steadily rising trend also stretched through the 1960s and 1980s. Economic explanations, such as the rising cost of college, do not seem to account for the trend. A desire for greater financial independence, especially among women, may well be the motivation.

The fact that most students now hold paid jobs during the school year can exacerbate problems of motivation and performance. Work time may crowd out homework time. Students who have spent the previous evening at work are sometimes tired in class the next day. Concerns about work may distract attention from school demands. Students who go to work every day do not have to rely on teachers to tell them what the outside world is like, and may therefore be more resistant to teachers' authority. There is evidence that students who work during high school get less postsecondary schooling (Mortimer and Finch, 1986), although they earn more money after they leave high school (this evidence is reviewed in Stern et al., 1990). This and other evidence caused Greenberger and Steinberg (1986) to warn that paid employment for students may make them "economically rich, but . . . psychologically poor."

Nevertheless, the fact that most students are working creates an important opportunity to "situate" more learning in the practical context of students' jobs. For instance, the vocational academies described previously arrange summer jobs for students that are related to the course content they have been studying. This kind of connection reinforces students' motivation at school, and enriches their experience on the job. If such connections were to occur more often, the fact of students' working could be converted from an educational liability to an asset.

A traditional mechanism for connecting school with paid employment is cooperative education, which was imported into the United States during the first decade of this century. It started in the four-year colleges, and still flourishes there, where it usually involves students spending a year or semester in full-time work between periods of full-time study (Cooperative Education Research Center, 1987).

In contrast to this "alternating" form of cooperative education, which prevails in four-year colleges, a "parallel" form predominates in high schools and two-year colleges. Students in the parallel mode spend part of the day or week in classes and the remainder of the day or week in paid employment. In high schools and two-year colleges, the co-operative method is most often used as part of vocational education, and is called cooperative *vocational* education. About 700,000 students were enrolled in these programs in 1981–82 (Craft, 1984).

Use of the cooperative method in vocational education has been sanctioned by federal policy, since regulations were written implementing the 1917 Smith–Hughes Act, which first provided federal support for vocational education. Students are given course credit for writing a paper, fulfilling their training plan, or taking a class in connection with their job. The defining characteristic of cooperative vocational education is the close connection between students' activities on the job and in the classroom. Normally the classroom instructor arranges job placements and writes a training plan that details what each student is expected to learn on the job. The job supervisor evaluates a student's performance in terms of these training objectives, and this evaluation becomes part of the student's grade in the "co-op" class. The classroom instructor usually has some release time to visit students' job sites and monitor the situation. "Cooperation" thus entails job supervisors taking on some of the responsibility of instructors, and vice versa.

Most cooperative education arrangements are worked out locally, between individual employers and school staff, subject to various state laws and local customs. One example of a cooperative education program that has been organized on a national scale is General Motors' Automotive Service Educational Program (ASEP), which prepares service technicians to work in General Motors (GM) dealerships around the country (Casner-Lotto, 1988). Local community colleges and GM dealers cooperate in supervising a planned two-year sequence of full-time work and full-time study periods lasting one or two months at a time. Before they begin the program, ASEP students sign employment agreements with the dealers. This in itself is not unusual: students in cooperative education programs other than ASEP may also be required to find their jobs at the outset. What is most unusual about ASEP is how a whole sequence of community college courses is integrated with related work experience.

Evaluations of cooperative vocational education have generally found that co-op students express more positive attitudes toward school and work than other students. After leaving school, co-op students generally have not been found to prosper any more than non-co-op students in the labor market. (A review of the research is in Stern et al., 1990.) However, much of this research has serious shortcomings, including inadequate control for the fact that many non-co-op students also have paid jobs, and some of these non-co-op jobs also have educational and economic value.

Ironically, the educational reform movement of the 1980s probably has cut into cooperative vocational education enrollments. A major feature of these reforms in almost every state has been to increase the number of academic courses required for high school graduation. A similar movement has occurred in two-year colleges. As a result, students have less time in their schedules to take vocational classes, especially those that occupy two-period blocks, as many co-op classes do. Cutting cooperative education seems perverse at a time when cognitive psychologists are calling for more situated learning, and cooperative education is specifically being advocated as a valuable program for the "forgotten half" of the high school students who do not go right to college (William T. Grant Foundation, 1988; Committee for Economic Development, 1985).

Apprenticeship

In the United States, approximately 300,000 individuals are enrolled in formal apprenticeships (U.S. Department of Labor, 1989). Most apprenticeships are governed by joint agreements between labor unions and employers' associations, and typically require three or four years to earn journeyman's papers. There is evidence that young men enrolling in apprenticeships after graduating from high school obtain higher earnings for at least 10 years than other young men who do not go to college or enter apprenticeships. Currently, the Office of Work-Based Learning in the U.S. Department of Labor is exploring the possibility of creating opportunities for "structured workplace training" where formal apprenticeships do not exist.

Worldwide, the most extensive and apparently successful system of formal apprenticeship is in the Federal Republic of Germany (Hamilton, 1990). Currently 1.7 million young people are apprenticing with approximately half a million employers to earn formal certification in 380 different occupations (Schmidt, 1989). About 70 percent of the 16–19 age group are enrolled in apprenticeships (Raddatz, 1989). In comparison, formal apprenticeships in the United States, which usually start at age 18, enroll only about 2 percent of the 18–21 age group.

German apprenticeship standards are developed and examinations given by the Federal Institute for Vocational Training, in concert with representatives of employers and labor unions. Unlike employers in the United States, German employers have opposed locating more training in the schools, and prefer to keep it at the workplace.

Government-SponsoredTraining Not Contracted Directly with Schools

The U.S. government sponsors a number of programs intended to prepare individuals for employment. The Job Training Partnership Act (JTPA) is currently the largest; it replaced the Comprehensive Employment and Training Act (CETA) in 1982. A large fraction of CETA funds had been supporting public employment; JTPA concentrates almost entirely on training.

This and other federal training programs are targeted for needy individuals: low income, unemployed, on welfare, and at-risk youth. Although not administered through the school system, training supported by federal programs in the end is often provided by schools, or by community-based educational organizations. For recent descriptions of federal training programs, see Barnow and Aron (1989) or Simms (1989). Many states also sponsor such programs (Creticos and Sheets, 1989).

CORPORATE TRAINING

In addition to education and training in schools, most employed people also have opportunities for learning in connection with their work. These opportunities are both formal and informal. Formal training occurs in classrooms or other settings away from employees' actual work locations. Opportunities for informal learning occur at the actual work location, while the learner is working.

What employed people learn in connection with their work ranges from what other people already know to how to solve new problems. As Carnevale and Schulz (1988, p. 18) put it, "The ability to seize and sustain a competitive edge requires two kinds of technical learning systems: one to teach employees and another to learn from them." Learning as problem solving is required in connection with new products, new technologies, or new organizational arrangements. This kind of learning is unique to the workplace itself; it cannot happen in classrooms separated from the work process. While simulations outside the work process may help develop the capacity to solve problems, actually solving a problem that has immediate, practical consequences is, by definition, part of the work process itself.

Given the potential benefits, how much time and money should be invested in work-related education or training? Each of the three partners in these investments—taxpayers, employers, and trainees (including unions representing them)—might answer that the others should invest more. But should the total investment be augmented, or is the current level about right? One approach to answering this question is to estimate the rate of return on investment in training. A high current rate of return implies that the level of investment should increase. Some recently estimated rates of return are reported below.

Another approach is to consider how learning can be achieved at less cost. Many employers have made deliberate efforts to enhance opportunities and motivation for learning in the work process to speed the pace of productive problem solving. As described below, some of these employers are manufacturing firms that have undertaken such efforts as part of the transition to more highly automated production. Building a "factory of the future" is widely seen to include redesign of jobs and relationships among jobs, adoption of new compensation systems, and making a greater commitment to employment security for hourly employees. These can be seen as investments whose payoff is learning—at a faster rate, and therefore at a lower cost.

How Much Company-Sponsored Training Currently Occurs?

Table 6.2 lists amounts reportedly spent by various firms on formal training. The last three entries show the ranges reported in three different surveys. Unfortunately, this listing is less informative than it may appear. The numbers on different lines are not all measuring the same things. Some include only the direct cost to the companies of formal training they do in house. Others also include training contracted to outside vendors. Some count, in addition, tuition reimbursement for work-related courses employees take on their own. Furthermore, the companies and samples listed in Table 6.2 are not representative of all U.S. employers.

With such mushy numbers, we can make only an order-of-magnitude estimate that the average employee works in a firm that spends between $100 and $1,000 a year on formal training for each employee, and probably less than $500. With total employment at about 110 million people in the United States, that implies a total expenditure somewhere between, very roughly, $10 billion and $100 billion a year on formal training by employers, and probably less than $50 billion. This is consistent with the often-repeated figure of $30 to $40 billion put forward by Craig and Evers in 1983—a figure they derived by supposing that the average employer spent about half of what AT&T did per employee! By way of comparison, U.S. institutions of higher education spent roughly $60 billion a year on instruction in the mid-1980s (Stern

Table 6.2. Reported Expenditure on Formal Training Per
Employee in Various U.S. Companies

Company	Source	Year	Expenditure per employee ($)
A.T.& T.	Eurich, 1985	1980	1,700
IBM	Eurich, 1985	1982	1,370
Travelers	Casner-Lotto, 1988	1986	500
New England Telephone	Casner-Lotto, 1988	1984	577
Pacific Bell	Casner-Lotto, 1988	1986	448
Corning Glass	Casner-Lotto, 1988	1986	74
Manpower Temporary Services	Casner-Lotto, 1988	1986	100
Motorola	Casner-Lotto, 1988	1986	430
Motorola	Business Week, 1989	1989	571
BNA survey	Mangum, 1989	1984	122–250
Delaney survey	Mangum, 1989	1986	350–1,400
Columbia survey	Bartel, 1989	1987	359–1,343

and Williams, 1986). These estimates do not include the cost of wages, salaries, and benefits paid to employees for time spent in formal or informal training during regular working hours.

Surveys that have inquired into the prevalence and duration of formal and informal training for employees are summarized in Table 6.3, from Brown (1989). Like the surveys on companies' direct expenditure, surveys of employees' time involvement also have used various definitions of training. However, it appears that roughly 20–30 percent of employees report having been involved in some kind of formal or informal training. Other studies, summarized by Mincer (1989), report that employees currently involved in training spend approximately 20–25 percent of their time on it. In any particular period, therefore, employees in the aggregate are spending something like 4–7 percent of their paid time in training.

Based on these percentages, Mincer (forthcoming) calculated that the value of employees' time invested in formal and informal training in 1987 was roughly $150 billion. Mincer also estimates the total investment by employers in training at roughly $150 billion a year based on findings from the Employment Opportunities Pilot Project survey.

An estimate of $150 billion a year for employers' investment in formal

Table 6.3. Summary of Extent of Employer-Provided Training

Type of measure	Study	Data set	Time interval	Specific measure	Proportion or average value
Received training	Haber (1985)	1984 SIPP	Time with current employer	Employer-provided training program	8%
	Lillard and Tan (1985)	1983 CPS	Time with current employer	Company (formal) training program	12%
				Informal OJT	15%
				Other training	5%
	Hollenbeck and Willke (1985)	1983 CPS	Time with current employer	Company (formal) training program	11%
				Informal OJT	14%
	Tierney (1983b)	1981 CPS	Last year	Employer-provided training programs	5%
	Duncan and Hoffman (1978)	1975 PSID	Currently receiving	Formal training or OJT	20%
Weeks of training	Haber (1985)	1984 SIPP	Time since 1980 with current employer	Weeks employer-paid training at work	6
	Tierney (1983a)	1978 CPS	Last year	Weeks of employer-provided training	9
	Bishop and Kang (1984)	1982 EOPP	NA	Weeks to become fully trained	7
	Duncan and Hoffman (1978)	1975 PSID	NA fully trained	Weeks to become	86
Hours of training	Tierney (1983a)	1978 CPS	NA	Hours of employer-provided training	120
	Bishop and Kang (1984)	1982 EOPP	First 3 months on job	Hours formal training	11
				Hours informal training by supervisors	51
				Hours informal training by co-workers	24

Source: Brown, 1989.

SIPP = Survey of Income and Program Participation;
CPS = Current Population Survey;
PSID = Panel Study of Income Dynamics;
EOPP = Employment Opportunity Pilot Project

and informal training combined is roughly consistent with the estimated expenditure of $50 billion on formal training alone, based on Table 6.2. As shown in Tables 6.1 and 6.3, most employees report somewhat less participation in formal than informal training. It is plausible, therefore, that if the costs of formal training (training department budgets) run to $40 or $50 billion a year, then the cost of informal training (supervisors' and co-workers' time spent teaching trainees) would be another $100 billion.

In sum, given the limited data available, a reasonable guess of what employee training currently costs is nearly $300 billion a year as of 1987. This figure includes close to $50 billion for the direct cost of delivering formal training, another $100 billion to deliver informal training, and $150 billion for trainees' time.

Little Incentive for Employers to Invest in Training

With such vast amounts of money spent for ongoing education and training of employees, it is understandable that employers say they wish schools could have done more of the job. Employees, for their part, see going back to school or into formal training as time consuming, stressful, and sometimes threatening to self-esteem. Neither employers nor employees can be expected to relish paying these costs.

Nevertheless, the benefits of company-sponsored training may more than justify the cost. Increases in productivity and earnings may be so large in proportion to the amount of time and money invested that the rate of return exceeds what is available from other investments. If so, more resources should somehow be invested in employee development.

The most authoritative estimates of rate of return to employee training and development have been calculated by Mincer (forthcoming), who found rates of return ranging from 8.5 to 31 percent for employees. Despite these rather high numbers, Mincer draws no firm conclusion about whether employees are investing too much or too little: "...there is no definite evidence of underinvestment, though it clearly cannot be ruled out, given the wide range of estimates."

Mincer and other economists have traditionally assumed that employees who get training on the job must accept a lower rate of pay, if that training would increase their potential earnings outside the firm that trains them. [Since Becker (1975, first edition 1964), such training has been called *general*, as opposed to *firm-specific*.] If jobs that included training did not offer a lower rate of pay than similar jobs where training was not included, the argument goes, an excess of qualified individuals would apply for the jobs that provided training, and market forces would bring pay rates down (Mincer, 1962; Becker, 1964; Rosen, 1972; Mincer, 1974). If employees had to sacrifice little or no pay in order to get general training, then the investment would cost little or nothing to them. Since on-the-job training does yield subsequent higher earnings for employees (Lillard and Tan, 1986; Tan, 1988; Mincer, 1989; Barro et al., 1989; Bishop, 1989a; Mangum, 1989), their rate of return would be very large—or infinite, if their cost is literally zero. Employees' appetite for training would then be limited only by their distaste for the effort required.

In fact, the assumption that employees must finance their own general training can be questioned on various grounds. Feuer, Glick, and Desai (1987) argue that, to protect investments in firm-specific training, companies may also share some of the cost (and benefit) of general training. Barron, Black, and Loewenstein (1989) propose a different theoretical rationale: that on-the-job training is complementary with ability, so that more able employees, who must receive higher wages, also receive more training, both specific and general. Feuer et al. and Barron et al. both tested their predictions with data sets that include direct measures of how much training individuals received. Both tests found that employees who were receiving more training (some of which is assumed to be general) did not have to accept lower wages. Bishop (1989a), based on findings from a different pair of data sets, also concludes that employees do not appear to sacrifice earnings while they receive general training at work.

A logical interpretation of this evidence is that employees' paid time spent in training really is a cost to employers, who also pay the direct costs of formal and informal training. In the aggregate, this adds up to the $300 billion figure derived above. But only about half of the additional output that results from this training is kept by employers; the other half is paid to employees. Since Mincer estimated that employees' rate of return would be somewhere between 8.5 and 31 percent if they were to absorb the cost of their own time in training ($150 billion), the rate of return to employers would only be about half of that, if employers were paying for employees' time plus direct costs ($300 billion total).

The social rate of return (gains to employers and employees combined, relative to total cost) would be 8.5–31 percent, according to this new interpretation. Employees would benefit greatly from expansion of company-sponsored training, but such expansion would not be very profitable for employers since more training entails additional direct cost as well as additional employees' time diverted from production.

LEARNING-INTENSIVE PRODUCTION

Diverting employees' time from production and investing it in training is one of the ways firms arrange for employees to learn, but it is not the only way. Some firms also deliberately incorporate learning into the work

process itself. When production becomes more learning intensive, acquisition of new knowledge and skill is built into the job, and improvements
in quality and productivity depend on the speed of learning.

As will now be described, firms use a variety of techniques to achieve
"learning intensive production." To the extent that learning becomes
an integral part of the production process, investment in training cannot
be estimated in the conventional way because it is not possible to
distinguish between time spent learning and time spent working. As
one manager put it, under these circumstances "training is like
breathing". In this situation, the important economic question is not
just whether firms sacrifice optimal amounts of employees' paid time
for knowledge or skill development, but also whether enough employers
have adopted a method of production that produces learning through
the arrangement of work itself.

Surprisingly, despite the extent of the literature about training and
skill formation in workplaces, the process itself remains a black
box. Appropriate compensation plans can increase employees' motivation to learn, employment security and a culture of collaboration
can create trust and further enhance motivation, new technology may
provide more opportunities to learn, a small plant size may facilitate
communication, and "doing by learning" (see the following discussion)
may increase the effectiveness of formal training—but neither researchers nor practitioners seem to have worked out any systematic account
of how learning *happens* in the work process itself.

To illustrate what a process model of learning through work might
consist of, Figure 6.2 sketches components of the process by which
an employee acquires the capacity to solve a nonroutine but recurrent
problem. For instance, an example of such a problem would be what
to do when successive heatings of a printed circuit in the process of
fabrication cause unanticipated changes in components that result in
defects. Engineers may need to redesign the circuit, but it is sometimes
possible to avoid costly redesign by tweaking the production process. How
can employees learn to solve such problems? Figure 6.2 suggests it
would be worthwhile to describe carefully how such learning occurs,
and to identify conditions that may facilitate learning. Underlying these
specific conditions lies a set of organizational arrangements that will
be described in the following.

Doing by Learning

Formal training can contribute to the integration of learning and production
by bringing the work process into the classroom itself. This approach uses
the class as an opportunity to produce specific ideas for improving efficiency
or quality in the production process. Such a class may begin by eliciting
statements from participants about problems they see in their own work

Figure 6.2. Process Model: Learning To Solve Non-routine Problems

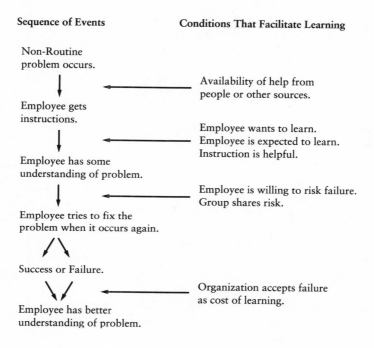

Sequence of Events   Conditions That Facilitate Learning

Non-Routine
problem occurs.

Availability of help from
people or other sources.

Employee gets
instructions.

Employee wants to learn.
Employee is expected to learn.
Instruction is helpful.

Employee has some
understanding of problem.

Employee is willing to risk failure.
Group shares risk.

Employee tries to fix the
problem when it occurs again.

Success or Failure.

Organization accepts failure
as cost of learning.

Employee has better
understanding of problem.

situations. After the instructor presents the new conceptual material, participants divide into small groups to practice applying the new information to real problems. An immediate outcome of the class, therefore, is a set of written suggestions that can be developed further outside class, or in some cases, implemented directly. Since the classes yield practical suggestions that have economic value, this may be called "doing by learning."

For example, at one company, a class for production workers on the concept of cycle time produced the following suggestions, among others: inspect samples of parts before they are sent out of the storeroom to the production line; make someone responsible for daily checking of prototype models (used by assemblers as guides) to ensure that they incorporate the most recent changes in engineering specifications; have downstream sections tell upstream sections if they spot defects; and start doing preventive maintenance on tools and certain equipment. These suggestions embody one of the key ideas from the class: that reducing cycle time and improving quality go hand in hand, because "doing it right the first time" saves time later in the production process. These and other suggestions from that class were compiled for use by a team consisting of production workers and supervisors, who were responsible for finding ways to reduce cycle time in their part of the factory.

At some companies, formal courses are developed and taught by production workers themselves, with training staff acting as resources and organizers. This gives classes more legitimacy for participants. It also increases the likelihood that class activities will have real payoffs, both from class exercises themselves and from future applications of the skills learned. A union leader remarked that the "key to success of the training is building on practical experience." At the union leader's firm, producing ideas to improve efficiency, quality, and safety is seen as part of a production worker's job. Other companies are trying to change their culture along the same lines.

Doing by learning—eliciting new ideas from participants in formal classes—expresses the principle that employees really are paid to think. In companies where this is not true, doing by learning is less likely to happen.

Using Slack Time for Informal Training

The real key to learning intensive production is learning through the actual work process itself. In part, this entails using slack time for problem solving, coaching, exchanging information, and other kinds of informal training.

I have observed this happening in a small (250 employees) insurance company. In 1984, following several years of experimentation with quality circles and work teams, approximately 30 employees from Premium Accounting, Policy Issue, and Policyholder Service were combined into a single Customer Service unit. Seventeen job titles were consolidated into one: Customer Service Representative. Within the unit, employees are organized in four teams, each responsible for serving a particular geographic region. Customer Service teams must perform the whole range of functions previously carried out in Premium Accounting, Policy Issue, and Policyholder Service. Within a team, any Representative may perform any function she knows how to do. (The group is entirely female.) However, since employees who came from the three separate units possessed different sets of skills, no single employee knew how to perform all the team's functions. Cross-training was necessary to prevent bottlenecks. Instead of providing this cross-training in formal classes, Valley Life is encouraging team members to teach one another.

To motivate Customer Service Representatives to use slack time for learning instead of pure relaxation, the company designed and implemented a "Pay for Learning" system. The ratio of potential top-to-bottom pay for Customer Service Representatives is approximately two to one. To climb the pay scale, an employee must rate herself "100 percent qualified" on the range of specific tasks performed by the teams. Self-ratings must be reviewed by the team and by management, and are subject to reversal if errors in a particular procedure were later traced to an employee who has claimed competence in that procedure. The amount of additional pay awarded for mastering each task or procedure is stated in terms of the estimated amount of time required to achieve mastery. The entire set of skills is worth 321 "weeks."

In addition to motivating individuals to learn, this company's system of pay for learning also reinforces the teams. All members of a team can earn up to 49 weeks' credit—a raise of 15 percent over base pay—if the team as a whole were to achieve a set of skills that includes scheduling work, selecting new team members (from a short list proposed by management), and testing new products or procedures. Thus, the socio-technical system and the compensation system both support continual learning with a minimum of formal, off-line training. The result is that employees are constantly asking each other questions about how to perform certain procedures, or trading information and insights about particular cases. These conversations take place on the fly, during short lulls that would otherwise not be used productively. As noted below, a growing number of companies have now adopted some kind of pay-for-knowledge system (see U.S. Department of Labor, 1988).

Even without pay for knowledge, use of slack time for learning can be motivated by other considerations. I have observed this in a manufacturing company where approximately 2000 production workers are employed in the firm's one large plant. About 400 of these are Team Leaders; the rest are called Team Members. Each team is responsible for a segment of the assembly line, where it balances job duties to allow team members to work at the same pace. Members rotate jobs and do much cross-training informally. "Versatility charts" displayed near the team's work area show each member's level of proficiency in each operation, along a four-step continuum: (1) has knowledge of the job, (2) can do the job with assistance, (3) can do it without assistance, (4) can teach the job. If a team member is absent, a glance at the chart will tell the team leader who is competent to fill in. Team leaders have an incentive to help team members become proficient in more operations, because the team leader is responsible for making sure the team still gets its work done when any member is absent. Team leaders therefore act as teachers and coaches, using occasional short lulls in the production process for informal training. The company does not have a pay-for-knowledge compensation plan, but team members are motivated to learn new operations by team spirit or peer pressure, since a more versatile member is more useful to the team, and also by their desire not to do the same operation all the time.

This company has a well-developed Just-in-Time inventory control system in operation that ensures that individual operators do not build up large buffer stocks. As a result, if a problem were to arise in one part of the assembly process, a whole segment of the line would have to stop moving. At this point, workers are expected to put their heads together to help solve the immediate problem and to figure out how to prevent such problems from happening again. Stopping the produc-

tion line and using down time for problem solving are important features
of the just-in-time system. At this company, the line is reported to be
stopped between 2 and 5 percent of the time. Other companies currently
in the process of transition to Just-in-Time manufacturing are also
expecting production workers to engage in continual learning and
problem solving during interruptions of the production process (see
Bailey's studies of the apparel industry, 1989a, c).

Collaborative Employment Practices*

To motivate employees to use their time and intelligence for continual
learning and problem solving, a number of American employers in recent
years have experimented with new forms of worker involvement and
collaboration. Often modeled after Japanese labor–management systems,
these experiments have included such innovations as greater use of work
teams, quality circles, greater flexibility in the allocation of workers and
in job classification, and restructuring of management rights. All involve
greater amounts of management consultation with employees as well as
some worker involvement in decision-making.

Varied in nature, and extending across public and private sectors,
manufacturing and nonmanufacturing, union and nonunion establishments, these experiments represent a substantial departure from traditional labor–management relationships in the United States. In contrast
to similar experiments in the 1960s and 1970s, these recent changes
have not been aimed at dispelling "blue-collar blues," but at improving
productive efficiency. As Deming (1981–82) pointed out, to improve
quality and efficiency it is necessary to "Drive out fear. Most people
on a job, and even people in management positions, do not understand
what the job is, nor what is right or wrong. Moreover, it is not clear
to them how to find out. Many of them are afraid to ask questions
or to report trouble. The economic loss from fear is appalling. It is
necessary, for better quality and productivity, that people feel secure."

The "Japanese-style" management philosophy includes the belief that
training is a necessary element of the system and learning is a never-
ending process (Bradley and Hill, 1983; Kochan et al., 1986; Cohen-
Rosenthal and Burton, 1987; Heckscher, 1988). For instance, at New
United Motors Manufacturing, Inc. (NUMMI), the joint venture between General Motors and Toyota in which GM is learning Japanese-
style management, production workers have been given classes in *kaizen*,
which means continuous improvement. One slogan repeated at NUMMI
is, "If you don't have a problem, that's a problem!" The status quo
can always be improved. Seeing problems as inevitable and learning
how to solve them are more productive than suppressing problems or
fixating on whom to blame.

Employers are asking workers to develop skills in human relations

---

*This section was written in collaboration with Michael Reich

that allow more cooperative and mutually beneficial labor–management practices. Such training is intended to advance the transition from adversarial to collaborative labor–management systems, and to increase the chances that new systems will last. Training is provided not only to production workers, but also for first-line supervisors and middle management, who are often most threatened by these changes, and for union leaders.

Workers are also being asked to be more flexible in their job assignments. Numerous automobile plants are now sharply reducing the number of job classifications and implementing the "team concept." In this system, employees work as part of a team, with the team leader taking over some of the duties of the traditional supervisor. Workers are asked to monitor quality and to solve as many production problems as possible by themselves instead of calling in specialized, skilled workers and management. As one union leader said with evident pride, "Our workers are now learning engineering skills and performing some engineering duties" (Brown and Reich, 1988). Similar trends are apparent in such industries as aircraft manufacturing and telecommunications.

Although these changes in employment practices can be introduced in the absence of any new technology—as at NUMMI—this kind of collaboration often increases the role of employees in adopting new technology. In unionized establishments, union leaders are increasingly being asked to contribute their perspectives, and those of their members, before new technologies are introduced. This requires that union leaders and members be given more training in the nature of new technologies.

Some kind of formal employee involvement is becoming more common throughout the economy, not only in manufacturing, but also in finance, trade, government, and other parts of the service sector. In 1982, the New York Stock Exchange surveyed a sample of U.S. corporations employing at least one hundred people, and estimated that 54 percent of employees in this group of companies were in firms that had adopted some kind of program to encourage more sharing of responsibility— for instance, through quality circles, job rotation, or participatory goal-setting. Other indications of increased experimentation with employee involvement in the 1980s are reported by Kochan et al. (1989), and by Levine and Strauss (1989). Improving the organization's ability to learn is one desired outcome of this activity.

Smaller Plants

In learning intensive workplaces, a production worker's job includes the production of ideas. As Reich (1983) put it:

Flexible systems can adapt quickly only if information is widely shared and diffused within them. There is no hierarchy to problem solving: Solutions may come from anyone, anywhere. In flexible-

system enterprises nearly everyone in the production process is responsible for recognizing problems and finding solutions. (p. 135).

Flexibility and employee involvement are easier to achieve in workplaces that are relatively small. There is evidence that, in fact, U.S. manufacturers have reduced average plant size. Based on research by Roger Schmenner, *Business Week* (October 22, 1984)reported the average plant built before 1970 and still operating in 1979 employed 644 people, compared with 241 people in the average plant opened between 1970 and 1979. *Business Week* estimated the average plant opening in the 1980s would employ 210 people. Smaller factories enable hourly employees to become "part of the flow of ideas," have "an impact on day-to-day operations," and feel "a sense of ownership." This contributes to continued learning.

New Compensation Systems

Financial participation is sometimes a concomitant of employee involvement. Workers develop a "sense of ownership" more naturally as actual owners. Since 1974, employers have been able to receive tax credits for contributing to Employee Stock Ownership Plans (ESOPs). The National Center for Employee Ownership (NCEO) estimates that approximately 8,000 companies had taken steps to establish ESOPs as of 1984. These companies employ approximately 8 percent of the workforce nationwide. The 1984 Deficit Reduction Act contained several provisions designed to spur the growth of ESOPs even further (see Blasi, 1989).

ESOPs are only one form of financial participation by employees. Conventional profit sharing is another. In addition, there are several established procedures—Scanlon plans, Rucker plans, Improshare—that award extra compensation to groups of employees when they improve productivity (Bullock, 1984). These plans have the advantage of tying financial rewards to the group's own efforts; they exclude factors beyond the group's control, such as fluctuations in product demand. For recent discussion of various pay-for-productivity plans, see Blinder (1990).

As illustrated in the insurance company discussed before, some firms are also experimenting with new compensation systems designed to explicitly stimulate employees' acquisition of new skills. "Skill-based pay" makes a person's current rate of pay depend on demonstrated mastery of certain skills and knowledge, not on the particular job the person is performing during the current period (Jenkins and Gupta, 1985; Lawler and Ledford, 1985; U.S. Department of Labor, 1988). Employees gain pay increments by progressing through a sequential "curriculum" of skills and knowledge used in the particular workplace. Skill-based pay epitomizes the integration of continued learning with work in participatory, learning intensive production systems.

Employment Security

While doing by learning produces an immediate payoff from training, the ultimate payoff to the company depends on how long employees remain employed there, and whether they are motivated to keep using what they have been taught in training. Granting some assurance of employment security addresses both of these concerns. Rosow and Zager (1988) argue that employment security is an essential part of a successful human resource strategy.

One way in which employment security increases the payoff from training is virtually self-evident: Firms collect the dividends of training only from employees who stay with them. Avoiding even temporary layoffs helps prolong the employment relationship because some employees—more likely those with better alternative opportunities for employment—quit when they are laid off rather than wait around to be rehired and wonder when they might be laid off again.

Employment security also enhances workers' loyalty and commitment to the company. They can appreciate that the firm is committed to a long-term relationship and is investing in that relationship through training. This appreciation can make employees more willing to take initiative, and to use slack time for learning and problem solving rather than nonproductive activity. Furthermore, employees can understand that, when the company follows a policy of filling new skill demands by training the existing workforce instead of dismissing them and hiring new people who possess the desired skills, it is then incumbent on existing employees to participate willingly in this training. Employment security thus fosters a reciprocal commitment that facilitates continued learning.

The complementarity of training and employment security is evident from statistical studies. Mincer (1989), using the Panel Study of Income Dynamics, found employees who said their 1976 jobs had required more OJT tended to stay longer with their 1976 employers. Tan (1988), using the Current Population Survey, found a lower incidence of company training in states where the unemployment rate is volatile or chronically high. Evidently, employment security promotes training and training promotes employment stability as both employers and employees try to maximize the payoff from the investments they make.

SOME POLICY IMPLICATIONS

This analysis of the strengths and weaknesses of the institutions and incentives for skill formation has several implications for industrial and public policy. These implications are especially important today, when many argue that insufficient "human capital" has become a constraint on the United States' economic competitiveness.

More Formal Training for Production Workers

Rate-of-return studies give reason to believe that employers on the whole may be providing insufficient opportunities and incentives for hourly employees to continue some kind of formal training after they are hired. Some formal instruction would seem to be increasingly necessary to understand new technologies, products, and procedures.

Cole (in this volume, Chapter 7) describes an extensive curriculum of formal training that, in combination with informal training, is designed to teach Japanese production workers how to use advanced "mechatronic" technology. Yet, in the United States, surveys such as those in Table 6.1 indicate that hourly employees traditionally have been given little or no continued schooling or formal training after they start work. In the automobile industry, Krafcik found that the annual hours of training for assembly workers in Japan were nearly 90 on average and more than 300 for new hires, compared to 30 on average and less than 50 for new hires in the United States (U.S. Congress, Office of Technology Assessment, 1990, p. 15). The wisdom of this practice should be reexamined.

United States employers should seriously consider increasing their investment in the training of hourly employees. Making better use of "doing by learning" (bringing the work process into the classroom) or techniques of cooperative education (enabling employees to accomplish certain instructional objectives in their actual work) can alleviate some concerns over the cost of formal training.

More Employment Security

Because employment insecurity reduces the return from both formal and informal on-the-job training, it follows that firms will provide less than the optimal amount of training if they provide less than the optimal degree of employment security. There are reasons to believe that firms do, indeed, provide less than the optimal measure of employment security because in the absence of proactive government policy no one firm has enough incentive to bear the first costs.

One reason for this reluctance has to do with aggregate demand (Levine and Tyson, 1990). It is costly for firms to maintain employment security when the demand for their product is low. But if they did, the wages and salaries they paid would contribute to the demand for other firms' products and thereby mitigate the effects of the decline in demand. By protecting security of employment for their own workers, firms would reduce the necessity of layoffs or discharges in other firms.

If firms provided employment security, they might also contribute to more stable aggregate demand by avoiding some of the inflationary pressure that occurs in tight labor markets (Stern, 1982). Inflationary pressure in tight labor markets results in part from high quit rates when employees see many tempting alternatives to their present jobs. High quit rates disrupt production and drive up unit costs. They also require employers to raise wages and salaries in an effort to retain existing employees or attract replacements, contributing directly to inflation. In contrast, employment security policies could increase employees' attachment to their jobs, leading to lower quit rates, less inflationary pressure, and therefore less need for antiinflationary recessions.

Given these and other possible positive externalities, the aggregate rate of unemployment would tend to be lower on average over time— creating another externality related to the cost of hiring. Some firms routinely discharge or lay off employees as a means of maintaining discipline, reducing excess inventories of finished goods, or changing the skill mix of their labor force. Normally, new employees are eventually hired to replace those who were discharged or laid off and unavailable for recall. Recruiting and hiring new people is costly. The cost is less when there is excess supply in the labor market, as indicated by a large number of unemployed people relative to the number of job vacancies. This kind of slack labor market, therefore, promotes high-discharge, high-layoff policies by firms. Conversely, tight labor markets would reward firms that attempted to maintain greater employment security to avoid the cost of new hires. If labor markets grew tighter because some firms provided employment security, there would be less cost to other firms in following suit.

Market incentives alone will not induce more firms to provide globally optimal levels of employment security; some collective mechanism is required to capture these positive externalities. Any collective action that promoted employment security would also, for reasons given above, promote more training of employees. In effect, such a collective mechanism creates a benign cartel in which employers and employees are all better off than when employers act individually. The kind of learning intensive strategy described in earlier sections of this chapter would be more feasible in an institutional context where all firms had to follow similar policies.

Streeck (1989) claims that collective agreements among employers in Germany, enforced by the government, have enabled that country to remain competitive by requiring more training than individual employers would otherwise provide. Similarly, Soskice (1989) sees the countries that have enjoyed the greatest economic success in the 1980s as "Coordinated Market Economies," which have enforced agreements providing for employment security and large amounts of on-the-job training, among other things. It remains to be seen whether individual firms can profit from this strategy in the United States, where this kind of benign cartel does not exist.

An example of a public program that helps employers offer greater security of employment is the Employment Training Panel in

California. This program supports retraining of employees who have been laid off or are in imminent danger of being laid off. Employers have used the training funds to teach current employees how to use new technologies, instead of discharging existing employees and trying to hire new ones with the requisite skill and knowledge. Case studies of companies that have received Employment Training Panel grants indicate that the availability of such funds has helped move some firms toward a policy of treating employees as long-term assets rather than as short-term costs (Schneider, 1988).

More Use of School–Work Hybrids for Teenagers

If adults are expected to continue learning while they work, how is this capacity acquired? Cognitive psychologists have argued that all learning is "situated" in the context where it occurs. This would seem to imply that the way to acquire a generalizable capacity for learning in the workplace is to become a learner in a variety of workplaces. Cooperative education and other school–work hybrid institutions can provide this kind of experience. By using the workplace as an educational setting, students can practice learning through the process of work itself.

NOTE

This chapter is based in part on research supported by the U.S. Department of Education through a grant to the National Center for Research in Vocational Education at the University of California, Berkeley. Conclusions do not necessarily represent official U.S. Department of Education Policy. Clair Brown and Michael Reich collaborated in the research and Paul Adler contributed insightful editing, but only the author is responsible for any errors in this chapter.

REFERENCES

Abramowitz, S., and E. Tenenbaum. 1978. *High school '77, a Survey of Public Secondary School Principals*. Washington, D.C.: National Institute of Education.

Adler, P. 1986. "New Technologies, New Skills." *California Management Review* 29: 9–28.

Aoki, M. (Ed.). 1984. *The Economic Analysis of the Japanese Firm*. New York: North-Holland.

Aoki, M. 1988. *Information, Incentives, and Bargaining in the Japanese Economy*. New York: Cambridge University Press.

Arrow, K. J. 1973. "Higher education as a filter." *Journal of Public Economics* 2: 193–216.

Bailey, T. 1989a. "Changes in the Nature and Structure of Work: Implications for Employer-Sponsored Training." New York: Columbia University, Conservation of Human Resources Project.

Bailey, T. 1989b. "Technology, skills, and education in the apparel industry, technical report." New York: National Center on Education and Employment, Teachers College, Columbia University.

Bailey, T. 1989c. "The Transformation of Technology, Skills, and Work Organization in the Apparel Industry." New York: Columbia University, Conservation of Human Resources Project.

Bailey, T. (unpublished). "Changes in the Nature and Structure of Work: Implications for Skill Requirements and Skill Formation." Unpublished manuscript, Columbia University, New York.

Barnow, B. S., and L. Y. Aron. 1989. "Survey of Government-Provided Training Programs." In U.S. Department of Labor Commission on Workforce Quality and Labor Market Efficiency, *Investing in People: A strategy to Address America's Workforce Crisis. Background_papers* Vol 1:493–564.

Barron, J. M., D. A. Black and M. A. Loewenstein. 1989. "Job Matching and on-the-Job Training." *Journal of Labor Economics* 7(1):1–19.

Bartel, A. P. 1989. "Utilizing Corporate Survey Data to Study Investments in Employee Training and Development." New York: Columbia University, Graduate School of Business.

Bartel, A. P. and F. R. Lichtenberg. 1987. "The Comparative Advantage of Educated Workers in Implementing New Technology." *The Review of Economics and Statistics* 69(1):1–11.

Becker G. S. 1975. *Human Capital* (2nd ed.). Chicago: University of Chicago Press.

Bell, T. 1975. *Hearings, U.S. House Subcommittee on Elementary, Secondary, and Vocational Education.* Washington, D.C.: U.S. Government Printing Office: 308–9.

Berg, I. 1970. *Education and Jobs: The Great Training Robbery.* New York: Praeger.

Bishop, J. 1989a. "Incentives for Learning: Why American High School Students Compare so Poorly to their Counterparts Overseas." In U.S. Department of Labor Commission on Workforce Quality and Labor Market Efficiency, *Investing in People: A Strategy to Address America's Workforce Crisis. Background Papers* Vol. 1:1–84.

Bishop, J. 1989b. "Occupational Training in High School: When Does it Pay Off?" *Economics of Education Review* 8(1):1–15.

Blasi, J. R. 1989. *Employee Ownership: Revolution or Ripoff?* Cambridge, Mass: Ballinger.

Blinder, A.S. (ed.) 1990. *Paying for Productivity: A Look at the Evidence.* Washington, D.C.: Brookings.

Bradley, K. and S. Hill. 1983. "After Japan: The Quality Circle Transplant and Productive Efficiency." *British Journal of Industrial Relations* 21(3):291–311.

Brown, C. 1989. "Empirical Evidence on Private Training." In US Department of Labor Commission on Workforce Quality and Labor Market Efficiency, *Investing in people: A Strategy to Address America's Workforce Crisis. Background Papers*, Vol. 1:301–30.

Brown, C., and M. Reich. 1988. "When Does Union-Management Cooperation Work?" In D. Mitchell (Ed.). *Can California be Competitive and Caring?* Los Angeles: University of California, Los Angeles.

Brown, J. S., A. Collins, and P. Duguid. 1989. "Situated Cognition and the Culture of Learning." *Educational Researcher* 18(1):32–41.

Bullock, R. J. 1984. "Gainsharing—A Successful Track Record." *World of Work Report* 9(8):3–4.

Burke, G., and R. W. Rumberger. 1987. *The Future Impact of Technology on Work and Education.* Philadelphia: Falmer Press.

Carnevale, A. P. and E. R. Schulz. 1988. "Technical Training in America: How Much and Who Gets It?." *Training and Development Journal* 42(11):18–32.

Casner-Lotto, J. 1988. *Successful Training Stategies.* San Francisco: Jossey–Bass Publishers.

Catterall, J. S. and D. Stern. 1986. "The Effects of Alternative School Programs on High School Completion and Labor Market Outcomes." *Educational Evaluation and Policy Analysis* 8:77–86.

Cohen, S. S., and J. Zysman. 1987. *Manufacturing Matters: The Myth of the Post-Industrial Economy.* New York: Basic Books.

Cohen-Rosenthal, E., and C. E. Burton. 1987. *Mutual Gains: A Guide to Union-Management Cooperation.* New York: Praeger.

Committee for Economic Development. 1985. *Investing in Our Children*. New York: Committee for Economic Development.

Cooperative Education Research Center. 1987. *Cooperative Education in the United States and Canada*. Boston, Mass: Northeastern University.

Craft, M. R. 1984. "A Look at Cooperative Vocational Education from the Federal Level." *Journal of Cooperative Education* 21:40–58.

Craig, R. L., and C. Evers. 1983. "Employers as Educators: The Shadow Education System." In A. P. Carnevale and H. Goldstein (eds.), *Employee Training: Its Changing Role and an Analysis of New Data*. Washington, D.C.: American Society for Training and Development.

Creticos, P. A., and R. G. Sheets. 1989. "State-Financed, Workplace-Based Retraining Programs." *The National Commission for Employment Policy and the National Governors' Association*. Washington, D.C.: National Commission for Employment Policy.

Dayton, C., A. Weisberg, D. Stern and J. Evans. 1987. *Peninsula Academies Replications: 1986–87 Evaluation Report*. Berkeley, Calif.: Policy Analysis for California Education, School of Education, University of California.

Deming, W. E. 1981–82. Improvement of Quality and Productivity Through Action by Management. *National Productivity Review*: 12–22.

Denison, E. F. 1962. *Sources of Economic Growth in the United States and the Alternatives before Us*. New York: Committee for Economic Development.

Eurich, N. P. 1984. *Corporate Classrooms: The Learning Business*. Princeton, N.J.: Princeton University Press.

Feuer, M., H. Glick and A. Desai. 1987. "Is Firm-Sponsored Education Viable?" *Journal of Economic Behavior and Organization* 88:121–36.

Freeman, R. B. 1976. *The Over-Educated American*. San Francisco: Academic Press.

Garen, J. 1984. "The Returns to Schooling: A Selectivity Bias Approach with the Continuous Choice Variable." *Econometrica* 52(5):1199–218.

Goodlad, J. 1984. *A Place Called School: Prospects for the Future*. New York: McGraw-Hill.

Gott, S. P. 1988. "Apprenticeship Instruction for Real-World Tasks: The Coordination of Procedures, Mental Models, and Strategies." In E. A. Rothkopf (ed.), *Review of Research in Education*, Vol.15. Washington, D.C.: American Educational Research Association.

Grant, W. J., and T. D. Snyder. 1983. *Digest of Education Statistics, 1983–84*. Washington, D.C.: National Center for Education Statistics.

Greenberger, E., and L. D. Steinberg. 1986. *When Teenagers Work*. New York: Basic Books.

Hamermesh, D. S. and J. Grant. 1979. "Econometric Studies of Labor-Labor Substitution and their Implications for Policy." *The Journal of Human Resources* 14(4):518–42.

Hamilton, S. F. 1990. *Apprenticeship for Adulthood*. New York: The Free Press.

Hanushek, E. A. 1986. "The Economics of Schooling." *Journal of Economic Literature* 24(3):1141–77.

Heckscher, C. C. 1988. *The New Unionism: Employee Involvement in the Changing Corporation*. New York: Basic Books.

Helfgott, R. B. 1988. *Computerized Manufacturing and Human Resources*. Lexington, Mass.: Lexington Books.

Hirschhorn, L. 1984. *Beyond Mechanization*. Cambridge, Mass.: MIT Press.

Jaikumar, R. 1986. "Postindustrial Manufacturing." *Harvard Business Review* (November–December): 69–76.

Jamison, D. T., and L. J. Lau. 1982. *Farmer Education and Farm Efficiency*. Baltimore, Md.: Johns Hopkins University Press.

Jenkins, D. G., Jr. and N. Gupta. 1985. "The Payoffs of Paying for Knowledge." *National Productivity Review* 3:121–30.

Jones, C., P. Sebring, I. Crawford, B. Spencer and M. Butz. 1983. *High School and Beyond 1980 Sophomore Cohort First Follow-up (1982) Data File Users Manual*. (Contract No. E-300-78-0208). Chicago: National Opinion Research Center.

Jorgenson, D. W. 1984. "The Contribution of Education to U.S. Economic Growth, 1948–73." In E. Dean (ed.), *Education and Economic Productivity*. Cambridge, Mass.: Ballinger.

Kearns, D. T. and D. P. Doyle. 1988. *Winning the Brain Race: A Bold Plan to Make our Schools Competitive*. San Francisco, Calif.: Institute for Contemporary Studies, ICS Press.

Kennedy, E. M. 1988. "When Students Dropout, We All Lose." *Vocational Education Journal* 9:34–35.

Kochan, T. A., H. C. Katz, and R. B. McKersie. 1986. *The Transformation of American Industrial Relations*. New York: Basic Books.

Kochan, T., J. Cutcher-Gershenfeld and J. P. MacDuffie. 1989. "Employee Participation, Work Redesign, and New Technology: Implications for Public Policy in the 1990s." In U.S. Department of Labor, Commission on Workforce Quality and Labor Market Efficiency. *Investing in People, Background Papers*, Vol. II:1831–92.

Lapointe, A. E., N. A. Mead and G. W. Phillips. 1988. *A World of Differences*. (Report No: 19–CAEP-01). Princeton, NJ: Educational Testing Service

Lave, J. 1988. *Cognition in Practice: Mind, Mathematics and Culture in Everyday Life*. Cambridge, England: Cambridge University Press.

Lawler, E. E. and G. E. Ledford. 1985. "Skill–Based pay: A Concept that's Catching on." *Personnel* 62(9):30–37.

Levin, H. M. 1987. "Improving productivity through Education and Technology." In G. Burke and R.M. Rumberger (eds.), *The Future Impact of Technology on Work and Education*. Philadelphia, PA: Falmer Press.

Levine, D. and L. D. Tyson. 1990. "Participation, Productivity, and the Firm's Environment." In Blinder, A.S. (ed.): *Paying for Productivity, a Look at the Evidence*. Washington, D.C.: Brookings. pp. 183–237.

Levine, D. and G. Strauss. 1989. "Employee Participation and Envolvement." In U.S. Department of Labor, Commission on Workforce Quality and Labor Market Efficiency. *Investing in People, A Strategy to Address America's Workforce Crisis*. Background Papers, Vol. 2:1893–948. Washington, D.C.: U.S. Department of Labor.

Levy, F. 1988. "Incomes, Families, and Living Standards." In R. E. Litan, R.Z. Lawrence, and C. L. Schultze (eds.), *American Living Standards: Threats and Challenges*. Washington, D.C.: The Brookings Institution.

Lewin-Epstein, N. 1981. *Youth Employment During High School*. Washington, D.C.: National Center for Education Statistics.

Lillard, L. and H. Tan. 1986. *Training: Who Gets it and What are its Effects?* Santa Monica, Calif.: Rand Corp.

Mangum, S. L. 1989. "Evidence on Private Sector Training." In U.S. Department of Labor Commission on Workforce Quality and Labor Market Efficiency, *Investing in People: A Strategy to Address America's Workforce Crisis. Background papers*, Vol. 1:331–86.

Mertens, D. M., P. Seitz and S. Cox. 1982. *Vocational Education and the High School Dropout*. Columbus: The National Center for Research in Vocational Education, The Ohio State University.

Mincer, J. 1962. "On-the-Job Training: Costs, Eeturns and Some Implications." *Journal of Political Economy* (Supplement) 70:50–79.

Mincer, J. 1974. *Schooling, Experience, and Earnings*. New York: Columbia University Press.

Mincer, J. 1989. *Labor Market Effects of Human Capital and of its Adjustments to Technological Change*. New York: Institute on Education and the Economy, Teachers College, Columbia University.

Mincer, J. (forthcoming). "Job Training: Costs, Returns, and Wage Profits." In D. Stern and J. M. M. Ritzen (eds.), *Market Failure in Training? New Economic Analysis and Evidence on Training of Adult Employees*. Berlin and New York: Springer-Verlag

Mincer, J. and Y. Higuchi. 1988. *Wage Structures and Labor Turnover in the U.S. and in Japan. Occasional Paper No. 6*. New York: National Center on Education and Employment Teachers College, Columbia University.

Mortimer, J. T., and M. D. Finch. 1986. "The Effects of Part-Time Work on Adolescent Self-Concept and Achievement." In K.M. Borman and J. Reisman (eds.), *Becoming a Worker*. Norwood, N.J.: Ablex Publishing.

Murnane, R. J. 1988. "Education and the Productivity of the Workforce: Looking Ahead." In R. E. Litan, R.Z. Lawrence, and C. L. Schultze (eds.), *American Living Sandards: Threats and Challenges*. Washington, D.C.: The Brookings Institution.

National Academy of Sciences, Committee on the Effective Implementation of Advanced Manufacturing Technology. 1986. "Human Resource Practices for Implementing Advanced Manufacturing Technology." Washington, D.C.: National Academy Press.

National Academy of Sciences, Panel on Secondary School Education and the Changing Workplace. 1984. *High Schools and the Changing Workplace, the Employers' View*. Washington, D.C.: National Academy Press.

National Academy of Sciences, Panel on Technology and Employment. 1987. "Technology and Employment." Washington, D.C.: National Academy Press.

National Commission on Excellence in Education. 1983. *A Nation at Risk: The Imperative for Education Reform*. Washington, D.C.: U.S. Department of Education.

Neubauer, A. 1986. "Philadelphia High School Academies." *Educational Horizons* 65(1):16–19.

New York Stock Exchange, Ofice of Economic Research. 1982. *People and Productivity*. New York:NYSE.

Oakes, J. 1985. *Keeping Track: How Schools Structure Inequality*. New Haven: Yale University Press.

Piore, M. J., and C. F. Sabel. 1984. *The Second Industrial Divide*. New York: Basic Books.

Psacharopoulos, G. 1985. "Returns to Education: A Further International Update and Implications." *Journal of Human Resources* 20(4):584–604.

Psacharopoulos, G. 1987. "To Vocationalize or not to Vocationalize? That is the Curriculum Question." *International Review of Education* 33(2):187–211.

Raddatz, B. R. 1989, November. "In–Company Vocational Education from a Teaching, Economic and Labour Market Viewpoint." Paper prepared for the Symposium on Vocational Education, Dignity of Work and Productivity, University of California, Los Angeles.

Raizen, S. A. 1989. "Reforming Education for Work: A Cognitive Science Perspective." National Center for Research on Vocational Education, Institute for Education and the Economy, Teachers College, Columbia University.

Reich, R. B. 1983. *The Next American Frontier*. New York: Times Books.

Resnick, L. B. 1987a. "Learning in School and out." *Educational Researcher* 16:13–20.

Resnick, L. B. 1987b. *Education and Learning to Think*. Washington, D.C.: National Academy Press.

Rosen, S. 1972. "Learning and Experience in the Labor Market." *Journal of Human Resources* 7:326–42.

Rosenbaum, J. E. 1989. "Empowering Schools and Teachers: A new Link to Jobs for the Noncollege Bound." In U.S. Department of Labor Commission on Workforce Quality and Labor Market Efficiency, *Investing in People: A Strategy to Address America's Workforce Crisis. Background papers*, Vol. 1:187–214.

Rosow, J. and Zager, R. 1988. *Training: The Competitive Edge*. San Francisco: Jossey-Bass Publishers.

Rothman, R. 1989. "Business Groups Back System to Measure Skills of Graduates." *Education Week* 9(11):1.

Schmenner, R. 1984. "Small is Beautiful Now in Manufacturing." *Business Week* 2865 (October):152–56.

Schmidt, H. 1989, November. "Vocational Education and the Dignity of Work." Paper prepared for the Symposium on Vocational Education, Dignity of Work and Productivity, University of California, Los Angeles.

Schneider, J. 1988. *Training and Employment Security: The Role of California's Employment Training Panel*. San Francisco, Calif.: Coro Foundation.

Schultz, T. W. 1975. "The Value of the Ability to Deal with Disequilibria." *Journal of Economic Literature* 13:827–46.

Schultz-Wild, R. and C. Kohler. 1985. "Introducing New Manufacturing Technology: Manpower Problems and Policies." *Human Systems Management* 5:231–43.

Scribner, S. and J. Stevens. 1989. "Experimental Studies on the Relationship of School Math and Work Math": Technical Paper Number 3. New York: National Center on Education and Employment, Teachers College, Columbia University.

Simms, M. C. 1989. "The Effectiveness of Government Training Programs." In U.S. Department of Labor Commission on Workforce Quality and Labor Market Efficiency, *Investing in People: A Strategy to Address America's Workforce Crisis. Background papers,* Vol. 1:565–604.

Sizer, T. R. 1984. *Horace's Compromise.* Boston, Mass.: Houghton Mifflin Company.

Soskice, D. 1989. "Reinterpreting Corporatism and Explaining Unemployment: Coordinated and Noncoordinated Market Economies." R. Brunetta and C. della Ringa (eds.), *Markets, Institutions and Cooperation: Labour Relations and Economic Performance.* London: Macmillan.

Spence, M. 1973. "Job Market Mignaling." *Quarterly Journal of Economics* 87:355–74.

Spenner, K. I. 1985. "The Upgrading and Downgrading of Occupations: Issues, Evidence, and Implications for Education." *Review of Educational Research* 55(2):125–54.

Stern, D. 1982. *Managing Human Resources: The Art of Full Employment.* Dover, Mass.: Auburn House.

Stern, D., C. Dayton, I. Paik, A. Weisberg and J. Evans. 1988. "Combining Academic and Vocational Courses in an Integrated Program to Reduce High School Dropout Rates: Second–Year Results from Replications of the California Peninsula Academies." *Educational Evaluation and Policy Analysis* 10(2):161–70.

Stern, D., C. Dayton, I. W. Paik and A. Weisberg. 1989. "Benefits and Costs of Dropout Prevention in a High School Program Combining Academic and Vocational Education: Third-Year Results from Replications of the California Peninsula Academies." *Educational Evaluation and Policy Analysis* 11(4):405–416.

Stern, D., M. McMillion, C. Hopkins and J. Stone. 1990. "Work Experience for Students in High School and College." *Youth and Society* 21(3):355–389.

Stern, D. and Y. F. Nakata. 1991. "Paid Employment Among U.S. College Students: Trends, Effects, and Possible Causes." *Journal of Higher Education* 62(1):25-43.

Stern, J. D. and Williams, M.F. 1986. *The Condition of Education.* Washington, D.C.: Center for Education Statistics, U.S. Department of Education.

Sticht, T. G. 1979. "Developing Literacy and Learning Strategies in Organizational Settings." In H. F. O'Neil Jr. and C. D. Spielberger (eds.): *Cognitive and Affective Learning Strategies.* New York: Academic Press.

Sticht, T. G. 1987. *Functional Context Education.* Workshop resource noteboook. San Diego, Calif.: The Applied Behavioral and Cognitive Sciences, Inc.

Streeck, W. 1989. "Skills and the Limits of Neo-Liberalism: The Enterprise of the Future as a Place of Learning." *Work, Employment and Society* 3:89–104.

Tan , H. W. 1988. "Private Sector Training in the United States: Who Gets it and Why." The RAND Corporation. Preliminary draft of paper for presentation at a conference on Employer-provided Training, Washington, D. C.: Sponsored by the Institute on Education and the Economy, Teachers College Columbia University, and the National Assessment of Vocational Education.

Thompson, H., and R. Scalpone. 1985. "Managing the Human Resource in the Factory of the Future." *Human Systems Management.*5:221–30.

U.S. Congress, Office of Technology Assessment. 1990. *Worker Training.* Washington, D.C.: U.S. Government Printing Office.

U.S. Department of Labor, Bureau of Apprenticeship and Training 1989. "Work-Based Learning: Training America's Workers." (Contract No. 1989–253–149:48381). Washington, D.C.: U.S. Government Printing Office.

U.S. Department of Labor, Bureau of Labor–Management Relations. 1988. "Exploratory

Investigations of Pay-for-Knowledge Systems." BMLR 108. Washington, D.C.: author.

U. S. Department of Labor, Bureau of Labor Statistics. 1985. "How Workers Get their Training," Bulletin 2226. Washington, D. C.: author.

University of the State of New York, and State Education Department. 1987. *Technology Education, Introduction to Technology, Grades 7 and 8*. Albany, NY: authors.

Weber, J. M. 1987. *Strengthening Vocational Education's Role in Decreasing the Dropout Rate*. Columbus, OH: National Center for Research in Vocational Education, Ohio State University.

Welch, F. 1970. "Education in production." *Journal of Political Economy* 78:35–59.

William T. Grant Foundation. 1988. *The Forgotten Half: Non-College Youth in America*. Washington, D. C.: Youth and America's Future: The William T. Grant Foundation Commission on Work, Family and Citizenship.

Willis, R. J. and S. Rosen. 1979. "Education and Self-Selection." *Journal of Political Economy* 87(5, part 2):S7–S36.

Wirt, J. G., L. D. Muraskin, D. A. Goodwin and R. H. Meyer. 1989. *Summary of Findings and Recommendations, Final Report*, Vol. 1. Washington, D.C.: National Assessment of Vocational Education, U.S. Department of Education.

Wozniak, G. D. 1987. "Human Capital, Information, and the Early Adoption of New Technology." *Journal of Human Resources* 22(1):101–12.

Zuboff, S. 1988. *In the Age of the Smart Machine*. New York: Basic Books.

7

Issues in Skill Formation in Japanese Approaches to Automation

Robert E. Cole

As American manufacturing managers flocked to Japan in the late 1970s and early 1980s to visit factories and grasp the Holy Grail of Japanese success, they were paying particular attention to technology. The reports they sent home, however, often commented that the answer was not to be found in highly advanced technology. They rarely saw technology more advanced than in their own plants. The managers however, did, note that Japanese plants were extremely well laid out and staffed by seemingly well-motivated workers.

Upon reflection, it is not surprising that these visitors did not often grasp the full import of the human and organizational infrastructure that underlay Japan's outstanding competitive achievements. Short visits and lack of knowledge of the Japanese language severely constrained learning opportunities. Moreover, the deployment of the new micro-electronic technology (for example, replacement of single-purpose automatic machines with multipurpose machines) has had less of an impact on the shape of the workplace (its work organization and plant layout) than the 1960s fixed automation technologies (Watanabe, 1989, p. 2), and, as a result, many of the most significant improvements in the infrastructure were not visible to the short-term visitors.

Japanese manufacturers have been less interested in being at the cutting edge of new technology than in being first to develop the reliable application of technology. They have excelled at the diffusion of simple applications of complex technology. The rapid diffusion in the 1980s of simple computer numerical control (CNC) machine tools and low-end industrial robots in large-, medium-, and even small-scale manufacturing firms has been a striking feature of the Japanese experience. Watanabe (1987) documents this diffusion in the automotive sector. In contrast, Americans have prided themselves on being ahead in large-scale computer-integrated manufacturing systems and state-of-the-art intelligent robots. Since Americans visited only a small number of facilities, they failed to see the breadth of diffusion of modestly advanced but reliable technologies.

The purpose of this chapter is to examine the general patterns of skill formation that accompany the broad-scale diffusion of automation technologies in Japan. In so doing, my intention is not simply to describe behavior but to capture the skill-formation strategy of large-scale Japanese manufacturers, particularly as it compares with American approaches. Skill-formation strategies designed to respond to the introduction of advanced technologies are a joint outcome of the historical experiences of Japanese managers and the circumstances in which they now find themselves. Consequently, I will devote some attention to historical and contextual factors. As Japan's own pattern of organizational borrowing from the West clearly demonstrates however, it is not necessary to replicate a historical pattern in order to adopt specific organizational practices. Japan's unique cultural elements do not preclude the relevance of Japanese technique for Western practitioners.

CONTEXTUAL FACTORS INFLUENCING APPROACHES TO AUTOMATION AND WORKER TRAINING

In thinking about the Japanese experience with automation over the past two decades, it is important to keep in mind some of the broad institutional and economic factors that conditioned the decision-making of Japanese manufacturing managers.

Institutional Factors

As is well known, a pattern of relatively long-term employment for males is characteristic of large Japanese firms compared to United States firms. Western European countries tend to constitute a middle case in this regard. Long-term employment covering a male worker's peak work years is more pronounced in large Japanese manufacturing firms and applies to both blue-collar and white-collar male employees (Cole, 1979). Some of the confusion in the literature over this matter stems from the collapsing of age categories in ways that blur important differences.

A recent large-scale study (Lynn et al., 1989) of engineering graduates from Carnegie Mellon and Tohoku University, both schools well known in their respective countries for the quality of their engineering graduates, provides further insight into this matter. The mean age for the U.S. and Japanese sample was 41.5 and 41 years, respectively. As anticipated, 74 percent of the Tohoku graduates in the sample were still with their initial employer. Perhaps more surprising was that a sizable proportion of the Carnegie Mellon graduates, 43.4 percent, were also still with their first employer. While the proportion of Carnegie Mellon engineers still with their first employer is larger than the popular literature might suggest, the gap with the Tohoku graduates is still substantial.

Figure 7.1 reports the percentage of respondents in the study who have ever changed employers by age. We can see some sharp differences in behavior by age and country. The proportion of the U.S. sample that has ever changed employers increases until a little below age 40, after which it stabilizes at about 60 percent. The Japanese sample, by contrast, displays relatively modest propensities to change employer (in the range of 20 percent) until age 45, after which it rises rapidly, reaching over 80 percent by age 60.

The steep rise after age 50 of the Japanese engineers who changed employers for the first time probably reflects the increase in those who have retired or have been transferred from their original company to a subsidiary. It is also possible that the older employees in the sample entered a less stable labor market in the 1950s and that, in the future, the curve will show a less dramatic upward turn for older Japanese engineers (Lynn et al., 1989, p. 28). The traditional retirement age at large Japanese companies, set at 55 for much of the post–World War II period, has risen significantly in recent years. Now it more commonly stands in the low 60s. Japanese employees retiring from large firms, however, typically stay in the labor force and become reemployed in small- and medium-size firms.

The institutional arrangements that produce these outcomes also shape worker skills and technological development. Because the arrangements are embedded in the norms that guide both employer and worker behavior, they exert a particularly strong influence. With less

Figure 7.1. Percentage Respondents Who Have
Ever Changed Employers by Age

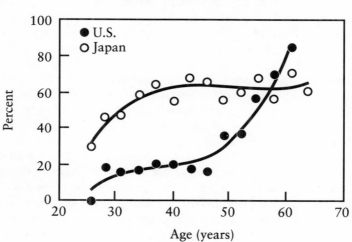

Source: Lynn, Piehler and Zahray (1989).

of a threat of losing skilled employees, management is more willing to invest in training its own employees. Moreover, Japanese employers seem willing to invest not only in providing specific skills usable primarily in their own firms but also in general skills, those that in principle would be in demand by other firms. As might be expected under such circumstances, large companies typically have major in-house training programs and in many cases they operate their own technical schools.

Employees who have internalized the prospects of remaining in the same firm for much of their work career are more willing to cooperate in technological innovation. Japanese workers in large firms display relatively little concern that their joint activities with management to develop and introduce new technology will lead to their displacement. Some exceptions include the response of the longshoremen, coal miners and train operators at the National Railways. Notwithstanding such exceptions, unions have by and large accepted as a matter of principle the idea that their members will benefit from the introduction of new technology and that the introduction of new technology is, in any case, inevitable (Kuwahara, 1987a, p. 8). Their sentiments reflect not only the context of employment security but also the broader context of rapid growth in the postwar economy. This growth has made employment security a feasible option for large-scale Japanese manufacturing firms.

With firms reasonably confident of retaining the employees they train, managers can cultivate a variety of firm-specific organizational skills. Umetani (1989) provides examples of these organizational skills: a sense of discipline and loyalty to one's firm, better teamwork among workers, "right attitudes" toward work and the company, better interdepartmental coordination, better communication between labor and management, and better human relations in the organization. Embedded in this list are the problem-solving skills that will be important to my subsequent discussion.

Not only is the probability of losing key technical personnel low, but the probability that those employees who do leave will be hired by direct competitors is also small (Cole, 1979). Consequently, large manufacturing firms are willing to share with their employees information on technological plans without fear that such sharing will lead to a loss of proprietary information. Indeed, such sharing provides the basis for building many of the organizational skills just described.

Employment security combined with the legacy of corporate paternalism and strong authority relationships have led to a situation in which job changes and career development within large Japanese firms occur very much at the initiative of management. In my initial research in this area in the early 1970s, I asked a representative sample of employees in Detroit and Yokohama the following question whenever they reported an intrafirm job change: "On the whole, was your next job at [employer] something you tried to get, or did it just happen?"

In the Detroit sample, 54.4 percent reported that they tried to get their next job, and 45.3 percent stated that it just happened. In the Yokohama sample, however, only 29.4 percent of the sample reported that they tried to get their next job, compared with 70.6 percent who stated that it just happened. Controlling for education had no effect on the Yokohama distribution, although there was a moderate rise in the "tried to get" response with increasing education among the Detroit respondents (Cole, 1979, pp. 113–14). These data suggest that intrafirm job movement and career development among the Yokohama respondents often had the character of an escalator. In contrast, intrafirm job movement in Detroit had more the character of individuals taking personal responsibility for directing their own careers.

More recent research confirms these perspectives, at least for engineers. In the previously mentioned study of the engineering graduates of Tohoku and Carnegie Mellon Universities, the researchers asked respondents to choose their reasons for taking their current position in the firm (first jobs in the firms were excluded from the analysis). Nearly 70 percent of the Japanese respondents reported that the most important reason for taking their current position was that they had been assigned to it by their firm. In sharp contrast, the researchers found that only 12.4 percent of the American respondents gave the same response. The researchers concluded that "the U.S. respondents placed much greater emphasis on individual ambition or convenience citing such factors as location, salary, and the opportunity for managerial advancement"(Lynn et al., 1989, p. 29). Sakakibara and Westney (1985, p. 14) came to identical conclusions in their study of the training and careers of engineers in the U.S. and Japanese computer industries. One further consequence of the two countries' differences was that engineering careers were much more standardized within each computer company in Japan, whereas U.S. personnel managers and engineers found it almost impossible to describe a typical career in their company.

These findings are important for our subsequent discussion because implicit in the data are the complementary behaviors associated with skill-formation and career development. In Japan, employers take primary responsibility for organizing skill formation, while in the United States, responsibility would seem more evenly divided between employers and the employee.

The formal reward systems in large Japanese manufacturing firms, based on "ability wages" rather than a "job wage" system, further encourages these outcomes. The informal reward systems contribute as well. The outcome is an environment in which employees are willing to learn, perform a variety of jobs, and are encouraged to do so by the organization of work, promotion systems, wages, and career structures (Dore et al., 1989).

Economic Factors

Much of the past two decades has been characterized by a labor shortage
in Japan (an exception being the period 1972–73 following the first oil
shock). This is true not only for the economy as a whole but also in the
manufacturing sector in particular. During the labor shortage of the late
1960s and early 1970s, manufacturing firms found it particularly difficult
to recruit production workers. The supply of middle school and agricultural
labor had dried up, and urban high school youth were not particularly
attracted to the physical demands and difficult work environment offered
by many manufacturing firms. In the 1980s, manufacturing firms increasingly complained that they were having trouble competing for recent college
graduates, including engineers, who were more attracted to the service
sector (for example, financial services). By the late 1980s, however, employers
also were complaining about an absolute shortage of production workers. From
the late 1960s through the 1980s, smaller firms with their poorer working
conditions and wages generally had difficulty filling all types of positions.

   Unlike some other countries, Japan found the prospect of filling these
gaps with foreign immigrant labor unacceptable. To some extent, the
movement of manufacturing firms toward direct investment in overseas
facilities was designed to break the bottleneck in production resulting
from labor shortage considerations (Cole, 1989). These labor-market
conditions placed significant pressure on management to pursue
automation as a solution.

   Just how severe the emergent labor shortage is becoming can be seen
in the August 1989 Labor Force Survey, which reported a seasonally
adjusted unemployment rate of 2.2. This was the lowest recorded levels
of unemployment in over seven years. The Ministry of Labor reported
that the shortage of regular workers in mid-1989 was the most acute
since the Ministry began conducting the survey. The results of a survey
by the Japan Federation of Economic Organizations (Keidanren) of
its 900 members on this matter appear in Table 7.1. They show that
the occupational category suffering from the most severe shortage is
the technical and research and development group, with the blue-collar
group in second place.

   Since the shortage has been greatest for the small- and medium-size
manufacturing firms, we might expect these firms—typically slower
to adopt advanced technologies—to be especially receptive to advanced
technologies. There is indeed evidence that suggests this is the case. For
example, the Ministry of Labor reported in the mid-1980s that 59.3
percent of private business establishments employing fewer than 1000
workers had introduced machines and devices in which integrated
circuits were used (Kuwahara, 1987a, p. 5).

   An additional factor conditioning the Japanese approach to technology lies in the strong corporate decentralization movement that

Table 7.1. Availability of Full-Time Employees by Occupational
Type (Share of Total, %)

	Severe shortage	Mild shortage	Appropriate level	Slight surplus	Large surplus	Total	No. of firms responding
Technical, R&D	18.6	0.8	28.6	1.9	0.0	100.0	(360)
Blue collar	9.9	26.3	37.4	20.7	5.7	100.0	(322)
Planning	7.7	38.1	52.0	2.2	0.0	100.0	(402)
Sales	6.3	47.5	43.4	2.5	0.3	100.0	(396)
Clerical	1.7	20.3	53.7	22.8	1.5	100.0	(404)
For information processing	18.8	56.7	24.0	0.5	0.0	100.0	(383)
For overseas assignments	12.9	48.5	37.7	0.9	0.0	100.0	(342)
All occupational types	3.7	45.4	37.0	12.3	1.5	100.0	(405)

Source: Japan Institute for Social and Economic Affairs (1982:2).

developed by the early 1960s. Japanese managers in the manufacturing sector identified operational decentralization as an important approach to reinvigorating their large organizations and thereby to improve quality and productivity. This decentralization did not stop at the divisional or departmental level, but reached down to the shopfloor. Production workers were expected to take responsibility for a variety of everyday decisions for which management representatives had hitherto been responsible (functions such as maintenance, quality control, and safety). It was this movement that eventually gave rise to the now well-known quality-control circles.

Aoki (1987) describes the economic benefits of decentralization in terms of its ability to economize on time and resources needed for organization-wide communication and its superiority over alternative systems in providing for continual adaptation when the environment is rapidly changing. The movement to decentralize employee responsibility rested on the capabilities of the labor force and had, as we shall see, far-reaching implications for the Japanese manufacturing sector's approach to technological innovation and skill formation. It opened options to management that were not available to more centralized- and specialist-oriented organizational systems.

APPROACHES TO SKILL FORMATION IN JAPANESE MANUFACTURING

In trying to capture the recent Japanese experiences with automation, it is important to understand the continuities that have characterized the Japanese approach to skill-formation and technological change. The specific practices with regard to the introduction of microelectronic applications, to be discussed below, must be understood in the context of these continuities.

The characteristic patterns associated with skill-formation in the manufacturing sector can be identified most clearly after the immediate postwar adjustments were completed in the late 1950s. However, we should not lose sight of the fact that some of these patterns have roots in prewar organizational practices. Of particular relevance is the distinctive way in which Japanese firms absorbed the ideas of scientific management in the interwar period. Not only did they not forge a strong tie between wage determination and the use of scientific management principles to organize work, but they maintained a continuing interest in having workers themselves participate in work-improvement activities (Cole, 1979, pp. 108–13).

During the early 1960s, Japanese manufacturing firms, especially in the metal-working industries, moved toward organizing flow production systems. Along with this change, they located individual production worker jobs in close proximity to a variety of related but different functions. To maximize productivity, management began to organize work so that workers would be able to conduct a variety of closely related jobs. This became the basis for the widely recognized feature of Japanese shopfloor operations: the multiskilled worker.

Kazuo Koike (1988) has given the most comprehensive treatment of the skill-formation process in the Japanese manufacturing sector. He found that production workers are given responsibility for solving both routine and nonroutine problems in Japan—in contrast to the United States, where the disposition of nonroutine problems is generally turned over to specialized experts such as skilled maintenance workers and engineers. Nonroutine problems, even in industries thought to be dependent on routine technlology, are far more common than outsiders recognize and stem from changes in product and labor mix as well as production methods. The Japanese believe that immediate on-the-spot resolution by the workers involved is a far more efficient approach than that embodied in a more centralized model. As a consequence, the Japanese have opted for an "integrated" rather than a "separate" system (Koike, 1988, pp. 158–61). To the extent that engineers are needed to help resolve the more complex problems, these engineers are located closer to the shopfloor than their American counterparts, and expected to be responsive to the problem solving needs of production workers.

QC circles are simply a parallel and structured approach to workshop problems that require study. They are the norm in large manufacturing firms, where typically over 90 percent of production workers are involved in circle activities. Moreover, it is not uncommon in manufacturing firms for production workers to constitute the actual improvement teams that implement QC circle suggestions. At Mazda, beyond the characteristically high percentage of employees participating in circle activities, two percent of the production workers were reported to be engaged in full-time improvement teams in 1988. These activities give workers yet another opportunity to accumulate additional skills and to exercise and extend existing ones. They also allow workers to engage in more challenging nonroutine work.

In effect, Japanese manufacturing firms have created a very large cadre of lower-level technicians who make enormous contributions to fine tuning the production system. At the same time, manufacturing engineers, while available to support production workers in these efforts, have much of their valuable time freed up to work on still more difficult problems. A lot of the firefighting and job redesign that so preoccupies management and engineering personnel in American plants is done in Japanese plants by production workers. In contrast, because many middle management and technical engineering personnel in American manufacturing operations are overextended, many pressing problems are not even addressed.

Why have Americans not been more willing to develop an integrated system that involves on-the-spot problem solving? The reluctance would seem to stem from an unwillingness to delegate authority and discretion to lower-level workers, which, in the end, may derive from the American application of Taylorism with its focus on separating planning from execution.

Skill-formation in large Japanese firms is organized to produce the outcomes just described. The primary mechanism of skill-formation is on-the-job training (OJT) over an extended period. New entrants are introduced by senior workers to progressively more difficult tasks through phased job rotation in their own and closely related workshops. This process requires an on-going and systematic assessment of worker training and skills. Management develops "job maps" for each employee. Their practices are well developed not only for engineers but for production workers as well.

At Honda Corporation, where I recently conducted interviews, management uses a clear and highly differentiated technical ranking system for evaluating all production workers. Honda devotes considerable administrative resources to monitoring and operating that system, including developing manuals for how to move up the ranking, tests for each grade, a self-report system, and individual employee interviews. A well-organized system assures that workers have the opportunity to exercise their skills. Production workers, for example, work closely with product and process engineers to design new products and processes.

The literature suggests that Honda's approach is quite common among large manufacturing firms, both in process and metal-working industries. When Koike refers to the "white-collarization" of production workers in Japan, he has in mind the way Western firms treat white-collar workers by creating career development paths. In Japan these paths are available to production workers as well.

Off-the-job training (Off-JT) in Japan is used for short periods to teach more theoretical material to employees. Off-JT emphasizes workers sharing skills with less experienced colleagues. Support from the wage incentive system is critical to producing such sharing of skills. Japanese firms typically rely on an ability-based wage system that rewards employees for acquiring skills rather than on a job-based wage system that rewards employees only if they are in jobs allowing them to use those particular skills. In principle, this ability-based system is quite similar to the knowledge-based pay systems that are gaining popularity in American industry, although the Japanese version usually combines the ability-based wage with strong seniority considerations. The ability-based wage system is founded on the assumption that learning is the key to productivity improvement and that a decentralized approach to problem solving and improvement is the most effective strategy for learning by encouraging information sharing among workers. Enhanced skills make it possible for workers to operate complex production systems and to switch easily across multiple product lines, and thereby enhance managerial flexibility and reduce the importance of economies of scale.

Thus far, I have focused on approaches to learning and training that are becoming more familiar to U.S. observers. It is also useful to dwell a little on a less-well-known mechanism for disseminating best practices: employee presentations of problem solving activities. In interviews conducted in 1989 with 20 major manufacturing firms famous for their quality achievements, such presentations were a standard practice. Presenters ranged from production worker QC circles to high status engineering departments. Employees shared methods and solutions related not only to quality problems but also to the introduction and operation of new technology. Through presentations, the firms encouraged broad employee participation and diffusion of best practice, thereby ensuring that the same mistakes are not made twice.

Presentations typically brought together management and members, with high-ranking managers often in attendance as well. The presentations usually included a history of the problem-solving activity and a discussion of the blind alleys and failed solutions pursued. By documenting a process by which failure and errors were overcome to produce success, the presentations treated errors and failures as part of a positive learning experience. The presence of senior managers reinforced this theme of learning from failure.

The contrast with U.S. approaches is striking. The American Productivity and Quality Center surveyed its membership and found that a majority (some 60 percent) of American top managers surveyed believed their failures were treated as positive learning experiences. However, the further down the hierarchy one went, the less this was the case. Only 33 percent of middle managers thought their failures were treated positively.

The steady stream of presentations makes the factory a school as well as a production facility. At Nippon Denso, engineers spend an average of 8 hours per week in education and training, 4 hours on company time and 4 hours on their own time. The primary approach to training involves the development and presentation of case studies.

REASONS FOR WORKER SUPPORT AND MANAGEMENT ADOPTION OF MICROELECTRONIC APPLICATIONS

To understand the skill-formation issues involved in automation, it is helpful to understand the motivations of management for introducing automation and the nature of worker reactions to automation. With the growing acceleration of microelectronic applications, a large number of surveys have been conducted in Japan on these matters.

In 1982, a wide range of employees at six large companies in the Kansai area (Osaka, Kyoto, and Kobe) were surveyed on the intro-

Figure 7.2. Reasons for Being in Favor of (or Opposed to) the Introduction of Mechatronics Equipment

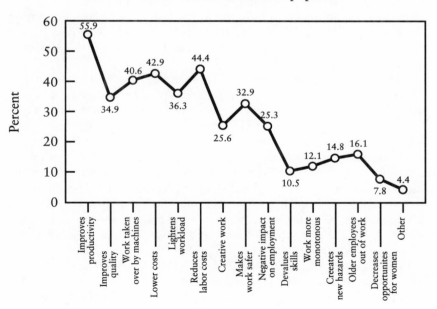

Source: Kansai Productivity Center (1985:32).

duction of "mechatronics" (Kansai Productivity Organization, 1985, pp. 31–32). The term *mechatronics* is in wide use in Japan and refers to a broad range of technologies based on the combination of mechanical and electronic systems (see McLean, 1983). The 2,438 respondents were asked their reasons for being in favor of or opposed to mechatronics. Figure 7.2 shows the distribution of their responses. Over 30 percent cited higher productivity, improved quality, greater reliance on machines, lower costs, lighter workload, labor savings, and improved safety as reasons for favoring mechatronics. These are all factors that management would regard positively. Decidedly fewer respondents cited negative reactions to the new technology. These findings are consistent with the observation that there has been very little resistance, or even less hostility, toward the new microelectronic applications in the Japanese manufacturing sector.

A Multiskilled Workforce

One possible explanation for the general acceptance of new technology is the multiskilled character of the workforce. Multiskilled workers have less reason to fear that the new technology will displace them. Kuwahara (1987b, pp. 3–4) discusses the view prevailing among Japanese unions that new technology usually leads to growth for the company through improved productivity and/or increased market share with no loss of total employment. If labor and management are both satisfied with the distribution of the benefits of such improvements, their attitudes will carry over to the next round of new technology. In this fashion, a positive innovation cycle is established. Kuwahara further argues that this cycle is facilitated by enterprise unions who have as their primary objective the long-term growth of the firm.

It should be noted that many surveys in the 1970s taken on the subject of the employment effects of new technology indicated that managers, government officials, and academics were concerned that there might be some negative outcomes and hostile reactions. Cases of job displacement resulting from the new technology were indeed identified.

Those academics writing in the Marxist tradition were concerned not only about the displacement effects associated with automation but also about effects on skill. Nakaoka Tetsuro (1971) focused on the polarization of skill he saw in steel and other industries. He described an emerging conflict between those few workers who were accumulating skills under the new technologies and those who were increasingly condemned to de-skilled jobs (Nakaoka, 1971, pp. 238–39).

In the mid-1980s, Hirohide Tanaka (1984), a high-level Ministry of Labour official, voiced considerable apprehension regarding the effects of microelectronics technology. He envisioned a sharp reduction of blue-collar labor as microelectronics technology took hold. He also anticipated that microeletronics technology would transform skill requirements. He feared workers' job content would change from a high degree of specialization to a new form of "generalization," "integration," and "composition." According to Tanaka, some of these developments were captured in the concept of the multiskilling of the Japanese blue-collar labor force. Tanaka, however, disputed the assumption that multiple skills necessarily led to a qualitative upgrading of job content. His concerns arose from his view that, because microelectronics technology simplified job content and reduced labor requirements, previously distinct jobs could be integrated into a single job. If all a worker need do in case of emergency is shut off a machine, hit an emergency button, report to his or her supervisor, and wait for instructions, then there is little reason why the worker cannot operate several different kinds of machines (Tanaka, 1984, pp. 272–75).

Tanaka's pessimistic views were not widely shared in either business or academic circles, and by the late 1980s most such concerns had dissipated. The burst of growth in the domestic economy in the mid- and late-1980s no doubt contributed to this outcome. In this broad context, the kind of debates in the Western countries about the job displacement effects of modern technology did not find much fertile ground in which to take root in Japan.

Flexibility and Quality

Apart from efficiency, Japanese business is particularly attentive to the flexibility and quality benefits of automation. This was very apparent in Watanabe's (1987) survey on the extent and purposes of adopting microelectronic machinery in the 5 largest automotive manufacturers, 22 of their major component makers, and 30 small subcontractors. Here I will discuss Watanabe's findings for the first two categories. Respondents in those cases were managers, and the focus of inquiry was on the introduction of NC machine tools, playback and other more advanced robots, and CAD/CAM. The term *CAD/CAM* is used roughly to refer to computer systems programmed to facilitate the design, manufacture, and testing of mechanical components.

The five automobile manufacturers reported that the primary reason for NC adoption was flexibility. The machines helped them to diversify products, contributed to a higher precision of work, and mitigated the worker shortage (that is, they were adopted for their labor-saving effects). For the adoption of robots, they listed the increase in flexibility of their production facilities as the first reason and dealing with difficult work environments as their second reason. Reducing labor requirements was rarely given as a primary motive; improving the quality of work through superior consistency was a far more common motivator.

Changing market conditions characterized by heightened competition and consumers who demanded a wider range of product choices encouraged the push toward greater flexibility. Manufacturers looked to the new technology to facilitate frequent model changes (long-term flexibility) and to allow them to produce in smaller batches (short-term flexibility). They explained the importance of improving the work environment in terms of the increased difficulty of recruiting young, well-educated Japanese workers to otherwise difficult and physically demanding jobs and to the rapid aging of their labor force. Such factors were particularly prominent in explanations for the adoption of painting robots.

CAD/CAM had been used by four of the five firms for about 10 years, and used especially intensively from the late 1970s. Watanabe found that flexibility and labor-savings among highly trained personnel were the major reasons given for its adoption.

For the large component companies, the primary reason given for the introduction of NC machine tools and robots were the same as for the automobile manufacturers: flexibility. The second most important reason was improved quality. Robot operations can be disrupted by the irregularity of materials, and such disruption is very costly to just-in-time operations. The new technology alleviated these problems by improving the consistency of parts, thus contributing to a smoother flow of production. The reasons given for CAD/CAM introduction (half of them had CAD while relatively few had a direct linkage from CAD to CAM) were, in common with the manufacturers, flexibility and labor saving of skilled workers.

While flexibility and quality stand out as the reasons for adopting the new technology, the need to respond to a growing labor shortage became more significant in the 1980s. Orders for machining centers, for example, accelerated starting in the mid-1980s with Japan's sharp economic expansion. The two major machine-tool makers, Yamazaki Mazak Seiko and Mori Seiki, explain the rapid growth primarily in terms of the need for manufacturing firms to increase efficiency in the increasingly severe labor shortage.

A Role for Workers

In reviewing these explanations for adopting advanced technologies, there is one theme that is not brought out by the survey data but nevertheless came through in my interviews with 20 major Japanese manufacturing firms in 1989. In the course of answering questions about the role of quality in equipment investment decisions, the respondents made repeated references to the role of small-scale automation and tooling investments that helped the worker do a better job and thereby improved the quality of the process. Indeed, many of these investments were proposed by the workers themselves. My experience in U.S. manufacturing firms is that management's stringent application of return on investment criteria and the difficulty of measuring paybacks for improvement in the process quality often stifle such worker initiatives.

TRAINING STRATEGIES FOR AUTOMATION

In this discussion of training strategies, I will begin with the broadest view of the subject, by noting the extent to which information about new technology is shared among all employees.

Business Plans

Japanese firms share detailed business plans with their employees. All large firms have mechanisms in place for producing long-term, medium-term, and annual business plans. These plans typically contain a good deal of information about technology. The annual business plan, typically known as the Presidential annual plan (*nendo hoshin*) typically provides information on technology objectives for the year and information on opportunities for relevant employees to participate in meeting those objectives. The planning process also affords employees significant participation opportunities. By contrast, the business planning process in most American firms has a strong hierarchical form. Key officials at various levels are expected to formulate plans to meet corporate (primarily financial) objectives. In large Japanese manufacturing firms, while the strategic objectives are set on high, the operational objectives specified in the annual plan are made the subject of large-scale employee involvement. Even QC circles are expected to formulate their themes to coincide with the annual plan objectives. The large-scale involvement carries over into plans for implementing new technology.

Union–Management Consultation Committees

Labor–management consultation committees are common in large manufacturing firms. They typically operate at the firm, division, and plant level. These committees developed from an amalgam of practices, including the prewar factory committees, the models offered by the Whitley Committee in Great Britain, and the Betriebsrat in West Germany. The modern phase got underway in the period 1955–65, during which time management began to make extensive use of human-relations techniques that stressed the importance of communication (Cole, 1979, p. 216). The labor–management consultation committees, which typically meet once a month, focus considerable effort on disseminating information about new technology plans to employees through union representatives.

The committees play a minor role in setting new technology directions for the firm. They do, however, function to ensure that management consults with union representatives. Kuwahara (1989) has documented this function in a number of case studies. In a reasonably representative case from the machine-tool industry, management presented its plans for the introduction of significant new technology some time between

6 months and a year before the proposed date of introduction. At that preliminary stage, management explained the anticipated effect of the new technology on its business prospects and on the workplace. Detailed discussions were then held between the union and management about the proposed plans, including time of introduction and impact on employment. Typically, discussion focused on the consequences of the new technology for redeployment and retraining of the labor force. The union seldom balked at the introduction of new technology, and rarely forced management into a fundamental change in its plans. However, the unions often did have an impact on issues regarding the redeployment of personnel. Union requests in this area involved changes in working conditions, workloads, the extent and nature of job transfers, and the nature of retraining activities (where they would be held, duration, and type of training program).

Educational Needs

In keeping with the joint union-management activities just described, the Mechatronics Labor–Management Committee of the Kansai Productivity Center conducted a number of case studies on microelectronics applications. These are reported in the Kansai Productivity Organization's (1985) *Mechatronics: The Policy Ramifications*. The findings of that study provide the basis for much of the following discussion.

The companies examined were identified as those that "have taken a progressive approach" to employee education upon the introduction of the new microelectronics technology. Specifically, the study focused on the relation between employee education and the adoption of industrial robots, NC machine tools, machining centers, and flexible manufacturing systems.

The study concluded that the demands of the new technology were considerable and therefore required an organized program of employee education. The authors saw three areas of educational need: (1) microelectronics for personnel engaged in research and development and production engineering, (2) the handling and maintenance of microelectronics equipment for middle-level production workers, and (3) introductory microelectronics technology for general workers in automated workplaces. Moreover, they found that human resource development in these areas required general education in the use of microcomputers and other devices incorporating microelectronics devices, education for the new jobs these new technologies create, and special retraining and/or reassignment for those employees who cannot adapt.

Table 7.2 summarizes the findings of the study, showing the skills and knowledge required for personnel working in an environment of microelectronics equipment. Obviously such a table can only provide

Table 7.2. Skills and Knowledge Required of Mechatronics Engineers[a]

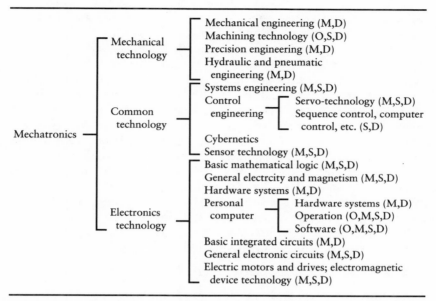

Legend: O=operator; M=mainteance personnel; S=systems engineer; D=development engineer.

Source: Kansai Productivity Center (1985), p. 80.

a general categorization, since the specific skills and skill levels vary by company, industry, and type of technology. Of the four types of personnel listed, the category of development engineer requires some clarification. Development engineers are those in-house engineers who develop peripheral equipment or prototype automation equipment beyond what is available in vendor products.

Education for microelectronics applications can be broken down into two categories. The first includes those programs that provide microelectronics skills and knowledge to all members of a company's plant or office staff but are not designed to prepare the worker for reassignment. The second type includes those programs that seek to provide a restricted group of people with skills that are immediately useful in their new assignments. The first type covers broad basic knowledge in preparation for the future introduction of microelectronics applications and serves to raise the overall engineering capability of the company. Typically, courses are stratified not only by the occupational types referred to in Table 7.2, but also by such factors as age, ability, educational level, and career history.

In-House Training

Most large manufacturing companies, as we have seen, have their own technical institutes already in place. In a study of 10,000 manufacturing facilities conducted by the Ministry of Labor in the early 1980s, over 60 percent of the companies reported that they had initiated specializing training programs in conjunction with the adoption of robotic and NC machines (cited in Office of Technology Assessment, 1984, p. 259). Such programs have a strong "hands-on" quality with practical exercises typically given equal weight with lectures. In designing the in-house training programs, the manufacturing firms have to contend with the sharp segmentation of electronic and mechanical engineering in Japanese high schools and universities. Most of the burden of combining the two disciplines falls on the firms themselves. In addition, the firms believe that rapid changes in both electronic and mechanical engineering require them to provide ongoing education to keep their employees—even younger employees— abreast of the latest information and techniques.

The Kansai Productivity Center study characterized the effects of microelectronics applications in the following terms:

1. Most skilled tasks were transferred to machines.

2. Setup and preprocessing tasks remained unaltered.

3. Programming machinery to perform the work became a new job task.

4. New jobs were created to maintain microelectronics equipment.

The researchers encouraged a program of modular training, with each module representing a single skill or unit of knowledge. As an example, the study presented the training needs for industrial robots. There are three elements in a robot drive systems: an actuator, a control mechanism, and a power mechanism, which is usually hydraulic. Each of these subsystems requires its own technical knowledge, programming, daily inspection, maintenance, safety measures, and skills. The researchers advised breaking these requirements down into smaller, self-contained modules for training. With the skills thus modularized, the training program would aim for step-by-step mastery of each of the building blocks. In this fashion, the study argued, all workers and managers can learn relatively easily and efficiently.

Avoiding Skill Polarization

The Kansai Productivity Center study also identified the possibility that the demands of new technology might lead to a polarization of skills between two classes of workers: those who could make the adaptation and those who could not master the new technology and requisite knowledge even when given the opportunity to do so. According to the study, older workers were most problematic in this regard, but the researchers also pointed out that older workers were often interested in studying new technology and that they could make important contributions if care were taken to tailor courses to their needs and capabilities.

Workers who in the end cannot master microelectronics equipment can still often be assigned to the preprocessing setup jobs and other tasks supporting microelectronics equipment. Sometimes, however, such employees must be moved to other workplaces.

With regard to age, Japanese corporate policy has a special concern with older workers. Japan has the most rapidly aging labor force among industrial nations, and corporate concern is fostered by the high priority given the effective use of older workers by the Japanese Ministry of Labor. According to Campbell (1992), "Efforts to encourage the employment of older people are the most unusual aspect of Japan's policy toward the elderly." In contrast, most European countries have focused policies on shedding older workers to cope with youth unemployment. In the United States, the emphasis has been on removing legal barriers to older workers' keeping their jobs. Only Japan has consistently pursued a positive policy of job maintenance and job creation for older people.

Programs pursued by the government through the Ministry of Labor include a requirement that companies raise the age of mandatory retirement; a quota for workers over age 60; a variety of subsidies to employers for keeping, hiring, and retraining older workers; targeted job-finding and counselling services; and better unemployment and job-training benefits for older workers than for younger workers.

Multiskilling

Japanese firms have been concerned about the possibility of a polarization of job skills and have typically sought to avoid creating a small labor aristocracy of skilled workers distinct from a larger core of unskilled workers by integrating old and new skills (Tanaka, 1984). The Kansai Productivity Center study reported favorably on Japanese firms' efforts to add new skills to old ones to produce, if not bona fide engineers, at least middle-level technicians. They also described a situation in which, by embedding intelligence in the new microelectronics machines, companies risked losing the workers' skills that underlay that intelligence. Such a loss could jeopardize future development calling for new kinds of capabilities and equipment. In response, the study also reported that some companies actively sought to retain general-purpose skills underlying the new technology.

At a different level, firms have faced the problem of a shortage of electronic engineers while being top heavy with mechanical engineers. A combination of both skills is now indispensable in many areas of product design and production technology. In a case study reported by the Kansai Productivity Center, the company decided that the best way to solve this problem was to develop the needed amalgam of skills by educating its mechanical engineers in advanced electronics. The firm developed an educational program based on a university-level course in electronics. A six-month course with 60 hours of lectures and 60 hours of practical exercises formed the heart of the program. Half of lectures were on the employees' own time. Instructors were recruited from among university faculty. The decision to develop its own engineering talent with a meshing of old and new skills seems characteristic of the approach of many Japanese manufacturing firms. Indeed the term for multiskilled workers in Japanese, *tanoko*, which in the past referred to the ability of production workers to master a number of different machines, today also refers to the ability of employees to master the integration of mechanical and microelectronics knowledge.

Well-developed systems of job rotation among departments also support multiskilling in many firms. There is extensive movement across product engineering, production engineering, and marketing departments (Watanabe, 1989, p. 11; Sakakibara and Westney, 1985). In one study reported by Watanabe, interdepartmental transfers between the product development and production technology departments were found to occur for 53 percent of the engineers in the automobile industry, 71 percent in the precision equipment industry, and 67 percent in the electrical and electronic machinery industry. Watanabe (1989, p. 12) concluded that, in mature industries such as the automobile industry, there was somewhat less need for such transfers than in industries where more dynamic product innovation was taking place. Nevertheless, these high frequencies contrast dramatically with U.S. practices.

In Japanese firms, career development policies seek to create broad levels of capability with respect to new technologies. The aim of these policies is to avoid creating unadaptable employees. As a recent OECD study reflecting on the overall nature of flexibility in Japanese labor markets put it, the assumption in Japan is that "everyone is a learner" (Dore et al., 1989, p. 52). It may be more accurate to say that the assumption is that all male employees are learners, since female employees have only limited exposure to job training and retraining opportunities. In addition, the OECD study stresses that employees with multiple skills can more easily learn to operate newly installed equipment. When they need to learn to program the new equipment, training programs can more easily upgrade the skills of those who already have a broad skill base. As with conventional technology, young workers are led through different modules and levels as they are converted to multiskilled workers.

A recent study of 3,000 manufacturing establishments gives us a more precise understanding of what is actually meant by the term *multiskilled*

Table 7.3. Percent of Multiskilled Employees by
Established Size, Kind of Industry, and Type of Task
(in % of 3,029 Sample Establishments)

| Task[a] | Total | Establishment size | | | Industry | | |
		1,000 or more	100-999	30-99	Metal engineering	Process industries	Light industries
A	40.2	67.1	44.3	35.3	45.1	48.3	34.9
B	35.6	53.6	41.1	31.5	42.2	39.3	29.7
C	16.3	20.4	15.4	16.4	20.1	13.8	13.7
D	14.7	39.3	19.4	9.6	14.8	25.7	12.7
E	7.8	20.8	9.5	5.4	10.7	11.0	5.0
F	6.6	8.6	7.9	5.9	13.2	2.9	2.0
G	0.3	0.9	0.5	0.2	0.3	1.6	0.1

[a]Types of task: A–Look after more than one production process; B–operate different types of machines; C–experience different tasks while young, for the purpose of preparing the worker for his middle and older age; D–do part of the repair and maintenance work in addition to machine operation; E–carry out mechantronic tasks; F–have technical knowledge/skills required for repair and installation of machines during a business trip; G–other.

Source: Watanabe (1989), p.10.

workers (cited in Watanabe, 1989, p. 10). The findings are summarized in Table 7.3. Despite the popular image of employees in smaller firms having to be "jacks of all trades," we find instead that the larger the firm, the more likely employees were to designate themselves as multiskilled workers. The proportion of such workers was impressively large in establishments with over 1,000 employees.

These tendencies can also be seen in the more automated of the new Japanese "transplants" in the United States. Michigan Automotive Compressor (MAC), for example, is a joint venture between Nippon Denso and Toyota. The plant opened in 1990, employing some 400 workers to manufacture automobile air conditioner compressors. At full production, it is expected to employ 800 employees. The plant will be Nippon Denso's most technologically advanced facility in its worldwide network, making heavy use of new technology such as robotics and CAD-to-robot interfaces. The official in charge of the local community college responsible for training employees for the new plant asked the plant manager: "How many of the 400 workers would you like to have trained in which of the nine production technologies?" The answer stunned him. The Japanese plant manager wanted all 400 employees trained in all nine of the production technologies—hydraulics, personal computer/programmable controls, electrical controls, numerical controls, electronic controls, sequence controls, robotics, surface finishing of materials, and assembly of specialized machinery. For the last three, the junior college needed assistance from Nippon Denso to be able to teach these subjects in ways desired by them. If the company were simply looking for workers to tend the robots while leaving high-paid engineers to do all the programming and specialized maintenance, there would have been no need for such an extensive set of skills. Clearly, this was not what the company had in mind. Rather, we see that Japanese managers aim to create a large cadre of middle-level technicians with broad, flexible skills.

The Nippon Denso managers made it clear that at their comparable Japanese facilities, production workers had these same broad skills, and the skills gave the firm tremendous flexibility. In Japan, the technical high schools have rigorous courses in all of these areas as well as background training in such subjects as statistics and quality control. When the graduates enter the company, they spend roughly another year in training for advanced skills. One issue of debate in Western firms has been the extent to which production workers should become involved with programming advanced microelectronics machinery. Japanese survey data indicate increasing production worker involvement in programming-related activities over time (Watanabe, 1989, p. 4).

JAPAN'S APPROACH

To summarize the Japanese approach to skill-formation for new technology is dangerous in view of the variability by industry, technology, firm, and occupational level. Only in the loosest fashion can we assert some general characteristics. These would include: a tendency to expose as many employees as possible to the new technology, formal training programs with a strong "hands-on" approach, a tendency to integrate old and new skills, an effort to avoid polarization between those who have the new skills and those who do not, and career development strategies designed to create multiskilling through job rotation and extensive training. For production workers, skill-formation goes well beyond the ability to operate more than one machine; it now includes maintenance and programming of much more complex equipment.

Although driven primarily by customer demands, competition, and labor shortage, flexibility and improved quality also served as major motivating factors for adopting the new microelectronics equipment. This adoption was facilitated by a highly capable multiskilled labor force. At the same time, the new flexibility and quality demands that result from the introduction of the new technology further encourage Japanese firms to upgrade and broaden their skill base. In Japanese manufacturing firms, with their commitment to skill formation, automation and skills tend to reinforce each other.

REFERENCES

Aoki, Masahiko. 1987. "Decentralization–Centralization and the Role of Small-Group Value in the Japanese Social System." Paper Prepared for Conference III: The Economy and Culture. Tokyo: Japanese Political Economy Research Committee.

Campbell, John. 1992. *How Policies Change: The Japanese Government and the Aging Society*. Princeton: Princeton University Press.

Cole, Robert E. 1979. *Work, Mobility, and Participation*. Berkeley: University of California Press.

Cole, Robert. 1989. *Strategies for Learning: Small Group Activities in American, Japanese and Swedish Industry*. Berkeley: University of California Press.

Dore, Ronald, et al. 1989. "Review of Flexibility in Japanese Labour Markets." Working paper. Paris: Manpower and Social Affairs Committee, OECD.

Japan Institute for Social and Economic Affairs. 1989. "Developing Human Resources to Cope with Restructuring," *Keizai Koho Center Brief* 53 (October):1–5.

Kansai Productivity Center. 1985. *Mechatronics: The Policy Implications*. Tokyo: Asian Productivity Organization.

Koike, Kazuo. 1988. *Understanding Industrial Relations in Modern Japan*. London: The MacMillan Press Ltd.

Kuwahara, Yasuo. 1987a. "Trade Unions and Developing New Technology." Paper presented to the Symposium on High Tech and Society in Japan and the Federal Republic of Germany. Berlin, Federal Republic of Germany.

Kuwahara, Yasuo. 1987b. "Organization and Policy of Labor Unions in the Advanced Technetronics Age." Paper presented to the International Conference on Labor Problems in the Advanced Technetronics Age. Tokyo.

Kuwahara, Yasuo. 1989. "Technological Change and Industrial Relations—Cases from the Printing, Banking and Machine Tool Industries in Japan." Working Paper. Geneva, Switzerland: International Labor Organization.

Lynn, Leonard, Henry Piehler, and Walter P. Zahray. 1989. "Engineering Graduates in the United States and Japan: A Comparison of Their Numbers, and an Empirical Study of their Careers and Methods of Information Transfer." Final Report of the project, "American and Japanese Engineers: A Comparative Study of Indicators of Their Number, Quality, and Utilization," National Science Foundation Grant No. SRS-84099836. Pittsburgh: Carnegie Mellon University.

McLean, Mick. 1983. *Mechatronics*. London: Frances Pinter Limited.

Nakaoka, Tetsuro. 1971. *Kōjō no Tetsugaku: Soshiki to Ningen* (Philosophy of the Factory: Organization and Mankind). Tokyo: Heibonsha.

Office of Technology Assessment. 1984. *Computerized Manufacturing Automation, Education and the Workplace*. Washington D.C.: Office of Technology Assessment, OTA.CIT-235.

Sakakibara, Kiyonori and D. Eleanor Westney. 1985. "Comparative Study of the Training, Careers, and Organization of Engineers in the Computer Industry in the United States and Japan." *Hitotsubashi Journal of Commerce and Management*, 20:1–20.

Tanaka, Hirohide. 1984. *Kaitai Suru Jukuren* (Dismantling Skill). Tokyo: Nihon Keizai Shinbunsha.

Umetani, Shunichiro. April 1989. "Training Policies and Strategies in the Context of Changing Technology, The Japanese Approach to Develop a Multi-Skilled Workforce." Paper Presented to the Workshop on Training Policies and Strategies in the Context of Changing Technology and Productivity Improvements. Delhi, India: The Commonwealth Fund for Technical Cooperation.

Watanabe, Susumu. 1987. *Microelectronics, Automation and Employment in the Automobile Industry*. New York: John Wiley and Sons.

Watanabe, Susumu. Dec. 1989. "The Diffusion of New Technology, Management Styles and Work Organization in Japan: A Survey of Empirical Studies." Report prepared for the OECD conference on "Technological Change and Society: The Role of Management Practices and National Institutions." Helsinki, Finland: OECD.

8

Technology, Industrial Relations, and the Problem of Organizational Transformation

Robert J. Thomas and Thomas A. Kochan

New competitors and new forms of competition have eroded the dominance of U.S. firms in the manufacture and sale of products, which has led, in turn, to a new "consciousness of manufacturing." Key elements of that consciousness include continuous improvement in quality, growth in product variety and differentiated marketing, and enhanced organizational responsiveness (especially in speed and flexibility) to changing global markets (Hayes et al., 1988). In short, American firms, like their counterparts in other advanced industrial economies, are searching for ways to gain strategic competitive advantage from the development and utilization of new technologies and organizational practices.

The central argument of this chapter is that the effort to achieve these advantages will precipitate fundamental transformations in the system of employment and industrial relations in the United States. Most significant will be a rapid erosion in the dominance of the traditional model, based on stability and predictability in the institutions and the philosophy of industrial relations and on a clear separation of the rights and duties of labor and management. The traditional model was characterized by a negotiated set of understandings between companies and unions that, though enshrouded in an ideology of shared values, in practice resulted in sharply defined and often antagonistic roles for personnel professionals, engineers, operations managers, and union representatives.

We will suggest that the transformation of traditional understandings and practices will require significant changes in the structure of organizational governance. However, we do not expect firms, unions, or employees to formulate a uniform response to similar external pressures. We will therefore identify the range of responses possible and then examine the behavior of stakeholders confronted by this choice.

While the traditional model will survive in some companies or even entire industries, we expect it will be rivaled first by a greater variance in approaches to employment and industrial relations practices and, second, by the emergence of alternative models adapted to specific market conditions and organizational strategies. Variance will increase as firms experiment with alternative competitive strategies, production locales, and product markets, and as they forge new types of relationships with partners and suppliers. Innovations in both product and process technologies will also be important catalysts to differentiation, particularly as efforts to "design for manufacturability" and to reduce time to market are assisted by new generations of programmable equipment and more sophisticated approaches to process control.

The appearance of alternative models will be precipitated by both adaptation to market conditions and technological innovation and by the recognition that adaptation (as well as overall firm performance) may be enhanced by employment and industrial relations practices that support higher levels of flexibility in work organization, integration of production and human resource policies, earlier and more meaningful labor–management consultation over business decisions, and power sharing in the design and development phases of technological change.

However, we do not expect the traditional model to disappear entirely, nor do we expect any single alternative model to predominate. Most broadly, managerial philosophy and organizational strategy will, we argue, continue to mediate the effects of market conditions and new technology. While competitive pressures may encourage some managers to emulate whomever they perceive to be the market leaders, other factors will allow for the coexistence of different models in the same industry and even within the same firm. For example, firms operating in the same markets may employ dramatically different models by drawing competitive advantage from sources other than their employment practices, as witnessed in the postderegulation experience of the airline industry. Alternatively, firms may seek to capture the benefits of a stable and predictable industrial relations system in one geographic region or political unit and, at the same time, build a more flexible new system in a different locale. Indeed, the expansion of competition across national boundaries and the proliferation of more flexible production technologies may actually facilitate greater choice in the construction of production and industrial relations systems.

New technology will be influential in the process of transforming employment and industrial relations systems, but it will not determine a singular set of responses. Instead, the relationship is reciprocal: The choice of technology will itself be profoundly influenced by shifts in business strategy, managerial ideology, and industrial relations theory and practice. In other words, the processes that underlie the transformation are interactive, not unidirectional, and that interaction will shape both human resource outcomes and firm performance. By making technology strategy and technological choice endogenous to a model of organizational decision making and industrial relations, we hope to avoid falling into the trap of simplistic technological determinism that has long plagued this field (see Davis and Taylor, 1976, for an exemplary critique).

This chapter is organized around three core questions. First, why is the traditional model of collective bargaining and personnel policy no longer adequate to the task of coping with contemporary changes in technology? That is, what has changed or is different about the current debates over new technology in comparison to previous debates? Second, how much change in industrial relations and personnel practice is possible within current organizational structures and governance arrangements? And, third, what changes in organizational structure and governance arrangements will be needed if new technology were to serve as a significant source of competitive advantage?

We address these questions in turn by, first, briefly reviewing the historical debates about the linkage between industrial relations and new technology and the institutional responses spurred by those debates. Second, we discuss why the debate is shifting from the "impacts" of technological change (for example, on worker skills, jobs and employment security) to a new focus on the integration of human and technical attributes in the production process. This section also summarizes the available empirical evidence on changes in organizational and institutional practice with respect to technology and industrial relations. We conclude in the third section by considering alternative definitions of employment and industrial relations that may coincide with the new "consciousness of manufacturing."

While this paper attends most directly to the relationship between technology and industrial relations, we will examine that relationship in the context of the broader array of forces operating on management and labor in contemporary industry. The key causal role played by technology in this complex web of relationships is, as argued by Walton and McKersie (1988), Pava (1988), Zuboff (1988) and others, to provide management and labor decision-makers the opportunity to "unfreeze" existing practices and to reshape the employment relationship.

HISTORY OF DEBATES ON NEW TECHNOLOGY AND INDUSTRIAL RELATIONS

Despite the recurrent specter of Luddism and the attention given in management and academic circles to overcoming worker resistance to change (Lawrence, 1954; Taylor, 1939; Roethlisberger and Dickson, 1934; and Noble, 1977), the historical record of industrial relations in the United States reveals few instances of overt union opposition to technological change. Clearly, companies and unions have clashed at times over changes in production methods and tools, especially when new methods or tools have threatened the livelihood of entire categories of employees or the existence of unions themselves (see, for example, Montgomery, 1987; Edwards, 1979; and Noble, 1984). However, the terms of the debate over technological change have historically been fairly narrow, focusing on the distribution of costs and benefits, that is, the consequences of change, not the legitimacy of technological change itself (see the review of contract language by Slichter et al., 1960, pp. 586–90). As Cockburn (1983, p. 121) has suggested, while unions may engage in collective struggle over skill, the struggle is less likely to be about skill than about its market value.

Thus, a conventional wisdom has evolved in the United States: Unions restrict themselves to negotiating over the impacts of technological change, and managements retain the right to organize work (Taft, 1963; Sorge and Streeck, 1988; Kassalow, 1989). As Slichter et al. (1960) argued in their classic analysis of the impact of trade unions and collective bargaining, when the employment base of a company is growing, unions are likely to accept technological change uncritically. Under highly competitive conditions, unions may have no alternative but to accept change—or even to promote it (Taft, 1963)— in order to maintain their members' jobs and their own institutional security.

It can be argued that the analysis by Slichter et al. is more true for industrial unions than for craft unions or the skilled trades sections of industrial unions (Montgomery, 1987). Achieving technological change in craft union settings has been more difficult, especially when the membership base, union jurisdiction, and/or the craft itself is threatened with extinction as in printing, railroads, longshoring, and segments of the construction trades (Bourdon and Levitt, 1980). Yet, even in these settings, labor and management have typically chosen to negotiate special agreements to deal with the job and institutional security issues at stake as an alternative to engaging in conflicts that might have severely weakened one or both sides. The mechanization and modernization agreement negotiated in 1960 in the West Coast longshoring industry is one example of this approach (Hartman, 1969). Thus, the evidence generally supports the contention that neither the presence of unions nor the creation of an industrial relations system has impeded technological change (Freeman and Medoff, 1985).

Separate Spheres of Influence

This narrowness in scope has been a product of both history and industrial relations theory and policy, although it is sometimes difficult to separate the effects of the two. With the eclipse of craft-based production, and the rise of scientific management, mass production, and industrial engineering in the 1920s and 1930s, decisions over the investment in and design of new technology were gradually pulled from the shopfloor into the realm of management (Piore and Sabel, 1985; Braverman, 1975). Concern for worker interests was largely relegated to the collective bargaining process or to personnel management professionals (Jacoby, 1985). This approach was later codified in the legislative enactments of the New Deal era. The "New Deal industrial relations model" sanctioned management's authority over strategic decision-making, including issues such as investments in new technology. Workers who had organized into unions were given the right to negotiate over the impacts of management decisions on wages, hours, working conditions, and other aspects of the employment relationship.

The practice of negotiating over the outcomes of technological change reflects the core assumptions underlying the New Deal industrial relations model and the "shared ideology" (Dunlop, 1958) of management and labor that supported the model. That is, it sustains the notion of a legitimate separation of spheres of influence. Management remains free to make strategic decisions and unions remain free from the political risks of being a party to decisions that may have negative consequences for their members. Both parties remain free then to use the collective bargaining process as an adjustment device. Unions retain the initiative to present claims for a share of the benefits of increased productivity as a means to offset the negative consequences of change.

However, as Sorge and Streeck (1988) have noted, this separation generated very different orientations for managers and union leaders with regard to technological change. Managers, especially top decision-makers, focused their attention outward to the market in search of signals to be translated into both product and production strategies. Their concern with the internal industrial relations consequences of market shifts and technological innovations were often secondary to the financial implications of environmental change. Union leaders, by contrast, paid little, if any, attention to the financial, product, or manufacturing process implications of market shifts and technological innovations. Instead, they devoted great attention to "trickle-down" or time-lagged effects on employment and industrial relations issues.

Since the collective bargaining process was the only arena in which unions could exert influence over these effects, and since union input came too late in the decision process to alter management's strategic responses, it is easy to see how a mismatch in orientation developed between management and labor. This mismatch also helps account for the increasing isolation of the collective bargaining process from core organizational issues. Kochan et al, (1987) make a similar argument in their explanation of how union leaders and industrial relations professionals became fixated with the routinization of collective bargaining.

Property Rights to Skill

While this analysis provides important insights into how the separation of spheres of influence and the creation of different orientations affected the manner in which companies and unions resolve conflicts of interest associated with technological change, there is another feature of the New Deal industrial relations system that we need to explore. Underlying the after-the-fact approaches to technological change was also a distinctive set of assumptions concerning the rights associated with property. These assumptions informed arguments about the claims workers and unions could make with respect to the strategic direction of the enterprise. This is an important issue in light of the rapid changes in skills (both upgrading and de-skilling) associated with the introduction of new technologies.

The ideological consensus described by industrial relations scholars relied heavily on specific conceptions of property rights (Stone, 1988). In the case of the modern corporation, owners and their representatives (managers) are accorded both responsibility for and control over the physical and financial assets of the organization. They can buy, sell, or deploy land, equipment, or other assets as long as they violate no legal regulations. They cannot, of course, buy laborers, but they are granted considerable latitude in deploying or allocating the labor (or the potential to work) they purchase through the employment contract.

With the rise of the industrial enterprise, the concentration of production activities, the growth of capital and energy-intensive machinery, and the eclipse of a craft-based division of labor, it became increasingly difficult to identify how employees' property rights, if they existed at all, figured into the process of technological change. In a situation where an employer not only supplied the equipment and materials, organized the work process, and determined the nature of the skills required to make it function, but also provided the training necessary to perform specific tasks within that process, property rights in skill were (and remain) ambiguous at best. If the employer were, for example, to change a job description in a way that reduced the skill requirements associated with the job, then, following the assumptions behind standard industrial relations practice and theory, the employer could seek to renegotiate the conditions of remuneration but neither the employees nor the union could make a legitimate claim to resist the job description change on the basis of destruction of the workers' opportunity to use their skill.

In other words, managers are held responsible for safeguarding and promoting the objectives of those who have a direct property stake in the enterprise (i.e., shareholders). In large measure, the legitimacy of managerial authority derives from that relationship. Unions and their members, by contrast, are deemed not to have a propertied stake; instead, by virtue of the contractual nature of the employment relationship, they are considered to have an "interest" in the enterprise, much as does a customer or a supplier (Williamson, 1986). Thus, while the model of organizational governance that emerged out of the early decades of the twentieth century did not explicitly address the relationship of new technology to industrial relations, it did impose effective limits on the claims workers and unions could make over the design of jobs and the investments in new technologies that might influence job design (except where health and safety are at issue).

Job-Control Unionism

Since unions ceded ultimate control over the organization of work to management, the only effective means available for unions to bargain on behalf of their members was rigorously to define and attach prices to the performance of specific jobs. This practice of "job-control unionism" established a system of industrial jurisprudence centered on what Selznick (1969) termed "industrial citizenship," with formalized contracts, detailed job descriptions, and a multistage grievance procedure to adjudicate disputes between rounds of contract negotiations.

Job-control unionism should not, however, be confused with a strategy to preserve skills. The practice of job control was intended to construct a landscape of positions defined well enough that any rearrangement undertaken by management would be obvious and would automatically activate contract provisions for such issues as determining wage and seniority levels (Katz, 1985; Chamberlain, 1986). However, since changes in technology originated at some remove from the shopfloor, this strategy did little more than ensure that the positions created or altered by new technology would have to be defined, classified, and ranked in ways consistent with precedents and practices already set by the contract (Slichter et al., 1960; Killingworth 1963; Cornfield, 1987). Negotiations over new job classifications might be tedious or even heated at times, but rarely would they lead to overt challenges to the appropriateness of the technology choices themselves.

At the same time that job control strategies and collective bargaining stabilized labor–management relations, they fostered growth of a thick underbrush of rules, customs and agreements governing the organization of many workplaces. Job descriptions, grievance procedures, and preset contract negotiations per se need not necessarily produce high degrees of formalization and rigidity. Over time, however, in instances where the relationship between the parties devolves into a dynamic low in trust and high in conflict, the potential flexibility of the job control model can give way to a deteriorating cycle of conflicts over rules, negotiation of further clarification, codification of rules, and the reinforcement of low trust levels (Fox, 1974; Katz et al., 1985).

Unintended Outcomes

Unintended though they might have been, such developments were, in many respects, the logical outcome of an industrial relations system (and the dominant theories underlying that system) that constrained unions to two principal foci: wage levels and industrial jurisprudence. That is, in partitioning the enterprise into distinct spheres and restricting the terrain of "bargainable" issues, industrial relations theory and practice promoted a perspective on human motivation based almost entirely on economic rewards and simple, but bureaucratic, notions of procedural fairness (Selznick, 1969; Dunlop, 1958).

While certainly not unimportant, economic rewards and bureaucratic rules did little to promote commitment or motivation to higher levels of performance; neither did they guarantee that workers will find the jobs they performed meaningful or satisfying. Moreover, they did not make factors such as job satisfaction or task significance central elements of (job-control) unionism. Quite the opposite, they encouraged unionists to ignore all but the economic dimensions of technological change. Indeed, not until the 1960s, when spurred by emerging theories of motivation in the behavioral sciences (McGregor, 1960; Hulin and Blood, 1968), did debates over job design begin to be entertained inside unions. Moreover, these ideas spread first in nonunion settings and were resisted by both industrial relations managers and labor union representatives in unionized facilities.

While managers in many industries chafed under what they perceived to be inelastic bonds of union work rules, the New Deal model did provide a measure of stability and predictability to union-management relations. This was especially evident in large unionized manufacturing enterprises whose bureaucratic structures easily assimilated another rule-driven process (Gouldner, 1954; Clawson, 1980). Indeed, in some cases industrial relations staffs came to prominence through their ability to "manage" unions (Serrin, 1970; Jacoby 1985).

Yet, as we will suggest in the next section, the New Deal model has proved inadequate to the task of coping with rapid economic and technological change. Separate spheres of influence may have provided a comfortable division of responsibilities, but it also encouraged managers and unions to adopt very different conceptions of the environment and the implications of environmental change. Restrictions on the flow of information may have enabled managers to exercise effective control over business strategy, but it isolated the parties and limited the intersection of their interests to that which could be negotiated under the rubric of collective bargaining. Collective bargaining, in turn, may have simplified organizational governance by expressing interests largely in terms of dollars and cents, but it reduced conceptions of human motivation to simple economic self-interest. Taken together, these "unintended outcomes" now represent a formidable barrier to organizational transformation and to the innovative use of new technology.

INTEGRATING HUMAN AND TECHNICAL ATTRIBUTES IN PRODUCTION

While responsibility for dealing with the impacts of technological change continues to reside within collective bargaining and the personnel function, the terms of the debate over technology and industrial relations have shifted dramatically in recent years. Three issues dominate the current debate: (1) whether labor–management relations built around a central institutional edifice—collective bargaining—are adequate to the task of coping with rapid technological change; (2) whether it is necessary to integrate worker interests, talents, and motivations with new technologies; and (3) whether such an integration requires a fundamental redefinition of the employment contract and with it a reformulation of the industrial relations system. All three issues reflect a deeper challenge facing policy-makers, managers, and union leaders in the United States and other advanced industrialized nations: how to use human resources and new technology to gain strategic advantage in today's marketplace.

Competitive Strategy and Technology Strategy

To unravel how new technologies will relate to industrial relations, worker interests, and organizational performance, we must begin by assessing how firms' business objectives influence their choice and subsequent use of technology. To make this assessment, we borrow a simplified summary of organizational choices and their consequences from the work of Kochan et al., (1984) and Kochan et al., (1986).

Intensifying competition, the shortening of product life cycles, and the increasing segmentation of markets have all heightened the pressures on firms both to lower costs and to increase the speed and accuracy with which they respond to changing market conditions and opportunities. Rather than produce a single response, however, these forces induce firms to reassess their competitive strategies and to choose whether to compete on the basis of lower costs and higher volumes for mass, standardized markets, or to search for single- and multiple-niche markets in which they can stress product quality, speed to market, or technological superiority. (For similar arguments, see Sorge and Streeck, 1988, pp. 27–31; Child, 1985; and Willman, 1987). While, in reality, firms may put some emphasis on both responses, the relative emphasis given to low cost versus differentiation strategies will have important consequences both for how new technology is developed and utilized and for how industrial relations will be conducted.

Nevertheless, even given these opportunities for the exercise of strategic choice, the *process* by which new technology is developed and deployed can be constrained by existing and historic labor–management relations (Wilkinson, 1983; Daniels, 1987). The more deeply committed either management or labor is to the traditional industrial relations system described earlier, the more difficult it will be to achieve the organizational reforms necessary to utilize fully technological innovations as they become available. Equally important, it will be more difficult to *devise* technological innovations that provide competitive advantage. In other words, technology strategy cannot be detached easily from the larger interrelated set of strategic choices and transformations in industrial relations.

Our central proposition is that reforms in industrial relations practice and in organizational governance are more likely to occur and survive over time in organizations that place greater emphasis on the differentiation/high-quality competitive strategy than in those that pursue the low-cost competitive strategy. The former requires a commitment to high productivity and substantial investments in human resource development. The latter implies the continuation—even intensification—of a low-wage/managerial control strategy.

We now turn to a more detailed discussion of the evidence that leads us to these propositions. The first body of evidence comes from efforts of the U.S. automobile industry to reform shopfloor industrial relations practices and production systems in order to improve manufacturing performance. The second comes from several intensive case studies of how new technology is traditionally developed.

Workplace Industrial Relations and Production Systems

The 1980s were a decade of intense experimentation and change in workplace industrial relations practices. In the early years of the decade, quality control circles and quality of work life programs proliferated (Simmons and Mares 1983; Walton 1981; Cole, 1989). While these programs served a useful function in unfreezing traditional practices and building trust, most were not powerful enough to create major improvements in productivity or product quality (Katz et al., 1983; 1985; Walton and McKersie, 1988). Many were "crisis driven" and/or undertaken without a clear connection to a broader agenda of organizational innovation and change. Thus, as crises abated or the programs exhausted the "housekeeping issues" (such as poor ventilation and lighting) they were allowed to address, interest waned and many programs withered away (Thomas, 1989).

Some, however, did take root and have contributed to improvements in performance. A growing body of evidence—including Cole's (1989) comparative analysis of workplace reforms in the United States, Japan, and Scandinavia and Walton's (1987) eight-nation comparative study of the maritime shipping industry—suggests that the successful cases integrated their industrial relations programs into changes in production policies that required greater teamwork, flexibility, problem solving, and decentralized decision-making. This conclusion is buttressed by case studies of Japanese transplants in the U.S. automobile industry and by recent quantitative analyses of automobile assembly plant productivity and quality.

Shimada and MacDuffie (1986) developed a model to describe the interactions between human and technical features in the Japanese production plants operating in the United States. From a review of the operating practices found in these plants, they proposed that the success of the technical production system rested on a foundation of high skill, motivation, and commitment by the labor force. These attributes were achieved through a complex, integrated approach to human resource policy that emphasized long-term employment stability, extensive training and development of a multiskilled labor force, compensation systems that rewarded both job performance and skill development, internal promotion, low status differentiation between workers and managers, elaborate vertical and horizontal information flows and suggestion systems, and extensive use of work teams to organize the production process.

These human resource attributes, in turn, supported a system of continuous improvements, decentralized decision-making, integration of quality control into the production process, just-in-time inventory practices, and tight interdependence across functional activities in the production process. Taken together, the researchers argued, the integration of these human and production system variables can create simultaneously high levels of quality and productivity.

It should be noted, however, that Shimada and MacDuffie regarded this arrangement as a "fragile" production system since it depended so heavily on attaining and maintaining the trust and cooperation of the workforce. For most Japanese transplants, trust and cooperation were built slowly through extensive programs of recruitment and selection, intensive pre-employment and on-the-job socialization, and, of course, efforts to sustain a "union-free" environment (Cole and Deskins, 1988; Parker and Slaughter, 1988). Although they enjoyed the inherent advantages of starting from scratch in a greenfield site, companies such as Honda and Nissan invested heavily in creating what they believed to be an essential foundation for their production system—that of reciprocal commitment among the company, its management, and its employees (or "associates").

Shimada and MacDuffie contrasted this fragile system with the traditional North American production approach that is designed to be more "robust" in order to dampen the impact of variability in human inputs. This more robust system emphasized narrowly defined jobs that can be filled by interchangeable, low-skilled workers; large inventory buffers that minimized the disruption caused by production errors or poor-quality parts; extra employees to cope with higher absenteeism; sophisticated quality-control inspection systems and specialized personnel to catch defects after production was completed; and technologies designed to minimize the number of workers and to control or limit worker discretion. All these attributes of a low-trust environment (Fox, 1974) make sense in the world of traditional industrial relations and all are deeply ingrained in the culture, educational training, and organizational experiences of American engineers, managers, and, as might be expected, union leaders as well.

In a test of the Shimada and MacDuffie model in an international sample of over 50 automobile assembly plants, Krafcik and MacDuffie (1989) and MacDuffie (1989) showed that the choice of fragile or robust strategies makes a difference in performance. That is, when more elements of the "fragile" human resource and production system were present, higher levels of quality and productivity were achieved. This is perhaps the most powerful quantitative evidence in support of the logic of these new systems.

Indeed, their results have been largely accepted—albeit grudgingly in some instances—and internalized as the appropriate strategy for the future of all the major American automobile firms. For example, General Motors has built on similar concepts in the design of the Saturn Corporation, in its Quality Network program, and in its efforts to introduce team systems of production into a variety of new and retrofitted plants. Chrysler has embarked on a strategy of negotiating "Modern Operating Agreements" or "Progressive Operating Agreements" with its local unions in various plants to reform along similar lines its labor relations practices, its work organization and management systems, and its production processes. Ford has adopted a more incremental approach to reform, linking employee involvement to quality and statistical process control.

With each reform, a brick appears to be removed from the wall dividing industrial relations strategy and practice from broader organizational goals and strategies. Narrow job definitions appear to be giving way to broader, multiskilled assignments even in the regimented assembly plant environment. Major investments in workforce training and long-term human capital improvement—ranging from basic literacy to manufacturing theory and business economics—give at least nominal support to the idea that employees are coming to be seen as a valuable resource. The gradual replacement of close supervision by semiautonomous work teams and more decentralized systems of responsibility for quality and work scheduling suggest that greater recognition is being given to the contributions nonmanagerial employees can make to company performance. The extension of longer-term employment guarantees in the major automobile companies and elsewhere have begun to erode traditional concepts of employment-at-will and the associated practice of mass layoffs in response to market fluctuations.

Encouraging as these developments may be, it is essential also to insert a note of caution. Both the models and the empirical analyses provide useful insight as to the difference between "fragile" and "robust" strategies, but they can only offer limited clues as to how far beyond the shopfloor those differences go, or, perhaps more important, how far they must go to support innovations at the workplace level. Put differently, for the new strategy to survive, we strongly suspect that it will have to be extended far beyond shopfloor-level reforms.

With specific reference to industrial relations practice, an important issue involves the extent to which the new strategy influences the *choice* as well as the *implementation* of new technology. Resolving this issue would require a detailed examination of the decision-making process as it takes place in the higher levels of the organization and at earlier points in time—an approach that is not customary for industrial relations theory and practice.

The Politics of Technological Choice: Upstream Decision Making

Reforms to shopfloor industrial relations practices may be important to the effective use of existing technologies, but their longevity and their potential contribution to broader organizational objectives are very much tied to upstream decisions about new products and new process technologies. As Kochan et al., (1987) and others (Sorge and Streeck 1988; Francis, 1986; Lansbury and Bamber, 1989; Poole, 1975) have argued, long-term support for innovations at the workplace level will require earlier and broader consultation on strategic decision-making around such issues as the selection and implementation of new production technologies. However, one should not expect planning and decision-making in all levels and functions to reflect automatically or immediately reforms in human resource and industrial relations philosophy. Despite the higher level of experimentation in work practices and the institutionalization of some industrial relations reforms, most organizations are and will remain complex assemblages of contending interests and visions that are extraordinarily difficult to infuse with a single operational philosophy.

Thomas' (forthcoming and 1991) examination of three technological changes in a large U.S. manufacturing firm provides a number of insights into the opportunities and obstacles facing companies and unions as they seek to change their traditional approach to technological change. The company and union involved in the study were among the pioneers in agreeing to contract language establishing joint committees to address new technology issues outside the confines of collective bargaining. The committees put in place were chartered to carry on advance discussions of the human and organizational consequences of technological change. However, after several years of meetings, briefings, and the like, both parties found themselves stymied by their failure to move beyond a few limited experiments in job redesign. With their cooperation, Thomas designed research to document the entire process of change—from proposal development to and through implementation—in order to uncover points where advance discussion/collaboration might yield innovations beneficial to both sides. Such innovations might include speedier and less troublesome introduction of new equipment and systems, fewer disputes over changes in job content and classification, and improvements in capacity utilization.

Thomas' case studies provide four findings of interest. First, they revealed how thoroughly pervasive traditional assumptions about motivation and authority can be even in an organization committed to change. Despite senior management's pronouncements signaling a shift in strategy, line managers and production engineers continued to believe that the only acceptable justifications for technological change were those that promised to reduce significantly the direct labor content of production activities. Even when aware that their requests often resulted in increases in indirect labor, managers and engineers relied on traditional accounting methods and evaluative criteria as their principal guides. On the one hand, they admitted dissatisfaction with accounting methods inappropriate to—and, indeed, often antagonistic toward—the development of a coherent manufacturing strategy. On the other hand, they despaired of their own ability to convince financial staff that alternative methodologies were available and appropriate to the task.

Second, the case studies strongly suggested that intraorganizational conflicts associated with the development and implementation of new technology can make it difficult to implement changes in labor–management relations without simultaneous change in other facets of the organization. Two key sources of intraorganizational contention were evident: (1) competition among subunits (for example, different functional groups) for a share of the finite resources available for process improvement led to closely guarded change efforts; and (2) proposed changes that commonly cut across functional boundaries ignited conflicts that reduced the willingness of change proponents to reveal their plans too broadly or too far in advance. In combination, these two sources of intraorganizational conflict made it exceedingly difficult to engage the union as a partner in crafting innovative approaches to technological change.

Third, the case studies showed that the existing division of labor between production engineering, operations management, and industrial relations further inhibited disclosure of information about technological change—especially to the union. For example, industrial relations (IR) staff were given responsibility for dealing with changes in staffing and wage levels, for estimating the impact of new technology, and for managing relations with the union. Yet, IR staff had neither the skills nor the resources to monitor incoming new technology adequately. Because IR lacked expertise and staff, it was often ignored by engineers and production managers until new machines were installed and needed to be put into use. Since they learned of the changes shortly before employees and the union, IR staff guarded the little information they had. Workers on the shopfloor heard only rumors of change—and rumors were frequent—until the new equipment was unloaded or unveiled. Rumor and surprise did little to promote trust and often provoked anxiety about job security and the need for mid-career retraining. These practices, in turn, challenged the union to invoke bureaucratic rules concerning job classifications and wage setting.

Engineers and managers who had been intimately involved in developing proposals and securing funding and who did have the data necessary for advance discussions refused to contact the union. On the one hand, they argued that this responsibility resided in industrial relations. On the other hand, production managers characterized advance discussion as a betrayal of company secrets to the union. They believed that disclosure of change plans would only give ammunition to the union for use in subsequent negotiations of wage levels and/or the next round of contract negotiations.

Fourth, the union itself posed a significant challenge to reform industrial relations practice. A central and unresolved question for the union was the price it might have to pay for participating in advance discussions of new technology. The costs in terms of resources expended in upgrading its technical staff were potentially enormous. The union also viewed the cost of accepting of a new set responsibilities as high. More extensive consultation with management provoked concerns that the union would be perceived by its members (and other unions) as having been coopted by management (Parker and Slaughter, 1988; Wells, 1987; Thomas, 1991).

By pledging themselves to advance consultation over new technology and then reaching an impasse in the implementation of their agreement, this company and its union confronted directly the legacy of the New Deal model of industrial relations. Workplace-level reforms had enabled substantial progress in promoting a common understanding of organizational objectives. Furthermore, the creation of collaborative efforts beyond the scope of collective bargaining had allowed for experimentation in industrial relations practice without interference from contract rules and regulations. Yet, the maintenance of distinct spheres of influence rendered both sides wary of instigating changes that would demand a redefinition of their relationship.

Further progress in developing a more flexible and responsive industrial relations system would require at least three changes in managerial philosophy and practice: (1) accepting unions as full and legitimate participants in the definition of a manufacturing strategy, complete with a reconceptualization of the criteria for selecting among alternative approaches to work organization; (2) confronting directly the forms and bases of contention among organizational subunits that inhibit information sharing across functional boundaries and between managers and union representatives; and (3) reorganizing the industrial relations function, or perhaps even eliminating it, to remove the limitations on consultation associated with bureaucratic rules and regulations.

For the union, progress in reshaping the form and content of the industrial relations system would pose three equally difficult challenges: (1) acquiring the expertise with which to anticipate the potential implications of embryonic technical concepts; (2) creating the organizational wherewithal to track technological changes from "cradle to grave"; and perhaps most important, (3) forming a willingness to refrain from using advance consultation, information sharing, and the like as points of leverage in a traditional approach to industrial relations and collective bargaining.

CHANGES IN INDUSTRIAL RELATIONS THEORY AND PRACTICE

Developments in the global economy have brought to the surface three fundamental problems for the structure and practice of industrial relations: (1) how to gain competitive advantage through the development of new technologies and organizational practices; (2) how to reduce or eliminate the historical barriers to flexibility in the deployment of physical, financial, and, most important here, human resources; and (3) how to recast the system of union-management relations to support competitive goals.

While research in industrial relations has yet to reveal a consistent pattern of responses to these problems, two general models appear to be emerging. One model, described earlier as a low-cost/managerial control strategy, represents a linear extension and, in some cases, an intensification of past practice. To the extent that labor cannot be "driven out" by technical means, adopters of this approach can be expected to seek alternative venues in which to implement their strategy—in particular, through the internationalization of production and sourcing—or to invest in campaigns to sustain their independence from organized labor.

The other model represents what we believe to be a decisive break with past practice. At its core resides a recognition that technological and competitive strategies can no longer be detached from organizational, industrial relations, and human resource strategy and practice. Buffering institutions, such as those found in the New Deal model of industrial relations, now represent obstacles to the creation of a system capable of producing high-quality goods. Strategies of control are slowly giving way to delegated responsibility, and tentative efforts at union-management cooperation are finding firmer footing in broader information sharing, job redesign, and workplace-level reforms.

The continued evolution of the latter model will depend on many things, including a consistent level of support for changed practice from top management. One critical factor stands out: the core definition of the employment relationship. That is, as we have argued in this chapter, the New Deal era model of industrial relations established a strict separation of rights and duties in the business enterprise that reduced the employment relationship to an economic nexus. As representatives of property owners, managers were given the right to organize work and workers and, as agents for propertyless employees, unions were given the right to bargain over the rewards for the performance of work tasks. The establishment of collective bargaining and industrial jurisprudence cemented that distinction. In the process, both management and unions were encouraged to focus their attention on the objective determination of wages and performance standards, and to ignore the subjective involvement of workers in the goals and the objectives of the enterprise.

Now it appears that subjective involvement is a key criterion of a flexible, responsive, and high-quality production system. New, expensive, and sensitive production technologies cannot be exploited effectively without knowledge, care, and attention from operators and technicians (Adler, 1987; Zuboff, 1988). Quality products cannot be produced without awareness of the limits as well as the capabilities of both mechanical and human systems (Heller, 1989; Hirschhorn, 1984). The costs of an illtrained and inattentive labor force are increasingly obvious. All these are undeniable indicators that, as Walton (1981) has argued, core organizational philosophies must shift from "control" to "commitment."

However, current definitions of the employment relationship, particularly the core principle of employment at will, stand in direct opposition to the cultivation of subjective involvement. Moreover, time-honored practices of hierarchical organization, especially the distinction between salaried and hourly or managerial and nonmanagerial employees, implicitly divide those from whom subjective involvement and commitment are both expected and rewarded and those from whom a set amount of work is expected in return for a set wage. At issue is more than simply the type and timing of economic reward; rather, the issue involves the claims that organizations make against the energies of their members and, in turn, the claims members can legitimately make against the collectivities of which they are a part.

Transformations in the system of industrial relations will both inspire and depend upon definitions of the employment relationship that transcend these historical limits. While the future can at best be dimly perceived, two alternatives are worth considering.

The "Vested" Worker

The first alternative may involve a redefinition of the basic model of organizational governance. That is, as organizations seek to employ the "whole" worker, as some Japanese firms claim to do (Shimada, 1984), they may be compelled to recognize the *reciprocity* of investments that employment entails. Organizations investing in their members as a key ingredient to the effective use of productive resources grant, as a result, a greater share of responsibility to workers for defining and achieving common goals; individuals invest themselves in organizational objectives in return for longer-term rewards, for example, in the form of employment security and lifelong skill development. More than simply a generalization of the limited Japanese practice of lifetime employment, the employment relationship would represent a "vesting" of workers in an organization to the point where workers can claim that membership gives them an expanded voice in the governance of the enterprise.

Such a redefinition could dramatically alter both the structure of unionism and the general distribution of employment opportunities. Employers seeking to secure their investments in employees and in a system of production and governance that employs the "whole" worker may take "protectionist" measures. They may be unwilling to risk losing the advantages they accrue by allowing knowledge about their practices to be transmitted to other firms through unions that also have contracts with their competitors. At the extreme, this could lead to efforts at corporatist solutions (Streeck, 1984) and/or enterprise unionism of the Japanese variety, and a serious threat of balkanization to the U.S. labor movement. Small steps in this direction have already been evidenced in the breakdown of pattern bargaining and, more directly, in the recent history of concessions and tailored contracts in the major unionized industries (Parker and Slaughter 1988). Resistance to such efforts has been growing in recent years, particularly as militant caucuses in the automobile industry (for example, New Directions) have voiced a more articulate opposition to programs of "jointness."

Employment opportunities could very well change should the employment relationship be redefined along the lines of the vested worker model. Here again, Japan and, to a lesser extent, Western Europe provide some useful lessons. As large Japanese industrial firms and enterprise-based unions evolved a complex set of rewards and incentives for long-term employment, they also contributed significantly to labor market dualism (Cole, 1979). A similar gap between increasingly skilled and secure job opportunities and less skilled and unstable employment could happen in the United States (Harrison and Bluestone, 1988) with added friction resulting from a likely parallel gap in the labor market along the lines of race and ethnicity (Wilson, 1987). As long as redefinition of the employment relationship—built around the notion of reciprocal commitments—remains largely a private affair, balkanization and increased labor market segmentation are at least two plausible consequences.

Public Policy Definition

An alternative redefinition of employment relations could take place as a matter of public policy. The New Deal model of industrial relations made it possible for companies and unions to develop privately an elaborate system of pensions and benefits based on the stable employment of workers with individual companies. A key implication of this model is that opportunities for skill development and retraining are only available through private employment, which contributes to labor market segmentation. If however, skill-formation were perceived as an essential foundation to economic growth in an environment characterized by rapid technological change, then the public sector would have a legitimate claim to helping redefine the employment relationship in ways that serve both managers and employees (Osterman, 1988).

While such efforts need not be restricted to the simple expansion of the traditional system of vocational education, the creation of a combined public/private investment fund in skill-formation would enable government, industry, and organized labor to have a voice in shaping the future of employment opportunities.

CONCLUSION

The circle is closed: changes in markets and technologies have set in motion a search for new models of industrial relations practice and theory, and success in these new market and technological conditions depends on the implementation of new industrial relations models. The experience of the 1980s further suggests that there is no guarantee that management and labor, on their own, will implement the reforms in organizational governance needed to produce and sustain new models. Instead, we have learned, once again, that all such organizational choices and changes, including technological choices and changes, are political choices and thus depend not just on objective external stimuli but also on the values, the distribution of power, and the historical relationships among the actors involved.

The private choices of firms, employees, and unions take place within and are influenced by a broader political and legal environment that many industrial relations and human resource scholars believe reinforces traditional practice and discourages needed innovations. Put simply, we believe that the industrial relations reforms needed to exploit new technologies fully will not diffuse broadly or dominate unless public policies change to strengthen the role and power of employee stakeholder interests in organizational decision-making and governance. We expect this proposition to be a central feature in future debates and research on the relationship between technology and industrial relations.

REFERENCES

Adler, Paul. 1987. "Automation and Skill: New Directions." *International Journal of Technology Management* 2:761–72.
Bourdon, Clinton C. and Raymond E. Levitt. 1980. *Union and Open-Shop Construction.* Lexington, Mass.: D. C. Heath.
Braverman, Harry. 1975. *Labor and Monopoly Capital.* New York: Monthly Review Press.
Chamberlain, Neil W., and James W. Kuhn. 1986. *Collective Bargaining.* New York: McGraw–Hill.
Child, John. 1985. "Managerial Strategies, New Technology and the Labour Process." In D. Knights, H. Willmott, and D. Collinson (eds.), *Job Redesign: Critical Perspectives on the Labour Process* London: Gower. pp. 107–41.
Clawson, Robert. 1980. *Bureacuracy and the Labor Process.* Berkeley: University of California Press.
Cockburn, C. 1983. *Brothers: Male Dominance and Technological Change.* London: Pluto.
Cole, Robert E. 1989. *Strategies for Learning.* Berkeley: University of California Press.
Cole, Robert E. 1979. *Work, Mobility, and Participation.* Berkeley: University of California Press.
Cole, Robert E. and Donald Deskins. 1988. "Racial Factors in Site Location and Employment Patterns of Japanese Auto Firms in America." *California Management Review* 31:38–54.
Cornfield, Dan. 1987. "Labor–Management Cooperation or Management Control." In D. Cornfield (ed.). *Workers, Managers, and Technological Change.* New York: Plenum
Daniels, W.W. 1987. *Workplace Industrial Relations and Technical Change.* London: Francis Pinter.
Davis, Louis, and James C. Taylor. 1976. "Technology Effects on Job, Work and Organizational Structure." In L. Davis and J. Taylor (eds.). *The Quality of Working Life.* New York: Free Press.
Dunlop, John T. 1958. *Industrial Relations Systems.* New York: Holt.
Edwards, Richard. 1979. *Contested Terrain.* New York: Basic Books.
Fox, Alan. 1974. *Beyond Contract: Work, Authority and Trust Relations in Industry.* London: MacMillan.
Francis, Arthur. 1986. *New Technology at Work.* London: Oxford University Press.
Freeman, Richard, and James Medoff. 1985. *What Do Unions Do?.* New York: Basic.
Gouldner, Alvin. 1954. *Patterns of Industrial Bureaucracy.* Glencoe, Ill.: Free Press.
Harrison, Bennet, and Barry Bluestone. 1988. *The Great U-Turn: Corporate Restructuring and the Polarizing of America.* New York: Basic.
Hartman, Paul T. 1969. *Collective Bargaining and Productivity.* Berkeley: University of California Press.
Hayes, Robert, Steven Wheelwright, and Kim Clark. 1988. *Dynamic Manufacturing.* New York: Free Press.
Heller, Frank. 1989. "Human Resource Management and the Socio-Technical Approach." In G. Bamber and R. Lansbury (eds.). *New Technology: International Perspectives on Human Resources and Industrial Relations,* London: Unwin Hyman. pp. 181–96.
Hirschhorn, Larry. 1984. *Beyond Mechanization.* Cambridge, Mass.: MIT Press.
Hulin, Charles L., and Milton R. Blood. 1969. "Job Enlargement, Individual Differences, and Worker Responses." *Psychological Bulletin.* 69:41–55.
Jacoby, Sanford M. 1985. *Employing Bureaucracy: Managers, Unions and the Transformation of Work in American Industry, 1900–1945.* New York: Columbia University Press.
Kassalow, Everett. 1989. "New Technology and Industrial Relations." In G. Bamber and R. Lansbury (eds.). *New Technology: International Perspectives on Human Resources and Industrial Relations.* London: Unwin Hyman.

Katz, Harry. 1985. *Shifting Gears: Changing Labor Relations in the U.S. Automobile Industry.* Cambridge, Mass.: MIT Press.

Katz, Harry, Thomas A. Kochan, and Kenneth B. Gobielle, 1983. "Industrial relations Performance, Economic Performance, and QWL Programs." *Industrial and Labor Relations Review.* 37:3–17.

Katz, Harry, Thomas A. Kochan and Mark Weber, 1985. "Assessing the Effects of Industrial Relations and Quality of Working Life Efforts on Organizational Effectiveness." *Academy of Management Journal.* 28:509–27.

Killingsworth, Charles. 1963. "Cooperative Approaches to the Problem of Technological Change." In G. Somers, E. Cushman, and N. Weinberg (eds.). *Adjusting to Technological Change,* New York: Harper and Row. pp. 61–94.

Kochan, Thomas, Harry Katz, and Robert McKersie. 1987. *The Transformation of American Industrial Relations.* New York: Basic.

Kochan, Thomas A., Robert B. McKersie, and Peter Cappelli. 1984. "Strategic Choice and Industrial Relations Theory." *Industrial Relations,* 23:16–39.

Krafcik, John F., and John Paul MacDuffie. 1989. "Explaining High Performance Manufacturing: The International Automotive Assembly Plant Study." Paper presented to the MIT International Motor Vehicle Program Policy Forum.

Lansbury, Russell, and Greg Bamber. 1989. "Technological Change, Industrial Relations and Human Resource Management." In G. Bamber and R. Lansbury (eds.). *New Technology: International Perspectives on Human Resources and Industrial Relations.* London: Unwin Hyman.

Lawrence, Paul. 1954. "How to Deal with Resistance to Change." *Harvard Business Review,* 32:49–57.

MacDuffie, John Paul. 1989. "Worldwide Trends in Production System Management: Work Systems, Factory Practice, and Human Resource Management." Paper presented to the MIT International Motor Vehicle Research Program Policy Forum.

McGregor, Douglas. 1960. *The Human Side of Enterprise.* New York: McGraw–Hill.

Montgomery, David. 1987. *The Fall of the House of Labor.* New York: Cambridge University Press.

Noble, David. 1977. *America By Design.* New York: Oxford University Press.

Noble, David. 1984. *Forces of Production: A Social History of Industrial Automation.* New York: Alfred A. Knopf.

Osterman, Paul. 1988. *Employment Futures.* New York: Oxford University Press.

Parker, Mike, and Jane Slaughter. 1988. *Choosing Sides: Unions and the Team Concept.* Boston: South End Press.

Pava, Calvin. 1988. "Managing New Information Technology: Design or Default." In R. Walton and P. Lawrence (eds.). *Human Resource Management: Trends and Challenges.* Boston: Harvard University Press.

Piore, Michael, and Charles Sabel. 1985. *The Second Industrial Divide.* New York: Basic.

Poole, Michael. 1975. *Worker Participation in Industry.* London: Cambridge University Press.

Roethlisberger, F. J., and W. J. Dickson. 1934. *Management and the Worker.* Cambridge, Mass.: Harvard University Press.

Selznick, Philip. 1969. *Law, Society and Industrial Justice.* New York: Sage.

Serrin, William. 1970. *The Company and the Union.* New York: Vintage.

Shimada, Haruo. 1984. "The Perceptions and the Reality of Japanese Industrial Relations." In L. Thurow (ed.).*The Management Challenge: Japanese Views.* Cambridge, Mass.: MIT Press.

Shimada, Haruo and John Paul MacDuffie 1986. "Industrial Relations and Humanware." Sloan School of Management Working Paper.

Simmons, John, and William Mares. 1983. *Working Together.* New York: Knopf.

Slichter, Sumner, James J. Healy, and E. Robert Livernash. 1960. *The Impact of Collective Bargaining on Management.* Washington, D.C.: Brookings.

Sorge, Arndt, and Wolfgang Streeck. 1988. "Industrial Relations and Technological Change: The Case for an Extended Perspective." In R. Hyman and W. Streeck (eds.). *New Technology and Industrial Relations,* London: Blackwell. pp. 204–19.

Stone, Katherine Van Wezel. 1988. "Labor and the Corporate Structure: Changing Conceptions and Emerging Possibilities." *University of Chicago Law Review*, 55(73):73–173.

Streeck, Wolfgang. 1984. "Neo-Corporatist Industrial Relations and the Economic Crisis in West Germany." In J. Goldthorpe (ed.).*Order and Conflict in Contemporary Capitalism*. London: Clarendon/Oxford.

Taft, Philip. 1963. "Organized Labor and Technical Change: A Backward Look." In G. Somers, E. Cushman, and N. Weinberg (eds.). *Adjusting to Technological Change*. New York: Harper and Row. pp. 61–94.

Taylor, Frederick. 1939. *Scientific Management*. New York: Harper and Row.

Thomas, Robert J. Forthcoming. *The Politics of Technology*. Berkeley: University of California Press.

Thomas, Robert J. 1991. "Technological Choice and Union–Management Consultation on New Technology." *Industrial Relations*, 30(2):167-92.

Thomas, Robert J. 1989. "Participation and Control: A Shopfloor Perspective." In R. Magjuka and S. Bacharach (eds.). *Research in the Sociology of Organizations*, Vol. 7.

Walton, Richard. 1981 "Establishing and Maintaining High Commitment Work Systems." In J. Kimberly et al. (eds.). *The Organizational Life Cycle*, San Francisco: Jossey-Bass, pp. 208–90.

Walton, Richard. 1987. *Innovating to Compete*. San Francisco: Jossey-Bass.

Walton, Richard, and Robert B. McKersie. 1988. "Managing New Technology and Labor Relations: Opportunity for Mutual Influence." MIT Management in the 1990s Working Paper Series #88-062.

Wells, Donald. 1987. *Empty Promises*. New York: Monthly Review Press.

Wilkinson, Barry. 1983. *The Shopfloor Politics of New Technology*. London: Heinemann.

Williamson, Oliver. 1986. *The Economic Institutions of Capitalism*. New York: Basic.

Willman, Paul. 1987. "Industrial Relations Issues in Advanced Manufacturing Technology." In T. Wall, C. Clegg, and N. Kemp (eds.). *The Human Side of Manufacturing Technology*, New York: Wiley. pp. 135–52

Wilson, William Julius. 1987. *The Truly Disadvantaged*. Chicago: University of Chicago Press.

Zuboff, Shoshana. 1988. *In the Age of the Smart Machine*. New York: Basic.

9

Union Initiatives to Restructure Industry in Australia

Max Ogden

Over the past 10 years, the Australian union movement's strategy has undergone a major transformation from what was virtually a sole concern with the distribution of wealth to a greater focus on the creation of wealth. Australian unions have broadened their advocacy efforts from a narrow preoccupation with issues specific to the worker, such as wages and working hours, to a wider concern with the health and global competitiveness of Australian industry.

Out of necessity—a necessity born of technological innovations and market shifts—and abetted by political forces, the Australian union movement has taken a position upon what was once considered exclusively management turf. The Australian union movement now is actively engaged in such issues as the efficiency of Australian industry, the need for new skills, training, and better management techniques, the use of technology, and the organization of work.

Australia Reconstructed (1987), a sweeping document produced by the Australian Council of Trade Unions, set forth the union movement's new vision: that industrial problems are best tackled in a comprehensive manner. The document also explicitly recognized that the methods or processes used in effecting change are as critical as the objectives. As a result of its efforts to implement this new vision, it is now widely conceded that the union movement has taken the initiative and in many cases set the pace for industry restructuring in Australia. This chapter surveys the change in the Australian union movement and describes the movement's approach of developing long-term national policies that both support and are supported by restructuring at the enterprise level.

A NEW UNION STRATEGY

The Australian union movement was born out of the British craft system, and retains many similarities. To this day, most union divisions are based on craft as opposed to industry, which accounts in part for the large number of unions. Of 308 unions, the largest 25 account for 63 percent of total membership, indicating considerable fragmentation in policies, resources, and areas of concern. Union membership has been declining in Australia from its traditional level of 60 percent, especially in service and high-technology industries. It now averages 42 percent of the workforce. All unions fall under the umbrella of the Australian Council of Trade Unions (ACTU).

From its British parent, the Australian union movement also inherited a pragmatic outlook, with little in the way of long-term political or industrial strategies. In particular, unions showed little interest in intervening in management decision-making areas and, even though they were the major founder of the Australian Labor Party (ALP) in 1891, tended to leave politics to the ALP except on issues that impinged directly on union rights or wages.

Beginning in the late 1960s and early 1970s, technological, market, and political changes conspired to change union thinking. The Communist Party of Australia had considerable influence in some sectors of the union movement, and played an important role in the early stages, arguing for greater worker intervention in management prerogatives; for unions to be more democratic; and for unions to take into account broader social issues such as the environment, social welfare, and the need for efficient industries.

Since then, the union movement has developed a rational overall strategy encompassing industrial democracy, technological change, skill formation, and environmental issues, as well as the more traditional concerns over living standards. Industrial democracy is no longer perceived as simply a nice issue to pursue, offering the reward of a warm inner glow, but a critical element of an efficient, wealth-producing industry, directly linked to the generation of jobs and the improvement of living standards.

This change did not emerge from a vacuum nor from the grand vision of any one person or group. Instead, the strategy unfolded step by step. Once the union movement became concerned about such things as the health of manufacturing industry and the national balance of payments, it became obvious that Australian industry had to become more efficient. This led to a focus on the role of management, and to the conclusions that Australian management was poor by world standards and that Australian industry required fundamental restructuring.

Issues that were traditionally peripheral to day-to-day negotiations became central. For example, workforce skills are now at the heart of union wage strategy, along with work organization, consultative processes, managerial decision-making, workforce morale, and union rights.

In addition, the new strategy requires long-term and sophisticated planning on the part of unions, rather than the generally reactive approach that characterized the earlier, more limited concern with wealth distribution.

The Ideological Context

It would be wrong to give the impression that there is unanimity within the unions about strategy even today. Traditional union views die hard, especially when both right- and left-wing elements used to concede that management had the sole right to manage. The right wing was not particularly interested in socialist change and believed that delving into management issues was too radical and might alienate union members and the public.

The left was committed to socialist change, but almost exclusively through changing the distribution of wealth and not industrial reform. The left led economic campaigns aimed at helping workers see the unjust nature of capitalism with the aim of inspiring workers to seek change. They viewed their task as helping capitalism collapse, not helping it run more efficiently. Therefore, the idea of a union movement concerned with the production of wealth as well as its distribution seemed an unacceptable compromise because it placed fetters on workers' activism. It is noteworthy that such a viewpoint fits perfectly with New Right ideology as demonstrated by the miners' and printers' disputes in Britain and some disputes in Australia.

When the concepts of worker control and industrial democracy were back on the agenda for debate in the late 1960s and early 1970s, they created confusion for the left. During this period, the Communist Party of Australia (CPA) took a leadership role in reshaping the union vision of workers' issues. Despite its small size and recent demise, the Communist Party in Australia supplied the union movement with many of its most able leaders for many years. Its reputation was enhanced by its unusual degree of independence. (It was one of the first Communist Parties in the world to condemn the Warsaw Pact invasion of Czechoslovakia and it had strongly supported the Dubcek reforms as elements of a democratic socialist society.)

The 1970 CPA document *Modern Unionism* presaged many of the elements of subsequent policy documents by the ACTU. The document's weakness, however, was its inability to link general strategy to the key day-to-day issues, especially wages and living standards, that concern workers. The union movement has since found the way to link all the issues in an integrated whole. Although there is still no unanimity on the union movement's new strategy, there is increasing agreement among member unions.

View of Technology

The impact of technological innovations has been one of the major forces shaping the stance of the Australian union movement. In 1984, the Australian Conciliation and Arbitration Commission (ACAC) issued a decision that was key to the evolution of the union's view of technology. Entitled *Technological Change and Redundancy Provision*, the decision required management to inform unions whenever it intended to make major changes, including technology changes.

The ACAC had been formed in 1904 by agreement between unions and the first national Labor Government and has ever since played the key role in centralized wage fixing and establishing national standards in working conditions. Its role was understood to preclude intervention in management. Its statement on notice of changes was therefore viewed as an infringement on management's right to manage and was challenged by employers in the High Court. The High Court, however, upheld the ACAC's statement and opened the door for management prerogative to be argued in the Industrial Relations Commission (IRC), as the ACAC is now known.

The *Technological Change and Redundancy Provision* was issued by the ACAC on application from the ACTU and reflected the ACTU's view that unions must take a proactive role in ensuring the optimum use of new technologies rather than stand flat-footed in opposition. This was a new position and represented an admission that it was not possible to save every job in mature and declining industries. Instead, the ACTU began to target the issues of how technology is designed and used, and who would control it.

The ACTU was also reacting to the introduction of new technology by management for the sole purpose of cutting jobs and direct labor costs. It believed this management focus was misplaced because direct labor costs in manufacturing usually amounted to less than 20 percent of total costs. With changing markets, the ACTU also saw that sales depended on criteria other than price, such as quality, prompt delivery, uniqueness, reliability, and environmental acceptability. Focusing exclusively on labor costs therefore dodged real problems of inefficiency elsewhere.

International best practice and Australia's own experience increasingly suggest that to make optimum use of new technologies, industry must have workers with higher skills and an integrated work organization that breaks with the traditional Tayloristic division of labor. The ACTU has therefore set a goal for the next 10 years of changing the whole culture of enterprises to make them more innovative, democratic, flexible, and able to provide the best basis for the design and use of technological systems.

View of the Market

Far from the criticism that unions pay no heed to the role of markets and thereby hinder Australian industry's competitiveness, the union movement believes the market is very important. However, the movement rejects blind faith in market mechanisms for three important reasons.

First, unions do not believe that a totally free market is the most efficient method of distributing wealth equitably. A totally unregulated market most often benefits the rich — those with control over resources — and moreover does not necessarily ensure efficiency. Second, unions are not so naive as to believe a free market exists anywhere, especially in international trade where all countries use various methods to try to direct the market, and often succeed. Third, unions believe they understand how the Australian manufacturing industry can respond to market demands better than most managements.

Historically, Australia's manufacturing industry, led by poor management with little entrepreneurial skill, has been highly protected. Managements served local markets, paid little attention to exports, and, when in trouble, sought the support of unions and government for ever-higher tariffs. As a result, the manufacturing sector was ill prepared to meet the avalanche of international competition that emerged in the late 1970s and early 1980s. Many companies went to the wall. Neither televisions nor machine tools, for example, are any longer manufactured in Australia.

Employers blamed a major campaign by the Amalgamated Metal Worker Union (AMWU)—the largest single union in Australia—in 1981 and 1982 for exacerbating industry's problems. The AMWU had won a 38–hour work week and a substantial wage increase that flowed through to the rest of industry. About 100,000 manufacturing jobs were lost during this period.

While this successful campaign may have contributed to some of the losses, it also began to reveal a much deeper malaise in Australian manufacturing. By the beginning of 1983, unemployment exceeded 10 percent and was at its highest level in Australia since the 1930s Depression. This situation combined with other factors swept the Labor Party into federal government in March of that year.

The collapse of commodity prices toward the end of 1983 followed by an $18 billion annual balance-of-payments deficit two years later brought a sudden realization that the only solution was to restructure manufacturing into a modern, efficient industry with the potential for import replacement and export expansion.

The Political Context

Political pressures for a change in Australia's industrial and labor policies began accumulating in the 1970s and early 1980s. Deep divisions on a number of issues between the Labor government and the unions from 1972 to 1975 prevented agreement on a wages and income policy and contributed to a massive wage explosion in 1974. This explosion along with an increase in unemployment helped bring about Labor's downfall in November of 1975 and the subsequent election of the conservatives, known in Australia as the Liberal Party.

The following seven years of conservative government saw policies that favored the export of energy and minerals and undermined manufacturing. Unions were able to negotiate wage increases that kept ahead of inflation, but taxes soared, pensions and spending on education dropped, and the national health scheme, Medibank, introduced by the Labor Party government, was scrapped. Overall, workers realized their standard of living was falling.

In the 18 months leading up to the March, 1983 election, leaders of the Australian Labor Party and the ACTU formalized an historic accord. The Accord committed government to improvements in the maintenance of real wages, the control of nonwage incomes, a fairer taxation system and social wage (government-funded employee benefits), and increased workers' rights, in return for a commitment by unions to establish a more disciplined wage strategy to start bringing unit costs down. In effect, individual industries and workplaces would not pursue wage increases outside a centralized wage-fixing system, which would be based on cost-of-living indexes and would be supported by government.

The Accord provided for removing antiworker industrial relations legislation and substantially increasing the rights for workers over the introduction of technology, redundancy and retrenchment, the formation of industrial development policy, and health and safety at work.

The Labor government committed to creating half a million jobs in its first term, succeeded, and added in excess of 1.5 million new jobs by its third term. Unemployment in Australia reached its lowest level since the mid-1970s, although it subsequently rose slightly again.

Australia Reconstructed

From the outset the Accord was seen as the basis for ongoing negotiation between government and unions on a wide range of issues. Union strategies were further developed and consolidated in the document *Australia Reconstructed*. This 200-page document was a watershed in the Australian union movement and consolidated the union movement's concern with production as well as wealth distribution.

Australia Reconstructed was the outcome of a joint study, partly funded by the Ministry of Trade, involving the ACTU executive members, leading union officials, and government representatives in 1986. The representatives examined industry in five western European countries

— Sweden, West Germany, Austria, Norway, and Great Britain — chosen for their similarities to Australia in size, trading situation, role of government and unions, and strategies they were pursuing.

Compared with Australia, the study found that the European countries:

1. had clearer long-term strategic goals for social change;

2. emphasized skill formation, work organization, and industrial democracy;

3. had unions that played a more proactive role in the introduction of new technology;

4. used their wage systems to help drive social change rather than only to preserve or raise living standards;

5. integrated key ministries to prevent policy fragmentation and contradiction; and

6. had governments that took a proactive role in industry and labor market policy.

The document adapted these findings in making numerous recommendations in six major policy areas: macroeconomic policies, wages, prices and incomes, trade and industry, labor market programs, industrial democracy, and strategic unionism. It represented the first time the union movement had adopted a comprehensive and completely integrated range of sophisticated policies. (Listed in Appendix A are some of the key recommendations from *Australia Reconstructed*.)

Objections to *Australia Reconstructed* were many. Nevertheless, over time, the document has changed thinking at the highest levels. It now serves as the basis for negotiations between the union movement and the federal Labor government.

MACRO ELEMENTS OF UNION STRATEGY

Australia's experience has made it clear that effective change at the enterprise level is not possible without a supportive macro framework. By the same token, the best macroeconomic policies will be useless unless the enterprise is able to capitalize on new opportunities.

To make industry modern and internationally competitive, Australian industry needs a highly skilled workforce, modern management techniques, the latest technologies, democratic work organizations and job designs, wage structures compatible with new skills and work organization, and an appropriate industrial relations system.

While some individual companies might assemble such a package, whole industries will not be transformed without an appropriate macro framework. Therefore, there needs to be national agreement on economic policy, training structures and standards, new directions for management schools, major change to all educational institutions, new national directions for wage policy, industrial relations, research and development, and so on.

This section outlines the union strategies for industrial policy, wage policy, award restructuring, education and training, and industrial democracy.

Industrial Policy

An extremely important part of the ACTU/ALP Accord of 1983 was for government to embark on major restructuring of industry with a commitment to manufacturing. The Accord called for forming a body known as the Australian Manufacturing Council to bring together unions, business, and government at the highest levels. In addition, a range of industry councils was formed to deal with problems specific to their industries. The councils were based in such industries as Metals and Heavy Engineering, Textile, Clothing and Footwear, and Forest Products. In total, eleven industry councils were established.

They have since enabled government, unions, and management to undertake joint research, discuss future strategy, produce joint documents, informally exchange views, and develop discussions at the workplace level.

Case Study: The Steel Industry Plan

During negotiations to establish the council structure, two of the industries in the most difficult circumstances, steel and automobile, developed their own plans and instituted authorities to oversee the plans' implementation. The steel industry was in a particularly perilous state. Many thousands had lost jobs in retrenchments in 1981 and 1982, when investment had virtually ceased. Moreover, there were signs that Australia's biggest company and only steel producer, BHP, was preparing to leave the steel business.

To help the steel industry, a five-year plan was put in place under which unions agreed not to pursue wage increases outside the centralized wage fixing system and to review work practices and demarcation. The company committed to no retrenchments during the five-year period—everyone who wished to continue working in the industry would have employment security—and to invest $800 million in upgrading their technology. The government undertook to maintain import duties (known as bounties) that would be activated whenever BHP's share of the Australian steel market fell below 80 percent; the bounties would be eliminated at the end of the plan.

The plan proved successful in providing the basis for the company to invest in excess of $1.4 billion, mostly in new technology. The unions worked to improve a number of important aspects of the operation, and, although problems still remain, BHP is now competitive in steel production on the world market, employment is stable, and new products are being developed.

After the five-year plan, the company and unions reached a further agreement to provide employment security for another four years. The new agreement focused on skills upgrading, consultative processes, new work organization, and a new award. BHP had adopted an integrated computer technology that required large retraining programs for both skilled and semiskilled workers, cross-skilling of electrical and mechanical tradespersons, workers involvement in traditional management areas such as production planning, and so on.

Case Study: Heavy Engineering Program

Heavy Engineering was another industry badly hit by the downturn in 1982 and subsequently helped by a cooperative effort among unions, management, and government. Heavy Engineering covers rail and tramway rolling stock, ship building and marine engineering, mining and crushing equipment, heavy machine tools, and some agricultural equipment.

The unions were unanimous that traditional tariff protection would not help, and that such protection had exacerbated the industry's malaise. The Metal Workers within Heavy Engineering eventually won reluctant agreement from the employers' organization, the Metal Trades Industry Association, and the government for a package that established new concepts for industry assistance in Australia.

After much negotiation, the government agreed to a three-year program known as the Heavy Engineering Adjustment Package, which involved $90 million of assistance. Unique features of the Package included:

1. Establishment of a tripartite (union, management, government) "Heavy Engineering Board" to administer the program.

2. Special conditions for receiving assistance: Companies had to present evidence of an agreement with the unions in their plant on work practices, development of new skills, consultative processes such as the formation of joint works councils, and detailed business plans. Management also had to provide unions with information on industry and company performance as well as potential markets, especially exports.

3. Funding specially directed to subsidies: Training, for example, attracted $125 a day for a person trained off the job for up to 36 days, or $100 a day for a person trained on the job. There was also aid for training development costs. The training programs themselves required both management and union approval.

4. Low-interest loans were provided for the purchase of new equipment and technology, and companies were strongly encouraged to invest in new design and production planning systems such as computer-integrated manufacturing.

Management was rather slow to make use of the Heavy Engineering Package because the Heavy Engineering Manufacturers Association was reluctant to seek funding that depended on agreement with the unions. Moreover, an unexpected market upturn shortly after the program began made companies busier than expected. Very few companies had business plans, and funding was needed, usually on a dollar-for-dollar basis, to help them develop plans.

In contrast to management's reluctance, the Metal Workers Union took the initiative by conducting seminars with shop stewards to acquaint them with the package, and suggesting that they approach management to reach agreement and apply for funds. In many cases, stewards were much better acquainted with the program details than management. Some managements had not even bothered to read the material, and had to have it explained to them by union representatives.

Other industry plans have since used the Heavy Engineering Package as a model. A recent independent report (Charlton West and Associates, 1989) found the Package generally successful. The report concluded that the Package increased and will continue to increase the efficiency and competitiveness of the Heavy Engineering industry. It cited the improvement in employer–employee relationships and an increase in the amount of forward thinking and planning as the two areas of greatest success. The report also concluded that the tripartite, "hurdle–reward" model of industry assistance was significantly more successful than previous industry packages of financial support, and that the Management Efficiency and Skills Enhancement element of the Package provided better value for the money than the Industry Development element.

The Package's approach at the micro level — targeting specific problem areas such as skills, management, and work organization, and involving unions and the workforce — not only made management more accountable, but directed attention to real problems in a way that general tariff policies never touched. Negotiations are now underway for a package for the whole of the metal industry, which consists of about 6000 workshops, based on the principles of the Heavy Engineering Assistance Package.

Wage Policy

The original ACTU/ALP Accord has passed through six stages, each of which saw changes in the form in which wage increases would be paid and how overall living standards might be maintained and improved. Since the first Accord, by agreement between unions and government, the Industrial Relations Commission (IRC) has increasingly modified wage policy to drive restructuring at the workplace level. Broad productivity and skill measures are now major elements of decisions where before they were peripheral.

The first major break with past wage policy occurred in 1987 when the IRC set a two-tier system of wage bargaining known as the "Restructuring and Efficiency Principle." The first tier consisted of an across-the-board payment of $10 a week to all workers. The second tier was a further four percent increase available for negotiation at the workplace with the proviso that it had to be "cost neutral."

Initially, this cost-neutral provision led to a mad scramble by employers to win back years of union gains. Employers targeted industrial awards, which cover the overwhelming majority of Australian workers, union and nonunion. Industrial awards specify legal minimums for wages, overtime rates, holidays, working hours, and working conditions. Employers avoided any serious study of management inefficiencies despite the fact that the IRC called for "an examination of restrictive work *and* management practices" (emphasis added).

In response, the Industrial Relations Commissioner responsible for the Metal Industry laid down, for the first time in Australian history, a 12–point program to be followed in workplace negotiations (see Appendix B). Generally left out of the list for negotiation were the longstanding award rights.

The second-tier wage negotiations represented the first time a national wage decision forced workers and management to examine the labor process, that is, the way work is organized and decisions are made. With a fairly buoyant labor market, some employers were happy to negotiate minimum change in order to start the four percent flowing quickly, but many others went to the other extreme and argued for ludicrous changes that would have extended management control and have very little, or even negative, effect on productivity and quality. The ability of unions to negotiate how management could be improved and how a company should be run was severely tested. Shop stewards and officials had to be trained for this new area of negotiations. In all, the negotiations required more than two years to complete.

The Metal Workers Union embarked on the task in a systematic way, listing issues of concern and following the guidelines from the IRC. It established an Australia-wide computer listing of all local agreements for comprehensive, cross-referenced records. This enabled the union to identify firms with consultative committees, changed work practices (for example, fitters undertaking welding work), changes in supervision, and new proposals for training.

By September, 1987, the metal unions had negotiated a couple of thousand workplace agreements and reached agreement with employers at the national level for some changes within the Metal Industry Award. This award is the biggest in Australia and covers half a million workers. As a result, the Industrial Relations Commission, satisfied with the progress, wrote the four percent into the award, allowing it to flow to all metal workers.

Both employers and workers were unprepared and untrained for the major change in negotiations called for by the *Restructuring and Efficiency Principle*. Nevertheless, by the time the four percent wage raise had flowed to most workers, there was discussion about a complete restructuring of the awards in the major industries to bring them into line with modern technology, work methods, and market requirements.

Wage Policy and Restructuring Awards

Wage policy was emerging as a key tool in the strategy for developing a modern industry with high skill levels. Starting with the two-tier system, wages were no longer seen as solely an instrument for maintaining living standards, but also as an important mechanism to drive industry restructuring. Because the unions had secured broader support for living standards—by broadening their focus from direct wages to include the social wage, taxation levels, and social welfare provisions—direct wages could now also serve other policy purposes as well.

Employers, government, and unions are now agreed that the rigid award structures that have determined wages, skills, work practices, and demarcation lines are outdated and need to be revamped. On April 12, 1989, the ACTU and the Labor government announced a complex package of economic policy, social welfare measures, and direct wage outcomes. Agreement on the package meant that the government would support the ACTU's wage claim in the Industrial Relations Commission. In return for this support, the unions agreed to restructure their awards as an important step to improving efficiency at the enterprise level. They viewed the new awards as the vehicle for changing the culture of Australian workplaces.

The old awards were based on the assumption that job descriptions, skills, and demarcation were the same for all workplaces covered by the particular award. New forms of work organization and skills, however, were forcing many workplaces to modify job titles and wage rates. To make the changes, unions had to present lengthy and costly cases before the Industrial Relations Commission. The new system supported by the Labor government is designed to allow changes to be made more easily so that awards can be more effectively modified to suit particular workplaces, while maintaining the very important national framework and safety net.

At the end of the first quarter of 1990, most of the new major awards had been approved by the Industrial Relations Commission. The next step is their detailed implementation at the workplace. Over the next few years, unions will be developing expertise in skills audits, job design, management techniques, and designing and using new technology. The new awards will facilitate the shift from the Taylorist paradigm to the paradigm of flexible specialization.

Case Study: Metal Industry Award Restructuring

The metal industry provides an example of restructured awards in action. In December, 1988, a study team of metal employers, unions, and government published a report, *Towards a New Metal and Engineering Industry Award*, that firmly committed the parties to major change in the biggest industrial award in Australia.

The skill component of the wages in the restructured Metal Industry Award started to flow in March 1990. Under the Award, workers will be listed in a skills hierarchy according to an analysis performed in each workplace. They will receive pay increments based on their skill level and new training provisions that include training during work time.

This pay structure is a major break with traditional Australian practice, in which all workers in one classification were paid the same regardless of skill level. The new structure replaces the 348 skill classifications that existed under the old Metal Industry Award with 14 skill levels ranging from process worker (the person who walks in off the street completely unskilled in the particular industry) to credentialed engineer for each of four streams of tradespersons: Electrical/Electronics, Mechanical/Machining, Structural/Fabrication, and Operator/Fitter. The skill levels are outlined in Table 9.1. There are some proposals to add clerical personnel into the new structure as well.

These changes were not without controversy. Greater cross-skill training was a boon for some but a threat to others. The Metal Workers Union, for example, proposed a 30 percent exchange of skills between mechanical and electrical during apprenticeship training. This proposal was strongly resisted by the Electrical Trades Union, which sought to maintain an elitist position especially in electronics. The unions eventually agreed that the exchange of such skills would begin from the tradesperson level upwards.

Incorporated into the award is the concept that everyone entering the metal industry at any level would have access to training. For example, unskilled employees starting at level 1 will receive 38 hours of training in their first six months, leading them to the next level. Beyond the second level, the equivalent of approximately 100 hours training is needed to reach each new level, except for those levels requiring recognized certificates, such as tradesperson and technician/draftsperson, or diplomas and degrees where the training will be much longer.

Through adult apprenticeships and training both on and off the job, it is now feasible for a person walking in off the street to work through to the tradesperson level and above. This would have been almost

Table 9.1. Skill Levels in the Metal Industry Award

Wage group	Classification title	Minimum training requirement	Wage relative to C10 level
C1	Professional Engineer	Professional scientist degree	170–185%
C2(b)	Principal Technical Officer	Diploma or formal equivalent	160%
C2(a)	Leading Technical Officer, Principal Engineering Supervisor/Trainer/Coordinator	5th year of Diploma or formal equivalent	150%
C3	Engineering Associate—Level II	Associate Diploma or formal equivalent	145%
C4	Engineering Associate—Level I	3rd year of Associate Diploma or formal equivalent	135%
C5	Engineering Technician—Level V, Advanced Engineering Tradesperson—Level II	Advanced Certificate or formal equivalent	130%
C6	Engineering Technician—Level IV, Advanced Engineering Tradesperson—Level I	1st year of Advanced Certificate	125%
C7	Engineering Technician—Level III, Engineering Tradesperson— Special Class	Post Trade Certificate or formal equivalent	115%
C8	Engineering Technician—Level II, Engineering Tradesperson— Level III	Completion of 66% of qualification for C7	110%
C9	Engineering Technician—Level I, Engineering Tradesperson— Level II	Completion of 33% of qualification for C7	105%
C10	Engineering Tradesperson—Level I, Production System Employee	Trade Certificate or Production/ Engineering Certificate III	100%
C11	Engineering/Production Employee— Level IV	Production/ Engineering Certification II	92.4%
C12	Engineering/Production Employee— Level III	Production/ Engineering Certificate I	87.4%
C13	Engineering/Production Employee— Level II	In-house training	82%
C14	Engineering/Production Employee— Level I	Up to 38 hours induction training	78%

Supervisory Training—Trainer/Supervisor/Coordinator

Level 1	122% of the highest rate paid to those supervised
Level 2	115% of the highest rate paid to those supervised
Technical	107% of the rate paid for the employees' technical classification

impossible in the past, when tradespersons would not receive recognition for new skills even if they undertook an engineering degree. By recognizing and rewarding skill levels, the new structure provides incentive for acquiring new skills.

Education and Training

In addition to wage policy and award restructuring, the Australian union movement has also been active in supporting the development of a new system of education and training to support industry restructuring. *Australia Reconstructed* had proposed to bring under one umbrella employment, labor programs, education, and training. Previously, education was a ministry on its own, and training came under one part of the Department of Labor, another part of which oversaw industrial relations.

In 1987, a new Department of Employment, Education and Training was established along with a new high-powered tripartite board, the National Board of Employment Education and Training, to advise the Minister. Below the board and feeding into it are several others with responsibility for areas such as Primary Education, Secondary Education, Training and Technical skills, and Aboriginal Education.

The new department and board signified the first time Australia had something approaching a national, coordinated system of education and training. Traditionally, most policy matters such as course content and accreditation were the province of state governments, which resulted in much variation and confusion in standards. Under the new system, each state must at least refer to the national bodies. The new Metal Industry Award for the first time established a "Metals and Engineering National Training Board" that will be mirrored in each state.

On their own, several states, especially those with Labor governments, have reorganized their education and training under tripartite organizations, such as State Training Boards. Their objectives are to bring education and training in line with modern requirements and with the new restructured Awards across the major industries.

In making these changes, policy-makers wrestled with the need for education to create both well-rounded, thinking individuals *and* workers with appropriate skills. Teacher unions, especially, fear that too great an emphasis on vocational training might strait-jacket workers into jobs, many of which might disappear anyway. Other unions worry about too great a discrepancy between education and work, especially in manufacturing. The union movement is committed to a solution that balances the two. It believes that creative, flexible, highly skilled, and responsible workers are needed to exploit modern technologies fully. An appreciation of the arts and social sciences, seriously lacking among today's engineers and scientists, would also contribute to the more effective design and implementation of these technologies.

The National Minister for Employment, Education and Training legislated for a compulsory levy on business to fund training, and issued discussion documents calling for national criteria on training standards and new methods for delivering training programs. The levy applies to companies with a payroll of $200,000 or more and amounts to 1.5 percent of the payroll. Qualifying companies must provide evidence by July, 1991, that they have committed 1.5 percent of their payroll to training in their own company, or be obliged to contribute the amount or the balance not spent into a general fund. The levy is aimed at those companies that spend virtually nothing on training their own workforce and poach workers trained by other companies or the public sector.

Industrial Democracy

The training levy along with wage policy have probably been the two most obvious and public manifestations of the strategy recommended in *Australia Reconstructed*. Another aspect has become so integrated into industry and award restructuring that few call it industrial democracy today.

The Labor government developed policies on industrial democracy as early as 1984, when Prime Minister Hawke, speaking at a one-day national gathering of several hundred union, employer, and government representatives, explicitly addressed the idea that industrial and participative democracy would be key ingredients in the revival of the Australian manufacturing industry.

Unions took advantage of government funding to create so-called "consultative processes" by which union members would identify their problems and then negotiate appropriate decision-making and information structures involving management to develop solutions for the problems. Compared with previous problem-solving, consultative processes sought to identify problems first rather than to create a structural solution in search of a problem.

The program quickly unearthed deep-rooted obstacles to industrial efficiency, such as lack of skills and weaknesses in management decision-making, that consultative processes alone could not solve. When the issue of award restructuring for work skills surfaced in the mid-1980s, it was clear that industrial democracy could not be kept separate.

Unions recognized that skilled workers generally had the potential to negotiate and intervene in decision-making more effectively than unskilled workers. Hence, industrial democracy became integrally linked with raising the skill level of the workforce.

In 1988, the ACTU and its employer counterpart, the Confederation of Australian Industry, issued a *Joint Statement on Participative Practices* stating that "participative practices" had an important role to play in creating a more efficient industry. Participative practices have been demonstrated in the metal industry and some other industries where groups of skilled workers have grasped the possibilities with some enthusiasm once they thoroughly understood the concept.

Despite vigorous conflicts both within the union movement and between unions and employers, consultative processes have been written into industrial relations agreements as a right of the workforce and a union matter. Industrial democracy has become synonymous with industry and award restructuring.

Workplace Resource Centers

Implementing new industrial agreements has often required expertise outside management and union circles. In response, the federal Labor government has established a network of "Workplace Resource Centers," tripartite structures controlled by management, unions, and government situated in states and regions. They are funded for three years but charge commercial rates with the intention of becoming self-funding.

The Centers are charged with employing experts in human resource and technical streams. Their charter requires that these experts only work in an enterprise by agreement between management and unions. In the main, the experts serve joint committees in carrying out the new industry awards, but they may address any problem. Unions have considerable input on what experts are employed by the Centers, but any information the experts obtain must be made available to both management and unions.

ENTERPRISE-LEVEL ELEMENTS OF UNION STRATEGY

All these changes at the macro level have to make an impact on the workplace or little will occur to improve industry. Union strategy at the enterprise level has insisted on treating the workplace as an integrated system. This strategy has created some difficulties for management, as managers now face proposals for comprehensive changes from unions. But unions themselves have been targets for change in these proposals as well.

In this section, union strategy for managing the impact of technology on the workplace is described. In Australia, we have found that new technologies typically require workers with higher skill levels. Certainly in the metal industry almost every manager complains of a workforce unable to handle new equipment. In some cases, equipment has lain idle because of the lack of skilled operators. This is one of the reasons the metal employers' organization has initiated some progressive changes and responded more positively than other employers to union initiatives.

Three cases of technology and work will be explored, exemplifying the effect of technology on, respectively, traditional job demarcations, the Taylorist division of labor, and problem-solving processes.

Technology and Demarcation

Technology is creating important problems for traditional demarcation lines between different job classifications. This is particularly true between electrical and mechanical work, operator and maintenance, between them all and supervisory staff, and between the skilled tradesperson and the technician. The integration of electronics with hydraulics, the move from mechanical and hydraulic instruments to electronic, the programming of Programmable Logic Controllers and other equipment such as CNC machining centers are all examples of how most traditional demarcation lines have become obsolete.

In the past, unions used demarcation as a defensive mechanism to save jobs and protect union organization. In recent times, it has become obvious in several industries that strict, narrow demarcation, along with poor management, was crippling productivity and creating an inefficient use of new technology and a loss of jobs.

The ACTU believes that all workers should have the right to upgrade their skills, and that demarcation should be eliminated if it stands in the way unless it is needed to protect workers' health and safety. The ACTU would like demarcation to be a natural division based on logical clusters of the skills needed to complete whole tasks. In changing demarcation, the union movement has found that an approach involving the total work process is best. Employees are much more likely to change work practices when they see the change as part of a package that offers job security, the opportunity for all to upgrade skills, a pay system that encourages skill acquisition, and have a genuine say in the change. By job security the ACTU does not mean individual ownership of jobs, nor that the number of workers in each occupation must remain the same. It means that people who wish to keep working in an industry over time can do so, even though the number employed in any given occupation and in any given enterprise might evolve. The real concern for the ACTU is that the national stock of jobs is maintained and expanding to enable people to move into new and better jobs.

Case Study: Reviving a Dockyard

A government-owned dockyard provides a good example of the benefits of eliminating or reducing demarcations. This dockyard had incurred increasing losses over a number of years because of government bureaucracy, incompetent management, extreme demarcation involving some 15 unions, and a demoralized workforce many of whom lacked necessary skills.

Despite several years' effort by the 15 unions and the ACTU along with the government, the dockyard's culture required radical overhaul. The government offered one last chance to save the dockyard by selling it to the private sector but only if the unions would agree to major changes. The unions reluctantly agreed to cut the number of unions to three, while the government provided a redundancy package that encouraged many employees to leave.

The yard reopened in July of 1988 with the three unions. A completely new agreement provided for consultative processes, substantial training, very little demarcation, and four wage levels allied to skill levels in each category (electrical, mechanical, and semiskilled). Management has developed an understanding of what is required to make the enterprise an international center of excellence in marine engineering.

The dockyard aimed to increase productivity eightfold over time, and, within 18 months of the opening, had succeeded in raising productivity to five times its level under the old system. Other improvements include the development of a more competent management, high workforce morale, a new $5 billion contract, and even one frigate launched slightly ahead of schedule—the first time in many years.

None of this would have been possible without the ACTU's firm resolve to come to grips with the requirements of modern industry. Nevertheless, for unions, the key issue in multiskilling is to ensure that workers' skills be upgraded into technical areas and areas of responsibility, and not just broadened to encompass more tasks. Employers often demand a simplistic breakdown of all demarcation for a horizontally multiskilled workforce. The union movement is more sensitive to vertical skill-building, which does not entail a frontal attack on demarcations but rather their reduction and modification.

Technology and the Organization of Work

A key strategic perspective in the new awards and agreements is that of reversing the traditional Taylorist division of labor. In particular, the union movement is determined to unite conceptual or intellectual activities with manual work. This means that the organization of work must provide for some planning, design, and responsibility on the part of workers, and a reduction of supervision.

With this in mind, unions have tried to secure the following key strategic elements in any agreement with employers:

1. A commitment from companies that no redundancies would arise from restructuring;

2. Provision for thorough consultation on all issues pertaining to the workplace;

3. Universal access to training;

4. Payment based on skills acquired, including responsibility and supervisory skills, although they may not be used all the time;

5. Training to take place on company time, meaning 5–10 percent of work time;

6. Commitments to redesign jobs and work organization;

7. A joint training committee on each site comprising a small number of union job representatives and management. This is often known as the "Joint Training and Job Design Committee." These committees must work closely with local Technical Colleges, and have authority to administer training programs, undertake skills audits, establish priorities, and develop training modules. These activities are to be undertaken within the national framework and principles as established in the award;

8. Training must include managerial as well as technical skills to allow workers to take increasing responsibility for their work;

9. Training must be a voluntary program and workers cannot be forced to retrain. Experience indicates that people overwhelmingly want to be involved;

10. Where there are migrants with English as their second language, there must be job programs for literacy;

11. Rights for union organization on the job if they do not already exist;

12. An agreement on subcontractors wherever that may be an issue, lest the process of subcontracting undermine restructuring. Comprehensive and systematic restructuring must be tailored to the unique characteristics of the workplace;

13. An agreement on occupational health and safety where appropriate;

14. Equal opportunity rights for women.

Employers have objected to some of these elements because they represent the union movement's attempt to begin dismantling the control mechanisms embodied in the bureaucratic, hierarchical systems that exist in most companies. Indeed, that is the objective. These concepts represent a radical departure for Australia, but are nothing new to western Europe, particularly Scandinavia.

The opportunity for every worker to upgrade skills and responsibility changes the role of the worker. In some cases, the change may merge some tasks and skills embodied at higher levels with the traditional direct labor or blue-collar workforce, eliminating the need for some forms of supervision. Such a blending might take place, for example, as the shopfloor gathers skills in planning, design, programming, and even in marketing and sales, by working more closely with groups responsible for those functions.

In such an environment, a career path would be based on skills, responsibility, status, and pay, and not necessarily on traditional structures. This alternative conception of a career path is needed to avoid replicating hierarchies at a higher skill level. Bureaucracies are the major problem in industry, and they are inefficient regardless of the level of skill.

Case Study: Technology and Work Organization at a Can Maker

An agreement between a major can manufacturer and the Amalgamated Metal Workers Union provides an example of one of the most advanced agreements on new technology in Australia. Reaching that agreement represented a major challenge to union strategy: balancing long-term goals with short-term exigencies.

The can maker wanted to expand into exports using new technology. Because the enterprise already had quality problems with an operation that was only five years old, both management and the union wanted to try a new approach. In doing so, they surmounted some unique challenges. They had to keep the old line operating throughout installation of the new automated line despite tight physical limitations that limited layout options. In addition, they faced severe time pressures, as the hardware had already been ordered and lay out plans had to be completed within six weeks of the first union meeting.

Despite these obstacles, management and union developed an agreement on principles and procedures for implementing the new automated can-making line that provided far more options than unions usually have. Furthermore, the agreement was allied to the design of the information and decisionmaking system. Guiding principles of the agreement were:

1. That there be no retrenchments arising from the new work system and technology;

2. That a joint project team oversee design and development, training, job design, and methods of coordination;

3. That the long-term objective was to create higher-skilled self-managing work groups;

4. That a seminar take place to plan the project. Participants in the seminar would consist of union representatives from each shift selected by members, personnel from management, and a representative of Technical and Further Education (TAFE). The seminar would decide the joint project team, which would include the TAFE representative and the AMWU organizer;

5. There be no loss of conditions or pay arising from the changes;

6. That the restructuring process follow the principles of the new Metal Industry Award;

7. That special attention be paid to occupational health and safety;

8. That, in the event of need for an outside consultant, the person be agreed to and work under the direction of the joint project team;

9. That any financial assistance that might be available from outside sources be controlled by the joint project team.

The introduction of the new automated can-making line is providing interesting lessons as it unfolds. The initial workers' seminar revealed a need to take the whole workforce through at least half a day of briefings to explain the expected effects of proposed changes. Some workers saw benefits while others saw threats in the new technology. Semi-skilled workers recognized that the self-managed work teams would provide good opportunities for increasing their skills and pay to the point where they might become tradespersons. Many skilled workers were already working at a lower skill level than their qualification would permit, and so they saw the work reorganization as a chance to create a context in which to utilize their skills more fully. By contrast, maintenance fitters and supervisors formed an unusual alliance that began to undermine the process until separate seminars for them showed how they too could develop new skills and roles under the new technology and self-managed work teams.

The local Technical College performed a detailed skills analysis that is now being integrated with the agreement on self-management to link current and future skills and to develop a skills career path that will fit with the new Metal Industry Award. The new self-managed work organization will require more planning and decisions to be undertaken by the group on the shopfloor.

In the middle of this complex process, management reverted to its traditional role and decided without consulting the unions that Christmas shifts would operate differently. This decision drew almost unanimous opposition from the workforce, which threatened industrial action. Many among the workforce once again became cynical and suggested dropping the whole restructuring effort and withdrawing from any cooperation with management.

The union decided to try to solve the short-term crisis within the context of the long-term strategy, and even to use the long-term changes as a negotiating device. The workforce agreed to cease negotiations on the new technology until the immediate dispute was resolved. Valuing the new technology, management reached agreement on the holiday shifts quickly, and promptly resumed negotiations on the technology project.

This exercise demonstrates one of the most difficult problems faced by unions in pursuing longer-term strategies: how to solve, in a principled way, day-to-day industrial disputes without jeopardizing progress on the more fundamental issues. Most managements are only prepared to discuss major change when confronted by a serious problem. But once restructuring begins, it can be stopped by other problems, such as insufficient work, market downturns, company takeovers, management crises, and so on. The only solution is a basic cultural change on the part of both union and management.

Processes for Change

From recent experience trying to implement industrial democracy and its links to award restructuring, Australian unions have developed some problem solving methods that represent new departures for the union movement. The methods follow two basic principles:

1. Strategies must be "problem centered"; that is, problems should be examined before establishing structures, not the other way around;

2. The development and implementation of strategies must be extremely democratic. Where democratization is the objective, the most thorough democratic methods must be used. Democracy cannot be imposed on people; people must be helped to arrive at democracy themselves.

When companies have approached unions in the past two or three years wanting assistance or a discussion about major problems or change, more forward-looking unions have avoided rushing into negotiations. Instead, unions have insisted on a holistic approach. This approach is warranted by the nature of issues to be addressed. A piecemeal approach will not be effective in tackling issues such as chronic industrial relations problems, new technology, shifting a workplace from one site to another, retrenchments, plant shutdowns, takeover by another company, poor product quality, and the introduction of new management techniques.

Unions therefore ask management to release a significant number of shop stewards and job representatives for a seminar conducted by the union in which the enterprise's problems will be discussed. The unions' assistance depends on what flows from the seminar.

The seminars move systematically from international and macro issues through to identifying major enterprise problems and establishing priorities among them. Participants then develop proposals within the context of the macro framework outlined in this chapter and the context of long-term strategic change for the enterprise. In many cases, the seminars represent the first time a group of people from the same workplace have discussed their problems in an organized way. They often realize that local concerns reflect problems across the industry.

The seminars usually result in a comprehensive document for negotiating with management. To ensure that union members and shop stewards are comfortable at each stage of the process, they are given a few days to discuss the document informally in the workplace. Then the unions ask management for time to conduct meetings during the work day to help workers understand the often complex and far-reaching changes. Final endorsement from a mass meeting is needed before discussions begin with the company.

Management is kept informed of developments at various stages of the process, but, regardless of the urgency of the problems, no negotiations with management take place until the employees have endorsed the proposals. While worker discussions appear time consuming, experience has demonstrated that they can proceed quickly and that they ensure a widespread commitment that minimizes the chance of worker disapproval in subsequent negotiations with management.

Dozens of workplaces have conducted such seminars, and unions have found that management's increasing need for union assistance in crises can be a useful bargaining device to ensure the resources necessary to conduct these seminars. Management is usually reluctant, but unions are insistent because they believe that management would otherwise seek quick-fix, superficial solutions to long-term problems. Furthermore, unions now have examples of how the process has saved or helped companies.

It is, however, still too early to tell whether the process described, once begun, will continue as the basis for an innovative, constantly changing culture. For the process to take hold, the on-the-job union organization (generally referred to as *union shop committees*) will have to be strengthened. Regular communication through newsletters distributed to employees, union seminars, and time off for small group meetings of union members would also help review progress on changes and identify new developments. More union training and development of shop steward confidence are also required to build a wider network of union activists to participate on consultative councils, joint training committees, and occupational health and safety committees.

Case Study: Problem Solving in the Railways

An interesting recent example of the union contribution to problem solving took place in the railways in Victoria. Following a number of seminars, a group of four shop stewards worked for many weeks to put together a comprehensive set of proposals totalling some 50 pages. The proposals called for extensive changes in skills, work organization, and pay systems for the four major railway workshops.

This 50–page document was distributed to over 1300 metal workers. Then, over a period of two-and-a-half weeks, some 26 meetings were conducted during work time to ensure thorough understanding. Subsequently, at mass meetings, there was only one vote against the proposals. Done the traditional way, with little preparation and an early mass meeting, the proposals would probably have met with overwhelming rejection because they represented a sharp break with the past. By helping workers understand the proposals within a broader context that included related issues such as changing the structure of management, the process was able to secure their support.

STRATEGIC UNIONISM

Although it may be too early to draw in-depth conclusions about the union activism of the past three years and the effectiveness of the new award structure, it seems safe to say that a strong, responsible union movement can provide a necessary stimulus for management to become more competent. A strong union can mobilize a collective, conscious, and committed response from the workforce. Combined with managements willing to tackle major change and with the consultative processes described, strong unions have successfully turned several companies around within a two-year period.

Ensuring strong unions, however, will involve a restructuring of the Australian union movement almost as extensive as the restructuring of Australian industry. Within the union movement, political and structural divisions and parochialism pose challenges for the future. There are also hurdles outside the union movement, of course. They include confusion among employers, conservatism in the technical and engineering fraternity, and ignorance that leads to equivocation on the part of some parts of government.

One Union in the Enterprise

The first task in restructuring the union movement is to pare the current 308 unions down to 20 key unions or groups of unions that can operate cohesively within industries. Amalgamating unions has been a very slow process in Australia, but there is no doubt that changes in technology and the need to upgrade skills and to reorganize work are providing the impetus for more rapid change. One union in the enterprise is very important, given the mobility provided by the new award structure and the strategy behind it.

At its most recent Congress, the ACTU decided to make union amalgamations one of its top priorities in the coming years, and established the objective of single union enterprises. The ACTU envisions national unions representing all employees in an enterprise where representation may now be divided among up to 20 unions.

Some breakthroughs have already been made. For example, the Amalgamated Metal Workers Union will join with the Association of Draughting, Supervisory and Technical Employees in the metals industry to provide single-union representation from the process worker through to supervisors and technical staff.

The biggest obstacles to single-union representation can be found in those industries with a major production workforce in one union and a much smaller workforce (sometimes as low as 10 percent) in several maintenance and services unions. This pattern occurs frequently in such industries as chemicals, petroleum, pulp and paper, textiles, and mining.

In this situation, some unions are excluding others to seek single-union coverage without regard to skill development or work organization. They establish agreements that cover the core workforce. One union, for example, negotiated total coverage of a plant but excluded skilled metal and electrical workers whose work is mainly subcontracted. By treating the most skilled work as not part of normal daily operations, the union limited the areas of skill development available to its own members.

Excluding the "peripheral" workforce from agreements can forfeit the chance to increase commitment to and understanding of the total production process among workers. The greater tragedy is that some shortsighted unions negotiate such agreements on green-field sites, which are precisely the areas where a creative use of skills and automation is most feasible.

Developing Union Leaders

A second major challenge to union restructuring is the development of more competent union activists and leaders. Considerable resources have been expended in the training of shop stewards as they expand their responsibilities beyond negotiating individual job problems and local wage increases.

The Trade Union Training Authority has been extensively reorganized to match industry groupings covered by awards and the ACTU structure. Training officers at national and state levels are allocated to industries where they integrate much of their work into workplace restructuring. As part of agreements, unions have insisted on shop steward committees with time to meet and train. Union members on consultative committees are taught that they are representatives of union members in their workplace and that consultative committees function as part of the normal negotiating process as in the collective bargaining sense.

To succeed in upgrading skills and restructuring the workplace, stewards and their committees must be proactive rather than reactive, and they must develop their own agendas for negotiation. This will require new skills on their part.

Parochialism in the Workforce

The third major challenge within the union movement is a workforce in most enterprises that is little concerned with developments in their industry and nation. The same can be said for much of union middle management and some local full-time organizers. Such parochialism adds to the difficulty of linking long-term strategy with short-term local issues, and could hold back change in Australian industry.

Problems with Employers

There is a combination of confusion, resistance, and incompetence among many employers. There are indications that up to 80% of employers have understood neither the essence of restructuring nor its potential. Most cling to outdated ideas and do not recognize what is in their own best interests.

It is often very difficult to get them to change until there is a crisis or major new issue to be confronted (for example, the appearance of a new technology). By then it is often too late. Sometimes agreements with top management are thwarted by middle management. Sometimes the board of directors makes decisions that are in direct conflict with agreements reached with top management.

Most Australian managements lack a long-term strategy and vision. In larger conglomerates, management is typically driven by the short-term profit demands of remote boards. The massive takeovers and speculative investments of recent years have seriously undermined strategic planning. This has brought in its wake a high rate of turnover among managers, which further weakens long-term planning.

Many managements cling to simplistic theories and the latest management fads when the problems and solutions are far more complex and require a comprehensive approach. One such fad is subcontracting all but the core business. The unions do not object to subcontracting in principle; some will always be necessary. However, our experience suggests that complex technological systems and idiosyncratic market demands require a highly skilled and committed internal workforce, whose endeavors are likely to be undermined by subcontracting to organizations that are often less skilled and less committed.

Some employer organizations, notably the Metal Trades Industry Association, are putting enormous effort into educating their member companies, and are cooperating with the unions on joint training programs. Often they do so in the face of opposition from other employer organizations, conservative political parties, and some prominent business people.

A divided business community means that no one national employer organization can make commitments and deliver. Warring factions in industry have allowed unions to take the lead in restructuring industry.

The Technical and Engineering Fraternity

In addition to employers, union strategy must also deal with the tradition-ally conservative technical and engineering fraternity. The development of effective skills in modern automation must include improvements in engineering education.

A recent report on the six engineering schools in the state of Victoria highlighted serious weaknesses in engineering training. It found too narrow a focus in the curriculum, which had little regard for the social consequences of technology, design as a social process, and industrial relations. Further evidence of the engineering fraternity's conservatism came when the Institute of Professional Engineers opposed the training levy on companies at their national conference in 1989.

Nevertheless, some engineering schools have given attention to offering a more well-rounded education and making students more knowledge-able about the new awards, work organization, potential for human-centered technology, and design. For the first time, some are asking unions for input into engineering training and increasingly express support for the fact that more engineers will now come from the ranks of the shopfloor, which they believe will make for better graduates.

Federal Government

Although substantial agreement has been reached between the current government and unions at the macro level, as exemplified by the regular negotiations around the Accord, there is virtually no minister who un-derstands the nuances and complexities of micro-level changes in technology and work organization. Some are prepared to be outspoken in criticizing management and calling for cultural change, but few if any understand the emerging new production paradigms or how the Taylorist division of labor functions as a fundamental barrier to efficiency. Most think simple consultation and cooperation is sufficient to restructure industry.

Government bureaucracies show an appalling lack of understanding of the requirements of modern industry and hence provide ministers with bad advice. The bureaucracies, especially Treasury, are rife with simplistic New Right thinking that the market can solve all when our everyday experience shows this to be false.

The ACTU works constantly to counteract Treasury advice and has succeeded in garnering significant government support. For example, after negotiations with the ACTU, the government set aside some $12 million to assist the award restructuring process with special emphasis at the enterprise level. This funding paid for specialists and special projects for both employers and unions, to focus on specific industries and enterprises.

A return to conservative national government in the future would

be a severe blow to union strategies; many employers have come to
doubt the value of such a change.

CONCLUSION

In its efforts to revive Australia industry through restructuring, the union
movement has so far focused mainly on skill improvement. In the future,
the spotlight is most likely to shift toward work organization. Already,
increasing numbers of union officials are recognizing that, unless they
negotiate changes in job design and the broader issues of production and
enterprise organization, their members and their industry would gain little
advantage from new skills or new technology.

The restructuring of Australian industry is an immense task, at this
stage driven largely by the union movement but with increasing support
from managements and government. The objective is a modern industry
using the latest technologies, allied to the highest level of skill and
efficiencies and most productive work organization, and managerial
methods appropriate to the twenty-first Century.

To summarize this chapter, the overall strategy, aimed at nothing
less than total change in the culture of the workplace, must link the
following elements:

1. *Long-term strategy.* There must be a long-term strategic plan on
   which to build short-term tactics. As outlined in *Australia Reconstructed*, the objective of this long-term plan is a world-
   competitive manufacturing industry that produces high-quality,
   profitable goods and services; has substantial democratic control; is
   environmentally sound; provides well-paid, skilled, and interesting
   jobs in a safe and healthy working environment; and maintains
   and improves living standards for the community at large;

2. *Macro agreements to provide framework.* There must be broad
   macro agreements in such areas as economic policy, wages, industry
   policy, education and training to provide the appropriate framework for union strategy to unfold and make effective changes
   at the micro level;

3. *Comprehensive change.* Changes at the micro level must be comprehensive in that they must encompass all aspects of the production process, namely, skills, work organization, management
   methods, use of the technology, work practices, union attitudes,
   and, in some cases, ownership structure;

4. *Problem-centered change.* At the micro level, the overall changes
   are best implemented by focusing on the practical day-to-day
   problems of the workplace. These could be any, or a combination,
   of such things as poor product quality, bad industrial relations,
   introduction of new technology, and inefficiency;

5. *Democratic process of change.* The methods for change must be extremely democratic, and reflect our democratization objectives. At every stage of every negotiation, the workforce must be kept thoroughly informed and be given the opportunity to provide effective input. Agreements should reflect the new levels of change with which the workforce is comfortable.

The Australian labor movement has sought to identify effective strategies from other countries and to apply these within the context of Australian culture and reality. Massive change, almost amounting to revolution, has occurred in a remarkably few years. The union movement hopes that much of this change will be manifest by the mid-1990s in a daily enterprise culture that takes for granted that industrial performance and social progress must be based on the close interdependence of new technology and high skill levels. There is no guarantee that the restructuring strategy will succeed. Without it, however, Australia will certainly become another third-world country.

APPENDIX A. EXCERPTS FROM *AUSTRALIA RECONSTRUCTED*

Macroeconomic Policy

Recommendation No. 1.1

Australia should develop a central national economic and social objective. This must be negotiated, set and given substantial support by all major parties, e.g., government, unions, business and community groups. The objective should be highly visible and actively embraced; it should be promoted by all parties.

Recommendation No. 1.2

Such a national objective for Australia should aim to achieve full employment, low inflation and rising living standards which are equitably distributed. This is dependent on maintaining the maximum possible level of economic growth and development. Australia must have an innovative, positive and consensual approach to the management of change and to the removal of all impediments to achieving these objectives.

Recommendation No. 1.3

To increase growth it is recognized that investment must increase. Provision of the correct macroeconomic setting is a necessary but insufficient condition for the generation of productive investment. Other means must also be developed.

Wages

Recommendation No. 2.1

Australia should maintain a centralized wage fixing system.

Recommendation No. 2.2

Increases in wages other than national adjustments should be within a specified limit which is itself centrally determined.

Recommendation No. 2.4

Adjustment should clearly take into account the income distribution effects of taxation and social wage policies.

Recommendation No. 2.7

In a centralized system, wage increases other than national adjustments should be in accordance with a set of acceptable principles. In particular, such principles should:

a. encourage a productive and efficient society, by providing incentive for training and skill enhancement; inefficient industries should not be subsidized through relatively lower wages (this should include the wages and working conditions of outworkers, without denying their right to work as outworkers); and

b. pay due regard to price and productivity movements in the internationally traded goods and services sector. In short, any community standard should, as far as possible, be set in this sector.

Industry Policy

Recommendation No. 3.1

The approach to industry development should be undertaken in four stages.

Stage One: Formulation of Industry Plans

Following extensive examination of an industry sector, including its strengths and weaknesses and workforce composition, there should be a process of consultation and negotiation to establish tripartite commitment to an industry plan.

a. Such tripartite agreements should involve Government commitment to provide the appropriate combination of incentives which maximize the growth potential of an industry sector and its capacity to provide a net benefit to the Australian community. It is recognized that there are different problems and prospects for each industry subsector and the assistance package must be tailored to suit those requirements.

b. There should be commitments by employers commensurate with the level of assistance being provided and the circumstances of the industry.

Stage Two: Implementation of Plans at the Company and Plant Level

While the first stage concerns formulation of industry development plans, the second stage (and the one that has now become central to industry development) concerns implementation at the company and plant level of agreements that should cover a range of issues including:

a. investment for import replacement, export expansion and industry modernization;
b. new product, process and new enterprise development;
c. management and work practices to improve the efficiency of the enterprise;
d. training for the fullest possible development of the Labor force's capacity to make a contribution to production;
e. dispute settling procedures;
f. occupational health and safety;
g. Industrial democracy structures and work organization;
h. programs to achieve the aims of equal opportunity; and
i. provision of paid study leave.

Stage Three: Monitoring

There should be continuous tripartite monitoring of every aspect of Stages One and Two for the entire duration of such plans.

Stage Four: Comprehensive Review and Evaluation

While Stages One, Two, and Three involve formulation, implementation, and on-going monitoring of industry development programs at the industry and enterprise level, Stage Four involves a comprehensive review and evaluation of the strengths and weaknesses of sectorial development plans after a three- to five-year period.

Labor Market and Training Policies

Recommendation No. 4.1

Employment and training plans/programs should be fully integrated with the tripartite industry plans, and the National Development Fund.

Recommendation No. 4.2

A National Employment and Training Fund (ETF) should be established.

Objective of the National Employment and Training Fund

Consistent with the national objective, suggested in Chapter 1, the Fund should operate under the following guidelines and principles:

a. The Fund provides for skill-formation and enhancement, training and general education of the workforce and will ensure that enterprises and governments are undertaking sufficient training and skill development for the future.

b. Enterprises, both public and private, are able to draw back from the fund 80 percent of the amount they have contributed to it, provided they have reached an agreement with their employees and unions on a training and employment package.

As with the National Development Fund, drawing rights should be publicly accountable on a similar basis as in the Steel, Heavy Engineering and Textiles Clothing and Footwear packages. In order to draw from the Fund, business and unions must reach agreement on the following matters:

i.   adequate arrangements for training (including the provision of paid study leave);

ii.   superannuation (including the removal of discriminatory pro visions);

iii. dispute settlement procedures;

iv.   work and management practices and work organization;

v.   job security and redundancy;

vi.   purchasing policy (so that firms submit prospective purchases to the State and National Industrial Supplies Office to ensure the maximum local content in their purchases); and

vii. reduction in Labor market segmentation in the workforce, particularly for women (including programs to achieve the aims of equal opportunity).

c. The Fund should operate in parallel with the National Development Fund. Formal links should be established to ensure that there is adequate coordination between each Fund.

d. In addition to the normal operation of the Fund, since firms are only automatically entitled to draw back 80 percent of the moneys deposited, the remaining 20 percent of the deposited funds should be available on a priority basis to firms undertaking additional training/employment packages which are specifically designed to enhance industry restructuring, modernization, import replacement and export expansion.

e. In the case of subsidiaries of international corporations, the prerequisite for the return of any of the deposited funds will be the removal of franchise restrictions on technology transfer (to the Australian subsidiary) and exports, and to justify, cease or limit transfer pricing activities.

f. Firms should not be able to retrieve their deposited funds unless they exhibit demonstrable price restraint in line with the policies of Federal and State governments; and

g. Access to deposited funds should be conditional on the provision of notice to the CES of any vacancies and on giving the earliest possible indication of any planned retrenchments.

Operation of the National Employment and Training Fund

a. The administration and operation of the fund at the national level should be through the National Board for Employment, Education and Training (NBEET) on the basis of agreement reached between industry and the trade unions.

b. At the local level, the application of the fund will be managed by tripartite committees of management and employees. The Government representatives on such committees will be drawn from both Technical and Further Education (TAFE) and Commonwealth Employment Service local centres.

c. The operation of the fund should be in addition to any existing training programs or package.

d. The NBEET needs to work very closely with the Australian Manufacturing Council and the Department of Trade in the formulation and implementation of its policies.

e. NBEET should also have a generously resourced research capacity. As a priority it should undertake forward planning for training needs including the early identification of skills shortages, the analysis of corporate plans for restructuring and the implications of industry plans, etc.

Funding the National Employment and Training Fund

The Fund should be financed by a tax on companies which could be levied in various ways.

In establishing the National Employment and Training Fund:

a. It is necessary to ensure that training is appropriate to meet Australia's current and future demands, and that effective consultation between the Commonwealth, the States, unions and employer organizations takes place. The Government should ensure that the National Board for Employment Training gives priority to this matter and is accorded the appropriate resources to see that it is carried out.

b. Consistent with the 1973 agreement between the Australian and Swedish Governments, the Swedish Labor Market Board or other appropriate sections of the Swedish Public Service should make available senior officers, for not less than 6 months, to provide advice to the Australian Government, business and unions on the establishment, structure, operation and programs of the National Employment and Training Fund.

Recommendation No. 4.3

The Government, as a matter of priority should examine in a tripartite framework ways of ensuring that the education system provides adequate, ever ambitious preparation for the world of work so as to exploit present and future opportunities in the labor market. A general 'technology' subject should be compulsory in school curricula. In particular, the education system should encourage all pupils, particularly girls, to participate in maths, science, economics and technical subjects, and also provide equal opportunity for girls to aspire to nontraditional employment through Work Experience and similar programs.

APPENDIX B. STATEMENT BY INDUSTRIAL RELATIONS COMMISSIONER M. KEOGH, MAY 1987

1. Committees comprising representatives of management, workers and relevant unions as appropriate, are to be established at each plant or enterprise no later than 5 June 1987. The objective of each committee shall be to negotiate a plant or enterprise restructuring and efficiency agreement no later than 21 July 1987.

2. In their negotiations, the members of the plant and enterprise committees are to take note of what the Commission said in its statement of 12 May 1987:

The restructuring and efficiency principle has a far wider compass than restrictive work and management practices and both employers and employees must treat the principle as providing the opportunity to undertake major and positive attitudinal and structural change. Inevitably the abolition of restrictive work and management practices must form part of this process of change and therefore there should be no barrier to their being considered in the current discussions.

3. Amongst the issues to be considered by the plant and enterprise committee during their negotiations are:

   a. organization of work, e.g., change of work methods;

   b. demarcation barriers and associated issues;

   c. flexibility in the arrangement of hours of work including shift work;

   d. changes in manning—nature and level—consistent with improved work methods;

   e. training and retraining;

   f. unproductive work patterns;

   g. guidelines for the introduction and use of new technology;

   h. management–workers communication and consultation procedures;

   i. the role of supervision;

   j. part-time employment of males (only females could be employed on a part time basis);

   k. payment of wages in forms other than cash; and

   l. the use of contractors.

This list was not to be treated as exhaustive.

4. Negotiations at plant or enterprise level should proceed in an environment free of industrial action and any areas of disagreement should be referred, through the respective national organizations, to the Commission for assistance in resolving those areas of disagreement.

5. Any agreement negotiated at plant or enterprise level must result in genuine improvement in efficiency and productivity and shall

be properly recorded and acknowledged by the employer and the workers or their union representatives.

6. The parties at both national and plant or enterprise level are to note that:

   a. improvements in pay or conditions under the second tier principles will not exceed four percent;

   b. it is inappropriate and contrary to the spirit as well as the objectives of the restructuring and efficiency principle for pay increases to be made before efficiency improvements are implemented; and

   c. the restructuring and efficiency principle recognizes that industry must strive to improve productivity and efficiency at the enterprise level in order to improve Australia's productive base and competitive performance; it follows that the immediate benefits for employees may not be commensurate with the value of changes to an enterprise.

ACKNOWLEDGMENTS

I would like to thank John Mathews (University of New South Wales), Richard Curtain (Monash University), and Paul Adler for their help and advice in preparing this chapter.

REFERENCES

Australian Communist Party. 1970. *Modern Unionism.*
Australian Council of Trade Unions/Trade Development Council to Western Europe. June, 1987. *Australia Reconstructed.*
Australian Metal Workers Union. 1983. *ALP/ACTU Accord—Agreement Unions and Government.* National Information Bulletin No. 1.
Charlton West and Associates. February 1989. *An In-Process Evaluation of the Heavy Engineering Adjustment and Development Program.*
Department of Industrial Relations, Metal Trades Federation of Unions, and Metal Trades Industry Association Mission to United Kingdom, Sweden, and West Germany. September 1988. *Towards a New Metal and Engineering Industry Award.*

10

Transforming the Routines and Contexts of Management, Work, and Technology

Claudio U. Ciborra
Leslie S. Schneider

Rapid changes in technology, markets, and competition are forcing corporations to reconsider what it takes to sustain competitive advantage. In particular, much recent literature has emphasized the importance of addressing decisions about business strategy, technology, and organizational structure as part of a coherent whole, rather than in isolation (Walton, 1989). In the ideal case, depending on multiple parameters such as the complexity of tasks, uncertainty of the environment, prevailing competitive strategy, and so on, corporations would select specific organizational structures, information systems, job designs, and systems development procedures and shape them into a coherent design that best fits environmental and internal constraints or "contingencies." When one or more of the main parameters change or when the existing design fails, the corporations would implement a new combination of structures, systems, and tasks (Kotter, 1978).

The process from perception of a bad fit between the existing design (such as technical systems and work organization) and present contingencies to intervention to achieve a better match among the various components of the whole is called *organizational learning* (Argyris and Schon, 1978; Duncan and Weiss, 1979; Fiol and Lyles, 1985; Starbuck, 1983; Hedberg, 1981; Levitt and March, 1988). The more rapidly contingencies are changing, the more the firm must be flexible and capable of moving swiftly from perception of inadequacy to action for change. Learning becomes a critical factor in dealing with the interdependencies among strategy, organization, and technology.

In periods of moderate growth, the capacity to manage the existing organizational design and create new activities through incremental diversification is paramount. But in periods of rapid change, corporations must engage in a process of continuous organizational renewal. At the corporate level, this entails creating new businesses at a fast rate and detecting at an early stage activities that should be discontinued (Lindholm and Hethy, 1990). At the business level, it also requires the ability both to react quickly to perceived problems and to look continually for new ways to reconceive and reshape the organization, its practices, and its purposes.

Given the challenges posed by rapid change, we argue that the recent emphasis on the need for coordinated technology, strategy, and organizational structure does not go far enough. Much of the literature assumes that once these areas are integrated, and people understand the new organizational logic, adequately planned change is a relatively straightforward and unproblematic process. Evidence of the great difficulty of organizational learning and change suggests that this is far from the case. Organizational inertia, rather than renewal, is a frequent outcome (Hannan and Freeman, 1984).

Effective innovation for business renewal requires going beyond the careful alignment of strategy, technology, and organization. It depends on what we can call "second-order organizational learning"—identifying and, where necessary, changing the background assumptions and institutional arrangements that shape an organization's approach to strategy, technology, and organization in the first place (see Argyris and Schon, 1978, for a general discussion of first- and second-order learning processes). We call these assumptions and their institutional embodiment the *formative context* (Unger,1987).

FORMATIVE CONTEXT

A formative context is a necessary part of organizational functioning. An organization's formative context gives meaning to its everyday practices and routines, defines acceptable and unacceptable behaviors, and determines the way they define problems and solutions. The outcome of a formative context is a texture of routines, roles and tasks, a division of labor, and a set of coordination mechanisms that come to possess an "aura of naturalness" for those who execute routines within that context. This context enables actors to perform organizational routines and practices without reflecting upon them first.

The notion of formative context is different from the more common concepts of mental frames and organizational culture (Swidler, 1986) because it simultaneously captures the institutionally embedded quality of work-related and social cognition and the cognitive dimension ever present in institutional arrangements (Simon, 1976). Furthermore, the distinction between the formative context and the lower-level routines that are executed, imitated, discontinued, and generated within its scope helps to highlight the implications of second-order learning (revising contexts) as opposed to learning by doing (revising routines within given contexts) for the implementation of technological and organizational innovations.

Precisely because the formative context is taken for granted, it is extremely difficult to identify, let alone change. Rarely does an organization know how to reflect on, question, or reinvent its formative context when the necessity arises. As a set of background assumptions and institutional arrangements, a formative context is stubbornly resilient.

Nevertheless, the difficulty of changing a formative context does not rule out organizational change completely. On the local level, for example, the concrete execution of a given work routine, operation of a machine, or use of a system, each element of the main design is subject to constant flux. As Brown and Duguid (1989) point out, ". . . people regularly invent ways around difficulties, discontinuities and unexpected irregularities in the course of their daily work and learn about their work in the process." This is an important and often-overlooked space for the creation of new practices and routines that can alter or transform the formative context. Local innovations contain the seeds of new possibilities, new horizons of action, new ways of framing things, and, thus, new directions for organizational change. The strategic challenge is how to sanction these local innovations, capture their insights for the organization as a whole, and exploit them as opportunities for second-order learning.

To establish a new agenda for strategic leadership in managing technology and work, this chapter investigates the theory and practice of technological innovation using the concepts of second-order organizational learning and formative context. We describe two cases of advanced automation to illustrate how the notion of formative context can explain why innovation is so difficult to implement or so subtle to appreciate when it occurs naturally. We also propose a set of alternative activities to help organizations develop second-order organizational learning and successful business renewal in connection with technological innovations.

THE FIRM AS A "THINKING ORGANIZATION"

To investigate how second-order organizational learning is critical to business renewal and technological innovation, it helps to consider the firm as the locus of complex and intertwined cognitive processes—a "thinking organization"(Weick, 1979).

Business firms can be regarded as organizations that "know how to do things." They are repositories of productive knowledge arranged as hierarchies of routines (Cyert and March, 1963; Nelson and Winter, 1982) linked to the execution of tasks. The knowledge embedded in these routines is represented by the skills of the members executing those tasks. A skill is itself a routine acquired by remembering and using answers to previously solved problems and avoiding previously encountered traps (Argyris, 1982).

These routines are generalized and stored in the brain and body of the individual or the work team (Zuboff, 1988). They are taken for granted; so they can be applied smoothly and competently. Such skills and routines lie at the core of the corporation, as they provide it with a unique, difficult-to-reproduce asset to support its competitiveness and growth. Given their tacit, opaque, and taken-for-granted character, these skills are not easily transferrable, and thus form the firm's distinctive competence (Polanyi, 1966).

The notion of routines as embodied in an organization's distinct competencies does not, however, exhaust what we mean by the thinking organization. We also need a concept of the dynamic process of creating and modifying routines and the knowledge the routines embody. In achieving higher levels of performance, both at the individual and the team level, in adapting to new environmental circumstances, and in being more flexible, the crucial process is the ability to integrate old knowledge and routines with the acquisition and use of new knowledge, that is, organizational learning.

The economic literature pictures this process as one of trial-and-error experimentation (Alchian, 1950; Rosenberg, 1982). As elaborated by Nelson and Winter (1982), such learning by doing allows not only for increased efficiency, but also for the creation of entirely new routines. They argue that the same simple trial-and-error mechanism can be used to search out, imitate, and recombine old routines to create new ones. Radical, Schumpeterian innovations are also considered to be the result of complex forms of learning by doing, that is, as successful recombinations of the routines that govern the firm.

Unfortunately, Nelson and Winter's qualitative accounts of the learning processes surrounding major innovations fail to recognize important aspects of learning as performed by human agents. First, the linearity between search, problem solving, and development and trial of a new routine is not automatic. New events may not trigger search routines at all when human agents consider the events threatening. Finally, and most important, routines aimed at correcting errors can lead to repetition of the performances that were considered faulty in the first place. Instead of new routines, vicious circles are unwittingly generated (Tversky and Kahneman, 1981; Masuch, 1985; Argyris, 1982). In other words, random events, anomalies, and disturbances, although ubiquitous in organizations, can be largely ignored, dismissed, or even actively repressed in the name of management control.

What is at stake in change as carried out by humans in organizations rather than through routines is the capacity to question the formative context that gives established routines their meaning.

LEVELS OF LEARNING

The distinction between routines and their background context allows us to differentiate between two levels of learning:

1. "Incremental learning," whereby organizational knowledge is

increased by performing or refining existing routines within a stable context that attaches the same set of meanings both to old and new routines.

2. "Second-order learning," whereby the context of meaning is changed. Old routines lose their original significance and acquire a completely new meaning, and routines previously ignored, suppressed, or unimagined are put into place and executed (Bateson, 1972).

Second-order learning implies appreciating disturbances and fluctuations as opportunities for new emerging designs, and not as objects for control or elimination. Such learning involves being aware of the tools, systems, artifacts, and ways of doing things that are usually taken for granted and left unquestioned. It requires "slowing down" in the execution of those routines in which we feel most confident and competent, and it involves facing threats or the fear of being or appearing incompetent (Argyris, 1982; Handy,1989).

Second-order learning is a process of putting into question the formative context that gives meaning to lower-order routines. If second-order learning is itself a routine, it is a qualitatively different kind of routine. Indeed, one may ask whether the variety of second-order learning paths has enough consistency to be considered a routine at all. Also, routines assume an unquestioned context and an agent or organization with a relatively stable identity and goals. We are concerned here with processes aimed at revising such contexts, identities, and goals (Ciborra, 1990).

How then can we usefully characterize this second-order learning process? We propose to put at the center of this analysis the notion of formative context. This insulating layer represents a bundle of mental and behavioral commitments—to technology, personnel, and methods—that cannot be altered easily or quickly. Its influence can be best appreciated from the perspective of action science (Schon, 1979; Argyris et al., 1985) as linked to action situations. Whenever an organizational member makes a decision, executes a routine, deals with a teammate or a customer, develops a vision of the business, or imagines alternative actions, he or she enacts a context in a local, specific situation and responds to it. The context provides the premises or programs for action that help people think and act, or that prevent them from doing so when they want to do it differently (Swidler, 1986).

Finally, the distinction and connection between organizational routines and formative context is of paramount importance when designing and implementing technological innovations. Effective technical systems consist not only of new routines, and procedures, but also of new organizational arrangements and new ways of seeing the world, that is, a new formative context (Hedberg and Jonsson, 1978). In the following sections of the paper, we will explore this thesis in greater depth.

Automation notably affects the most standardized routines and skills in an organization. It changes the boundary between the tacit and explicit routines, although often in unexpected ways, and necessitates new routines and skills (Adler, 1990). It also has the potential to support second-order learning; that is, systems can be designed and implemented to provide a context that facilitates the emergence of new organizational forms and new technical systems.

Such a response requires an organization and technology design strategy that lets people concentrate on what Brown et al., (1989) call "situated invention and innovation." The phrase means helping people reflect on their work practices and routines and connecting them to the formative context of their organization. Doing so is complicated since, like formative contexts, technology often remains in the background of thought and action—as the following two cases suggest.

Case One: Manufacturing Resources Planning at an Aircraft Instruments Plant

Our first case describes the implementation of a computerized "manufacturing resources planning" (MRP) system at an aircraft instruments plant owned by a major United States corporation (Schneider and Howard, 1987). It illustrates what happens when an organization's formative context is not adequate to the demands of new technology and how a "bad fit" between a formative context and new technology can undermine the possibilities offered by the technology.

The aircraft instruments plant is a manufacturer of high-technology products such as engine sensors, displays, and monitoring systems. Management set out to overhaul completely its inventory control and factory scheduling by implementing the new computer-based information system, MRP. MRP is a factory-wide information system designed to rationalize inventory planning and scheduling. It collects information from the various departments of the factory, and, depending upon factors such as plant capacity, orders, and material on hand, schedules where every part should be at any particular time. MRP not only tracks information and parts, but coordinates the entire production process. As such, it is often referred to as the "central nervous system" of the modern factory.

Just as MRP pulls together information from locations throughout the factory, it also links the work of the various departments—marketing, sales, stock room, and shopfloor. Workers depend upon each other to maintain the database and to ensure that the information in it is up to date and accurate. Poor data integrity ripples through the entire system and undermines everyone's performance.

Like any computer system, MRP is basically a "simulation." In this case, it is a model of the complex process by which thousands of parts are turned into a specific set of manufactured products. No matter how accurate the data or carefully planned the software, the MRP program will never be able to take into account all the possible contingencies that can occur on the shopfloor. So the work of those who run the system is to "maximize the fit" between the computer simulation of the MRP system and the complexities of production in the factory. Put another way, they apply the general rules of the information system to the particularities of each specific case on the shopfloor.

Since the major task in working with MRP becomes fitting the system to the circumstances of the work, it is not sufficient for workers simply to follow the rules of the system and take its instructions for granted. Instead, they have to participate in a constant round of evaluation and decision-making: Are the data really accurate? Are the instructions coming from the system really adequate to the circumstances of a particular situation? As Kling and Iacono (1984) write, "Workers [using MRP] . . . must make skilled judgements, based on projections about the repercussions of their actions rather than simply according to fixed rules."

To accomplish this, they need at least three distinct cognitive skills: (1) a formal, abstract knowledge of the system itself—its logic and rules; (2) a highly concrete knowledge of the work organization—how different departments function, what their formal procedures and informal practices are; and (3) the capacity to make their organizational models explicit and available for reflection, so they can better relate them to the formal model of the work organization embodied in the software.

At first glance, it seemed that management at the aircraft instruments plant had a relatively clear understanding of the technological and organizational challenges associated with implementing and successfully using the MRP system. A key goal was to use the new system to replace the obsolete production control technology of the plant. Managers understood that the problem with the old system (based on an obsolete, unintegrated, and inflexible technology) was not merely a matter of technology. It was also a result of what managers referred to as the "inadequate work disciplines" of the entire production planning and control system. Because the current technology was so unreliable, shopfloor personnel tended to depend on their own informal knowledge of materials on hand and breakdowns on the shopfloor, for example, to smooth the production process.

Management felt it needed to systematize work practices in order to counter the loss of the crucial informal knowledge and skills of older workers, who were beginning to retire, and to replace the messy informal practices that had developed. In the words of the systems manager of the MRP II project, "we are moving from making products by art to making them by science."

Thus, the ultimate goal of the strategy—and the MRP system—was to introduce a new concept and philosophy of management, to establish "a new set of values." Management wanted to eliminate the traditional methods of inventory and production control, which they considered overly informal, too dependent on the personal judgments and initiatives of the planning and control clerks, and replace them with a more rational, more automated, and more consistent system.

Managers of the MRP project talked about the system as a "people system" and emphasized the importance of "sensitivity to the user." Following Wight (1981), they maintained that managing the organizational issues surrounding technological change was the key to the ultimate success of their efforts. "One reason the old system never worked is that people never really felt a part of it," said one system manager. "This time, we've recognized that people play at least as important a part as the computer—if not more so. We're emphasizing people as being the most important part." Managers said that their biggest area of concern was "dispelling the 'it's not my job, man' mentality." Or, as one systems designer put it: "Throughout any computerized system, the judgment factor is very important. We've got to instill a new set of values about how people go about their work."

The managers' attitudes seemed to reflect a general understanding that MRP entailed a new way of thinking, a new philosophy. However, when it came to planning and designing the system, and defining the roles of workers, the managers' espoused values were inconsistent with the values embedded in their practice. Although they said they recognized that people were the key to a successful system, their unconscious assumption—grounded in a formative context based on managerial control over a recalcitrant workforce—that "people were the key problem" remained unquestioned. This assumption was buttressed by corporate procedures. When it came to justifying the cost of the MRP investment to corporate management, the standard operating procedure encouraged managers to focus on projected reductions in head count and labor costs. Management's assumptions were further reinforced by the procedures adopted by systems designers, who saw their task as solving a technical problem. The designers focused on "getting the system in" in a manner that left no room for local experimentation. Not surprisingly, when it came to training the workforce, managers emphasized narrow technical skills, such as learning how to identify the computer codes of the system, rather than the broad organizational expertise crucial to using MRP effectively.

Ten months into the implementation process, none of the expected gains in efficiency had yet to materialize. There was so much emphasis on working with the system and following its rules that clerks often hesitated to override the system's commands even when they knew the commands did not make sense. While MRP brought new tools to the aircraft instruments plant, workers and managers were still ensconced in old roles and an old formative context.

Workers and their supervisors received contradictory signals from the information systems staff about just how to function with MRP. According to one production planning supervisor, "When you don't do what the system says, they're up here saying, 'What the hell are you doing?'" On the one hand, they were told to follow the rules. On the other hand, they were informed that "the system only suggests; it doesn't run the show. It's up to you to decide."

Unlike the clerical personnel, when shopfloor personnel could not make sense of the system, they developed new informal procedures for "doing end runs around the system." "In case after case," said one production supervisor, "you have to say 'forget the system.' We don't say 'second-guess' because that drives the information systems people crazy. What it is is good common sense. Making judgments."

One example of tinkering with routines concerned weekend work. The plant runs a seven-days-a-week operation, and many changes happen over the weekend. But on weekends, the MRP system is down and the stockroom is closed because parts must be released by the computer. To avoid stopping production altogether, the supervisor and programmers would estimate on Fridays what steps in the production process could be completed over the weekend, then feed those steps into the system as if they were already done. They bypassed the rules and "covered up" the bypass.

Dealing with such mismatches required two important skills. Of course, people needed to understand the logic and operations of the new system. But work with MRP also involved using their concrete knowledge of the work organization—how different departments function, how they fit together, what their formal procedures and informal practices are—to interpret what the computer was telling them to do at any moment. Workers had to pay attention to all the messy and unexpected things that could go wrong as a particular part made its way through the production process. It was this ability to reinterpret the new system in the context of the work organization itself that allowed workers to operate MRP in a way that avoided major interruptions. Only then did they know when to override the system, when to "bend or manipulate the rules" creatively in order to anticipate problems and come up with the best fit between two parallel but often quite different systems—the computer simulation and the reality it is meant to mirror.

The idea of MRP as a "simulation" of production at the plant, the possibility of a serious "mismatch" between the computer model and the shopfloor, the necessity for learning and local innovation to make the computer and the shopfloor work together rather than in opposition—all are elements of an effective MRP development and implementation strategy. But because of the prevailing formative context, the MRP design team and plant management were ill prepared to recognize, let alone address, these issues.

Even worse, the formative context drove local innovations and learning underground. The insights gained from people's "end runs" were hidden because workers felt that these practices were not sanctioned by management. Thus, almost without knowing it, the firm's formative context created obstacles to the success of the technology.

Managers at the plant developed a technological change strategy that was logical, consistent, and coherent. But their actions were influenced by a pre-existing formative context that betrayed a set of assumptions that were inadequate to the unique opportunities and demands of computer-based systems like MRP. This led managers to underestimate and misconstrue the kinds of changes in organizational structure, skills, and motivation that would be needed to operate MRP effectively. In other words, even though they began the MRP project with an accurate intuition that it would necessitate a substantial redesign of the organization and human resources management, managers were unable to bring the key elements of their formative context (for example, economic evaluation procedures and systems development methods) to the foreground. Instead of an organizational change effort, they ended up with a technical change project.

This case shows the resilience and pervasiveness of management's formative context. Implicit assumptions of control and technical rationality prevail over an espoused theory about "people at the center" of the innovation. The automatic enactment of routines, the development of organizational arrangements, training, and role definitions all serve to reinforce each other.

The intertwining of assumptions, routines, and systems development procedures indicates that the formative context is more than a set of cognitive frames or assumptions. Rather, it consists of individual cognitive frames reflected and reinforced by *social* actions such as executing specific tasks, dealing with people and artifacts, and a specific way of organizing work and doing business.

The end result is that, despite clearly defined goals and plans, a sound economic evaluation, and a structured implementation, the new system did not lead to the expected outcomes. Even the useful local innovations, such as shortcuts and new rules of thumb, remained private know-how and did not augment the knowledge base of the organization. Learning from mistakes was also limited. New effective routines were kept unofficial, while problematic solutions were not discussed, since designers thought they had adhered to the best technical practice and were not willing to question their competence—or to have it questioned.

One can imagine the trajectory of the MRP project given the lack of effective learning and inability to reframe the roles of systems, management, and workers. The "innovation" will be further undermined when modifications are made. The existing formative context will lead management to interpret the failure of the present project as confirmation of the need to rationalize production and centralize control more effectively. The new, informal routines developed by the workers will be interpreted as a sign that work discipline is still lacking and that the entire production process needs further stream-lining. Moreover, efforts to redesign the system will start from the existing automated routines instead of discarding them altogether. Inertia rather than innovation will be the most likely outcome of any new project carried out within the existing formative context.

Finally, the case suggests that the MRP system itself shares the characteristics of a formative context. It contains a view, or simulation, of the entire production organization, a set of assumptions about how production should be managed (although concealed in hypotheses, parameters, and algorithms), and how labor should be divided into jobs and tasks, how information should flow and be stored across departments and between people in the organization. In a way, MRP was developed as an extension of the firm's formative context, as a means to reinforce its basic assumptions and routines of centralized control.

However, because complex systems are open, they allow for tinkering and the local generation of new routines and skills. This case study reports on some of the tactics and routines developed locally to circumvent the MRP system. But since local experiments are never recognized officially by management at the plant, the result is a patchwork of institutional arrangements, routines, assumptions and systems, and much of the new technology's potential was wasted.

Case Two: The Computer Network for Software Development

Our second case concerns the use of network-based systems for software development. It illustrates that, when dealing with systems such as electronic mail, networks, and groupware that are more open than MRP, the paths that lead to innovation are often surprising. Planned changes do not materialize, while unexpected ones take place but are ignored because of the existing formative context.

The Research and Development department of a large European computer manufacturer was assigned by top management the task of developing the operating system of a new minicomputer line. The challenge of coordinating about 400 programmers working simultaneously on the same piece of software raised concerns about the already precarious internal organization of the department.

To prepare for this complex task, the chief software designers reshaped the department's structure according to the functional organization of the new minicomputer system. Thus, a team of programmers was set up for each function the system was designed to perform, with a hierarchical structure connecting the various teams. After some time, the project became plagued by problems that software developers often face in this type of endeavor: delays, sky-rocketing costs, poor documentation, and so forth.

To increase productivity and improve the organization of work, two major innovations were introduced. The first was a structured methodology for rationalizing software development, that is, a set of guidelines that organized work by dividing it into stages and defining precise goals and activities for each stage, such as analysis, programming, and documentation. The idea of a methodology appealed to programmers as well as managers because it supported key values of the software culture: rationality, order, transparency, and consistency. Its application, however, turned into a costly disaster.

The second innovation turned out to be an undisputed success. It was called the "software factory" and consisted of a computer network connecting hundreds of workstations on which a set of programs, or "software tools," were available to support the programmers' work. The software factory linked each programmer to fellow workers through electronic mail, creating a new programming environment for interactive software development. The software factory became the basic infrastructure for the daily work of the programmer: Everybody soon took it for granted as an effective programming environment.

The success of the second innovation points to the problems of the first. At the time, various explanations were given for the repeated failures to impose order on the systems development work flow. Some blamed politicking by chief designers; others argued for more formality and automation; union members proposed an altogether different approach based on "democratic" work groups.

In contrast, the second innovation supported group work that was already widely practiced "below the surface." Although not officially acknowledged, electronic mail and tools of the software factory supported that group work. The messaging system provided an informal channel for direct communication among programmers; the tools allowed for the integration of different pieces of code and would automatically update the parameters of one program when other interlinked programs were changed. The software factory was not just a production tool but also a "coordination technology" (Malone, 1988), well suited to the complex task of the Research and Development Department. It both improved individual productivity, and allowed for flexible coordination and bargaining between the workplaces linked to the network.

The enlarged work groups supported by the network crossed both the physical barriers defined by the R&D department's geographical layout and, more importantly, the organizational boundaries among the units of the hierarchy. As a result, the real tasks, roles, and communication patterns were governed neither by the formal structure defined by Personnel nor by the functional chart set up originally by system designers. They were, instead, the product of informal cooperation and bargaining that took place through the computer network.

Unfortunately, the actors, irrespective of their position in the hierarchy, their particular interests, and their influence on the process, seemed to be blind to the significance of the emergent work organization, and were therefore unable to intervene in an effective way to facilitate the process of organizational innovation.

When implementing innovations and imagining alternatives to improve their effectiveness, the actors, no matter what their specific stance or goals, are under the influence of that deep-seated structure we have called formative context. The context that conditioned the members of this Research and Development Department can be characterized as a cluster of institutional arrangements, beliefs, and procedures: a hierarchical division of labor; a hierarchical, functional decomposition of problem solving strategy; the drive toward structured formalization; the conflicts between technical and managerial roles; and the assumptions regarding the paramount value of technical rationality, structured methodologies, and the dysfunctionality of the informal organization of work.

This hierarchical formative context was retrieved and enacted by the actors in situations when they needed to make sense of their everyday routines or invent changes to achieve higher effectiveness. Because the formative context was internalized and taken for granted, it blinded them to the mismatch between structured methodologies and the uncertainties of the development process, and thereby blocked the learning of the department's members. To recognize the mismatch and reflect upon it would have threatened large regions of the context itself.

It is interesting to note that the conflicts between those arguing to maintain the existing organization and those seeking it to change it in various ways (like the structured programming proposal and democratic work groups proposed by the union) served primarily to reinforce the existing formative context. The conflicts hindered the creation of a set of concepts and a language to describe those changes that were not leading to greater or reduced formalization and standardization. The union members, for example, advocated radically new forms of work organization, but their proposals were still organized along the centralization–decentralization axis, and they paid little attention to the emergent work practices, especially those tried out locally.

This case shows that the interaction between daily work routines and the underlying formative contexts to which they are linked is a complex one, especially in periods of transformation when new events bring about sweeping changes. The introduction of the software factory, although implemented within the hierarchical framework, led to the unexpected establishment and extension of new horizontal links between workplaces and the emergence of routines and behaviors, such as working and bargaining in a network, that may point to a formative context of a different kind.

An unrecognized emergent networking formative context had come to coexist uneasily with the prior, hierarchical formative context. This suggests another, more general and theoretical conclusion: that formative contexts often have a collage, makeshift nature, where old and new routines are continually tested, discarded, retrieved, and combined alongside and in partial conflict with a mainstream sense-making pattern. Formative contexts in real organizations are rarely completely coherent.

Finally, the case suggests that, when developing a system like the software factory, the object of design and construction—be it deliberate or unintended—consists of new routines, programs, procedures, databases, and flows, but, more important, of a new formative context. A new context can shape both the organization of work and the set of social scripts that govern the invention of alternative forms of work.

STRATEGIES FOR INNOVATION AND CHANGE

The theory and cases discussed so far illustrate how pre-existing formative contexts can either limit learning and radical change or provide the raw materials to support new designs and innovations. The makeshift outcomes described in the cases are not merely anomalies or aberrations, or simply the result of incompetence that can be corrected by a more comprehensive organizational design. They are the emerging norm, not the exception, as organizations attempt to capture the accelerating expansion of technical opportunities. If this were true, what sort of organizational strategy could systematically lead to radical change and effective innovation? We make some suggestions in this section.

The Learning Organization: Deconstructing the Hierarchy

To foster second-order learning, organizations should encourage local experimentation. This requires a shift in organizational structure from one on the hierarchical end of the spectrum toward a form characterized by semiautonomous units (Brown and Duguid, 1989). Flexible coordination among these units can foster the exchange of local, valid knowledge, and present an overall picture of the organization and how it evolves locally and globally as experiments are carried out.

The MRP system, although a simplified simulation of the production process, contains a global model that interconnects tasks, departments, people, and systems, and includes in its database a rich picture of production flows. Such an integrated view and the routines that it supports are only an approximation of the complexities of the production system. At its boundaries, ad hoc problem solving routines are tried out locally by those who diagnose the mismatch between the model and actual production events (Ciborra et al., 1984). This boundary activity implies that MRP conceived as a system that *manages* production information more efficiently can function only if new information were continually *created* at its boundaries by people experimenting with routines to fill gaps in the system. Such a pattern corresponds to the "informating effects" of systems (Zuboff, 1988).

Had management at the aircraft instruments company realized that *information creation* and not *management control* was what MRP was about, and that local problem solving was the key to making the system work, they might have tried to transform the running of MRP into a kind of research and development laboratory. This would have entailed a totally different set of organizational arrangements, job design, coordination and incentive mechanisms, and possibly a formal change in the organizational location of the production department. Moreover, in a research and development laboratory, the rules of the win–lose game between management and workers would have changed dramatically from control and domination to inquiry based on trust. Only through this different formative context could new, more appropriate routines have been generated and the MRP system effectively implemented.

One example of a firm that has successfully created new organizational forms by breaking its traditional formative context is the Japanese corporation Yamazaki Machinery (Harvard Business School, 1987). Yamazaki management was able to draw on all the lessons of its highly automated production operations when it implemented a new flexible manufacturing system (FMS). Realizing that the key to successful FMS operation is looking for problems and diagnosing them, not running the machines, they suggested a radical shift in organization. Production and engineering activities were to be integrated in such a way that engineers would run the shopfloor operations and production management would provide the staff support. Suddenly the taken-for-granted nature of the location of manufacturing in the organization vanished and various units co .d be combined in totally new ways. This is the institutional outcome of what we mean by the capacity to change a formative context. Reflecting on the new constraints and possibilities opened up by the new technology and questioning existing structures and established ways of thinking are essential ingredients for creative organizational change.

Another example is the story of Canon's creation of the personal copier (Nonaka and Yamanouchi, 1989). At a time when demand for copiers seemed to be leveling off and a further decline was expected, Canon rethought the concept of the copier as well as its own strengths as a corporation. The result of this systematic process of organizational reflection was the idea of the mini-copier, a product that has proved extremely successful.

But a key condition for this radical innovation was the creation of a special unit outside the traditional bureaucratic structure of the organization. Members of the unit were drawn from throughout the corporation and had reputations for innovation within their own departments. Canon's idea was to develop dynamic cooperation among a diverse group of people. The unit also emphasized alliances with others groups both inside and outside Canon. Because members of the team stayed in close touch with outside sources of information, they could evaluate and respond to changing market conditions quickly.

Alliances

More generally, we see a promising new line of thought emerging in the context of interfirm alliances. These alliances are increasingly interpreted as opportunities for firms to challenge their formative contexts and to encourage second-order learning.

In high-technology sectors, especially, the pace of technological innovation requires structures that are extremely adaptive and flexible. No single company is able to keep up with all the potential new developments that emerge daily in its own and potentially related industries. As a response to these structural conditions, alliances or coalitions are emerging even among competing firms (Porter and Fuller, 1986).

The logic of these alliances is that companies can share research and development results and efforts in order to exploit complementarities at the precompetitive stage (Fusfeld and Hacklish, 1985). To be sure, alliances fail because of the opportunism of the partners. Nevertheless, alliances are becoming increasingly common despite strong arguments in favor of the internal development of crucial innovations.

Alliance participants commit themselves to cooperative behavior in order to force themselves to learn how to shake up their traditional way of doing things. The ability to question established routines through the alliance is based on a process that Nonaka (1988) calls "learning by intrusion." The alliance exposes the members of one organization to arrangements, mindsets, and routines that belong to different firms and different formative contexts. In the process, it unfreezes old behaviors and mindsets and generates completely new ideas and new possibilities for growth, innovation, and second-order learning.

One can find examples of changes in corporate identity and evolution in important alliances, including those that have "failed." Take the example of the AT&T–Olivetti alliance. Thanks to that partnership, Olivetti made a quantum leap in the computer industry. Today Olivetti is one of the very few computer vendors in Europe that not only makes a profit but is also able to interact as a peer with major suppliers such as Intel and Microsoft for developing new generations of chips and systems.

New Skills: Everybody is a Designer

When implementing a technological innovation or designing a new complex organization, the key challenge is the continual generation of new knowledge. We have argued that in an increasingly dynamic, competitive world, it is risky to limit the emergence of new knowledge, new institutions, and new systems to learning by doing.

These changes must come from the bottom up, and that is possible only if actors are able to go beyond the skilled execution of current routines. They must try out new ways of doing things and deliberately risk mistakes. Furthermore, this experimentation must be valued and encouraged by management. The actors must also be able to make sense of this local experimentation in a way that links it to the organization's formative context. They must become what Schon calls "reflective practitioners" (Schon, 1979).

The considerable investment of Japanese firms in the statistical training of shopfloor employees exemplifies the kind of new skill-formation policy that is needed to empower employees to contribute to this experimentation process.

Focusing on local experiments alone, however, is not enough. An organization must be able to capture local insights for the organization as a whole. This requires future leaders to be both "designers and operators" and organizations to be giant networks of interconnected nodes (Stata, 1989).

That is, if the source of innovation is bound to be local and linked to marginal fluctuations, and the firm as a formative context is loosely connected, then the institutional infrastructure for communicating knowledge must be loosely coupled and shaped by the network. It must encourage the flexible sharing of innovations among scattered units. Actors at the multiple nodes of the network must play the role of "smooth network operators" who use planning as an organizational learning process in itself (De Geus, 1988).

New Systems to Support New Contexts

The orientation towards second-order learning also requires technologies that possess an open nature and are subject to continuous reinvention, that is, to an innovative adaptation process carried out by the users themselves (Rice and Rogers, 1980).

As the two case studies illustrated, two features of computer-based systems give them a dynamic character with almost a life of their own that defies attempts by members of the organization to harness them fully for their own purposes. First, systems are increasingly platforms for creating applications, routines, languages, communication modes, and simulated, virtual environments that go beyond the limited set of purposes and functions initially laid out by designers and sponsors. Second, they are laboratories where the more visible artifacts associated with the execution of everyday routines can be designed, engineered, and assembled (Hewitt and De Jong, 1984).

If these are the qualities of systems as currently designed and implemented within the existing, hierarchical formative contexts, what would be the characteristics of information systems that are conceived not just to reinforce the existing order, but to support innovation and second-order learning? New systems for information creation (Nonaka, 1988) rather than information management should possess the following properties:

1. They should facilitate the process of reinvention that any complex technological artifact undergoes when put to use.

2. They should not conceal the relations between routines embedded in systems and formative contexts. On the contrary, they should make those relations explicit and available for questioning.

3. They should function as media for enhancing coordination and communication within and across teams (Winograd and Flores, 1986). Problems and solutions shift all the time, and because systems are open and pasted together by nature, they should support loosely coupled forms of organization.

4. They should provide real-time feedback to users on their current organization of work and the emerging coordination and communication patterns.

5. They should function as "systems for experts," but not in the way implied by current conceptions of "expert systems." That is, in addition to supporting or replacing the knowledge-based routines of professionals and managers in specific domains of expertise, they should support people's capabilities for reflection and inquiry within the contexts in which they are embedded. They should help people build up, question, and modify practical knowledge according to the emergence and the shift of problematic situations and contexts (Ciborra and Lanzara, 1990).

Peter Senge of Massachusetts Institute of Technology's Systems Dynamics Group (Senge, 1990) has developed an innovative software program to help managers model the impacts of their decisions. Using the program, managers explore their assumptions about the dynamics underlying their own strategic choices. The very process of explicating critical assumptions always proves useful and very often reveals startling inconsistencies.

Using the program, the Chief Executive Officer of one firm discovered that his assumptions about the relative productivity of new and experienced sales personnel were inconsistent with projected hiring by a factor of two. He had never thought through how projected rapid hiring rates would dilute the overall yield of sales personnel, forcing experienced salespeople to divert more time to training junior staff and resulting in increased turnover of senior staff.

Another instance of using technology as a tool for second-order organizational learning comes from the World Bank (Howard and Schneider, 1989). It concerns the use of portable computers by Bank professionals in the field. When professionals began experimenting with portables on missions, they knew it would help them produce the necessary documents more quickly and efficiently. But they also found that the use of simple analytical software as a way to make the reasoning processes behind their analyses and decisions explicit, transformed their relations with clients. It brought sources of disagreement out into the open, allowing discussions to focus on the real issues of analytical assumptions and policy and not just differences of opinion. As a result, the professional–client relationships became more of a partnership. A real dialogue developed to the mutual satisfaction of both sides. Once again, a system affected both routines—computing with a spreadsheet— and contexts—seeing the relationship in a new way, enacting the premises for a new institutional arrangement that was a partnership instead of a market relation.

New Systems Development Strategies: The Role of Intervention

According to the conventional view, information systems consist of routines, procedures, and technologies to process data electronically. From this perspective, designing an information system means designing and implementing functional requirements and specifications in terms of data flows, work routines, or economic transactions. In other words, the conventional approach limits its inquiries and methods to the explicitly visible patterns of activities, albeit segmented and grouped in different ways.

Taking a different perspective, we submit that the components of an information system—data flows, work procedures, transactions— are the visible embodiments of ways of organizing reality, cognitively and institutionally, that are deeply entrenched in the formative contexts we bring to projects and organizational situations (Boland, 1982; Hedberg and Jonsson, 1978). This view has a number of important implications for the design and use of new technology. According to this view, designing a new technical system means to a large extent changing and restructuring the institutional bonds and background conditions upon which people establish and enact their practical dealings and relations.

It is unlikely that a routine, even a payroll application, can be designed without at the same time affecting its formative context. It is also difficult to restructure organizational practices without restructuring the underlying context as well. The design of such powerful artifacts cannot escape the issues of how to analyze and design formative contexts.

Information systems, then, should always be treated and designed at two distinct levels: the formed routines and the formative contexts. To meet this challenge, we must redirect current design practices. They need to involve more than property determination, requirements specification, routine problem solving, and interest accommodation. Instead, they should deal with the structures and frameworks within which these exercises take place. That is, successful design practices deal with shaping and restructuring formative contexts (Leonard–Barton, 1987).

One can change formative contexts only by intervening in situations. The logic of intervention is in many respects different from the logic of analysis because its epistemology draws on a theory of action (Argyris and Schon, 1978; Argyris et al., 1985). Intervention is concerned with understanding and acting in situations by enacting practical experiments to test formative contexts, to bring conflicts and inconsistencies to the surface, and to explore deviations from routines and identify contexts to which they may lead.

One example of how this process might work comes from the work of one of the authors as a consultant to the World Bank. In the early 1980s, the Bank wanted to develop a strategic approach to technology management. At first, management left this task to technical personnel. However, the operational staff rejected the proposed centralized, control-oriented solution. They too had been experimenting with the new technology and felt their insights needed to be included in any plan. As a result, top management initiated what it called the Action Research Project. The project was an attempt to capture all the local learnings associated with information technology and to develop a new strategy based on them.

Consultants acted as free-floating anthropologists collecting stories of "best practice" from local divisions. They trained Bank staff to develop a series of cases profiling distinct work and technology "cultures" within the Bank, and these were disseminated throughout the organization. Project members developed a methodology for helping work units reflect on and change their own technology practice. As a result, local innovation and learning were captured for use by the organization as a whole. This process proved so valuable that the position of a free-floating technology-and-organization consultant was institutionalized in the Information Technology and Facilities Department.

CONCLUSION

The problem with existing frameworks on strategy, technology and work is that they assume people and institutions will and can change their behavior automatically. They rarely acknowledge cognitive or organizational barriers to learning. As a result, the changes they generate are usually based on general prescriptions or the requirements of the technology. Moreover, they are implemented in a way that is disconnected from the implicit influence of cultural backgrounds, frames, routines, and institutional arrangements. Often the outcome of this approach to strategizing is exactly the opposite of what was intended. Individuals and organizations seem blind to radical changes, vicious circles develop, and little of the planned innovation takes place.

To establish a new agenda for strategic leadership, this chapter has investigated the theory and practice of technological innovation from the perspective of organizational learning. We argue that business renewal can only take place through "second-order learning." In particular, firms and systems are not just artifacts, but what we call "formative contexts" that shape strategies, behaviors, routines, and actions.

The actions that appear to be critical for organizations to develop second-order organizational learning and successful business renewal can be summarized as follows:

1. Sanction local experimentation, reflection in action, and the development of ways to capture and build on local experiments and interventions organization-wide.

2. Make second-order organizational learning a tool for strategic planning.

3. Develop an institutional infrastructure based on a loosely coupled network, using information technology to enhance coordination and the flexible sharing of information and innovation among scattered units.

4. Create managers and "free-floating" experts who can assist members of the organization to understand and change the formative context.

5. Encourage alliances among organizations. Second-order learning requires the ability to make connections among different routines, norms, cultures, and contexts (Ohmae, 1990).

REFERENCES

Adler, P. S. 1990. "Managing High-Tech Processes: The Challenge of CAD/CAM." In M. A. Von Glinow and S.A. Mohrman (eds.). New York: Oxford University Press.

Alchian, A. A. 1950. "Uncertainty, Evolution, and Economic Theory." *Journal of Political Economy* 53(3):211–21.

Argyris, C. 1982. *Reasoning, Learning and Action*. San Francisco: Jossey–Bass.

Argyris, C., R. Putnam, and D. M. Smith. 1985. *Action Science*. San Francisco: Jossey–Bass.

Argyris, C. and D. Schon. 1978. *Organizational Learning: A Theory of Action Perspective*. Reading, Mass.: Addison-Wesley.

Bateson, G. 1972. *Steps to an Ecology of Mind*. New York: Ballantine.

Boland, R. 1982. "The Process of Systems Design: A Phenomenological Approach." *Proceedings of the 3rd International Conference on Information Systems*. Ann Arbor, Michigan (December).

Brown, J. S., A. Collins, and P. Duguid. 1989. "Situated Cognition and the Culture of Learning." *Educational Researcher* 18(1):32-41.

Brown, J. S. and P. Duguid. 1989. Learning and Improvisation—Local Sources of Global Innovation." Xerox PARC Working Paper (September).

Ciborra, C. U. 1990. "X-Efficiency, Transaction Costs and Organizational Change." In P. Weiermair, *On X-Efficiency Theory*. Ann Arbor: University of Michigan Press.

Ciborra, C. U. and G. F. Lanzara. 1990. "Designing Dynamic Artifacts: Computer Systems as Formative Contexts." In P. Gagliardi (ed.). *Symbols and Artifacts: Views of the Corporate Landscape*. Berlin: de Gruyter.

Ciborra, C. U., P. Migliarese, and P. Romano. 1984. A Methodological Inquiry into Organizational Noise in Socio-Technical Systems." *Human Relations* 37(8):565–88.

Cyert, R. M. and J. G. March. 1963. *A Behavioral Theory of the Firm*. Englewood Cliffs, N.J.: Prentice–Hall.

De Geus, A. P. 1988. "Planning as Learning." *Harvard Business Review* (March–April):70–74.

Duncan, R. and A. Weiss. 1979. "Organizational Learning: Implications for Organizational Design." In B. M. Staw (ed.). *Research in Organizational Behavior*, Greenwich, Conn.: J. A. I. Press. pp. 75–123.

Fiol, C. M. and Lyles, M. A. 1985. "Organizational Learning." *Academy of Management Review* 10(4):803–13.

Fusfeld, H. I. and C. S. Hacklish. 1985. "Cooperative R and D for Competitors." *Harvard Business Review* 63(6) November–December:60–67.

Handy, C. 1989. *The Age of Unreason*. London: Business Books, Ltd.

Hannan, M. T. and J. Freeman. 1984. "Structural Inertia and Organizational Change." *American Sociological Review* 29:149–64.

Harvard Business School, 1987, Yamazaki Mazak (A), Case 9-686-083 rev. 3/87, Boston Mass.

Hedberg, B. L. T. 1981. "How Organizations Learn and Unlearn." In P. S. Nystrom and W. H. Starbuck (eds.). *Handbook of Organizational Design* (2nd ed.). New York: Oxford University Press.

Hedberg, B. L. T. and S. Jonsson. 1978. "Designing Semiconfusing Information Systems for Organizations in Changing Environments." *Accounting, Organizations and Society* 3(1):47–64.

Hewitt, C. and P. De Jong. 1984. "Open Systems." In M. L. Brodie et al. (eds.). *On Conceptual Modeling*. New York: Springer Verlag.

Howard, R. A. and L. Schneider. 1989. "Portables in the Field." *Office Technology and People* 5(2) September.

Kling, R. and S. Iacono. 1984. "Computing as an Occasion for Social Control." *Journal of Social Issues* 40(3):77–96.

Kotter, J. 1978. *Organizational Dynamics: Diagnosis and Intervention*. Reading, Mass.: Addison–Wesley.

Leonard-Barton, D. 1987. "Transferring Technology from Developers to Operations: A Conceptual Framework." Harvard Business School, Working Paper #87-049. June.

Levitt, B. and J. G. March. 1988. "Organizational Learning." *Annual Review of Sociology* 14:319–40.

Lindholm, R. and L. Hethy. 1990. *Business Policies and Management Strategies*. Forthcoming. Geneva: I. L. O.

Malone, T. W. 1988. "What is Coordination Theory?" Center for Information Systems Research, MIT, Working Paper #182.

Masuch, M. 1985. "Vicious Circles in Organizations." *Administrative Science Quarterly* 30(March):14–33.

Nelson, R. R. and S. G. Winter. 1982. *An Evolutionary Theory of Economic Change*. Cambridge, Mass.: Harvard University Press.

Nonaka, I. 1988. "Creating Organizational Order out of Chaos: Self-Renewal in Japanese Firms." *California Management Review* 30(3) Spring:57–73.

Nonaka, I. and T. Yamanouchi. 1989. "Managing Innovation as a Self-Renewal Process." *Journal of Business Venturing* 4:299–315.

Ohmae, K. 1990. *The Borderless World*. New York: Harper Collins.

Polanyi, M. 1966. *The Tacit Dimension*. Garden City, NJ: Doubleday.

Porter, M. E. and Fuller, M. B. 1986. "Coalitions and Global Strategy." In M. E. Porter (ed.).*Competition in Global Industries.* Boston: Harvard Business School Press.

Rice, R. E. and E. M. Rogers. 1980. "Reinvention in the Innovation Process." *Knowledge* 1(4) June:488–514.

Rosenberg, N. 1982. *Inside the Black Box: Technology and Economics.* Cambridge: Cambridge University Press.

Schneider, L.S and R. A. Howard. 1985. "Office Automation in a Manufacturing Setting." Office of Technology Assessment, Washington, D.C.

Schon, D. A. 1979. *The Reflective Practitioner.* New York: Basic Books.

Senge, P. M. 1990. *The Fifth Dimension: The Art and Practice of the Learning Organization.* New York: Doubleday.

Simon, H. A. 1976. *Administrative Behavior: A Study of Decision Making Processes in Administrative Organization* (3rd ed.). New York: Free Press.

Starbuck, W. H. 1983. "Organizations as Action Generators." *American Sociological Review* 48:91–102.

Stata, R. 1989. "Organizational Learning: The Key to Management Innovation." *Sloan Management Review* (Spring).

Swidler, A. 1986. "Culture in Action: Symbols and Strategies." *American Sociological Review* 51(April):273–286.

Tversky, A. and D. Kahneman. 1981. "The Framing of Decisions and the Psychology of Choice." *Science* 211(January):453–8.

Unger, R. M. 1987. *False Necessity.* Cambridge: Cambridge University Press.

Walton, R. E. 1989. *Up and Running.* Boston: Harvard Business School Press.

Weick, K. E. 1979. *The Social Psychology of Organizing* (2nd ed.). New York: Random House.

Winograd, T. and F. Flores. 1986. *Understanding Computers and Cognition: A New Foundation for Design.* Norwood, N.J.: Ablex.

Wight, O. 1981. *MRP II: Unlocking America's Productivity Potential.* Williston, Vermont.

Zuboff, S. 1988. *In the Age of the Smart Machine—The Future of Work and Power.* New York: Basic Books.

11

Innovation and Institutions: Notes on the Japanese Paradigm

Thomas B. Lifson

Trends in technology compel us to seek more effective institutional means for producing knowledge in our industrial sectors. In the 1990s, strategists guiding America's major manufacturers through the tangle of issues surrounding technological change and human resources will have to take account of Japan. In many consumer, intermediate, and capital goods industries and segments, Japanese companies either set the competitive pace in product improvement or threaten to do so in the future. In addition, they are continually upgrading their manufacturing technologies, thereby lowering costs, improving quality, shortening cycle times, and otherwise enhancing competitiveness. This pattern is based on a complex organizational system able to sustain near-continuous improvement in both product and manufacturing technologies.

The capability to upgrade products and processes continually is not universal in Japan or wholly absent in the United States. Industries such as aerospace, supercomputers, and pharmaceuticals, where innovation is a basic competitive strategy, are among America's best performers relative to Japanese competitors. But many other sectors, previously considered to be mature according to the product life-cycle theory (Wells, 1972), are "de-maturing" (Abernathy et al., 1983). Analysts have found that developments (many of them by Japanese companies) in the techniques of flexible manufacturing and new combinations of product technologies such as mechatronics and optoelectronics are accelerating the rate of change and creating uncertainty in basic product and process parameters.

As technology becomes more specialized, requiring greater depth of focus, opportunities to profit from innovation increasingly arise out of the intersection of different fields. At the same time that the need for specialization becomes greater, the ability to link specialized knowledge becomes more valuable. Successful innovation thus requires both a higher degree of differentiation and a greater capacity for integration (Lawrence and Lorsch, 1967). While U.S. industry has finely tuned mechanisms for promoting new specializations, Japanese industry has important strengths in their integration.

The increasing importance of automation and technological innovation demands that American firms develop more effective integrative mechanisms—mechanisms capable of assuring the requisite inter- and intrafirm cooperation. Members of different firms and subunits—such as production engineers, product designers, and factory personnel, including operators—must share information, accumulate knowledge out of its application, quickly incorporate improvements into their work, and evaluate and adjust to one another's suggestions. Traditional bureaucracy, even assisted by new data collection and distribution technologies, is often too cumbersome to compete with the pace of innovation set by Japanese competitors. Can we expand our understanding of the range of institutional tools available?

The differing cultural and institutional foundations of Japan's business system have led to organizational forms and social forces comparatively undeveloped in Western organizational thought and practice. These forms and forces present a new paradigm to Western business strategists. Johnson (1987) puts it well when he states, "We are only beginning to recognize that Japan has invented and put together the institutions of capitalism in new ways, ways that neither Adam Smith nor Karl Marx would recognize or understand."

If imitation is indeed the sincerest form of flattery, it is time to repay the compliment. There will be many complications along the way. Cole (1989) explores the complexity of the borrowing process in some detail. His concise words of caution are worth quoting: "Borrowing is not simply a matter of copying as commonly portrayed in popular discussions, but rather a complex process involving adaptation and *invention of new social practices*." (Cole, forthcoming, emphasis added).

There are many lessons to be learned from Japan. For example, techniques such as small-group-based learning (Cole, 1989) and lean inventory systems can be studied and adapted to great advantage. But the Western business strategist who hopes to adapt to the Japanese paradigm of business organization needs a way of sorting out the basic insights from the specific form they take in Japanese culture. An institution can be considered an enduring social construct that sustains a pattern of human behavior over time. In a specific time and place, an institution is always built on the artifacts of a specific culture or set of cultures. To transfer a new institution into U.S. industry, the basic forms and forces that shape the behavior of potentially all human cultures must be uncovered. The shock of the unfamiliar can be minimized by clothing the new institutional practices in the garb of American cultural artifacts.

Bluntly stated, the thesis of this chapter is that the Japanese paradigm taps into a richer mix of basic social forces and forms than the dominant paradigm of the United States. It is able to tap a spectrum of institutions that are very effective at synthesizing knowledge. The modern business institutions that have developed in Japan's premier industries are robust. They are capable of adjusting to some kinds of change with remarkable agility. But there is nothing inherently Japanese about the institutional territory they occupy. Americans can use indigenous symbols, traditions, concepts, and other social constructs to build functionally equivalent systems based on the same underlying mix of basic forms and forces.

This chapter proposes a theoretical framework for understanding the spectrum of institutions and the culturally nonspecific basic social forms and forces that have been employed more extensively in Japan than in the United States. The evolution of organizational forms in Japan will then be traced. The process of innovation in Japan, both within firms and among groups of firms will be examined. The final section will consider the process of adapting American organizations to the lessons of the Japanese approach.

FORMS, FORCES, AND INSTITUTIONS

The characteristics of Japanese institutions can be viewed within a framework adapted from that proposed by Oliver Williamson (1977). Williamson posited that markets and hierarchies are alternative basic forms for integrating the efforts of actors. Of course, as forms, markets and hierarchies are abstractions. As soon as they are manifest in the social realm, imperfections or mixed forms appear. The contrast is nevertheless instructive. According to Williamson, firms can gain efficiency by breaking down hierarchies and replacing them with the multidivisional M form based on market-like relations between profit centers. The extensive information that an efficient market requires must be produced by human interactions. As a result, when the market and its informational requirements are complex, hierarchy may be an essential supporting element.

The image of a continuum linking pure markets at one extreme with pure hierarchies at the other has served as a powerful heuristic device for exploring a variety of institutional arrangements (Imai and Itami, 1984; Eccles, 1983). I submit, however, that to the two basic forms of market and hierarchy must be added a third, the network. Figure 11.1 and Table 11.1 portray the resulting range of institutional possibilities, which I propose to call the *institutional triangle*. The area comparatively well developed in Japan and underdeveloped in the American tradition is indicated by the shaded area.

All complex human institutions draw on some mix of the three forms and on the basic social forces corresponding to them. Exchange corresponds to the market form, and dominance, the setting of one actor apart from the others to issue orders and rules, corresponds to the hierarchy form. Networks of spontaneous sharing of information with those socially available, that is to say those with whom an identity

Figure 11.1. The Institutional Triangle
Territory of Japanese Institutional Development

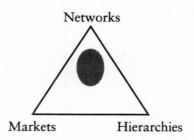

is possible, is just as basic and ancient a social form as exchange and dominance. All are fundamental approaches to organizing socially to cope with uncertainty, change, and risk.

A pure network is as much an abstraction as a pure market or a pure hierarchy. At its most general level, a network can be defined as the "totality of all the units connected by a certain type of relationship" (Jay, 1964). But for purposes of comparison with markets

Table 11.1. Three Basic Organizational Forms

	Market	Heirarchy	Network
Example	Spot oil	Corporation	Scientific community
Behavior orientation	Buy/sell	Earn	Give
Cohesive force	Self-interest	Dominance	Identity
Legitimating concept	Invisible hand	Authority	Purpose
Nexus	Exchange	Action	Spontaneous sharing
Energizer	Currency	Rank	Information
Reward	Money	Promotion	Priority (wisdom)
Information	Atomistic	Centralized	Self-generating
Goal	Wealth	Power	Knowledge
Signals	Price	Commands	Introductions

and hierarchies, a network can be considered to be a self-organizing collectivity of actors spontaneously sharing information.

Just as self-interest is the force powering markets, and dominance the force animating hierarchies, identity gives life to networks. Identity is a powerful motivating force in institutional life. Some of the most extreme and heroic acts, such as the voluntary sacrifice of life in wartime, are motivated by the form of identity called *patriotism*.

Sharing Knowledge

For the production of knowledge, spontaneous sharing is critically important. Knowledge is useful information; it is tied to use. When an actor using information spots an anomaly and spontaneously communicates with other actors in the hope that they might also use the information, the process of refining and extending knowledge begins. The other actors can bring more data. The scientific community is a modern example of this principle at work.

Adler (1989) shows how the increasingly important role of technology and other forms of knowledge in competition creates a shift toward the network form. Knowledge is not only what economists call a public good—it is not diminished by consumption—but is what Adler calls a *super-public good*—the more it is used, the more it expands. Neither markets nor hierarchies nor any mix of the two can optimize the production of public goods. Market forms that lock up property rights to knowledge create incentives to make the risky investments needed to create new knowledge, but then society loses by the lack of general availability of the resulting knowledge. Hierarchies such as centrally planned economies can command broad dissemination of existing knowledge, but cannot create incentives to create new knowledge. The spontaneous sharing and commitment to a higher purpose characteristic of the network form is far better adapted to knowledge growth than either the exchange characteristic of markets or the authority characteristic of hierarchy. Not surprisingly, the professions are the sector of our institutional structure most dependent on the network form since they have historically been more concerned with information and knowledge than the sectors of our economy dominated by market and hierarchical forms.

In each of the three forms, there is a characteristic type of signal that influences the behavior of the actors. While commands and price are the signals in hierarchies and markets, introductions, the intermediation linking an actor with a new source of information, are the signals characteristic of networks. This intermediation can connect an actor with another actor, or with a nonactor source of information such as a book, blueprint, or digital code. Note that in the purest sense of a network, such intermediation does not constitute part of an exchange. It is rather an act of sharing, undertaken to advance the shared goal. Kumon's (forthcoming) distinction between pure networks and reciprocity systems is important.

Reciprocation, a particularly robust process, comes into play when a network is being used for economic purposes and its form shifts toward the market pole. The mutual understanding that develops out of sharing information and adherence to a common goal provide assurance that, eventually, there will be a satisfactory balance of contribution and return. Reciprocation consists of nonspot exchanges, in which something of value (such as information, assistance, or any other resource) is given for an unspecified return to be received at an indefinite time in the future. Meanwhile, the actor that made the contribution holds an obligation from the actor that received the contribution. Earlier we called this mixed form *obligated reciprocity*.

The actors that are members of networks may be individuals, or they may be collectivities themselves, such as companies, departments, or divisions. Thus, networks exist at different levels of aggregation. Real-world networks of managers within a single corporation, used for achieving the economic goals of the firm and individual, may be called *administrative networks* (Yoshino and Lifson, 1986). Imai (forthcoming) discusses *corporate networks*, networks among firms used to advance the information stock of member actors.

Interfirm Systems

Corporate networks are one form of a broader category of complex organization—the interfirm system. In Japan, they produce much of the continuous innovation and are thus an important feature of the Japanese economy. Nevertheless, they are only beginning to be understood and systematically examined by scholars. Interfirm systems may be self-organizing networks, but most often they also have some degree of formal structure and are influenced by historic forms of organization. They take the form of groups of companies interacting in a regular pattern, which jointly contribute resources to and share resources generated by a collective endeavor to produce and deliver complex goods and services. Imai (forthcoming) argues that, "The long history of coordination between firms may be a crucial factor in explaining the special adaptability of the Japanese economy."

The language of organizational analysis is still ill equipped to describe interfirm systems. Although the reasons behind this are complex, fundamentally, interfirm systems have played a much smaller role in the development of the economies (Scotland, England, Europe, and the United States) that gave birth to most economic and organizational theories.

Today, with the rise of Japanese commercial and industrial institutions self-evident, theorists in Japan and overseas are beginning to devise new concepts and explanations of the economic successes of Japan. Features of the Japanese economy previously regarded as particular to Japanese culture or remnants of a "premodern" recent past are being proposed as models of institutions with considerable logic and efficiency in this high-technology age. In the universal aspects of these models, we can begin to discern elements that might be adapted to American circumstances. First, however, it is useful to review briefly some of the important features of the institutional history of Japan.

THE EVOLUTION OF ORGANIZATIONAL FORMS IN JAPAN

Japan began building its modern industrial infrastructure about 1870, in response to grave external threat. After more than two centuries of isolation, overwhelming military force compelled it to open its borders to trade and diplomacy. The old order toppled, pushed by those convinced that there was no choice but to learn to play the game of survival the Western way. These people thought that, unless Japan were able to amass quickly the technological and economic resources necessary to build and maintain a modern army and navy, the nation would fall prey to the West. China provided stark evidence of what lay ahead should Japan fail to marshall the resources necessary to fight a modern industrialized war: military defeat, followed by loss of sovereignty, mass opium addiction, and cultural decay.

Japan had no grand strategic plan. Knowledge about the outside world, its business, technology, and institutions, was virtually nonexistent. In addition, exportable resources were scarce. Japan could not purchase the needed facilities and supplies in larger than sample quantities. In the subsequent process of industrial and commercial development, there was plenty of muddling, and many mistakes. Few if any observers could have predicted that, in 35 years, Japan would have built the military might to defeat Imperial Russia, much less recover from its twentieth-century defeat to be reborn as a world industrial, financial, and technological power.

The Context for Industrialization

One of Japan's secret weapons, invisible to all but the Japanese themselves, was the high level of organizational sophistication Japan had achieved in a pre–Industrial Revolution technological context. Early eighteenth-century Japan supported three cities as big or bigger than the capitals of preindustrial Europe; they dwarfed the settlements of prerevolutionary America. By 1720, Edo, the capital, had a population of at least a million (Rozman, 1974). Osaka, the mercantile center, had a population of about 400,000 (Hirschmeir and Yui, 1981), as did Kyoto, home of the Imperial Court and many craft producers (Sansom, 1963). London is thought to have had 500,000 inhabitants in 1700 (Braudel, 1982), while at the same time Boston in 1700 had 7000 and Philadelphia 4000 (Braudel, 1981).

Japan had a national financial market, the Osaka Rice Exchange, where investors dealt in puts and calls. Artisans in various locales, under the auspices of local feudal authorities, organized into guilds that standardized and improved production techniques and the quality of goods. Goods themselves were wrapped in standardized packages (woodblock-printed wrappers) and distributed nationally. Retail outlets included large multistore enterprises using a low-price, cash-and-carry format.

In the West, institutional development of a comparable order in the commercial infrastructure took longer and was intimately involved with, if not driven by, the development of industrial means of production. It is only a partial exaggeration to say that Japan developed some of the commercial institutional software of a modern economy prior to the arrival of the hardware of the Industrial Revolution. When industrialism arrived, it did so as an import, and was perceived as an essential key to national survival in the face of an overwhelming military threat.

Feudal Roots of an Organization Form: the *Ie*

Japan went rapidly from feudalism to industrialization without the centuries of transition experienced by European countries. Under feudalism, Japan was a decentralized political economy, whose foundation was the domain (*han*). There were approximately 260 *han* in Japan toward the end of the feudal period. Each of these was ruled by a lord (*daimyo*). An overlord (*shogun*) ruled the federation (*bakufu*) to which the lords and their domains pledged fealty. It was the *bakufu* that kept peace among the lords. When a *bakufu* collapsed, there was an extended period of war among the *daimyo* as they vied to enlarge their domains and dominate smaller lords. The final *bakufu*, ruled by the Tokugawa clan, lasted from 1603 to 1868.

Driven by a need for revenue, the *han* administration was commercially active despite a Confucian bias against merchants. Each lord's bureaucracy, staffed by noble warriors (*bushi* or *samurai*), collected taxes from the peasants, and sold part of the rice harvest to Osaka merchants.

A particular organizational form, the *ie* (literally, "house"), evolved from the clan agromilitary groups that vied with the Imperial court and nobility for power eight and more centuries ago (Murakami et al., 1979; Murakami, 1984; Murakami, forthcoming). The *han* governments were based on the *ie*. Late in the twelfth-century a *bakufu* (literally, "tent government") formed that enabled the agromilitary clans, organized as *ie*, to establish partial political and economic hegemony. But this *bakufu* federation dissolved into an extended period of war among the clans that ended only in the early seventeenth-century. The two and a half centuries of subsequent Tokugawa *bakufu* rule that preceded industrialization saw the power of the *ie* clans challenged by mercantile houses, which themselves mimicked, built upon, and adapted some of the crucial features of the *ie* form. Under the Pax Tokugawa, these *ie*-based mercantile houses flourished.

The *ie* form has several notable characteristics. It was capable of replicative extension; that is, an *ie* could grant one of its components a charter as a subhouse with allegiance to the main house. The subhouse would adopt the same *ie* form for its internal structure. An *ie* could likewise affiliate with a larger house. Thus, like networks, an *ie* could be part of a multilayered structure, with each level sharing similar basic characteristics.

Membership in an *ie* was based on what anthropologist Francis L. K. Hsu (1963) called a *kintract*—a word combining kinship and contract. Through a very loose notion of kinship, extending to relatives of in-laws and especially through the extensive use of adult adoption, it was possible to recruit outsiders into the kinship structure on the basis of ability. Once inside, however, the solidarity of family ties, particularly the high barriers to exit, functioned to ensure continuity of membership. Hsu wrote that these practices "transform the *ie* into a sort of corporation." The ultimate goal of this quasifamily collectivity became "eternal continuance and expansion of the group" (Murakami, 1984). For a large group that lasted many generations, it was necessary to embody the group in a symbol, and for the Japanese this symbol became the head of the house.

Due to the widespread use of adoption, blood line was not the principle upon which succession in the *ie* was based, as was the case for noble houses in Europe, China, and indeed a vast majority of traditional political systems. Instead, the principle of the "stem succession line" (Nakane, 1970) or "stem linearity" (Murakami, 1984) symbolized the continuity of the group over generations. The stem consisted of an unbroken linear chain of succession, recognized as legitimate but not necessarily based on the accident of birth. Hirschmeir and Yui (1981) have translated this into a job description:

> To become head of the House meant taking up the holy responsibility of exerting all efforts towards the prosperity and continuity of the House, following closely the rules handed down, and never defiling the House name.

Within the *ie*, the hierarchy was predominantly a functional one, related to role rather than to status, and there was competition from below. Although the Tokugawa clan attempted to make the class structure of Japan rigid between the seventeenth and nineteenth centuries, its efforts were not fully successful. Samurai competed with one another for bureaucratic posts as well as for distinction in the martial and aesthetic arts. The display of wealth at the Tokugawa court was nearly mandatory for each *daimyo* lord. And the rise of extensive commercial empires, such as the House of Mitsui, was a troubling factor.

The domains themselves were largely autonomous. Within the domains, the village (*mura*) was the basic unit of production. Since wetfield paddy techniques of rice growing demanded tight coordination of planting and harvesting, as well as collective construction and maintenance of a hydraulic system, farming villages in some respects functioned almost as a single economic unit. But each household was also a distinct entity with responsibility for its own survival. Villages were largely autonomous, as long as they paid their taxes and avoided troubling the authorities with disputes or externally visible crimes. Within the village, prosperous farm families themselves took on characteristics of the *ie*.

Thus, Murakami (1984) characterized the *ie* as featuring both decentralization and autonomy. Functional hierarchy, goal congruence, and stem linearity supplied the unifying forces that balanced centrifugal tendencies.

Tokugawa era merchant houses adapted many of the characteristics of the *ie*. Many Osaka merchants practiced adoption for the head of the ie "almost as a matter of principle" (Hirschmeier and Yui, 1981). Many would "spin off" branch establishments run by experienced professional managers. These branches would operate as independent profit centers, but they followed House rules, used the House name, and were obligated to the House. It was possible to establish a national branch system this way, as the Mitsuis most prominently did (Roberts, 1973).

Industrialization and Organization

The forcible opening of Japan to the West under the guns of the "black ships" forced these institutions of the past to change. The Meiji Era (1868–1912) provided an environment of great dynamism and challenge. Adaptability became the key survival skill for the business organizations that were to modernize the Japanese economy. There was an entire world outside to understand. Whole new systems of thinking, organizing, learning, and doing had to be mastered.

Many feudal-era business organizations could not adapt. A handful, including Mitsui, Sumitomo, Hitachi, and Kikkoman (Fruin, 1983), through a process of trial and error, evolved and flourished. Entrepreneurship created many new firms. Some entrepreneurs, such as Iwasaki Yataro, the founder of Mitsubishi, came from the nobility, while many others came from well-to-do families in rice-farming villages (Smith, 1988). All their businesses faced the challenge of grafting elements of the modern corporation onto their own institutional tradition.

Up through World War II, Japan's industrialization and modernization was dominated by *zaibatsu* organizations, which were large-scale, family-owned conglomerates. Industrializing Japan, lacking markets or other institutions for obtaining the necessary scale and type of resources for coping with risk, developed the *zaibatsu* form of enter-prise–group capitalism (Yonekura, 1985). "Doing this required a combination of the capital of rich merchant families, the organizing capabilities of elite warriors, and the professional knowledge of university graduates" (Imai, forthcoming). A number of other developing econo-mies also turned to similar groups as institutions of industrialization (Leff, 1977–78; Leff, 1979).

The *zaibatsu* drew on the *ie* extensively while adopting distinctly Western notions, such as the limited liability corporation. Stem linearity continued as the principle of succession to leadership, although membership became open to all who met functional (mostly educational) criteria. Driven by the lack of a domestic supply of advanced products and by an inability to import them, the *zaibatsu* extended up and down the chain of production. Mitsubishi grew from shipping to shipyards, engines, and metallurgy; Mitsui, from textiles to looms and chemicals; Sumitomo, from copper to wire and electrical machinery. With the advantages of capital, business experience, and access to the human resources being turned out by Japan's new system of public education and universities, the *zaibatsu* became the central institution of private industry in Japan.

In legal form, the *zaibatsu* became holding companies. In spirit, they practiced replicative extension. Departments established to supply a necessary raw material became corporations. A centralized personnel function guided elite university graduates among the operating com-panies, producing a kind of stem linearity and functional hierarchy for the necessary coordination. Trading companies (*sogo shosha*) provided another kind of coordination, managing the commercial and physical flows among operating units. *Zaibatsu* banks and insurance companies provided a degree of centralization of financial flows. Nevertheless, within their own specialties, the operating units had substantial au-tonomy (Allen, 1940).

The combination of centralization and decentralization was well suited to facilitating the absorption and even the enhancement of technologies learned from abroad. For example, in cotton textiles, the first great modern production sector in the historic course of indus-trialization, the *sogo shosha* focused on buying stable and uniform supplies of cotton and marketing large quantities of the mills' output. This left the management of the cotton mills free to devote itself to maximizing production efficiency through long production runs and close moni-toring of technical factors. Chao (1977) found that Japanese cotton mills in Shanghai in the late nineteenth-century were able to pay higher wages and charge lower prices than local entrepreneurs because of the focus and consistency fostered by the division of labor.

Japanese firms trained and developed managers and workers inter-nally, rather than relying on training and credentials from outside bodies (Dore, 1971). Workers' qualifications were thus firm-specific, and not necessarily transferrable to other firms. This reinforced the barriers to exit for trained personnel, who were usually in short supply, and promoted a diffusion of skills and knowledge throughout the firm and into related firms.

The Looser Postwar Structure of Interfirm Systems

World War II and its aftermath decisively changed the organizational geography of Japan. Occupation authorities seized the *zaibatsu*, broke them into the smallest practical units, outlawed holding companies, and sold off the seized assets to the public (Hadley, 1970). But as soon as Japan regained her sovereignty, the old affiliates remerged within industrial sectors and exchanged stock with cousins in other sectors. New companies also opened. Major industrial firms, such as Hitachi and Toyota, developed their so-called *keiretsu* (literally, "line-up in order") structures of upstream suppliers, subcontractors, and subsubcontractors, and downstream distributors, through similar control mechanisms. Product flows led to financial ties, including enormous trade credit (often 180 days), loan guarantees, equipment leases, and exchanges of equity. These interfirm systems fostered coordination through personnel exchanges, open information flow, and risk sharing, and helped Japanese companies to assimilate quickly the many new imported technologies.

Imai (forthcoming) argues that the oil crisis of 1973 provided a far greater shock to Japan than to any other industrial economy because of Japan's heavy dependence on imported oil. The crisis triggered a broad consensus that virtually all Japanese industrial firms would have to pursue efficiencies through energy-saving technologies and through the application of microelectronics. Each company turned inward to examine its own rationalization possibilities, and this focus fostered a higher degree of specialization. At the same time, the specialization forced each company to look outward for other highly specialized resources. The old structural ties became less important. The more loosely structured interfirm systems, which Imai termed "corporate networks," were playing an increasing role in the development of innovative products and processes.

INNOVATION IN INTERFIRM SYSTEMS

There has been a gradual proliferation of forms among collectivities of industrial production units in Japan, and a long-term trend in the direction of looser ties and increased autonomy for operating units. Although interfirm systems manifest a variety of forms, it is worthwhile examining the general process of innovation within them. We shall use a simple hypothetical example.

Company A is a Japanese manufacturer of widgets. Its widget is an assembly of several mechanical, electromechanical, and electronic components, mounted on a frame, and enclosed in a box. The components range in level of sophistication from moderate to high. Many of the components are sourced from outside suppliers, companies B through F. Most of the suppliers have longstanding ties to A, including cross-holding of equity, loan guarantees, equipment leases, and personal ties among staff. The collection of firms may be termed the *product system* for A's widgets. A's widget competes with the products of several other Japanese manufacturers, as well as foreign firms.

Because competition is intense, A and its suppliers are conscious of the need to cut costs, improve quality, design, performance, or otherwise add value. They also see themselves as sharing a common source of prosperity in the sales of their widgets to end users. This sense of a collective fate provides them with a basic goal congruity. They know that if A were to lose market share to more innovative rivals, Japanese or foreign, they would all suffer. The management of A encourages this perspective in many ways, from forming equity and other ties as mentioned, to group meetings and formal organization of its suppliers. As the lead firm, it views itself and is seen by others as most responsible for ensuring collective prosperity.

Each firm knows its specific product and process technology, and is constantly scanning the environment for developments of relevance to it and to other members of the product system. This information is rather freely shared. Instead of hoarding information as proprietary, suppliers seek to enhance their relative bargaining position with A by offering information as a source of potential value to the collectivity. They want to enhance the collectivity's competitiveness with rival product systems.

Firm B manufactures the frame on which components are mounted. It discovers a new molding process that would enable it to cut the cost of producing the frame while also making the component and end product lighter. However, the change would also require some alterations in the way certain components are mounted. To accommodate the changes, A as the assembler would have to expend effort and other resources. The manufacturers of components C and D would also have to expend resources to change their products to accommodate B's proposed change.

Who is to bear the costs of these changes, and how shall they be compensated for these costs? Under a pure market regime, intense bargaining among A, B, C, and D would be required. A and B face an easier problem because each is potentially able to capture some benefit from the cost reduction. But C and D, forced to modify their products, but not necessarily enjoying cost reductions, might resist changes without direct compensation. Since the technologies involved are new and uncertain, it might not be clear until later exactly how great their costs might be.

The returns to the entire product system are also uncertain. If the weight and cost reductions were to cause volume and market share to rise, the payoff might be substantial, particularly for those members of the system whose unit costs decline most steeply with volume. But if rival product systems were quickly to match the improvements, preservation of market share and volume might be the only effects. Thus, the parties must make uncertain expenditures for a return that can only be known sometime in the future.

The agreement the parties would have to construct is an example of what Williamson (1977) would call a *contingent claims contract*, the most time-consuming and costly sort of contract to negotiate. To protect its own bargaining position, each member of the product system would have incentives to withhold information from the others. Under such circumstances, it is easy to see that developing and implementing technological change on a timely basis would be difficult.

But members of most Japanese product systems do not operate under a pure market regime. Instead, their mutual identification with the health of the entire product system directs them to share freely the information they have created or uncovered for the benefit of the entire product system. For example, Firm C may have discovered the frame-molding technology through its contact with other firms and brought it to the attention of B and A, despite the possibility that implementing the change could require costly modifications of its own product.

However, goal congruence is not the only factor at work. For goal congruence to persist as an effective motive, there must also be the assurance that the returns to individual firm will be at least roughly proportional to the resources and effort expended. Instead of using spot market or formal contractual exchange as the mechanism for achieving a division of effort, risks, and returns, the product system uses obligated reciprocity. Each party to the system understands that, when another party's efforts result in benefits to it, an obligation is created. If reciprocation were refused, then the party denying its obligation would be subject to ostracism from the system. The parties therefore freely search for and offer information that might be of value to others in the system with the relative assurance that each will receive a just return. In practice, a kind of rolling credit system has emerged. C and D would accommodate change this time to the benefit of A, B, and the collectivity, while next time, others may accommodate changes that benefit C or D.

This form of coordination has another important benefit: Changes tend to be implemented one at a time in sequence. Holding other variables constant while jointly carrying out one change significantly lowers the levels of risk and uncertainty. By comparison, a marketlike negotiating arrangement would lead to the bundling of several unrelated changes at the same time once the contract was "unfrozen." This result vastly complicates the innovation process, making mistakes more likely and adding to the difficulty of balancing effort, risk, and reward. Without the secure framework of functioning obligated reciprocity, each party is likely to attempt to maximize its own performance, bargaining position, and therefore welfare (in the narrow sense) at each iteration of change.

Japan is not at all unique as a country in which obligation counts in business relations. Williamson (1979) recognizes the practical importance of obligational contracting, and Macaulay (1963) found that personal trust and informal give and take were significant factors governing the conduct of American business managers. The Japanese approach, however, differs from the American in two ways. The Japanese use obligational contracting more extensively, and they experience no institutional or intellectual/emotional conflicts in doing so. In the United States, on the contrary, the law tends to assume a contract either exists or does not, and the legal system is currently hard at work defining employment relationships and authority in hierarchies through extensive litigation in the field of employment law. In a land ruled to such an extent by laws, there is little place for obligated reciprocity in important affairs. The intellectual presumption that allocative efficiency requires short-range profit maximization predisposes many Americans to believe there is something wrong with "log rolling," "back-scratching," or any of the other pejorative expressions Americans have developed to describe acting on the basis of obligations to others.

Dore (1983) takes the position that the Japanese use of obligated reciprocity, or as he calls it, *relational contracting*, is rooted primarily in culture. He cites the long-term orientation of the Japanese, their highly developed sense of duty, and the preference for avoiding open conflict. However, obligational contracting has been a feature of many ethnically and extended-kinship-based business systems throughout the world. These include the Lebanese traders in Africa, Hasidic Jews in the diamond trade, and overseas Chinese in Southeast Asia, not to mention the Mafia and other dealers in covert goods. These systems have two basic features in common. First, it is difficult to make explicit written contracts to cover economic exchanges, either because local officials would tax or otherwise interfere with business deals, or because the costs, risks, and rewards attending a transaction are difficult to know at the time the exchange is consummated. The second common feature is structural. There are strong boundaries for group membership, and expulsion from the group is a serious sanction, virtually precluding the ability to engage in future business in the same field.

The contemporary Japanese business system has developed structures and practices to ensure that ostracism is a potent sanction both within the "society of firms" and the "society of individuals." Business firms are typically members of various forms of groups, ranging from the different types of interfirm systems we have mentioned, to trade and industry associations and locality-based associations, such as chambers of commerce. These groups provide a social context for interfirm transactions. For example, if a firm could not obtain satisfaction from another, the other members of the group would bring pressure to bear on the alleged offender.

The Japanese also have a rather strong presumption that a business relationship once begun should endure. Arbitrarily terminating a promising relationship is often regarded as a failure to behave properly. Thus, once a relationship becomes public knowledge, the reputation of each firm becomes somewhat hostage to the relationship's success. Any termination must be explained. Circumstances beyond the control of a firm (such as a rise in raw material costs that might make it uncompetitive) are not enough. Its partner is expected to help overcome the problem as quickly as possible, for example, by developing substitute raw materials or finding other sources of cost reduction. Only when a firm fails to devote its utmost energies to overcoming the problem (or as the Japanese would say, lacks "sincerity") is the associated firm justified in terminating the relationship. The termination then becomes a black mark on the seller that makes other potential customers somewhat wary of entering into anything more than a marginal purchase arrangement with it. Similarly, the buyer that behaves arbitrarily in terminating a relationship with a seller who is making its best efforts to preserve the relationship would become the subject of disapproval, and other potential vendors would be reluctant to make it a preferred customer.

INNOVATION IN ADMINISTRATIVE NETWORKS

Network-based forms of coordination operate within corporate hierarchies as well. Administrative networks combine spontaneous sharing with obligated reciprocity inside the boundaries of a single firm. The boundary of the firm is kept high, and is sustained by the latent power of the ostracism sanction (Yoshino and Lifson, 1986). For large firms, recruitment to the roster of permanent employees is largely limited to the entry level. Once having joined a prestigious firm, a worker's options for interfirm mobility are limited to lower-status companies and foreign corporations.

Concepts of authority, and the formal structures allocating it, create a large volitional element in the efforts of most Japanese managerial workers. Detailed assignments of exclusive authority to individuals and detailed formal measures of an individual's impact are rare. Rather, interdependence and collective results are assumed. The levels of activity formally required by a particular job posting are only the beginning of the expected level and range of work. Under these circumstances, managers find themselves dependent on the semivoluntary or volitional efforts of others (Lifson, forthcoming). They thus have to depend on their ability to offer eventual reciprocation. Poor track records or prospects in this regard would lead others to hesitate to honor their requests. Unable to leave their firm for an equally attractive alternative post, and unable to mobilize the efforts of others within their own company, such managers are relegated to a kind of purgatory.

Administrative networks exist in many firms, although their comparative degree of development and use differs with circumstances. Administrative networks are most useful in situations with a high degree of change and uncertainty and a high level of complexity and interdependence. These circumstances require innovation, that is to say, the creation of information. Fundamentally, successful innovation requires integrating information derived from a variety of sources, and making decisions based on analyses of the data. As Nonaka (1988) notes, "The systematic incorporation of the opportunity for creating information into daily work at the operator level has been precisely the major characteristic of Japanese organizations." Administrative networks are the primary vehicle by which these opportunities are realized.

I have previously examined the role of administrative networks in studies based on research in several *sogo shosha* trading companies (Lifson, 1978; Yoshino and Lifson, 1986). These firms, professional intermediaries straddling countries, industries, and markets, are perhaps the purest and most extreme cases of administrative networks as a management system. They must combine information originating in different industries in many locations, and make decisions quickly, under the discipline of rapidly changing markets and low margins.

Innovation in manufacturing requires a similar discipline. It rests on the systematic creation of information by the combining of a variety of sources of on-the-spot information, each of which is obtained by an "actor on the spot" doing business in Hayek's sense (Hayek, 1945; Imai, forthcoming). This information must be selectively put to use by the efforts of various individual actors located within different subunits of the firm. The impact of the use of the information on performance, as measured by formal mechanisms of the control system, is often difficult to assess in advance.

Opportunistic Scanning

One type of environmental scanning most useful to the creation of usable information may be called *opportunistic* scanning because it requires the judgment and volition of the actor on the spot, and cannot be formalized or planned in advance. An example will illustrate the idea. A manager, whom we shall call Suzuki, working in one arm of a firm may come across a development that might affect another part of the firm. Since the firm is presumed to be a Japanese industrial producer, we shall use the male personal pronoun. If Suzuki has established a relationship with someone in the other arm of the firm, call him Kato, Suzuki would be more likely to understand some of the potential impact of the development on Kato and be motivated to undertake some effort (over and above anything required of him in his current position) to communicate the issue to Kato.

The performance of such "ad hoc" or "opportunistic" acts as just described, over and above the formal, bureaucratic, mechanistic linkage processes designed into an organization, is very useful to an organization in helping it cope with change. Because infinite possibilities for action face any manager with a generalized commitment to the firm over and above those formally designed into the manager's position, there must be a mechanism for setting priorities and channeling activity. The structure and dynamics of an administrative network system provide such a mechanism. When Suzuki took the trouble to investigate and communicate his finding to Kato, he began to create an obligation for Kato to him. For the Suzuki–Kato relationship to continue into the future, Kato would have to acknowledge the obligation, both would implicitly put a value on it, and eventually Kato would reciprocate. One can thus identify at least four stages in any network transaction, as shown in Figure 11.2.

Reciprocation

Assessing the value of an obligation is often a long-term process, for there are two components of value: the effort that went into the action by Suzuki and the value of the outcome to Kato. In most cases, Suzuki's effort may be readily known, but there may also be complications. For example, Suzuki may have incurred some obligation of his own in obtaining the data, or Suzuki may have had to put aside other work to do it, which could create future problems for him. In most cases, the assessment of value to the receiver, in this case Kato, requires the most time and judgment. Information that enables Kato to suggest actions to the firm that ultimately prove important would powerfully benefit Kato's own career progress. In such a case, one form of reciprocation might involve sharing credit with Suzuki openly. Or, if credit sharing were not feasible or desirable, reciprocation might involve employing Kato's influence to obtain some kind of decision favorable to Suzuki's interests at some point in the future.

Reciprocation therefore is an event that itself requires an outcome and assessment, as shown by a feedback loop in Figure 11.2 from the

Figure 11.2. Stages of a Network Transaction

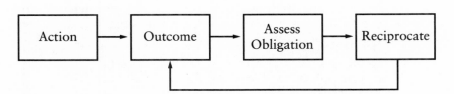

last of the four boxes to the second. In reality, it is impossible to draw an endpoint for the chain of favors and reciprocation that links two individuals who enjoy a solid, continuing, and important network relationship. There is no "zero balancing" within a healthy relationship. Instead, the squaring of accounts (*karikashi nashi*) is really a way of distancing oneself. In a satisfying relationship, each party strives to maintain either an approximate equilibrium of obligation owed between the two, or perhaps a slight positive balance in his own favor. Thus, each party is constantly thinking of ways to add (at minimal personal effort) obligation at the highest ratio of value added to the other's "accounts payable" obligation column.

Although Suzuki and Kato may occasionally keep the depth of their relationship secret, or may sometimes choose to conceal its use in certain instances, their dyadic relationship does not exist in isolation. It must be understood in the context of the other relationships Kato and Suzuki maintain. Context is important in several ways:

1. Kato and Suzuki may need to rely on others, especially mutual associates, to help them measure obligation owed and discharged.

2. Mutual associates are an implicit enforcement mechanism, ensuring that obligations are fully discharged. If Kato were to refuse to satisfy Suzuki, and others were to side with Suzuki, then Kato's reputation, and his ability to call on others for their help, would suffer. In a system where formal sanctions are few, and job responsibilities and authority are kept to a low level of specificity, the result could be a fatal disability. Formal authority of position can become all but meaningless without the support of members of the firm.

3. Third parties can provide a supple currency for balancing obligation:

   a. By making Suzuki's meritorious deeds known to others, Kato can add to Suzuki's prestige and credibility easily. This is more than an abstract consideration, for it improves Suzuki's ability to form new relationships and to call on others' help readily.

   b. Kato may go a step further, and actually introduce and recommend Suzuki to a third party, say, Ikeda, when Suzuki is in need of a resource over which Ikeda has discretionary control. In so doing, Kato stands as a guarantor of Suzuki's ability to use Ikeda's resources well, and of Suzuki's ability to discharge any obligation that might be incurred toward Ikeda.

   c. Alternatively, Kato may have a store of obligation owed to him by Ikeda, and may realize that Suzuki, to whom Kato owes obligations, could use Ikeda's resources. In this case, Kato may act as a "broker" or reticulator, simultaneously collecting obligation from Ikeda and discharging it to Suzuki.

4. Inevitably, rotation policies mean that Kato and Suzuki will transfer to new positions, and the institutional component of their relationship will devolve onto others. When personal or organizational relations are strained, rotation may be a welcome means of avoiding or escaping from obligations, although there may be a reputational price to pay. In most instances of satisfactory relationships, the personal component of the obligation balance between Kato and Suzuki must be correlated with an institutional or positional component.

Personal and Institutional Obligation

Whether a particular action, and the obligation that results from it, is considered personal or institutional is a matter of signaling among the actors involved in a transaction and those around them. For instance, if Suzuki were to have consulted with others, or sought his superior's sanction for devoting time to his information search, the obligation would probably be more in favor of the unit than Suzuki. Kato's actions also help determine who owes the obligation, himself or his unit. If he were to keep himself centrally involved in using and dispersing the information, he would tend to receive more personal credit for the benefits that occur in the future and be owed more personal obligation. If he were to involve others from his unit early on, or if his activities were to receive other resources from his unit early on, then the obligation would accrue to the work unit.

Kumon's (forthcoming) distinction between networks based on the spontaneous offering of information and exchange systems based on reciprocity is helpful here. Pure network interaction is based not on the expectation of receiving something eventually in reciprocation, but on sharing without a direct return. To the extent a particular action is open and public, it tends to have the nature of a network rather than that of an exchange reciprocation. To the extent that an act is seen as benefitting the entire firm rather than certain subunits or individuals, it is network rather than exchange in nature. Network interaction requires no reciprocation.

Administrative networks are not pure networks in Kumon's sense. They are relationships that can be used both for the spontaneous sharing of information and for reciprocal exchange of obligation. In most instances, both modes of action are present, but to differing degrees. One might envision a spectrum between (reputational) markets and (pure) network: At the market end managers privately help each other in a reciprocal way, whereas at the network end, managers interested in advancing the overall company welfare publicly offer each other the most valuable information they possess. In the middle would be situations where managers expect both some degree of reciprocation and some degree of recognition for their access to valuable information. Most real situations probably contain some degree of latent tension between private and public motives.

Selectivity

In forming and maintaining a network, any manager, even a young one, is faced with the necessity of being selective. His time is, after all, finite. By choosing to maintain one relationship, he diminishes the time available for others. Thus, he must draw priorities, even if subconsciously. Over the long term, the most valuable network will consist of managers in important positions throughout the firm whose ability to draw on others, through their own ample store of obligation, is highest. From a coldly calculating point of view, it makes sense to invest one's time in establishing relationships with those young managers who are likely to rise the highest and to perform the most activity of a value-adding nature. If Suzuki were such a manager, and Kato had previously established a relationship with him, then Kato would have the good fortune to have potential access to Suzuki's large and valuable network of resources in the future. As Suzuki progresses, his obligation would take on a higher value to Kato. This might be termed the "catch a rising star" effect.

Suzuki, meanwhile, finds himself at the center of a virtuous circle. As his network expands, so does his ability to call on more diverse resources. This puts him in a position to pay back obligation faster. Moreover, the value that others, such as Kato, place on Suzuki's obligation to them also rises. I call this valence applied to a manager's obligation his *credibility*. As more people are attracted to the reputation of a high-credibility manager, they become interested in bringing information and other resources to him in the hope of establishing or reinforcing a network relationship. The fortunate Suzuki will thus have even more resources at his disposal.

Credibility Markets

Suzuki's credibility in this case is analogous to the price of a commodity in short supply. But it is a market based on reciprocation over time rather than immediate exchange. In fact, the entire reciprocity system of obligation accounting bears close comparison with a market system. I would contend that, over time, through the credibility mechanism, quasimarket prices are established for the obligation of managers, and that these prices closely reflect the real executive worth of individuals. As one rises up the hierarchy of any organization, but especially so in a Japanese firm, one finds executive positions that are more and more concerned with coordination, planning, relationship maintenance, and other skills that tend to draw heavily on a network such as the one described. Of course, the same sorts of market imperfections, especially imperfect information, apply to this system as they do to economic markets.

Efficiencies of Administrative Networks

Administrative networks are important more for the kind of interactions they facilitate than for the volume of interaction that may take place through them. Administrative networks are useful in managing the most difficult kinds of situations—where quick change is necessary and new paths must be explored, when a whole series of "what if?" questions have to be worked out, and where efforts, rewards, costs, and efficiencies must be balanced among different units. In stable and familiar circumstances, decision rules, formal procedures, and other tools that can be written down in the organizational manual can provide the appropriate coordination of behavior. In somewhat more complex situations, marketlike mechanisms such as profit centers and transfer pricing provide flexibility and decentralization. But innovation and coping with change require the ability to rise above ordinary procedures, to take account of information not routinely reportable and perhaps not quantifiable, and to mobilize resources in portions of the organization over which a manager may have less than full authority.

The efficiencies offered by administrative networks are thus threefold:

1. Speed, because no adjustments to or constraints arising from the formal procedures are involved.

2. Lower costs, because no new procedures have to be established formally, and the people involved already communicate efficiently. The establishment and maintenance of an administrative network is by no means a costless endeavor. Lower incremental costs are offset by high fixed costs. But once the infrastructure is present, the incremental cost of a transaction is low, encouraging more thorough communication and weighing of various factors.

3. Quality, because the surveillance is thorough and constant, and the incentives are not perverse. Not only the two parties to the transaction, but others around them, monitor outcomes.

How then can American organizations begin to realize some of the innovation efficiencies of administrative networks, interfirm systems, and self-organizing networks, as practiced in Japan? The following section proposes some initial answers.

ADAPTING THE JAPANESE PARADIGM TO THE AMERICAN CONTEXT

Given the great differences between Japanese and American culture and history, invention will have to be a significant component of any American attempt at adapting the Japanese experience. We humans tend to be so deeply attached to social institutions, processes, and intellectual or emotional orientations, that a powerful motive is necessary to convince us to change. The kind of open discussion and evaluation needed for an iterative, long-term change process does not come naturally when the process questions the foundations of one's behavior. It is perhaps salutary that the competitive threat of Japanese innovation is so severe. To paraphrase Dr. Johnson, powerful competition concentrates the mind wonderfully.

Cultural Hostility

Any strategy for more fully developing networks as an integrative form in American institutions must squarely face our strong cultural and institutional bias against them. Americans are very uncomfortable with the idea that networks can be powerful. In our cultural and institutional history, networks are predominantly identified with conspiracies, racism, elitism, and market-rigging.

Ethics therefore has to be the cornerstone of any strategy involving the institutional use of networks in America. Due to the peculiarities of our history, we are vitally concerned with the issue of access for diverse groups of people. Most of the other advanced economies attach a lesser degree of importance to this consideration. Networks thrive on a common identity. We insist on diversity among the members of our institutions, and we leave it to lawyers and judges to lay down guidelines to achieve this. The legal issues in the formation of American networks will be formidable. We have yet to evolve equal-access measures that most of the populace would seriously describe as fair.

The core issue of the network form in America is openness. What information has to be made public, at what time, and in what way? What information is properly left to the discretion of actors to distribute selectively through opportunistic scanning? Privacy is a particularly resonant dimension of American culture. Private people, it comes as no surprise, view networks with suspicion. But if we could build special-purpose networks, with strong norms guiding equitable and efficient information sharing, there would be a possibility of overcoming the bias.

A strong identity of purpose or collective goal can be very helpful in soothing cultural discomfort with the network form. A perception among members that they are serving a transcendent purpose through their work together would unleash immense energies. Also, a network with a purpose that transcends its own boundaries and private needs, to identify with the interests of society, has a better chance at institutional legitimacy. In sum, American institutions with a strong network character must identify themselves with a public purpose to achieve and maintain legitimacy.

The Management of Identity

American management has shown much interest in using participative methods, corporate culture, and small-group-learning techniques to develop and deploy a sense of identity as a social force in producing desired behavior. Nevertheless, identity management has yet to gain widespread acceptance as a principal focus for management efforts. Early efforts to introduce identity as a more potent tool of management in American corporations will likely center on formal and emergent information systems. Familiar information tools such as performance measurement and evaluations, publications, electronic mail, memoranda, satellite teleconferences, management education sessions, retreats, and, most of all, daily interactions will probably be used to help members build accurate and fair public identities.

In managing identity, the contemporary American business institution must also meet the demands of its members for outside identities. A number of U.S. institutions demand and get close to complete acceptance of the institutional component of identity. Investment bankers, high-priced lawyers, the top managers of big corporations, White House staff, and other select groups are expected to live and breathe their jobs in return for marketplace rewards and prestige. But not everyone wants to or should identify with work so strongly. While they may choose to reward those who do make such a total commitment, most organizations must provide satisfactory membership options for those who see outside roles, such as parent and citizen, as at least equally important.

Symbols play a major role in the construction, maintenance, and modification of identity in institutions. Management needs to cast a wide net to identity and invent a lexicon of useful symbols in the management of identity. The Japanese have an important lesson to teach us on the value of archaic symbols in the process of paradigm adaptation. In the Meiji Restoration, the Japanese reached into their history to use the Emperor as a symbol of identity while fundamentally altering their government, economy, society, and culture.

We can find in our collective past many similarly useful symbols. The Middle Ages were a time in which network organizations flourished as important, legitimate institutions. Freemasonry and various guilds had a strong element of network to them, as they were the custodians of expert knowledge. Identity within these relatively stable communities may have flourished more so than in our current dynamic times. We may be able to adapt work imagery from medieval guilds and many other historical contexts to the identities of modern technology networks within and among our manufacturing firms. Pondering symbols and images to embody their individual and collective identities can be a creative and enjoyable exercise for various members of an organization. It is true that in the Anglo-American variant of economic evolution, guilds and unions have tended to be associated with self-protective resistance to change, but the Japanese have shown that network organizations can be instruments of dynamic innovation.

Fostering Networks

In addition to identity management, American firms can develop human resources policies that systematically create opportunities for networks to develop. Actors in different organizations can be given the opportunity and incentive to form key, public relationships. Evaluation systems can be adapted to measure effectiveness along the network dimension under an appropriate time horizon for measurement and reward. Firms might have to supplement their fundamental concept of work as the job slot, which presumes that work is divisible into discrete temporal segments that can be appropriately measured and rewarded.

Moreover, satisfactory credibility markets will have to evolve. Managers must be able individually and collectively to evaluate one another when they share information and begin to build up obligations. It might be necessary to design forums for peer evaluation. These can serve to mark steps upward on a functional hierarchy. Depending on the circumstances, organizations may choose to conduct reviews through a wide variety of processes. Rituals and competitions, both very effective means of addressing issues of identity, can be employed on certain occasions.

Internal credentialing may come to be more important. Every person in a firm should have access to learning or other means to earn internal credentials and rewards. White- and blue-collar groups both need to be involved. With greater learning possibilities must come increased emphasis on retaining valued employees. In firms where administrative networks are seen as real assets, the loss of a contributing member is considered to affect many others adversely. The costs of such losses must be weighed against the costs of incentives to reduce turnover. Methods to ensure a continuity of relationships would be most effective if they were keyed to the future value of the firm.

Vast opportunities exist to draw on the richness of cultural artifacts that constitute our collective American heritage. To sustain and build on a collective identity as Americans, we must exploit, not ignore, the variety of our institutional raw materials.

Managing Interfirm Systems

To adapt the Japanese paradigm, American companies and managers must also become more adept at managing interfirm systems. A trend in this direction is already well established, with many major manufacturers cutting the number of their suppliers and working more intensively with the remaining core. It will be necessary to invent the means of establishing and reinforcing a greater sense of collective identity and destiny, or goal congruence, among members of the entire chain of value-adding activity.

In a way, the rugged individualism that characterizes American culture extends to the firm level and stands in the way. In the past, we have rarely acknowledged how deeply the fate of a company depends on those firms with which it regularly interacts. The standard Japanese corporate reference book, the *Kaisha Shiki Ho* (*Quarterly Directory of Companies*), published by the *Nihon Keizai Shimbun,* Japan's largest business daily newspaper, lists as a matter of course the five largest suppliers and five largest customers of companies, along with total sales and assets. Neither the "*Fortune 500*" nor the "*Forbes 500*," nor any of the listings in *Business Week,* contain this type of data.

To the extent that antitrust doctrines permit, it may be helpful to exchange symbolic amounts of equity, or use loan guarantees or other financial ties to reinforce the notion of collective fate among members of a product system. It will also be necessary to reinforce a sense of the "society of firms" through periodic gatherings for seminars, reviews, and similar functions of various personnel from all the companies in the value chain. Exchanges of staff members for varying periods of time is another possibility.

The focus of the lead assembly firm must change from managing a series of bilateral relationships to managing multilateral relationships involving a heterogeneous community of associated companies. As discussed, not only do companies that deal with the same major supplier or customer have a common interest, but they also act to reinforce codes of conduct. The management of one relationship inevitably has repercussions for other relationships in the same interfirm system.

Top management has the responsibility for developing clear protocols of collaboration within the firm and within the interfirm system. Employees must understand the boundaries of confidentiality as well as those of the community of interest. It will not be simple to develop such protocols. Role modeling by leaders at all levels will be the most effective tool for disseminating these standards. The opportunity to consider openly the effectiveness of previous collaborations and to devise clearer guidelines for the future must be given to people at all levels of the firm.

Learning from Japanese Partners

The very best way to assimilate the lessons of the Japanese experience with innovation is to foster close relationships with Japanese companies. Most major American industrial companies are already engaged in a variety of relationships with Japanese firms that are sometimes also their rivals. Learning from those firms while competing with them requires a delicate balance.

Although the balance of trade in information within collaborations between American and Japanese firms has usually favored the Japanese, it can change in the future. All too often, American companies have ill-defined learning objectives. In addition, time and effort are required to get knowledge out of a Japanese organization since there tends to be much less formalized documentation and codification in Japan. Instead of expecting a Japanese partner to lay out all the relevant facts and concepts, detailed and repeated questioning is necessary.

Above all, the creation of strong and trusting personal relationships between members of one's own organization and members of the partner's organization is the key to learning. Unfortunately, the rotation and reward practices of many American companies work against this. Just when an engineer or manager has established one or more such close relationships, he or she is shifted to another slot. Since there is no incentive for the person in question to maintain the relationship in the new capacity, the relationship lapses. The person coming into the slot as the replacement must start from the beginning. Both sides are then frustrated.

Measuring and rewarding an employee's ability to construct and maintain a network of relationships in a Japanese partner would help alleviate this problem. Travel budgets can be seen as part of a research and development effort instead of an additional overhead expense. Recognizing that interfirm networks are a productive asset is essential for the balance of trade in information to be righted.

Americans who take the time to establish solid interpersonal relationships are often surprised at the degree to which their Japanese colleagues share information, even proprietary data, with them. Japanese people and companies respond extremely well to those who adopt the posture of interested student. The arrogant assumption that one's own firm knows everything is most counterproductive.

There is still a window of opportunity for Americans to learn from Japan. A reservoir of goodwill still exists. But it is being drained all too rapidly by the aggressive posturing of "Japan bashers," who find the source of all our troubles in Japan. The company that can create a community of interest with its Japanese suppliers, strategic allies, and customers that emphasizes the "win–win" aspects of their competitive game will be able to tap a rich source of experience in managing a complex commercial and industrial system.

We should be grateful for the legacy of our own mix of civilizations, but all legacies can be dissipated by heirs who are not sufficiently attentive to changing circumstances. The rise of Japan, based on a distinctive hybridization of Eastern and Western civilizations, is too important to ignore any further. We owe it to ourselves and our children not to waste the chance to make our ways of working and living more reflective of the best the world has to offer, no matter where ideas, institutions, and customs originate.

REFERENCES

Abernathy, W. J., K. B. Clark, and A. M. Kantrow. 1983. *Industrial Renaissance*. New York: Basic Books.

Adler, ..P. S. 1989. "When Knowledge is the Critical Resource, Knowledge Management is the Critical Task." *IEEE Transactions on Engineering Management*. 36, 2 (May):87-94.

Allen, G. C. 1940. "Japanese Industry: Its Organization and Development to 1937." In E. B. Schumpeter (ed.).*The Industrialization of Japan and Manchukuo, 1930–1940: Population, Raw Materials, and Industry*. New York: Macmillan.

Braudel, F. 1981. *The Structures of Everyday Life*. New York: Harper and Row.

Braudel, F. 1982. *The Wheels of Commerce*. New York: Harper & Row.

Chao, K. 1977. *The Development of the Cotton Textile Production in China*. Cambridge, Mass.: Harvard East Asian Monographs.

Clark, R. 1979. *The Japanese Company*. New Haven, CT.: Yale University Press.

Cole, R.E. 1989. *Strategies for Learning: Small Group Activities in American, Japanese, and Swedish Industry*. Berkeley, Calif.: University of California Press.

Cole, R.E. Forthcoming. "Some Cultural and Social Bases of Japanese Innovation: Small Group Activities in Comparative Perspective." In H. Rosovsky and S. Kumon (eds.). *The Political Economy of Japan, Vol. III: Cultural and Social Dynamics*. Stanford, Calif.: Stanford University Press.

Dore, R. 1971. *British Factory–Japanese Factory: The Origins of National Diversity in Industrial Relations*. Berkeley, Calif.: University of California Press.

Dore, R. 1983. "Goodwill and the Spirit of Market Capitalism." *British Journal of Sociology* 34 (4):459-82.

Eccles, R. 1983. "Control with Fairness in Transfer Pricing." *Harvard Business Review*. 61 (6):149-61.

Fruin, M. 1983. Kikkoman: *Company, Clan, and Community*. Cambridge, Mass.: Harvard University Press.

Gerlach, M. Forthcoming. *Alliance Capitalism: The Strategic Organization of Japanese Business*. Berkeley, Calif.: University of California Press.

Hadley, Eleanor. 1970. *Antitrust in Japan* Princeton, N.J.: Princeton University Press.

Hamel, G., Y. L. Doz, and C. K. Prahalad. 1989. "Collaborate with your Competitors–and Win." *Harvard Business Review* 67 (1):133-39.

Hayek, F.A. 1945. "The Use of Knowledge in Society." *The American Economic Review* 35 (2):519-30.

Hirschmeir, J., and T. Yui. 1981. *The Development of Japanese Business* (2nd ed.). London: George Allen and Unwin.

Hsu, F. L. K. 1963. *Clan, Caste, and Club*. New York: Van Nostrand.

Imai, K. 1985. "Network Organization and Incremental Innovation in Japan." Institute of Business Research, Hitotsubashi University, Discussion Paper No. 122.

Imai, K. Forthcoming. "Japan's Corporate Networks." In H. Rosovsky and S. Kumon (eds.). *The Political Economy of Japan, Vol. III: Cultural and Social Dynamics*. Stanford, Calif.: Stanford University Press.

Imai, K. and H. Itami. 1984. "Interpenetration of Organization and Market: Japan's Firm and Market in Comparison with the U.S." *International Journal of Industrial Organization* 2 (4):285-310.

Jay, E.J. 1964. "The Concepts of 'Field' and 'Network' in Anthropological Research." *Man* 177.

Johnson, C. 1982. *MITI and the Japanese Miracle*. Stanford, Calif.: Stanford University Press.

Johnson, C. 1987. "How to Think about Economic Competition from Japan." *Journal of Japanese Studies* 13 (2):415-28.

Kumon, S. Forthcoming. "Japan as a Network Society." In H. Rosovsky and S. Kumon (eds.). *The Political Economy of Japan, Vol. III: Cultural and Social Dynamics*. Stanford, Calif.: Stanford University Press.

Lawrence, P. and J. Lorsch. 1067. *Organization and Environment*. Homewood, IL.: Irwin.

Leff, N. 1977–78. "Industrial organization and Entrepreneurship in the Developing Countries: The Economic Groups." *Economic Development and Cultural Change* **26** (4):661-75.

Leff, N. 1979. "Entrepreneurship and Economic Development: The Problem Revisited." *Journal of Economic Literature* **17** (1):46-64.

Lifson, T. 1978. *The Sogo Shosha: Strategy, Structure, and Culture*. Ph.D. thesis, Harvard University.

Lifson, T. Forthcoming. "The Managerial Integration of Japanese Business in America." In H. Rosovsky and S. Kumon, (eds.). *The Political Economy of Japan, Vol. III: Cultural and Social Dynamics*. Stanford, Calif.: Stanford University Press.

Lincoln, J. 1989. "Employee Work Attitudes and Management Practice in the U.S. and Japan." *California Management Review* **32** (1):84-106.

Macaulay, S. 1963. "Non-Contractual Relations in Business: A Preliminary Study." *American Sociological Review* **28** (1):55-67.

Mitchell, J. C. 1974. "Social Networks." *Annual Review of Anthropology* 3:279-300.

Murakami, Y. 1984. "Ie Society as a Pattern of Civilization." *Journal of Japanese Studies* **10** (2):279-363.

Murakami, Y. Forthcoming. "Ambiguity of Ie culture: Culture and Civilization." In H. Rosovsky and S. Kumon (eds.). *The Political Economy of Japan, Vol. III: Cultural and Social Dynamics*. Stanford, Calif.: Stanford University Press.

Murakami, Y., S. Kumon, S. Sato. 1979. *Bunmei To Shite No Ie Shakai (Ie Society as Civilization)*. Tokyo: Chuo Koron Sha.

Nakane, C. 1970. *Kazoku No Kozo (Family Structure)*. Tokyo: University of Tokyo Press.

Nonaka, I. 1988. "Creating Order Out of Chaos." *California Management Review*. **30** (3):57-73.

Okimoto, D. 1982. *Between MITI and Market*. Stanford, Calif.: Stanford University Press.

Piore, M. J. and C. F. Sabel. 1986. *The Second Industrial Divide: Possibilities for Prosperity*. New York: Basic Books.

Roberts, J. 1973. *Mitsui: Three Centuries of Japanese Business*. New York: Weatherhill.

Rozman, G. 1974. "Edo's Importance in Changing Tokugawa Society." *Journal of Japanese Studies* **1** (1):91-112.

Sansom, G. 1963. *A History of Japan: 1615–1867*. Stanford, Calif.: Stanford University Press.

Smith, T. 1988. *Native Sources of Japanese Industrialization, 1750–1920*. Berkeley, Calif.: University of California Press. .

Wells, L.T. 1972. "International Trade: The Product Life Cycle Approach." In L.T. Wells, (ed.). *The Product Life Cycle and International Trade*. Boston, Mass.: Harvard Business School Division of Research.

Westney, D. E. 1987. *Imitation and Innovation: The Transfer of Western Organizational Patterns to Meiji Japan*. Cambridge, Mass.: Harvard University Press.

Wheelwright, S.C. and R.H. Hayes. 1985. "Competing Through Manufacturing." *Harvard Business Review* **63** (1):99-109.

Williamson, O. E. 1977. *Markets and Hierarchies*. New York: The Free Press.

Williamson, O. E. 1979. "Transaction-Cost Economics: The Governance of Contractual Relations." *Journal of Law and Economics* **22** (2):233-62.

Yonekura, S. 1985. "The Emergence of the Prototype of Enterprise Group Capitalism: The Case of Mitsui." Hitotsubashi University Institute of Business Research, discussion paper No. 125.

Yoshino, M.Y. and T. Lifson. 1986. *The Invisible Link: Japan's Sogo Shosha and the Organization of Trade*. Cambridge, Mass.: MIT Press.

Name Index

Abernathy, W. J., 292
Abramowitz, S., 157
Adler, Paul, 3, 56, 66, 69, 76, 90,
  105, 226, 274, 296
Alchian, A. A., 272
Allen, G. C., 302
Aoki, Masahiko, 149, 193
Appleby, Arthur, 82
Argyris, C., 269, 270, 271, 272, 273,
  288
Arnold, E., 100, 103
Aron, L. Y., 164
Arrow, K. J., 156
Attewell, Paul, 10, 46, 54, 56, 59, 72,
  74, 78, 150
Ayres, R., 67

Badham, R., 76
Bailey, T., 149–50, 174
Baldry, Chris, 90, 101
Baldwin, George, 56
Bamber, Greg, 222
Barnow, B. S., 164
Barron, J. M., 169
Bartel, A. P., 155, 166
Bateson, G., 273
Becker, G. S., 168–69
Bednarzik, Robert W., 57
Bell, R. M., 90, 92, 93–95, 97
Bell, T., 159
Berg, I., 156
Berg, Maxine, 52
Bessant, J., 108
Beynon, H., 7
Bishop, J., 154, 156, 157, 158, 167,
  169
Black, D. A., 169
Blackburn, M. L., 52

Blasi, J. R., 176
Blauner, Robert, 6, 56
Blinder, A. S., 176
Blood, Milton R., 217
Bloom, David, 52
Bluestone, Barry, 227
Boddy, D., 91, 96
Boland, R., 287
Borys, Bryan, 66, 89, 90
Bourdon, Clinton C., 213
Bradbury, J., 94–95
Bradley, K., 174
Brady, T. M., 93
Braudel, F., 299
Braverman, Harry, 7, 51, 52, 59, 90,
  95, 97, 214
Brentano, Lujo, 142–43
Bright, James, 90, 93
Brown, C., 166, 167, 175
Brown, J. S., 151, 271, 274, 282
Buchanan, D. A., 91, 96
Bullock, R. J., 176
Burke, G., 150
Burnett, David, 74
Burns, B., 68
Burris, Beverly, 51
Burton, C. E., 174
Butera, F., 54

Cain, P., 57
Campbell, A., 103, 105
Campbell, John, 205
Carnevale, A. P., 164
Casner-Lotto, J., 162–63, 166
Catterall, J. S., 159
Chalmers, A. D., 94–95
Chamberlain, Neil W., 216
Chao, K., 302

Child, John, 104, 218
Ciborra, C. U., 269, 273, 282, 286
Clague, Ewan, 56
Clark, Peter, 48
Clark, R., 47–48
Clarke, Jon, 55, 56
Clawson, Robert, 217
Cockburn, C., 54, 213
Cohen, S. S., 149
Cohen-Rosenthal, E., 174
Cole, Robert E., 71, 178, 187, 188, 190,
    191, 192, 194, 201, 219, 220, 227
Collins, A., 274
Committee for Economic
    Development, 151, 160, 163
Conference of Socialist Economists, 96
Connolly, Anne, 90, 101
Cooley, Michael, 100–101, 103
Cooperative Education Research
    Center, 162
Coopers and Lybrand Associates, 103
Cornfield, Dan, 216
Craft, M. R., 162
Craig, R. L., 165
Creticos, P. A., 164
Crompton, R., 53–54
Cross, M., 99–100, 107
Crossman, E.R.F.W., 56, 67, 93
Cyert, R. M., 271

Daly, A., 71
Daniels, W. W., 218
Davis, Louis, 212
Dayton, C., 160
DeGeus, A. P., 285
De Jong, P., 285
Deming, W. E., 174
Denison, E. F., 155
Dennison, Edward, 80
Department of Scientific and
    Industrial Research, 91
Deskins, Donald, 220
Desai, A., 169
Deutsch, Steven, 82
Dewey, John, 157
Dickson, W. J., 212
Dore, Ronald, 191, 206, 302, 306
Dostal, Werner, 71
Doyle, D. P., 151–52

Duchin, Faye, 74–75
Duguid, P., 271, 282
Duncan, R., 167, 269
Dunlop, John T., 214, 217

Eccles, R., 294
Edwards, Richard, 8, 213
Eurich, N. P., 166
Evers, C., 165

Faunce, William, 56
Feldberg, Roslyn, 53–54
Feuer, M., 169
Fidgett, T., 89
Finch, M. D., 161
Fiol, C. M., 269
Flores, F., 286
Forslin, J., 76
Fox, Alan, 216, 221
Francis, Arthur, 222
Fraser, Bryna Shore, 81
Freeman, C., 106–7
Freeman, J., 270
Freeman, Richard, 213
Freyssenet, M., 7
Friedman, A. L., 54
Fromm, Erich, 143
Fruin, M., 301
Fuller, M. B., 284
Fusfeld, H. I., 284
Fyrth, H. J., 91–92

Gallie, D., 8
Garen, J., 156
Geiger, Theodor, 144
Gent, M., 71
Gerwin, D., 71
Giuliano, V., 55
Glenn, Evelyn, 53–54
Glick, H., 169
Goldsmith, M., 91–92
Goldstein, Harold, 81
Goodlad, J., 157, 159
Gorz, André, 146–47
Gott, S. P., 151
Gouldner, Alvin, 217
Grant, J., 155
Grant, W. J., 155
Greenberg, Leon, 56

Greenberger, E., 161
Gupta, N., 176

Haber, 167
Hacklish, C. S., 284
Hadley, Eleanor, 303
Hamermesh, D. S., 155
Hamilton, S. F., 163
Handy, C., 273
Hannan, M. T., 270
Hanushek, E. A., 156
Harrison, Bennet, 227
Hartman, Paul T., 213
Hartmann, G., 68, 71, 91, 98, 99
Hayek, F. A., 308
Hayes, Robert, 210
Hazelhurst, 67
Heckscher, C. C., 174
Hedberg, B.L.T., 269, 273, 287
Helfgott, R. B., 151
Heller, Frank, 226
Hethy, L., 269
Hewitt, C., 285
Higuchi, Y., 149
Hill, S., 174
Hirschhorn, Larry, 15, 55, 56, 66, 69,
    82, 150, 226
Hirschmeir, J., 298, 300, 301
Hollenbeck, 167
Hoffman, 167
Howard, R. A., 274, 287
Hsu, F.L.K., 300
Hulin, Charles, 217

Iacono, S., 275
Imai, K., 294, 297, 303, 308
Institute of Manpower Studies, 103
Itami, H., 294

Jacoby, Sanford M., 214, 217
Jaikumar, R., 150
Jamison, D. T., 155
Japan Institute for Social and
    Economic Affairs, 193
Jay, E. J., 295
Jenkins, D. G., Jr., 176
Johnson, C., 293
Jones, Bryn, 49–50, 68, 71, 91, 96

Jones, C., 157
Jones, G., 53–54
Jonsson, S., 273, 287
Jorgenson, D. W., 155

Kahneman, D., 272
Kalleberg, A., 54
Kang, 167
Kansai Productivity Center, 197–98,
    202–6
Kaplinsky, R., 69, 90, 99, 101
Kasarda, John D., 52, 82
Kassalow, Everett, 213
Katz, Harry, 216, 219
Kearns, D. T., 151–52
Kelley, Maryellen, 68, 69
Kennedy, E. M., 159
Keogh, M., 266–68
Kern, Horst, 7, 111, 142
Khamis, C., 89
Kidd, John, 74
Killingsworth, Charles, 216
Kling, R., 275
Knights, D., 8
Kochan, Thomas A., 174, 175, 210,
    214, 218, 222
Kohler, C., 150–51
Kohn, Melvin L., 50
Koike, Kazuo, 194, 196
Kostner, Klaus, 71
Kotter, J., 269
Krafcik, John, 178, 221
Kumon, S., 297, 311
Kuwahara, Yasuo, 190, 192, 198,
    201–2

Lan Xue, 69
Lansbury, Russell, 222
Lanzara, G. F., 286
Lapointe, A. E., 156
Lau, L. J., 155
Lave, J., 151
Lawler, E. E., 176
Lawrence, Paul, 212, 292
Lazarsfeld-Jahoda, M., 143
Ledford, G. E., 176
Lee, David, 55
Leff, N., 302

Leonard-Barton, D., 288
Leontief, Wassily, 74–75
Levin, H., 57, 150
Levine, D., 175, 178
Levitt, B., 269
Levitt, Raymond E., 213
Levy, F., 155
Lewin-Epstein, N., 161
Lichtenberg, F. R., 155
Lifson, Thomas B., 292, 297, 307, 308
Lillard, L., 152, 167, 169
Lilley, S., 91, 92
Lindholm, R., 269
Littler, Craig, 51
Loewenstein, M. A., 169
Lorsch, J., 292
Lukasiewicz, John, 75, 81
Lund, R. T., 67
Lundgren, E. R., 67
Lutz, Burkhart, 143
Lyles, M. A., 269
Lynn, Leonard, 188, 189, 191

Macaulay, S., 306
MacDuffie, John Paul, 220–21
McGregor, Douglas, 217
McKersie, R. B., 212, 219
McLean, Mick, 198
McLoughlin, I., 101–2
Majchrzak, Ann, 54, 70–71, 76, 82
Mallet, S., 6
Malone, T. W., 280
Malsch, Thomas, 146
Mangum, S. L., 152–53, 166, 169
Mann, Floyd, 56
Manske, F., 76
March, J. G., 269, 271
Mares, William, 219
Martin, R., 54
Marx, Karl, 7, 52, 90, 95, 143, 198
Masuch, M., 272
Medoff, James, 213
Mertens, D. M., 159
Miller, S. M., 67
Mincer, J., 149, 155, 166, 168–69, 177
Mishel, Lawrence, 80

Mokray, Joan, 15
Montgomery, David, 213
More, Charles, 46, 48, 49, 51
Mortimer, J. T., 161
Mueller, E., 57
Murakami, Y., 300, 301
Murnane, R. J., 156

Nakane, C., 300
Nakaoka, Tetsuro, 198
Nakata, Y. F., 161
National Academy of Sciences, 54, 70, 82, 150, 160
National Commission for Employment Policy, 81
National Commission on Excellence in Education, 156
Nelson, R. R., 271, 272
Nichols, J., 7
Noble, David F., 67, 68–69, 81, 212, 213
Nonaka, I., 283, 284, 286, 308

Oakes, J., 159
Office of Technology Assessment, 99–100, 178, 204
Ogden, Max, 232
Ohmae, K., 289
Organization for Economic Cooperation and Development, 56
Osterman, Paul, 228

Parker, Mike, 220, 224, 227
Pava, Calvin, 212
Penn, Roger, 47, 49–50, 56, 59
Perrolle, Judith, 54
Perrucci, Carolyn, 47
Personick, Valerie, 80
Phillimore, J., 99
Piore, Michael, 69, 149, 214
Pirker, Theo, 143
Polanyi, M., 272
Poole, Michael, 222
Popitz, Heinrich, 143
Porter, M. E., 284
Prais, 90
President's Commission on International Competitiveness, 82

Psacharopoulos, G., 155
Pullen, R., 71

Raddatz, B. R., 164
Raizen, S. A., 151
Reich, Michael, 174–75
Reich, R. B., 149, 175–76
Resnick, L. B., 151
Response Analysis Corporation, 57
Rice, R. E., 285
Roberts, J., 301
Roethlisberger, F. J., 212
Rogers, E. M., 285
Rosen, S., 156, 168–69
Rosenbaum, J. E., 157, 158
Rosenberg, N., 272
Rosenthal, Neal, 81
Rosow, J., 177
Rothman, R., 157
Rozman, G., 298
Rule, James, 72
Rumberger, R. W., 57, 150

Sabel, Charles, 69, 149, 214
Sakakibara, Kiyonori, 191, 206
Salzman, H., 75, 76
Samuel, Raphael, 46, 48
Sansom, G., 298
Sayles, Leonard, 76, 79
Scalpone, R., 150
Scattergood, Hilda, 47, 49–50, 56
Schelsky, Helmut, 144
Schmenner, R., 176
Schmidt, H., 164
Schmoller, Gustav, 142–43
Schneider, J., 180
Schneider, Leslie S., 269, 274, 287
Schon, D. A., 269, 270, 273, 285, 288
Schooler, Carmi, 50
Schultz, George P., 56
Schultz, T. W., 155
Schultz-Wild, R., 150–51
Schultz, E. R., 164
Schumann, Michael, 7, 111
Scribner, S., 151
Seltz, Rüdiger, 146
Selznick, Philip, 216, 217
Senge, P. M., 286

Senker, Peter, 67, 89, 99–100, 102, 103, 104, 105, 108
Serrin, William, 217
Shaiken, Harley, 67, 68
Sheets, R. G., 164
Shimada, Harvo, 220–21, 227
Silvestri, George, 75, 81
Simmonds, P., 102, 105
Simmons, John, 219
Simms, M. C., 164
Simon, H. A., 270
Singelmann, Joachim, 59
Sizer, T. R., 157
Slaughter, Jane, 220, 224, 227
Slichter, Sumner, 213, 216
Snyder, T. D., 155
Sorge, Arndt, 71, 213, 214, 218, 222
Soskice, D., 149, 179
Spence, M., 156
Spenner, Kenneth, 57, 150
Starbuck, W. H., 269
Stata, R., 285
Steinberg, L. D., 161
Stern, David, 149, 159, 160, 161, 163, 178
Stern, J. D., 166
Stevens, J., 151
Sticht, T. G., 151
Stone, Katherine, 54, 215
Strauss, G., 175
Steeck, Wolfgang, 149, 179, 213, 214, 218, 222, 227
Susman, Gerald, 70–71
Swidler, A., 270, 273
Swords-Isherwood, N., 67

Taft, Philip, 213
Tan, H., 152, 155, 167, 169, 177
Tanaka, Hirohide, 198–99, 205
Tapp, J., 93–95
Targ, Dena, 47
Taylor, Frederick, 212
Taylor, James C., 212
Tennenbaum, E., 157
Thomas, Robert J., 210, 219, 222, 224
Thompson, H., 150
Thulestest, B. M., 76
Tidd, J., 105–6

Tienda, Marta, 59
Tierney, 167
Touraine, A., 6
Treiman, D., 57
Turner, H. A., 49–50, 51
Tversky, A., 272
Tyson, L. D., 178

Umetani, Shunichiro, 190
Unger, R. M., 270
U.S. Department of Labor, 151, 152, 163, 173, 176

Verbatim Corp., 57
von Friedeburg, Ludwig, 143

Walker, Charles, 52
Wallace, M., 54
Walton, Richard, 212, 219, 226, 269
Warner, M., 103, 105
Watanabe, Susumu, 187, 199–200, 206–8
Watson, W. F., 48
Weber, J. M., 159
Weber, Max, 143
Weick, K. E., 271
Weinstein, A., 71
Weiss, A., 269
Welch, F., 155
Wells, Donald, 224
Wells, L. T., 292
Westney, D. Eleanor, 191, 206
Wight, O., 276

Wilkinson, Barry, 55, 68, 97, 218
William T. Grant Foundation, 151, 163
Williams, C. Brian, 69
Williams, Lawrence, 69
Williams, M. F., 166
Williamson, Oliver, 215, 294, 305, 306
Willis, R. J., 156
Willke, 167
Willman, Paul, 218
Wilson, William Julius, 227
Winograd, T., 286
Winter, S. G., 271, 272
Wirt, J. G., 153
Wolf, H., 76
Wood, Stephen, 54
Woodward, J., 6
Wozniak, G. D., 155
Wright, E. O., 59

Yamanouchi, T., 283
Yonekura, S., 302
Yoshino, M. Y., 297, 307, 308
Yui, T., 298, 300, 301

Zager, R., 177
Zeisel, Hans, 143
Zicklin, Gilbert, 49, 65, 69
Zimbalist, Andrew, 52
Zuboff, Shoshana, 150, 212, 226, 271, 283
Zysman, J., 149

Subject Index

ACAC. *See* Australian Conciliation and Arbitration Commission

ACTU. *See* Australian Council of Trade Unions

Administrative networks, Japan, 297
  described, 307–8
  efficiencies offered by, 313
  management credibility in, 312–13
  mechanisms for opportunistic scanning, 308–9
  reciprocation of information in, 309–12

Advanced manufacturing technology (AMT), emphasis on high-skilled work force, 70–71

ALP. *See* Australian Labor Party

Amalgamated Metal Workers Union (AMWU), Australia, 236
  agreement with can manufacturer on new technology, 251–53
  and metal trades industry adjustment package, 240–41

AMT. *See* Advanced manufacturing technology

AMWU. *See* Amalgamated Metal Workers Union

Apprenticeship program, 163–64

AT&T-Olivetti alliance, 284

Australia. *See also* Australian Council of Trade Unions
  Heavy Engineering industry, 240–41
  macroeconomic policy strategies for industry, 239–41
  manufacturing industry, 236, 239
  metal industry, 240–47, 266–68
  policies on industrial democracy, 247

railways, union problem-solving in, 255
  restructuring of unions: by amalgamation, 256–57; by broadening outside interests in, 257, 258–59; by developing more competent leaders, 257; employer resistance to, 257–58; prospects for, 259–61
  technological innovations, 234–35
  unemployment, 237
  union movement: changes in, since 1960s, 233; craft divisions, 232–33; early attitudes toward politics, 233; education and training for industry restructuring, 11, 244–46, 256–61; ideologies, 234; views of market, 235–36
  union strategy for handling new technology, 11, 234–35; development of problem-solving methods, 253–55; integration of workplace jobs, 248–50; on role of worker in organization of work, 250–53
  wage policy, 233, 241–44, 245
  workplace resource centers, 247–48

Australian Conciliation and Arbitration Commission (ACAC), on technological change, 234–35. *See also* Industrial Relations Commission

Australian Council of Trade Unions (ACTU), 233
  Accord with Australian Labor Party, 237

327

Australian Council of Trade Unions
  (ACTU) (cont'd)
  Australia Reconstructed union
    strategy, 232; comparison of
    Australia with European
    countries, 237–38;
    macroeconomic policy
    recommendations, 238, 261–66
  on job security, 249
  on optimum use of new technology,
    235
  union amalgamation as priority of,
    256
  on workplace demarcation between
    job skills, 249
Australian Labor Party (ALP), Accord
  with ACTU, 237
Australian Liberal Party, 236
Automation. See also Research on
  automation and work;
  Technological innovations
  effect on maintenance and design
    skill, 99–103
  limitations on, 5–6
  organizational design to support,
    38–41
  staffing for, 4, 107–8
Automobile industry
  Japan: competitive advantage of,
    107; technological ranking
    system for production workers,
    195, 196
  U.S.: efforts to reform industrial
    relations and production system,
    219–21; introduction of
    multiskilled jobs in, 221;
    Japanese transplants in, 220–21
  West Germany: competitive
    pressures on, 113; integrated
    work organization in, 113–14;
    market strategy for, 113;
    projected automated production
    jobs in, 117–19; skill
    requirements in, 115–16; systems
    controllers as percent of
    workforce, 118; workforce
    makeup, 114–15

Brighton Labor Process Group, Great
  Britain, 96

Bureau of Labor Statistics, U.S.
  on manufacturing employment, 60
  occupational projections, 57, 80,
    83 n

CAD. See Computer-aided design
California, vocational academies, 160
Canon, new organization to
  implement innovation, 283–84
Capitalism
  creative versus destructive effects
    of, 46
  Japanese zaibatsu enterprise-form
    of, 301–2
  organization of labor process, 96
Carnegie Mellon engineering
  graduates, 188–89, 191
CETA. See Comprehensive
  Employment and Training Act
Chemical industry, West Germany,
  125
  electronic computer controls in,
    125–26
  importance of R&D leadership in,
    125
  manual work in, 128, 129
  need for technological and
    organizational change in, 125
  systems controllers, 128–29
  workforce, by sectors, 128
  work organization, 126–27
Chrysler Motors, labor relations
  reforms, 221
CNC. See Computer numerical
  control machines
Commerce, U.S. Department of,
  workplace job studies, 57
Communist Party of Australia (CPA),
  233, 234
Competence of employees, 13
  as function of tools, 20–23
  as function of skills, 18, 23–27
  as function of skills and roles,
    42–43
  model of, 16, 18–20
  plant organization to support,
    38–39
  proposed research on, 44–45
  role systems for: automation effect
    on, 40–41; complementarity
    principle and, 34–38; by direct

and indirect personnel, 27–28, 30–33
workers experience of, 28–30
Competitiveness, 8–9, 12, 13
 Japan: institutions influencing, 293–94; product and process improvements for, 292; U.S. versus, 292
 U.S.: institutional changes to improve, 314–15, 316, 318–19; technology improvement as source of improving, 11, 210, 212, 218–19; union-management relations to support, 225
Comprehensive Employment and Training ACT (CETA), 164
Computer-aided design (CAD)
 described, 74
 in Great Britain: for drafting, 100–101; effect on engineering, 102–3, 104–5; research on skill implications of, 89
 in U.S. manufacturing: de-skilling from, 54; results of, 75–76
Computer-aided design/computer-aided manufacturing (CAD/CAM), 74
 in Japanese manufacturing, 199–200
Computer numerical control (CNC) machines, 65
 British research on skill implications of, 89, 98–99, 100–103
 German machine manufacturer use of, 120–21
Computer systems
 computer-aided design, 54, 74–76, 89; and computer-aided manufacturing, 74, 199–200
 computer numerical control, 65, 89, 98–103
 de-skilling effects of, 54, 100–103
 effect on production worker, 64–65
 integration of mechanized systems with, 65–66
 interaction among, 72–73
 management information system, 65, 66, 76–79
 Manufacturing Resource Planning,

64, 66, 70, 274–79, 282–83
 for software development, 279–82
 support of innovations by creating new, 285–87
 U.S. versus Japanese development and application of, 187–88
Corporate training, 164. See also Learning-intensive production; On-the-job training
 company expenditures on, 165–66, 167–68
 and employee productivity, 168
 extent and duration of, 166–67
 formal versus informal, 164
 rate of return on investment in, 165, 168–69
 social rate of return on, 170

Databases
 interactive computing and, 72, 73
 management information system, 76–79
De-skilling effects of new technology, 3, 9, 48
 computer-aided design and, 100–103
 criticism of de-skilling thesis, 54–55
 under early British industrialization, 52
 from erosion of craft labor, 53–54
 labor-management conflicts over, 52–53
 NC machine tools and, 68–69
 under Taylorism, 53, 71
 work-upgrading approach versus, 51–52, 55–56, 59
Digital Equipment Corporation, Westfield computer manufacturing plant
 case study: interviews for, 17–18; theoretical framework for, 15–16
 competence of employees: barriers to, 31–32; dimensions of, 33–34; interdependence of, 34–38, 39; management to support, 30–34; model of, 18–20, 42–45; personnel role system to support, 27–30, 40–41; plant organization to support, 38–39

Digital Equipment Corporation
(*cont'd*)
plant description, 16–17
tool system automation: disruption
from, 33–34; skills for, 23–27;
worker problem solving and,
20–23

Earnings. *See* Wages
Education. *See also* Corporate
training; Learning-intensive
production; On-the-job training;
Schools apprenticeship, 163–64
contribution to productivity,
155–56
cooperative, 151; in four-year
colleges, 162; recommended
increase in, 180; in vocational
schools, 162–63
functional context, 151
government-sponsored training
program, 164
institutions providing work-related
149, 152–54
measurement of skills by attained, 57
proposed incentives for increasing,
158
reform movement of 1980s in, 163
required level for manufacturing
employment, 82
Electrical/electronic equipment
industry, West Germany
flexibility in work organization,
130
integrated work organization for,
131–33
Taylorism in, by type of operation,
129–30
technocratic model for work, 131
Employee Stock Ownership Plans
(ESOPs), 176
Employment security
collective employer agreements for,
179–80
cost of maintaining, 179
employee training and, 177–78
Engineering
British versus German use of
electronic skills in, 103–4
Great Britain, 89; computer-aided
design effect on, 102–3, 104–5

profile of U.S. versus Japanese
graduates in, 188–91
projected employment in U.S., 81
ESOPs. *See* Employee Stock
Ownership Plans

Flexible manufacturing system (FMS),
105
Great Britain, 105–6
Japan, 106, 199–200, 283, 292
U.S. 149, 150, 224–25
Fordism, assembly-line technology
and mass production, 106–7
Ford Motor Company, reforms in
labor relations practices, 221
Formative context
for functioning of business
organizations, 270–71
and information systems, 287–88
and organizational routines, 272,
273
and technological innovations:
aircraft instruments plant case
study, 274–79; computer
network software case study,
279–82

General Electric, implementation of
NC technology, 68–69
General Motors
Automotive Service Educational
Program, 162–63
implementation of NC technology,
68
Quality Network program, 221
Great Britain. *See also* Research on
automation and work
automation effect on skills:
contextualist analysis, 96–99;
labor process analysis, 95, 96; in
maintenance and design
operations, 99–103; policy
analysis, 91–95
engineering, 89, 102–5
microelectronics production, 103–4
robotic technology, 105–6

Heavy Engineering Manufacturers
Association, Australia, 240
Honda, production worker evaluation
system, 195–96

Industrial Relations Commission
    (IRC), Australia, 235
  wage bargaining: 12-point program
    for metal industry, 242, 266–68;
    two-tier system, 241–42
Industrial relations system, U.S.
  basic model of organizational
    governance, 225–28
  low-cost/management control
    model, 219, 225
  New Deal model, 214–17, 225, 226
  and property rights to skills, 215–16
  to support competitiveness, 225
  technological change under, 210,
    211; craft unions and, 213, 215;
    integration of shop-floor
    production with, 219–21; job
    definition reforms to encourage
    multiskills, 221; and
    organization's competitive
    advantage, 218–19; reforms
    relating to choice and
    implementation of, 221–22;
    union focus on economic effects
    of, 217; union-management roles
    in decision making on, 212–14
  traditional model of: continuing use
    of, 211; described, 210; in
    meeting technological
    innovations, 212; problems in
    changing, 222–25

Japan. See also Manufacturing
    industry; Organization, business
    firm; Technological innovations
  automobile industry, 107, 195–96
  competitiveness: automobile
    industry, 107; organizational
    infrastructure evolution and, 12,
    187
  labor unions, 197–98, 227
  machine-tool industry, 150, 187
  management philosophy, 175
  robotics, 105, 106; diffusion of
    technology for, 187
Job Training Partnership Act (JTPA),
    164
JTPA. See Job Training Partnership
    Act

Kansai Productivity Center, case

studies on microelectronics
    applications, 201–5, 203–4, 205

Labor unions
  Australia: described, 232–36;
    problem solving by railway, 255;
    for metal workers, 241;
    restructuring of, 244, 246,
    256–61; strategy for handling
    new technology, 248–55
  Germany: systems controllers and,
    137–40
  Japan: attitude toward
    technological change, 197–98;
    enterprise-based, 227
  U.S.: challenge to reform industrial
    relations system, 224–25; craft-
    based, 213, 215; job control,
    216; proposed organization
    changes effect on, 227; and
    technological change, 212–14,
    216, 217
Learning-intensive production, 149
  described, 170
  effectiveness, 151
  formal classes for, 171–72
  motivation for, 170; employee
    involvement in labor-
    management relations, 175–76;
    employment security, 177–78;
    financial participation by
    employees, 176–77; pay-
    for-learning system, 173–74;
    smaller plant size, 176
  process model for, 170–71
  in workplace: for flexibility in job
    assignments, 175, 176; by using
    slack time, 172–74

Machine building industry, West
    Germany
  fabrication versus assembly work
    in, 121, 122
  manual work in, 121, 123
  predicted development of new
    technology in, 122, 124
Management
  barriers to best practice use of
    automation, 107
  British attitude toward automation,
    103; in dealing with skill

Management (*cont'd*)
  requirements, 105; for flexibility
    in staffing workforce, 107–8; for
    work organization, 103–4
  U.S.: identity, 315–16; increase in
    employment in, 62–63;
    introduction of MIS for, 76–79
Management information system
    (MIS), 65, 66, 76–79
  clerical skills for, 72–74
  design of, 287–88
  for manufacturing managerial
    employees: advantages of,
    76–78; criticism of, 78–79; skills
    required for, 79
Manufacturing employment, U.S.
  CAD system effect on designers and
    drafters, 74–76
  comparison with other industries,
    58
  educational level for, 82
  non-production: clerical and
    administrative, 61–62; effects of
    interactive computer and
    database systems on, 72–74;
    increase in, 58, 59; managerial,
    62, 63, 76–79; professional and
    technical, 62, 63; sales force, 62
  occupational makeup of, 60–64
  on-the-job training for computer-
    related, 81–82
  predicted increase in high-skill,
    70–71, 82, 83
  production, 63–64; computerized
    systems influencing, 64–65;
    increased responsibility for,
    66–67; potential for high skills,
    70
  projections of, 80
  role of new technology in changing,
    211
  slowdown in growth of, 60
  total, 61
Manufacturing industry, Japan
  approaches to skill formation: for
    multiskilled workers, 194; off-
    the-job training, 196; on-the-job
    training, 150, 195–96; quality
    control procedure, 71, 194–95,
    201; U.S. approach compared
    with, 196–97; for worker

routine and nonroutine problems,
    194
  availability of employees for,
    192–93
  competitiveness, 292
  factors affecting technological
    innovations in: corporate
    decentralization movement, 193;
    economic, 192; institutional,
    188–89
  flexibility in, 199–200, 283, 292
  hours of training for assembly
    workers, 178
  industrial relations: employment
    relationships, 200–1, 203–7,
    227; labor-management
    consultative committees, 201;
    union attitude toward
    technological innovations,
    197–98
  innovations in interfirm system,
    304–7
  microelectronic and mechatronic
    applications in, 197; education
    requirements for, 201–2;
    flexibility and quality benefits
    from, 199–200; motivation
    factors influencing, 208;
    multiskilled workforce for,
    197–98
  training for automation in: business
    planning process for, 200–201;
    in-house training for robotics and
    NC machines, 203; job rotation
    system for, 205–6; by multiskills,
    205, 206–7
Manufacturing industry, U.S. *See also*
    Manufacturing employment, U.S.
  flexible systems in, 149, 150,
    224–25
  integrated systems for problem
    solving in, 194, 195
  and return on investment criteria,
    200
  skill and occupational changes in:
    compensatory theory of, 48–49;
    educational requirements for, 57;
    social determination versus task
    analytic approaches to, 49–51;
    upgrading approach to, 55–60
  technological innovations in, 46;

company and union roles in choice and implementation of, 222–25; and demand for skills, 46; employee training for, 152, 153; required continual learning for, 150–51

Manufacturing Resource Planning (MRP), 64, 66
advanced manufacturing technology combined with, 70
failure of, 276–79
management goals for, 275–76
recommended operations for, 275, 282–83
required creation of new information for, 282–83

Marxist theory
on capitalist labor process reformulation of, 1920s, 142–43

Metal industry, Australia
participative practices in, 247
program for workplace negotiations, 242, 266–68
union, management, and government cooperation for, 240–41
wage policy, 242, 243–44, 245

Metal machine trades, U.S., skill replacement and reformulation, 48–49

Michigan Automotive Compressor, 206–7

Microelectronic products, 103–4, 199

MRP. See Manufacturing Resource Planning

NC. See Numerical control

New Deal era, industrial relations model, 214
on employee property rights to skills, 215–16
job control strategy, 216
obstacles to producing high-quality goods, 225, 226
and stability of union-management relations, 217
and technological innovations, 217

New United Motors Manufacturing, Inc. (NUMMI), 175

New York State, vocational curriculum, 160

Numerical control (NC) machine tools. See also Computer systems, computer numerical control
British research on skill implications of, 89; 93–95; comparison of CNC and, 98
in Japanese manufacturing, 199, 203
in U.S. manufacturing, 65; as de-skilling technology, 68, 69; implementation of, 68; low productivity of, 69; skill requirements for programming and maintenance of, 67, 68

NUMMI. See New United Motors Manufacturing, Inc.

Occupations
changes in manufacturing, 60–64
expansion of white collar, 58, 59
employment projections by, 80–81
measurement of skill levels across, 57
on-the-job training for, 152, 153
overall upgrading of skills in, 59

OECD. See Organization for Economic Cooperation and Development

On-the-job training. See also Corporate training; Learning-intensive production
for computer-related manufacturing employment, 81–82
and employee earnings, 169
and employment security, 177–78
occupations requiring, 152, 153
and problem solving, 164, 170–71
recommended increase in, 178

Organization, business firm
formative context for: functioning of, 270–71; and organization routine, 272, 273; in technological innovation implementation, 273
Japan: administrative networks for innovation in, 297, 307–13; comparison of U.S. and, 293–94; corporate network interfirm system in, 297, 303–7; evolution of, 298–303; forms of, 294–97; zaibatsu form, 301–2

Organization (cont'd)
  reshaping of, 269–70
  strategies for implementing
    innovation, 282–88
  to support worker under
    automation, 38–41
  U.S.: ability to adopt efficiencies of
    Japan, 313: cultural factors
    working against, 314–15;
    identity management and,
    315–16; by interfirm mechanism,
    317; potential for, 293, 318–19
Organizational learning
  defined, 269
  incremental, 272–73
  second-order, 270, 271; actions for
    developing, 289; described, 273;
    local experimentation for,
    282–83; skills and routines for,
    271–72; technology as tool for,
    285–87; use of formative
    context, 273
Organization for Economic
  Cooperation and Development
  (OECD), 55–56, 206

Philadelphia, vocational academies,
  160
Productivity
  education and, 155–56
  employee compensation plans and,
    176–77
  formal corporate training and, 168
  learning-intensive production and,
    170
  strict job demarcation and, 249–50

Research on automation and work
  changes in, 6–7
  Great Britain, 89; contextualist
    analysis, 90–91, 96–99; in
    engineering firms CAD,
    100–103; labor process analysis,
    90, 95–96; and maintenance and
    design skills, 99–100; policy
    analysis, 90, 91–95
  industrial sociology and, 144–45
  new generation of, 3, 8–9, 13
  on qualitative versus quantitative
    issues, 4–6

  in robotics, 105–6
  on role of management, 103–5
  on U.S. employee competency,
    44–45
Robotics, 89
  international differences in,
    application of technology for,
    105–6
  Japanese technology for, 105, 106,
    187; in-house training for, 203,
    204

Scholastic Aptitude Test (SAT),
  scores, 156
Schools. See also Education
  contribution to economic
    productivity, 155–56
  earnings related to number of years
    in, 155
  proposed incentives for staying in,
    158
  vocational education: cooperative,
    162–63; curriculum expansion
    of, 160; federal support for, 159,
    162; increased demand for
    academic subjects in, 160–61,
    162; students attracted to, 159
  weaknesses in U.S.: curriculum
    deficiencies, 158; failure to
    prepare for workplace, 156, 159;
    lack of student motivation,
    156–58
  working students in, 161–63
Scientific and Industrial Research,
  Great Britain Department of, 91
Scientific management. See Taylorism
Skills. See also De-skilling effects of
  new technology
  Australia: as component of wage
    policy, 241, 244, 245; effort to
    raise level of, 247
  British debates on automation
    effect on, 90–91; contextualist
    analysis, 96–99; labor process
    analysis, 95–96; in maintenance
    and design operations, 99–103;
    policy analysis, 91–95
  competence and, 18, 23–27
  defined, 271
  hierarchy of, 24–27

Japanese approaches to formation of, 194–97

research on: compensatory theory of, 48–49; measurement of level of, 57; replacement and reformulation of, 48–49; social determination versus task analytic approach to, 49–51; upgrading approach to, 51, 55–60

tool system automation and, 20; emphasis on mental skills, 23–24; work problems and, 20–23

U.S. mechanism for developing work-related, 149–53

SOFI. See Soziologisches Forschungsintitut

Soviet Union, adoption of assembly-line technology and Taylorism, 107

Soziologisches Forschungsintitut (SOFI), data on industry workforce, 114–15, 120, 127

Systems controllers. See under West Germany

Sweden, organizational changes for skilled and semiskilled work, 140

Taylorism
    Australian union efforts to reverse, 250
    de-skilling effect of, 53
    in German electrical and electronic equipment industry, 130–31

Technological innovations
    Australia, 234–35
    formative context in implementing, 273; case study in aircraft instruments plant, 274–79; case study in computer network software development, 279–82
    Japan: administrative networks to implement, 307–13; interfirm system to implement, 297–98, 303–7; network form of organization for, 296–97
    organizational learning to implement, 270, 273; second-order, 271–72, 273, 282; skills and routines at core of, 271–72

qualitative versus quantitative effects of, 4–5

recommended organizational strategies to implement: information systems, 285–86; interfirm alliances, 284; local experimentation, 282–84; new skills development, 284–85

U.S.: continual learning in the production process for, 149, 150; high level of skills for, 149–52; human problems resulting from past, 47; learning-intensive production and, 151, 170–74; need for workforce experimentation with, 47–48; as source of improving competitive advantage, 11, 210, 212, 218–19; union attitudes toward, 212–13, 214, 216, 217

West Germany: new approaches to, 111–12

worker competency for, 15–16

Tohoka University, engineering graduates
    career development, 188–89
    reasons for current job choice, 191

Tools
    changing nature of, 20, 21
    competence as function of, 18–20
    skill changes with automation of, 21–24

United Kingdom. See Great Britain

United States. See also Automobile industry; Industrial relations system; Labor unions; Manufacturing employment; Manufacturing industry; Organization, business firm; Technological innovations
    competitiveness: institutions to improve, 314–15, 316, 318–19; Japan versus, 292; technological innovations as source of improving, 11, 210, 212, 218–19
    metal machine trades, 48–49

Wages
    Australian policy, 233, 241–42; for metal industry, 242, 243–44, 245

Wages (*cont'd*)
  education and, 156
  on-the-job training and, 169
  pay-for-learning system and, 173
  pay-for-productivity plan and,
    176–77
West Germany. *See also* Automobile
    industry; Chemical industry;
    Electrical/electronic equipment
    industry
  apprenticeship program, 163–64
  humanization of working life
    program, 111, 141, 145
  industrial sociology: early changes
    in, 142–43; political effects on,
    145; post-World War II research
    on, 143–44; technological
    change and, 144–45; and
    understanding modern society,
    146–47
  machine-building industry, 120–24
  manufacturing: preference for high-
    skill workforce, 71; productivity
    in, 71; time for employee training
    in, 150–51
  microelectronics production, 103–4
  new approach toward automation,
    111–12
  oil companies, 125, 126
  on-the-job training, 150–51
  research on automation and work,
    case studies, 112; in automobile
    industry, 113–18; in chemical
    industry, 124–29; in electrical

and electronics industry,
  129–33; in machine building
  industry, 120–24
systems controllers, 118, 122, 127;
  attitude toward education,
  136–37; functions, 133–34;
  knowledge and skill requirements
  for, 134–35; problems in
  supervising, 135–36; qualities of,
  136; relation to unions, 137–39
work structure: efficiency based on
  integration of functions, 139–40;
  increase in systems control work,
  140; international comparison
  with, 142; need for political
  regulation of transition in, 141;
  rise in skill level in, 140–41
Work organization
  Australian strategy for role of
    worker in, 250–53
  implications of automation for:
    Great Britain, 96–97, 103,
    104–6; Japan, 106; U.S. 105,
    106; West Germany, 103–4
  West Germany integrated, 113–14,
    126–27; defensive versus
    offensive integration, 132;
    technocratic versus integrated
    models, 131–33

Yamazaki Machinery, flexible
  manufacturing system, 283

Zaibatsu organization, 301–2